Social Evolution, Economic Development and Culture

Social Evolution, Economic Development and Culture

What it Means to Take Japan Seriously

SELECTED WRITINGS OF RONALD DORE

Ronald Dore

Centre for Economic Performance, London School of Economics, UK

Edited by

D. Hugh Whittaker

Faculty of Oriental Studies and Centre for Business Research, University of Cambridge, UK

Edward Elgar

Cheltenham, UK • Northampton, MA, USA

Published by
Edward Elgar Publishing Limited
Glensanda House
Montpellier Parade
Cheltenham
Glos GL50 1UA
UK

Edward Elgar Publishing, Inc.
136 West Street
Suite 202
Northampton
Massachusetts 01060
USA

A catalogue record for this book
is available from the British Library

Library of Congress Cataloguing in Publication Data

Dore, Ronald Philip.
Social evolution, economic development and culture : what it means to take Japan seriously / Ronald Dore, D.H. Whittaker.
Includes bibliographical references and index.
1. Japan—Economic conditions. 2. Japan—Social conditions. 3. National characteristics, Japanese. I. Whittaker, D.H. (D. Hugh) II. Title.

HC462.D68 2001
306′.0952—dc21 00–055117

ISBN 1 84064 498 2 (cased)

Printed and bound in Great Britain by Bookcraft (Bath) Ltd.

Contents

Figures

Tables

Acknowledgements

First of all I would like to thank Ronald Dore for his co-operation, assistance and good humour throughout the preparation of this book. His willingness to go the extra mile made a big difference to the outcome. I would like to thank Joanne Bennett-Murray and Zöe Conway Morris for their help in scanning the articles and putting them into a format ready for abridging, and the Japan Foundation (London office) for a grant to make this possible. Takeshi Inagami provided valuable comments on a number of occasions, and Geoffrey Hawthorn and Richard Bowring gave helpful feedback on an earlier draft of the Introduction. Makoto Fujimoto tracked down a number of articles and helped to fill gaps in the list of Japanese publications. Finally, Edward Elgar's enthusiasm, stemming in part from his long association with publishing Ronald Dore's work, helped to see this project through to completion.

Introduction

D. Hugh Whittaker

Ever since he first arrived in Japan in 1950, Ronald Dore's fascination with the 'real world' has generated a rich and distinctive scholarship, appreciated by readers in many social science disciplines. That he has made enormous contributions to our understanding of modern Japan is without doubt. But his contributions extend to the fields of development, education, political economy, sociology and more. The breadth of this scholarship, however, means that most readers only see a piece of the proverbial 'elephant'. The first aim of this book is to present the various pieces and show how they fit together.

This is not something that can be done simply with scissors and paste. It means trying to identify common themes and underlying orientations, a task not helped by the fact that Dore's fascination with interpreting the 'real world' has been far greater than any desire to advance any theoretical or methodological 'school', or found one around himself. (He laughs off labels like 'neo-institutionalist' which some have tried to identify him with.) Yet most readers will know that there is something in his work that goes beyond a keen eye for detail, jargon-free description and rigorous use of logic for analysis. A second aim of this book is to identify what this something is and assess its contribution to social science.

First I make my own attempt. This Introduction provides a biographical sketch which shows how his research interests developed and the context in which they developed based on my discussions with him, interviews and biographical notes published in Japanese, and his major published works. It then assesses his contributions.

Perhaps the best description of Ronald Dore is 'comparative sociologist'. I use the term recognizing first that, although his approach is sociological, he has no great commitment to sociologists as a professional group - in fact he more frequently mixes with economists and political scientists. His research interests straddle conventional disciplinary boundaries. Second, comparison is endemic to sociological research. Some of it is done very badly, however, while his is very sophisticated. I use 'sociologist', then, in a non-tribal sense and 'comparative', not to further narrow down his contribution, but to point to contributions fundamental to social science research. As historically-created disciplinary boundaries blur, these contributions become even more noteworthy.

The main body of the book is a collection of readings - articles and chapters written by Dore, and also abridged or extracted by him - organized around four themes which have been vital in his research. The first is a classical sociological concern - social evolution, or common patterns of developmental change that supposedly all societies go through. The second is his late development twist to social evolution: the argument, first, that late developers are not bound to follow the same evolutionary path as early developers, and second, that late developers share systematic institutional features. The third theme is that culture matters; the interplay of culture and evolutionary development is what creates national differences.[1] Culture here is neither an all-powerful stamp, nor a residual category into which unexplained phenomena are swept. It is the combination of his conception of social evolution and his sophisticated view of culture, based on detailed empirical studies, which accounts for the conceptual richness of Dore's work. The fourth springs from his own interests as a 'political animal',[2] and methodologically from the belief that the previous three may pose constraints, but they are not deterministic; there is scope for human agency and policy choices, for hope and reason, to make a difference. Dore's contributions to policy debates, therefore, are consistent with his own comparative sociology.

The choice of these four themes, and the selection of papers, is the result of discussions between Ronald Dore and myself. Some readings are heavily abridged, representing the need to balance inclusion and a word count limit. Where appropriate, details of related readings are provided. One or two of his more famous articles, such as 'Goodwill and the Spirit of Market Capitalism' have not been included, as they have been widely reproduced elsewhere.

Finally, a list of Ronald Dore's publications arranged by year further attests to the development and scope of his research, as well as his enormous productivity. Compiling this list was no easy task since Dore himself has not fully recorded or collected his own writings. It required considerable detective work and some small gaps may remain. Perhaps this attests to the fact that he is remarkably modest, despite all his achievements.

BIOGRAPHICAL SKETCH

Encountering Japan, and Sociology

Ronald Dore would be the first to concede the importance of chance in historical events. In 1942 a state scholarship took him from Poole Grammar School to the School of Oriental Studies (now the School of Oriental and

African Studies, SOAS) to study an enemy language for the war effort. Turkish was his first choice, but he was assigned to Japanese, which he proceeded to study for the next eighteen months. An accident and an injured leg saw him staying on and teaching Japanese at SOAS instead of being sent to India along with the rest of his classmates. The university atmosphere and the steady improvement of his Japanese as he was teaching it induced academic ambitions. He took evening classes to do his A levels and then, with the help of his teaching colleagues, took an external London degree in Japanese language and literature:

> all at the army's expense. And then, when I was demobbed in 1947 they gave me a Further Education and Training Grant on the grounds that my education had been interrupted by the War![3]

He used the grant to do post-graduate work, but reluctance by General MacArthur's Occupation GHQ staff to admit foreign students prevented him from using his London University travelling studentship for a year's study in Japan. His first demobilized summer he spent cataloguing the Satow and Aston collections of Japanese publications in Cambridge University Library.[4] It was there that he came across Arai Hakuseki's account of learning Chinese characters in *Oritaku shiba no ki.*[5] This autobiography alerted Dore to the scope and depth of education in Tokugawa Japan (1603–1868), and prompted him to choose it as a research subject. He was registered as a PhD student at SOAS studying 'Japanese Confucianism':

> It made a good, traditionally Orientalist subject but reading, not just about schools, but also the moralistic writings about education of the Confucianists, taught me a lot, as you can see from my frequent references back to Confucian ideas, contrasted with those of 'individualistic' Christianity.[6]

He supplemented the material in the SOAS and British Museum libraries with works sent by a Tokyo University professor, in return for which he sent books on British education. He was increasingly drawn towards educational sociology and, ultimately, sociology. While he was waiting for his visa for Japan, the newly established 'Scarborough posts' for Japanese language, literature and history at SOAS were filling up. Eventually only one post was left – vaguely specified as 'Japanese institutions'.[7] This post was kept open for him and, in anticipation, he attended introductory sociology and psychology courses at the London School of Economics (LSE) for a term.

> If I'd been asked then what I was doing, I would have said Japanese studies. I started going to sociology classes at LSE a couple of months before I went to Japan for the purely self-interested reason that by that time the only job left was something curiously called Japanese institutions, which to most people then meant festivals

and folklore. As it was the only job likely to be available for me afterwards, I started thinking, and decided I needed some general sociological background.[8]

In 1950, under the pretext of being assigned 'honorary secretary to the Cultural Advisor to the United Kingdom Liaison Mission to the Supreme Commander of the Allied Powers', he was able to enter Japan. He lived with the Cultural Advisor - George Fraser - and his family in Seijo while commuting to the sociology department and library of Tokyo University to further his research on Tokugawa education. Six months after arriving in Japan he placed an advertisement in the *Asahi* newspaper, seeking a room to let. He found a six mat (about twelve square metres) room in Hanazono-chō, Taito Ward, behind a *sake* shop, facing onto a small alley, which was always bustling with people doing subcontracting work for a nearby factory.[9] The sheer vitality of the district, and Tokyo in general, prompted him to put his library-based research to one side and look at the Japan around him. The seeds of the idea had been planted by Fraser 'somewhere off the coast of Malaysia' when they had talked about Lynd's classic study of *Middletown* (Lynd and Lynd, 1929) in the USA. Dore decided he would attempt to shed light on Japanese social structure and culture through a study of Hanazono-chō (which he named 'Shitayama-cho'). The purchasing power of a £150 special Treasury research grant enabled him to recruit research students, mainly from Tokyo University, to distribute questionnaires and conduct interviews. He brought the data with him back to London in late 1951, and proceeded to write *City Life in Japan* (1958) whilst lecturing at SOAS, and attending further sociology lectures and seminars at LSE.

The lectures included Ginsberg's 'Theories of Progress', and Marshall's 'Elements of Social Structure'. He was admitted to the 'awesomely formal' sociology staff seminar, but got his greatest intellectual stimulation from the informal Thursday evening seminar, organized by graduate students such as David Lockwood and Ralf Dahrendorf between 1952 and 1954.[10] While many of the departmental staff perfunctorily dismissed the US sociologist Parsons for his verbiage and/or lack of empirical relevance,[11] in the Thursday evening seminar he was 'all the rage - "real sociology" in contrast to the Ginsbergian bland mixture of history, philosophy plus empirical sociology, which typified the department'.

Dore had no great liking for Parsons' grand theory-building scheme - and his own rejection of the library in Tokyo in favour of the bustling alleys of Hanazono-chō provides a sharp contrast in sociological orientation with Parsons' sojourn in Heidelberg, where the latter studied Weber and Sombart - but he did find some of Parsons' concepts useful for his *City Life* analysis. Indeed he acknowledges a debt to Sprott's 1952 article for alerting him to the usefulness of Parsons' recasting of earlier evolutionary ideal-typical dichotomies – Toennies' *Gemeinschaft* (community) and *Gesellschaft* (association) in particular – through his 'pattern variables'. These provided useful conceptual tools for considering social change during Japan's industrialization and urbanization.[12] In the final chapter of *City Life (*Chapter 1 in this volume*)*, however, Dore provided a twist. Although the past eighty years had brought greater individuation in terms of personal choice to 'Shitayama-cho' residents, they could not be called 'individualistic'. He quotes a Japanese author who berates his countrymen for their 'spirit of dependence' and lack of individual awareness:

> The Westerner must guard against the fallacy of assuming (like the author quoted, together with most other Japanese intellectuals) that the stages of social development which Western countries have experienced are right and natural stages deviation from which is somehow unhealthy (for the Westerner the historicist fallacy may become tinged with arrogance). But it was difficult for someone who left Japan in 1951 to think other than in these terms of a nation whose leaders of opinion had decided that theirs was a 'backward country', a 'following-behind country', committed to imitating the development of the West now in its social and political as well as in its industrial forms. Japan had, owing to its peculiar circumstances, *skipped a stage* in the proper order of social development. The damage had to be repaired. (1958, 393, italics added)

Dore left open the question of whether the 'damage' could be repaired – whether it was possible for the Japanese to become as individualistic as the Westerners they wanted to emulate – but he did endorse the Japanese sociologist's stage-skipping diagnosis. In this he was influenced by Riesman's (1950) notions of 'mass' society and its 'outer directed' individuals. Riesman saw guilt-control as one aspect of the 'inner direction' of individuals in early capitalist, competitive societies. It is this stage which Japan had missed, Dore believed, moving directly from the 'collectivity orientation' of Tokugawa Japan to a 'new collectivism', albeit with greater individuation than the former stage.

In this evolutionary perspective, culture – which in later writings Dore describes as 'modal behavioural dispositions' – is something that can change over time and vary according to place, even within Japan. This was quite a different conception of culture to that advanced by the cultural anthropologist Ruth Benedict (1946). It was impossible in the 1950s to write about Japan without taking a stand on Benedict's depiction of Japan as a 'shame culture' as opposed to Western 'guilt cultures'. Dore criticized first her assumption of the 'immutability' of Japanese culture, and second her 'Japanese as totally alien' exaggeration of cultural differences (using moral concepts from the West).[13]

He identified a variety of sanctions on behaviour which were important not only in Japan but elsewhere, too – personal shame, family/we-group shame, punishment for breaking the law, displeasure of particular individuals, and guilt from failing to live up to personal standards – and showed how different combinations applied in different situations. According to Dore's view, it was meaningful to say that Japanese culture is distinctive, but only in the sense that the *average* Japanese man or woman is inclined to think or behave in different ways and with different weightings compared with the average man or woman in similar circumstances in other societies. On the one hand, therefore, he rejected the 'historicist fallacy' and its universalist (and ethnocentric) assumptions, while also rejecting the cultural particularism of Benedict.[14] These twin positions are fundamental in Dore's writings, and were already evident in his first monograph.

A further feature of *City Life* was a strong emphasis on what is nowadays called grounded research. He recalls discussing his *City Life* survey with the US sociologist John Bennett at the Culture, Information and Education (CIE) section of the Occupation GHQ in 1951, and being berated for not having a clear guiding hypothesis.

> He said, 'You can't do research unless you've got a hypothesis.' Actually I didn't have one until I was writing up, and even then it wasn't really a hypothesis. I did write it in the context of theories of modernization – the foreshortening, skipping a stage notion.[15]

In sum, in *City Life* we can already discern the main elements of Dore's sociology. First, he shares with classical sociologists a broad interest in community, social change and social evolution. Second, however, he rejects the ethnocentric assumptions of some of them – that there is only one path to development, the one pioneered in the 'West'. Third, he rejects static and deterministic views of culture in favour of studying the interplay of human agency, institutions and cultural values or norms in specific settings. Fourth, and related to this, his 'open' approach contrasts with that of the 'closed' systems theorists of the times; in this sense it is closer to that of Weber.[16]

Digging deeper, we can discern certain attitudes which underlie these orientations. First, a respect for the Japanese and Japanese society, the seeds for which were sown, ironically perhaps, during his early language classes during the war (Dore, 1994a, 274), and while cataloguing at Cambridge University Library, but reinforced during his first stay in Japan. This meant a reluctance to accept the prevailing view of the backwardness of Japanese society, whose peculiarities would have to be abandoned if Japan were successfully to modernize.

Second, a reluctance to accept the innate superiority of British (or Anglo-Saxon or 'Western') civilization. Dore was born into a working-class family. His father worked at a butcher's shop before working on the railway, starting as an engine cleaner, and retiring as a locomotive driver. He grew up with a working class disparagement of, but discomfort in the presence of, the 'nobs' of the middle and upper classes. Japanese academics who expected him to exemplify English gentlemanship got on his nerves. Switching his research from Japanese Confucianism to the hustle and bustle of Hanazono-chō was consistent with these sentiments. The affinity he felt towards the residents made him reluctant to see them as unique or peculiar, let alone backward. We shall return to this later.

Affinity, however, did not mean unreserved admiration. There is a brief discussion at the end of *City Life* about the implications for democracy of skipping a stage. Without a stage of small-scale, competitive, independent economic activity, could independence of thought and action become and remain established? The ambiguity of this discussion reflects an attitudinal dilemma; a desire to avoid ethnocentric assumptions about social evolution on the one hand, but a positive value placed on 'inner direction' on the other. Although he writes sympathetically of Japan, and often critically of Britain, his preference has always been to live in the latter (or in recent years, Italy).[17]

Studies in Development

After four years back in the UK, Dore was anxious to return to Japan. His chance came fortuitously. The Royal Institute of International Affairs (RIIA) was looking for someone to study Japan's land reforms. Land reform was widely seen as a prerequisite to establishing a stable democracy and for economic growth. There were reports that in Japan it had been a spectacular success, but were these accounts exaggerated? The RIIA was willing to fund someone to look at this. In his earlier stay Dore had occasionally accompanied village survey teams with the sociologist Fukutake Tadashi. Now he had the chance for a systematic study. With a year's leave from SOAS, he arrived in Japan in time for the February 1955 elections, in which land reform debates figured prominently. He spent the following months in three villages in different parts of Japan, with different crop and tenure patterns, finishing off with a questionnaire survey conducted by Tokyo University students before burying himself in the village he subsequently wrote about as 'Shinohata' to write up his findings.

In studying land reform, Dore was entering a minefield of politicized and entrenched views, with which his findings brought him into conflict. On the one hand, General MacArthur had credited himself with the most successful land reforms since the Roman Gracchus brothers in the second century BC. MacArthur may have championed the reforms, Dore reasoned, but their success and durability had much more to do with indigenous social forces and endowments, which the Occupation had unblocked. On the other hand, he could not agree with the British cynics who derided the Americans for their naïvety in believing that they could march in and democratize Japan: the 'leopard cannot change its spots' view as he called it.[18] In his view, not only had Japan changed, but the leopard wasn't so spotty in the first place, at least in terms of rural fascism.

More significantly, his upbeat assessment of the progress and effects of land reform clashed with the views of those (*kōza* school) Marxists within Japan who argued that the semi-feudal nature of Japanese agriculture remained intact, and that the landlords would make a comeback since, among other reasons, the land reforms had not touched their forestry holdings. He argued that changes in postwar Japan meant that a return to the 1930s was inconceivable, and that markedly improved standards of living were widely shared. Finally, he disagreed with his friend and mentor Fukutake, and most other rural sociologists, who believed that progress and democracy required individuation and a breakdown of community cohesion and hence of community constraints on the individual. He argued – against the evolutionary perspective of his own urban study – first that the shift from vertically organized, landlord-dominated communities to more egalitarian owner-farmer communities had actually increased cohesion, and second that this was a good thing and not inimical to democracy.

Dore did, however, share the pessimism of all those Japanese scholars who foresaw a chronic labour surplus problem in the villages, at least until the benefits of Japan's compressed demographic revolution were felt, because of an incapacity to generate sufficient jobs elsewhere in the economy. Within five years, as he has reflected on a number of occasions, growing labour shortages in a booming economy were to provide him with a graphic lesson in the dangers of prediction, although they reinforced his views about the benefits of economic growth experienced in rural Japan.

Dore resigned from his SOAS job in 1956, in part so that he could spend an extra six months in Yamanashi writing up his findings, and then to take up a post in Canada, launching Japanese studies at the University of British Columbia. There he returned to his notes and the books he had collected on Tokugawa education, but with new questions as a result of his research on contemporary Japan, and with the growing interest amongst foreign scholars in the 'pre-modern' facilitators of Japan's rapid 'modernization'. Again employing Parsons' pattern variables, he showed how ascription (in which status is determined by the family into which one is born) was tempered by achievement in Tokugawa schools and how, by the end of the period, the balance had been decisively tipped towards the latter, both in education and the bureaucracies, as a result of internal and external crisis, introduction from the West of new branches of learning, and the quantitative expansion of education. His emphasis on social institutions contrasted with that of Parsons' own student, Bellah (1957), whose use of the Weberian tradition was to look for the emergence in Tokugawa Japan of a functional equivalent of the Protestant ethic.

Dore's estimates of literacy rates, which are still used today, pointed to levels of literacy in the 1870s which were at least comparable to those of many European countries, Britain included, at the same time. While Japan was only just embarking on industrialization, however, the industrial revolution was well underway in the latter. This finding marked the beginning of his 'late development' thesis, a development of stage-skipping evolution:

> Education seems to have become the major mechanism of social selection at an earlier stage of industrialization in Japan than in Western countries. Learning was the royal road not only to the professions and to government, but also to business success as well – as the very high proportion of university graduates among Japanese business-men suggests. Undoubtedly one explanation of this fact is that Japan was a late developer, catching up by learning, and hence having more practical use for already systematized knowledge. (1964, 293)

The concluding chapter of *Education in Tokugawa Japan* was presented at the first of a series of conferences on Japan's modernization which resulted in a number of volumes later published by Princeton University Press, the second of which Dore organized and edited (1967). The moving spirit of the group was celebratory. Recent Japanese history was not, as contemporary Japanese intellectuals were inclined to present it, a story of wicked predatory aggression and imperialism. It was also a heroic tale of successful industrialization under dedicated modernizing leadership. Dore's 'balance sheet' account, including the way the ultranationalists corrupted the Confucian legacy, showed his characteristic reluctance to side wholly with either simplification. Later, when one of the 'modernization' group, Edwin O. Reischauer, became US ambassador to Japan, the modernization story, and his courting of Japanese intellectuals, became branded by the Japanese left as part of the 'Reischauer offensive', designed to further America's Cold War aims.[19] It was partly in response to that criticism that the last book of the series was a somewhat more critical collection of papers under the title *Dilemmas of Growth in Prewar Japan*, to which Dore contributed a paper jointly with Marxist economic historian Ouchi on the landlord's role in the development of Japanese fascism (1971).

On the debate itself, Dore criticized those who flatly spurned, as part of the 'Reischauer offensive', attempts to look at Japan for development lessons for 'less developed countries'. He also wrote (Chapter 2 of this volume) on the need to distinguish between modernization as a conscious 'transitive' process – what people deliberately do to their society when they are trying to catch up with more 'advanced' countries – and modernization postulated as an 'intransitive' evolutionary process, as in 'the Reformation was the start of European modernization'.

These views grew out of his work the previous year, which he spent with the Food and Agriculture Organization (FAO) in Rome reading about Africa, Latin America and south and east Asia in order to write the FAO's fourth *Progress in Land Reform* report. (The rural co-operatives chapter was deemed insufficiently optimistic by the International Labour Organization [ILO] co-operatives division, and he was happy to withdraw it for publication in his own name [1971; Chapter 4]). It questioned Engels' claim that primordial village communities cannot directly develop modern co-operatives without an intervening stage of individuation.) Now back in London in the sociology department of LSE,[20] he had already taught a course on the sociology of development with Tom Bottomore (who had spent a year in India) and Ernest Gellner (who had done anthropological work in North Africa), but his year in Rome made development his prime preoccupation. He later recalled that the FAO year put a new perspective on the different starting points in the drive to industrialize and modernize, and reinforced the significance he attached to the legacy of Tokugawa education and administration (1983a, 34; see Chapter 16).

This preoccupation, too, ensured 'late development' a central place in his next major project – a comparative study of industrial relations in British and Japanese factories. Dore had spent a couple of months in the summer of 1965 interviewing in two Seiko watch factories. He was drawn to industrial relations because it seemed – as Abegglen (1958) had demonstrated – that there were marked differences between Japan and Western countries, and these were likely to raise interesting questions. As the differences were more pronounced in the modern, large-firm sector than the traditional small-firm sector, it was unlikely that they could simply be attributed to Japan's backwardness. And as there were also considerable sectoral differences *within Japan* to be accounted for, a simple cultural explanation was not convincing, either.[21]

He joined a comparative project with Keith Thurley and Martin Collick in the UK, and Hazama Hiroshi and Okamoto Hideaki in Japan. Thurley and Okamoto were to concentrate on the construction industry; Collick, Okamoto and Hazama on steel; and Dore and Hazama on electrical engineering, from which they chose two matching factories in each of Hitachi and (then) English Electric. All notes and collected materials were to be pooled, and each was to write his own book.

This was Dore's first fully comparative study using matched cases, and *British Factory–Japanese Factory* has become a classic for both its rich empirical detail, and the use of this method. It was published at the same time that a series of French–German comparisons were being conducted, also critiquing universalist and culturalist approaches to industrial relations and work organization.[22] However, while the 'societal effects' group was attempting to construct a framework to show how social and economic institutions differed, and fitted together differently, in the respective countries (rather statically at first), Dore's main interpretive interests lay in relating his findings to evolutionary change.

In particular, he attacked widely-held assumptions that Japan would have to reform its distinctive, 'backward' institutions if it were to develop successfully. He did so on three counts. First, as a result of late development, Japan had developed an 'organization-oriented' industrial relations system as opposed to Britain's (earlier, ossified) 'market-oriented' system. The former conferred technological advantages. Second, late development offered the benefits of greater social equality, the movement towards which was another social evolutionary trend. Third, late development conferred advantages in related social institutions, such as education and personnel management. If anything, it was Britain that would change, as a fledgling organization-oriented system struggled to break out of the restraining market orientation.

Not surprisingly, the book proved controversial, on a number of grounds. First, regarding the empirical and historical evidence, it has been argued that it did not adequately represent the chequered industrial relations history preceding the 'co-operative line' which emerged in Hitachi in the 1960s, as well as lingering resistance and conflict (e.g. Kawanishi, 1992). Critics of Japanese industrial relations and management concede that there is indeed a high degree of equality in terms of status and wage differentials in large Japanese companies, but this has been gained at the expense of worker self-determination, and the subordination of individuals' interests to those of the company. In the words of one, Japan's unions pressed for and gained 'citizen's rights' in the corporation, but lost 'villager autonomy'.[23] Logically speaking, this is not inconsistent with Dore's own views (cf. his earlier interpretation of Riesman), but he stressed the value of 'citizen's rights', and saw the professed intention of Japanese union leaders to 'transcend' enterprise unions and create British-style industrial unions as misguided.

Second, and more controversial, were the arguments about 'late development', and 'reverse convergence' as it came to be called. 'Late development' effects, and the converse 'penalty of taking the lead', had been expounded by a number of economists, including Veblen (1915; 1934) and Gerschenkron (1962), but Dore took the concepts further, into institutions of training, employment and industrial relations (cf. Chapter 9). In part, the controversy hinged upon just what, and how much, of Japan's employment and industrial relations system derived from (1) its late-development status (which should be evident in other late developers); (2) its own socio-cultural distinctiveness, particularly its pre-industrial legacy; and (3) idiosyncratic or historical factors such as war.

In the exchange between Cole and Dore in the *Journal of Japanese Studies*

(1978 and 1979 respectively), Dore denied that he was holding up Japan as a normative model for Britain. Instead, he was suggesting that later developers were more likely to develop institutions closer to Japan than Britain, and that 'the British system was getting closer to the Japanese system a good deal faster than vice versa'. This was due, in part at least, to an evolutionary trend towards the greater prominence of (bureaucratic) organizations in economic and social life, a view echoing not just Weber but, more recently, the writing of Shonfield (1965), further developed subsequently by scholars of corporatism (e.g. Schmitter, 1979). Cole questioned this tendency:

> [S]ome scholars maintain that bureaucracy is on the wane in advanced industrial societies, ill-suited as it is for the condition of rapid environmental change and the growth of people and idea-oriented service jobs. I have yet to see convincing evidence on this score, but were the thesis correct, it would certainly invalidate the Dore hypothesis. (1974, 392)

On the face of it, history would seem to have vindicated Cole's view. Deregulation and market resurgence, the demise of tripartite corporatism and rise of the Silicon Valley entrepreneur would appear to mark a reversal of the earlier evolutionary trend. Dore held to his view of the bureaucratic future until the late 1980s (cf. Chapter 13; also Chapter 7 on its recent evolution), but in recent writings has become clearly uncertain (e.g. 2000). In the mid 1970s, however, neither Cole nor Dore could foresee the complex socio-economic developments that the industrialized countries were soon to experience. We shall return to some of these below.

After spending a year in Princeton in 1969–70 to write up *British Factory–Japanese Factory*, Dore moved to the newly formed, interdisciplinary Institute of Development Studies (IDS) at Sussex University as its sociologist, joining economists such as Dudley Seers and Paul Streeten. His next major monograph, combining analysis with polemic, stayed with 'late development', but in the context of education. Again it posits a trend towards bureaucratic organization, but the analysis also draws on Young's (1958) notion of the rise of meritocracy. Dore was first drawn back to education by going to Japan in 1970 as an OECD examiner to prepare a report on the Japanese education system. The following year, as a member of an ILO employment mission looking at large-scale youth unemployment in Sri Lanka, he spent six weeks visiting schools and talking to educational administrators in that country. There he experienced:

> for the first time a country with a sharp division between a modern sector offering salaries and security far superior to life in the traditional peasant economy; and the tremendous strains set up because that modern sector grew only slowly, while the school system, whose certificates had hitherto acted as license to enter that modern sector, expanded at a much more rapid rate. I saw this as one more 'late

> development effect', vastly accelerating processes which were common to all modern societies. (1997b, 24)

Observations on those missions, and in England, generated the arguments for *The Diploma Disease,* an expression which has entered common discourse. The 'diploma disease' (or 'credentialism') is not a personal affliction, but a social one. It occurs when 'genuine' learning - learning for its own sake, or learning how to do a job - is displaced by learning in order to get a job. Late developers, which use education certificates for occupation selection from an early stage, and which experience an expansion of education relative to employment growth at a rate which generates 'qualification inflation', are particularly prone to the disease.

In terms of polemics, the book strongly criticizes human capitalist writers on the one hand, and deschoolers on the other. It is not against examinations and meritocratic selection *per se*, but it tempers the more optimistic image of late development and bureaucratization of *British Factory–Japanese Factory* by explicitly (re)introducing a pathology which inhibits the development of inner direction, promotes the development of a 'managed society' (*kanri shakai* in Japanese), and ultimately a new form of social stratification. Japan is a good example (1983a, 37–8; although its experience of the 'diploma disease' was less severe than in other late developers: Chapter 16).

Dore argues that the process eventually takes hold in earlier developers as well; indeed nowhere has qualification inflation been more evident in recent years than in Britain, which has seen a massive expansion in tertiary education, and increased use of certificate-based selection. Yet this has occurred alongside the market reforms of the 'Thatcher revolution', modified but carried on under the Blairite banner of universal flexibility. The two trends are not necessarily contradictory, he suggests. The latter reforms may have an effect in shortening job tenures, reducing the importance of seniority in pay and promotions, and so on, but they have not affected the growing importance of certificates for getting jobs, which is a key aspect of bureaucratization in *The Diploma Disease*.[24]

Returning to industrial relations, Dore began to look at whether Japan's 'organization-oriented' employment system could be found in other late developers and, if so, whether it needed consolidating by advocacy in the face of all the experts advocating Euro-centric (or American) models. In 1973 he organized a project to study industrial relations in Mexico, Senegal and Sri Lanka, again extending and refining the late development thesis. It was this research, as he noted in his exchange with Cole, that brought home the importance of ingrained 'behavioural dispositions' of culture (Chapter 16). And there were limitations to any simple advocacy of a 'Japanese model' as a recipe for developing countries, as he notes in the Epilogue to *Shinohata*

(1978; Chapter 13), written after a '20 years on' spell in his Yamanashi village (and also in an article (1984; Chapter 12) written after a three month spell at the Institute for Economic Growth in Delhi in 1980). Some of these limitations stemmed from differences in culture and institutions, others from the changing political and economic context of development, and yet others from thorny issues such as intergenerational distribution; even current Japanese villagers, beneficiaries of visibly growing wealth, would be unlikely to support Japan's model of industrialization which brought harsh privations for their grandparents.

Political Economy of Capitalisms

By the mid 1970s development studies itself was in a state of flux, racked by internal criticism. The 'missions' of the 1960s and early 1970s had dried up as developing countries now had their own specialists, and master–pupil relations were replaced by bargaining for resources. There was a debate within the IDS over its role, and whether it should extend its scope to look at development in Britain. Dore's view was that the problems of a stagnant Britain were completely different from those of development in Tanzania, that attempts to draw lessons from one to the other were futile but, ironically, it was he who switched his research focus to Britain. His study of the textile industry in Blackburn was intended not as a study of processes of development, but:

> I came around to the view that if one was at an Institute for Development Studies, which had the function of providing intellectual backup to help poorer countries become richer, that one of the best things one could do when sitting in England, and one of the things one had a better *right* to do than preaching to developing countries' governments, was to look at the possibilities of running down in as humane and efficient a way as possible the British industries which were subject to the competition of trade from developing countries. Like textiles.[25]

The project involved a comparison of the textile industry in Britain, France and Japan. Parts of this study were published (Dore, 1982, Chapter 23; 1986b), but difficulties with collaborators meant that the planned book based on a Blackburn–Kishiwada comparison never materialized. However, a related ILO project on structural adjustment led to *Flexible Rigidities* (1986a), which contains a substantial case study on the textile industry in Japan.

These studies of the textile industry marked a new transition in Dore's scholarship, in four ways. First, he was moving away from development studies *per se*, which had been a key interest for the past decade and a half. Second, he was drawn towards the growing debates on technology, technological innovation and the social context of innovation. In 1981 he became assistant director of the newly formed Technical Change Centre (TCC), set up by the Leverhulme Trust, Science and Engineering Research Council (SERC) and Economic and Social Research Council (ESRC), with a double brief - exploring how to make technical change happen to promote competitiveness on the one hand, and how to anticipate and if necessary ameliorate the consequences of technical change on the other. Under the first brief he studied the introduction and use of CNC (computer numerical control) machine tools in British (and Japanese) factories, and innovation in the British (and Japanese) pump industry, and under the second, the Youth Training Scheme and unemployment.[26] Third, his studies of textiles, and a 1980–81 study of energy conservation measures in Japan, fuelled his keen interest in industrial policy and, hence, what is nowadays called 'political economy'. Fourth, although to some extent he had always been interested in policy debates, his writing became more explicitly advocative.[27] In particular, he felt the new right agenda for curing Britain's economic malaise was misinformed and socially regressive. Japan was the platform for his critique.

As he argued in *Flexible Rigidities*: 'Japan ... has grown to be the second biggest Western economy precisely by incorporating these features which are deplored elsewhere, as integral functioning elements of its system of "organized capitalism". It has seen the shape of the future and made it work' (1986a, 250). His prescription was to make rigidities (of long-term commitments) produce the flexibility that comes from willing co-operation, not removing the rigidities by making commitments short term as in auction markets. Those who attempt the latter course, he argued, have a limited concept of efficiency; in stressing allocative efficiency - the efficiency that comes from the constant reallocation of labour and capital to the use that brings the highest returns - they ignore what Leibenstein (1966) calls '*x*-efficiency', which encourages work based on conscientiousness, diligence, caring about the quality of work, but is less amenable to algebraic manipulation as it depends on how people are educated, trained, motivated and integrated. The argument - and the transition - is most clearly expressed in *Taking Japan Seriously*. The main themes in the book are given as:

> 1 '*x*-efficiency' or 'production efficiency' is as important as, and probably for explaining differences in national economic performance *more* important than, allocative efficiency.
> 2 A sense of fairness of social and economic arrangements is a crucial precondition for that kind of efficiency.
> 3 That sense of *fairness* cannot be achieved in the rough and tumble which results when each actor in the market is encouraged to maximize his own short-term benefits, unconstrained by anything except the hard reality of market forces - not, at any rate, in modern societies, with modern concepts of citizenship and the accompanying rights to be respected and consulted and to receive a minimum level of income and security. (1987a, 18)

The subtitle of the book – 'A Confucian Perspective on Leading Economic Issues' – deserves some comment. Dore clearly saw a Confucian legacy in modern Japan (e.g. Dore, 1996; Chapter 18), but strictly speaking, that is not what the subtitle referred to. It was actually being used as a polar construct, to contrast the assumptions of 'original virtue' of the Mencian Confucianists on the one hand, and those of 'original sin' on the other. These give rise to very different views as to why people work, why they co-operate, why they compete and notions of fairness. The latter, he argued, have influenced the evolution of Western economic doctrines and more recently the policy programmes of Mrs Thatcher and Mr Reagan, while the former have been embedded in Japanese economic policy (p. vii). By means of comparison and contrast, he sought to stimulate debate on policy alternatives in Britain (and the USA):

> One starts off taking the role of the state and views of its limitations current in Britain today for granted. The next step is a sense of the polarized dichotomy: Japan/developmental state – Britain/regulatory state. The third step is the realization that this is not in fact a dichotomy but a spectrum, that in getting a sense of the contrast between the two polar states at the ends of the spectrum, one has got hold of a new tool of analysis, a new dimension, a new means of measuring changes as a shift along that dimension, a new means, say, of analyzing the compatibility of different institutions which may belong to different parts of that dimension. (1987a, 7)

Through the contrast, he sought to challenge widely-held views of employment, unemployment, social participation and citizenship. Technological change creates new jobs and destroys others. The jobs it creates tend to be the so-called 'symbolic analysts' jobs' (demanding logical reasoning and verbal exposition associated with a university education) and those that disappear are jobs which can be learned without much special training. The 'ability demanding-ness' of jobs shifts upwards, but the supply of abilities does not keep up, even with concerted efforts to extend participation in education, given that ability endowments vary and not everyone can become a symbolic analyst.

Work, however, is critical for a sense of first class citizenship, he argued, by giving people a sense that they are contributing to society, that society needs their contribution, by providing the money to live a 'normal' or 'decent' life-style, and so on. Yet one result of the above trend is growing long-term unemployment and/or people engaged in 'Mcjobs' which do not yield a wage sufficient to meet either a welfare or dignity minimum. On the other hand, those at the other end of the spectrum have no fear or experience of unemployment, find themselves in great demand, enjoy considerable power and prestige, and command high wages for doing work which more and more is of a kind which gives its own intrinsic satisfactions. Given a long-term secular trend towards egalitarianism, this new type of inequality is amplified, he argues, and creates if not a new Two Nations, then a New Hierarchical Order, with debilitating social consequences (Chapter 24).

Instead of developing theories to justify the New Hierarchical Order, Dore proposed we change our conception of work to conform to the actual nature of the 'good jobs' which the technology we use still leaves to be done by humans, from one of irksome duty to privilege, and that those enjoying the privilege share with those that do not. Specifically, he argued for a universal 'citizen's income' which would form a base income, to which salaries of those privileged to work would be added (*ibid.*). This would require a massive redistribution of income, hence a rediscovery of fraternity, the forgotten French Revolution value, or a new communitarianism. Rather than a utopian vision, he considers this to be the best of a number of painful alternatives to dealing with ever greater inequality of rewards resulting from increasing technological complexity which, rather than unemployment itself, he considers to be the real problem.[28]

In the late 1980s, Japan was being taken very seriously, especially in the USA, though not necessarily in the sense advocated by Dore. USA–Japan trade friction was reaching new heights, and was followed by 'investment friction' as cash-flush Japanese companies bought US icons like the Rockefeller Center. The USA was attempting to chip away at Japan's 'invisible' trade and investment barriers through the Structural Impediments Initiative, which highlighted differences in Japanese and US capitalism. In this context the end of the Cold War marked not so much the end of history, but a new era of competition, if not between civilizations, at least between different forms of capitalism. Dore became a visiting professor first at Harvard University (1986–9) and then MIT (1989–94).[29] In the polarized, highly-charged clashes between the so-called revisionists and free-traders in the USA, he sought to bring an 'outsider's' view, which led to his 'IIIRQ' (Investment Inviting Import Quantity Restrictions) proposal (1990b; 1993; Chapter 26).

The Japanese economic juggernaut of the late 1980s also produced a spate of 'Japanization' writing, which seemed to support the 'reverse convergence' thesis, although Dore had suggested convergent independent evolution, and had not, in 1973, contemplated imitative borrowing. Dore returned to this and late development in the Afterword to the 1990 edition of *British Factory-Japanese Factory*. On the whole, he found evidence, as originally proposed, of a trend towards greater organization-orientation in employment systems, albeit for core workers. This was tempered in some cases, however, by the casualization of employment of non-core workers, and what he judged a minority trend towards market-oriented employment in Britain and the USA. He also stood by his view of an evolutionary trend towards greater egalitarianism, though again with the exception of peripheral groups in Britain and the USA, and with the twist of attempts to turn (core) employees into shareholders rather than improve their rights at the expense of shareholders.[30]

As co-ordinators for a major study of corporatism in the UK, Crouch and Dore (1990) found that corporatist arrangements had not been swept aside *in toto*, but rather that tripartite neo-corporatist institutions had been replaced by quangos and quagos, while old forms of corporatist arrangements, particularly in the professions, were largely intact. They found a 'return to the old British pattern'. A 'return', however, is not the same as continuation of an evolutionary trend, even with blips. The 'return' was evident, not only in the attempt to impose market solutions to Britain's economic malaise, but in the reassertion of shareholder power in corporate governance, and a revival of the 'company law' model of the firm. This revival, moreover, was being exported with evangelical fervour, fanning the 'clash of capitalisms'.

Dore gradually became more equivocal about the outcome of the 'Darwinian contest', not just within Britain, but in Japan itself (1994c). In his Ishizaka Lectures of 1989, he explored whether the Japanese were bound to become more individualistic - in various senses of the word - in the twenty-first century. At this time he still concluded that:

> I do not believe that the world of the 21st century will be dominated by consumerist rather than productivist values ... [and] I do not believe that the productivist ethic will be of a market individualist kind such as prevailed in the heyday of the yeoman and the small entrepreneur. It is much more likely to be a group corporatist ethic. (1990a, 112-13)

The question which he was becoming increasingly preoccupied with, however, was not whether Japan would finally experience its missing stage, but whether it was suffering from, in Hirsch's (1977) term, the 'depleting moral legacy of capitalism'. Hirsch's argument was that to be in some overall sense efficient, capitalist societies rely on pre-capitalist moral constraints, but it is these very constraints which are eroded by capitalism. When he cited Hirsch in his 'Goodwill and the Spirit of Market Capitalism' article (1983b), it was still in the context of how Britain could replenish the 'depleting moral legacy' by learning from Japan. In the 1990s, however, the question was whether Japan's moral legacy was itself being rapidly depleted.

Albert had argued that 'Rhine capitalism' might eventually give way to neo-American capitalism despite being more economically efficient and socially equitable because of the latter's seductive appeal: 'In the ideological beauty contest, it is easy to see who will score more points. The neo-American model proudly presents itself as a hard-headed professional, undisguised and untroubled by sentiment or second thoughts. Its main rival comes across as complicated, opaque - if not obscure - and cloaked in too many overlapping folds of social considerations, financial constraints, cherished traditions and good intentions.' So much so that: 'even the good grey burghers of Zurich and Frankfurt are beginning to wonder what it feels like to win the jackpot with one spin of the roulette wheel'.[31]

Dore saw this beginning to happen in Japan as well. He explained recent trends in Japan partly as a consequence of the way Japan's post-bubble recession and the US boom had eroded Japanese self confidence, but also in terms of generational change. The newer generation – *chūryū nisei* (second generation middle class) – raised in relative urban prosperity, with no direct experience of collective efforts to overcome postwar hardship, and inheritors of financial assets their parents had accumulated, might well succumb to the temptations of the roulette wheel, or at least to the attractions of market 'allocative efficiency' arguments which justified higher returns to shareholders and less concern for employees. 'Making money' in financial markets was beginning to take precedence over 'making things'.

> What a world we are away not only from Shitayama-cho, but also from the economic structures and values of Japan in 1950–51. Then banks performed the wholly necessary function of collecting savings from depositors and lending them to people who were engaged in producing and trading real goods and services. Their income came from the difference between deposit rates and loan rates. Now, increasingly, they serve only to mediate the relationship of their clients to volatile financial markets, creaming off fees for that service and meanwhile juggling their clients' and their own money in elaborate risk pyramids of swaps, futures and options, thereby helping to cause the very volatility they charge their clients for protecting them from. Finance, once the handmaiden of industry, is rapidly becoming its master (1999, xxix–xxx).

Feelings about egalitarian social justice were also changing: modern elites, segregated from an early age from those they would eventually manage and attending the best schools their parents went to, with the financial benefits that schooling bestowed, would be less able or inclined to identify with those they led. The led, in turn, would be increasingly deprived – by enlarged equality of opportunity in the meritocratic education selection system – of voices competent to articulate their concerns, in contrast to the early postwar labour movement. As a result, Japan's capacity to develop measures to replenish the 'depleting moral legacy' would be reduced.

In his writing for publication in Japan he turned from addressing the criticism that he had paid insufficient attention to the unhealthier consequences and victims of Japan's economic growth (two volumes of interviews with non-establishment and anti-establishment people: 1994e; 1997d), to warning against paying insufficient attention to the unhealthier consequences of Anglo Saxon neo-liberalism. He did this through a regular column in the *Tokyo Shinbun*, various other newspapers and journals, and through a 'global standards' research group, in which he brought together a number of senior businessmen, bureaucrats and academics to study the issues at stake in the late 1990s debates about changing corporate governance. With the implementation of Japan's Big Bang, the rapid inroads of foreign institutions in its financial markets, globalized transactions, and the growing importance of credit-rating agencies on the one hand, and a recognition of the need for strategic change in its manufacturing heartland on the other, it was in the area of corporate governance that he saw the decisive Darwinian battles being fought. These concerns are also the major theme of his latest book (Dore, 2000a).

Is US-style finance capitalism – or more appropriately 'investor capitalism' (e.g. Useem, 1996) – the next stage in the evolution of Japan's 'producer capitalism', or are there alternatives which Japan might realistically adopt? We appear to be back where we started, only this time Dore is somewhat more pessimistic. His pessimism contrasts, for instance, with the easy optimism of Fukuyama, who foresees the recreation of moral values and community after the 'great disruption' because human beings are, by nature, social beings (Fukuyama, 1999, 6). Is his pessimism evidence that he has become a jeremiad, as he sometimes suggests? Is he seeking to warn the Japanese about a potential loss of community? Or are Japan's 'post-industrial' options really more limited than those open to it when it was industrializing or recovering from World War II? In less pessimistic moments, he suggests that Japan might offer 'stiffer resistance' than Germany because its distinctive institutions are based not simply on law and class compromise, but (presumably less fragile) communitarian traditions. Much depends, he suggests, on whether the respective experiences of the Japanese and US economies in the coming years permit a revival of Japanese national self-confidence. And also on developments in Korea and China. Continued rapid growth in East Asia may lead the Japanese to reassess their Asian-ness and hence their institutions (Dore, 2000b). The issues are crucial, and attest to the continued relevance of Dore's research in understanding community, social evolution, and modern political economy.

LOCATING DORE AND HIS CONTRIBUTIONS

Like many of Halsey's 'provincial thirteen', Ronald Dore was of working class background, 'won the scholarship' to grammar school, and only went to university because of World War II.[32] Like them, he was an outsider in Britain's status hierarchy, but came to London to study in an environment removed from the traditional 'Oxford–London–Cambridge axis' of politics, power and letters. Indeed Dore mixed with many of the thirteen at LSE, particularly in the Thursday evening seminars, in a pulsating postwar intellectual milieu.

Yet Halsey does not include Dore in the group, for good reason. Based at SOAS, Dore was an outsider, even here, and although he has always borne the sociologist label, and taught in the sociology department at LSE for ten years, he did not particularly espouse the profession of sociology. Though British, with 'occasional pangs of pride over Britain's possession of the BBC, the NHS (National Health Service) and FT', and keenly interested in making Britain a better social democracy, he has spent considerable periods of his academic career outside the UK, and his primary research interests have lain abroad as well, particularly in Japan.

He once described his lack of interest in the demarcation and maintenance of academic disciplines in the following terms:

> I had the *good luck* never to have been brought up from an early age - never to have been socialized, a proper sociologist would say - into any disciplinary tribe. I came to sociology by the autodidact's back door. I got a job in a sociology department because Japan was considered exotic and important, and I had accidentally acquired some knowledge of it ... I myself have never really been aware of being in possession of any particular disciplinary expertise, or of having anything in the way of theoretical tools of the trade that were specifically sociological. (1994d, 1425, emphasis added)

One who does not show allegiance to a particular tribe is unlikely to be honoured by it. And so it has been, to some extent, with Dore. His preference has been to move across disciplinary boundaries in his pursuit of answers to his questions, and to use rigorous reasoning and empirical evidence in the formulation of those answers. His success in doing so, however, has gained him at least honorary membership in a wide range of tribes, including anthropology, education, sociology, economics and political economy.

The reason he considers himself lucky (according to the above quote) is that when disciplinary tribalists are faced with the dilemma, in the competition for funds and prestige, of whether to appeal to wider-world relevance or the superior intellectual quality of their discipline, they tend to opt for the latter. The dilemma and the tendency are particularly apparent in economics departments, where a scholar's prestige is often 'in inverse proportion to the number among them who can understand his algebra' (1995, 102), but it happens in other disciplines as well.

Even if it began with 'luck', then, Dore's lack of interest in academic tribalism is not the result of indifference. On the contrary, it is based on definite views of good and bad, useful and useless, beneficial and injurious social science:

> A line of division much more important than any disciplinary boundary - important

> because it has clear political implications – is that between what one might call the rationality-obsessed economists, political scientists and sociologists, and those who are *struck with wonder at the world about them, seek explanations of their own and their fellow humans' behaviour,* and in seeking such explanations, allow for the possibility, not only of irrationality but also of altruism, and of adherence to norms – norms driven by conscience of concepts of self-respect, by guilt or shame. *In part it is a division between theorists and social scientists.* But it is also, if you like, a division between those whose feet are planted joyously and firmly in the traditional Christian doctrine of Original Sin, and those who would find more congenial the Confucian doctrine of Original Virtue. (Not 100% virtue, of course, even according to the most optimistic of Confucianists such as Mencius or Mao Tse Tung...)
>
> That line of division is one which cuts across conventional disciplinary divisions. While it is true that many economics departments are dominated by the rationality-obsessed because their rationality obsession provides the essential axiomatic base for their mathematical pyrotechnics, some of the most socially – if you like sociologically – perceptive and empirical reality-rooted social scientists are economists. Some of them lead a *double life*; doing their professional stuff in the journals to build up their claim to a Nobel prize, talking about the real world in casual journalism, and only actually daring to bring their two selves together when they come to give a presidential address to some economic association. Others actually concentrate their professional work on the study of real-world economies, keeping alive the political economy tradition of Smith and Marshall. (1994d, 1429–30, emphasis added)

'Theorists' here are those whose preoccupation with theoretical advancement or confirmation leads them to extract a very limited number of factors from complex webs of real life causation – or else simply to work with 'stylized facts' which the theory requires and are *assumed* to approximate real life causation – and to work out the logical implications of what would happen if only those factors operated. The result may well be clever models and theoretical advancement, but limited relevance to real life, and limited ability to make real life situations intelligible. Principal–agent theory in economics, for instance, is built on 'uni-dimensional man', ignoring the fact that 'principal and agent in Lagos are often uncle and nephew, that Yokohama principals are often business firms engaged in some R&D joint venture with the firm of their so-called agent, that an Idaho principal is often some junk-bond-issuing asset stripper' (1995, 102). While sociologists might be expected to step in and pick up such 'tosh' or 'irrational residue' (according to Samuelson's infamous demarcation), increasing numbers are themselves succumbing to the same tendencies, adopting the same view of 'uni-dimensional man'.

The rejoinder to such criticism may be summed up by Coase's blunt assessment of the (older) institutional economics tradition: 'Without a theory they had nothing to pass on except a mass of descriptive material waiting for a theory or a fire' (1984, 230). To this Dore might well respond that being remembered by posterity is a dubious motive for research; a more immediate motive, apart from intellectual curiosity, should be improving the human lot through informing policy with sound social science research. And policies based on the assumptions of the theorists who win Coase's approval - assumptions that human beings move solely out of self-interest, with the propensity for guile - may well accelerate the 'depleting moral legacy' of capitalism, bringing the real world into closer alignment with theory. It would be better to have no lasting legacy than one of this sort.

If we accept Dore's distinction between theorists (bad) and social scientists (good), who are the social scientists? In general, they are researchers who examine the world about them and seek for recurrent regularities, or generalizations arrived at by induction, which may be translated into predictions, the falsification of which gives rise to better propositions and predictions. They *strive for* objectivity by constant self-examination, and listening to critics who have different views. (Herein lies a danger of academic tribes, or rather bands within tribes, who read and write largely for each other, because everyone else is either wrong or not worth bothering with.) And in general, they tend to be methodological individualists, although they tend to leave the study of the micro mechanisms of human behaviour to psychologists (Dore, 1995, 98–9).[33]

As for Dore himself, being 'struck with wonder' at the world about him has always been his motivating drive, and he much prefers to explore that world than to become involved in debates on methodology or theory, his one notable exception being an article on 'Function and Cause' (1961, reproduced in several collections on sociology theory), which coincided with his taking up a readership in sociology at LSE. He has not even attempted to spell out exactly what he means by 'social evolution', for instance, unlike his late friend Gellner (1988), much less develop a general theory like Ginsberg or Hobhouse. Being 'struck with wonder', however, has always been coupled with an insistence on rigorous reasoning and avoidance of obfuscation. This may owe something to formative years at LSE, to Popper's lectures on logic for instance.[34] But it probably owes more to his own research ethics. 'Seeking explanations of their own and their fellow human's behaviour' means an insistence on avoiding a 'double life' in the sense described in the quote above.

This insistence takes on a special significance when it comes to Dore's comparative sociology. As Lipset states in his book on American particularism: 'It is impossible to understand a country without seeing how it varies from others. Those who know only one country know no country' (1996, 17). But there are many ways of making comparisons, some of them crude and lazy, some of them reflecting a researcher's 'double life'. Dore's refusal to accept the complete 'otherness' of the Japanese in 1950 (and perhaps also his earlier fascination with the rationality of Confucian ethics) posed a conundrum which could not be resolved reasonably through a double life, or by subscribing to existing theories or disciplinary schools. Rather than placing the conundrum to one side, he used it creatively to generate his research agenda, and to discipline his thinking.

His criticism of Benedict's guilt and shame cultures concerned not just her oversimplified dichotomy, but her basic stance of seeking out and emphasizing the 'other' in Japan. His reaction, he explains in the new preface for *City Life in Japan*, was to try to show how the 'essentially Japanese' notions of *on* and *giri* and 'shame culture' were reorderings of elements familiar enough to non-Japanese. Fundamental here is the attempt and ability to empathize with the subjects of study, to strive towards bridging the gap between self and other, while at the same time, not to assume that there are no differences.

> The institutional constraints which surrounded their lives, and their choices, might be different, but it rarely seemed to me difficult to empathize with the citizens of Shitayama-cho. I always felt fairly confident that I could ... reconstruct what people thought and felt from what they said and did. And with the empathy mostly went sympathy. (1999, xi)

In addition, and this was a further major criticism of Benedict's approach, the particular reorderings or differences were not simply a product of Japanese culture, but also a product of Japan's history as a latecomer to industrialization. This evolutionary perspective goes beyond empathy and introduces a variety of possibilities in which self and other might be linked. Benedict's particularist view of Japanese culture on the one hand, and universalistic (or unilinear) views of social evolution on the other, both become much more nuanced and dynamic. The incorporation of an evolutionary perspective into the comparative method - or vice versa - generates a conceptual richness which is the hallmark of Dore's scholarship, but it is based on empathy, and an insistence on avoiding a double life. Those who have wrestled seriously with the issue of 'self' and 'other,' particularly in relation to Japan, and with static conceptions of culture mobilized to account for the 'other', can readily appreciate the importance of this contribution.

Dore has been a pioneer in his sociological attempts to take a non-Western country seriously and without condescension. His concern with social evolution (the increasing specialization of social institutions and co-ordinating mechanisms brought about by the accumulation of scientific knowledge and its application to technology) is in the classical tradition of sociology, but his work is a far cry from the Oriental despotism and Asiatic mode of production treatment of the non-West by many of sociology's founding fathers (whose 'Orientalism' is alive and well today, as shown in the outpouring of 'crony capitalism' commentary following the 1997 Asian Crisis). It is a far cry, too, from probing the mind and mores of the savage, however noble. Coming to terms with the 'other' has been a major problem for social science, and Dore has made a major contribution.

Dore sums up his own approach as 'looking around the world at the enormous variety of situations and solutions to problems that human beings have arrived at, evaluating them, and asking whether what are considered better solutions can be applied elsewhere, particularly to your own country. And in order to know whether or not they can be applied depends on whether or not, in the places they are operating, they are to be explained by certain historical factors or contemporary cultural factors which are not present in the place you want to transplant them to. The only way of ascertaining this is by detailed, historical, analysis.'[35] Detailed, socio-historical analysis has always characterized his research; the policy orientation came later. The case is set out in the Preface to *Taking Japan Seriously*.

For those seeking to overcome the late nineteenth-century general methodological dispute (*Methodenstreit*) between the historical and social sciences, and the artificial division of labour between sociology and economics, to rescue Veblen from Coase's fire through evolutionary economics, or to forge a new economic sociology, Dore's work merits particular attention. And his approach to dealing with the 'other' will become even more important as cautious attempts are made once more to incorporate insights from the biological sciences into social science.

STRUCTURE OF THE BOOK

The rationale for the selection of papers and their organization into four parts now needs little further explanation. In a very rough sense the four parts follow the chronological development of Dore's thinking and, at the same time, depict the logic of his approach to his research. Part I is titled 'Technology-driven social evolution'. As Figure 6.1 suggests, ideas and philosophies also have an exogenous role in this conceptual scheme, and in this sense, at least, his approach is Weberian. The major chapters have been selected to show how his concept of social evolution has been applied. There is the added twist, however, of late development, taken up in Part II. The notion itself was not new, but Dore perhaps applied it more determinedly than earlier exponents to various institutional settings, as the five selected chapters show.

While Dore addressed the question of culture as early as his *City Life* book, his early inclinations were to stress the scrutability of Japanese society, in reaction to the approach adopted by Benedict. As he developed his thinking on social evolution and late development, however, it become necessary for him to spell out more clearly how culture fitted into his evolutionary framework.

The chapters in Part III show how he did this, although the ordering is designed to show how the pieces fit together rather than chronological development. (Chronologically we would begin with Chapter 16, which stresses the importance of starting points in industrialization, specifically educational and other institutional heritages.) Eventually Dore adopts Weberian ideal types, particularly in the (British/Anglo-Saxon) 'company law' model of the firm versus the (Japanese/Japanese–German) 'community' model. These are an expository device, and are also intended to portray how different institutions fit together, as well as institutions and behavioural and motivational dispositions, to form 'systems' (Chapter 19).

Further, they are used as polemical devices, to draw attention to different possibilities for reform, as suggested by the 'Confucian perspective' quote above (cf. 1987a, 7). His concern that 'real world' research be employed for 'real world' policy solutions was already evident in his Diploma Disease 'modest proposals' (Chapter 22, and before that in numerous Letters to the *Times* and other newspapers), but became more prominent in the 1980s, when he started doing research on technological innovation in the UK and its consequences. The chapters in Part IV present a range of his advocatory writings, which as noted earlier, are consistent with his view that structure and culture are not deterministic, but that there is scope for human agency and policy choices, for hope and reason, to make a difference. No double life, but a sociologist who (in his words) 'cannot keep quiet when he thinks he can see ways in which people could be made happier, richer, or less at each others' throats if only they could be made to understand the world as he does'.

A few words about the abridging and editing processes are necessary. The abridging was done by Dore himself. Omissions are indicated by '…' and bridging or summarizing abridgements are put in square brackets [ ]. Any impulses to rewrite were resisted; the only other changes are the correction of grammatical or typographical errors, and stylistic changes made by me to produce a consistent style for the book. Romanization of Japanese words has not been made consistent, however, and generally follows that of the original publication. For the sake of balancing inclusion and overall word length, some chapters were pruned more drastically than others. Decisions about the extent of pruning were also made by Dore; I have attempted to indicate the outcome by designating them 'slightly abridged', 'abridged' or 'extracted'.

NOTES

1. Genes and (chance) historical events can be added; see Figure 15.1.
2. His own term; see note 27.
3. Personal communication in response to a preliminary draft of this Introduction. Brief,

unattributed quotes come from this source. Dore's mastery of Japanese, it goes without saying, is a vital foundation for his scholarship.
4. The results fed into an ongoing effort, published as Hayashi and Kornicki (eds), 1990.
5. Arai Hakuseki was a mid-Tokugawa period Confucian scholar and shogunal adviser. Japanese names appear with the family name first, personal name following.
6. Discussion, 21 July 1999.
7. The original plan was for ten posts in Japanese language and literature, two in history, two in religion and folklore, one in economic institutions and one in social institutions and the law. The total number was reduced to six, with economic and social institutions rolled into one, called 'Japanese institutions' (Dore, 1994a, 274–5).
8. Discussion, 10 January 1997.
9. Yanagihara, 1995, 224.
10. Cf. Dahrendorf, 1995, 379.
11. Glass dismissed Parsons without argument, according to Halsey (1985: 159). Sprott provided an assessment of Parsons in the *British Journal of Sociology*, but it was clearly intended to save others from having to embark upon the 'time-consuming task' of venturing into the murky 'waters' themselves (1952, 203, 221).
12. See, for instance, Dore's 'Introduction' to *Aspects of Social Change in Modern Japan*, 1967.
13. Dore's first seminar at LSE, in 1952, was on the subject of Ruth Benedict's *Chrysanthemum and the Sword*.
14. Cf. Inagami, 1999.
15. Discussion, 10 January 1997.
16. By 'open' I mean starting with particular phenomena and working out what other phenomena are involved in causing them, rather than starting from the notion of a social system as a whole and trying to establish where the phenomena fit in. Relatedly, however, he exhibits a disciplinary openness (cf. Inagami, 1999).
17. He says that the sentence most often quoted back to him in Japan is from the Preface to the Japanese translation of *British Factory-Japanese Factory* (1973; 1990) about the relative merits of British and Japanese industrial relations and employment systems: 'I think the Japanese system is better, but I'm glad I don't have to live in it.' Italy's synthesis of 'inner direction' and communitarian attitudes and institutions to some extent resolves this ambivalence.
18. Dore, 1958, xvi. He recalls being confronted with this attitude, tinged with arrogance, when giving his first talk at the RIIA (Dore, 1997a; discussion).
19. Cf. Dower's criticism of scholars whose work 'has tended to be congruent with the objectives of the American government' (1975, 33). He was attempting to resurrect interest in E.H. Norman's work, which they had 'courteously shelved'.
20. He was appointed a reader at the LSE in 1960, and taught courses on Japanese society, social structure and social change. As professor from 1965, he held a joint LSE-SOAS appointment until 1969, when he spent a year at Princeton writing up the *British Factory-Japanese Factory* study.
21. Dore, 1983a, 35–6. Abegglen had generally avoided attributing the distinctiveness of Japan's employment system to backwardness, emphasizing instead socio-cultural distinctiveness.
22. Maurice, Sellier and Silvestre (1982; 1986) brings together this work.
23. Kumazawa, 1982. Gordon, 1998, is an exponent of this view. It is interesting that Hazama, Dore's partner in the research, framed his analysis in terms of association-based British workplaces versus community-based Japanese workplaces. He was distinctly ambivalent about the evolutionary implications of this framework, and the respective merits of each. His concluding chapter follows the convention of asking what Japan can learn from Britain, and calls for greater individualism, but towards the establishment of a new democratic type of workplace, rather than British shop-floor relations (Hazama, 1974).
24. Personal communication in response to draft.
25. Discussion, 10 January 1997.
26. Dore suggests he ended up as 'a dabbler in both, expert in neither' (discussion), but the following discussion shows that he took them seriously. The TCC closed in 1986.

27. E.g. Chapters in Part IV. Regarding his political activities, he joined the Labour Party and went to branch meetings in the 1950s, but did not enjoy politics. ('If I had had a more forceful personality, and the prospect of being elected a candidate soon, I might have stuck with it...') He was associated with the Tawney Society, and subsequently the Social Democrats in the early 1980s (prior to the merger with the Liberals), and was opposed to Britain's see-saw politics, in which successive Labour and Conservative governments scrapped the institutions set up by their opponents once they gained power and then set up their own, with the result that few could ever become established.
28. The concepts were first explored in the final chapter of *The Diploma Disease*. Cf. also Dore, 1987a, b; 1994b.
29. He was simultaneously a visiting professor and then director of the Japan-Europe Industry Research Centre at Imperial College, and from 1991 senior research fellow at the Centre for Economic Performance, LSE.
30. At this stage he had still not taken on board the evidence of growing income differentials in the UK and USA, although they were consistent with his technology change and unemployment ('scissors effect') thesis (Chapter 21).
31. Albert, 1991, 207, 195 (English edition).
32. Halsey, 1985, 154. The 'provincial thirteen' were students of sociology at LSE from 1950-52, many of whom helped to establish sociology departments throughout Britain in the 1960s. They were J.A. Banks, Olive Banks, Michael Banton, Basil Bernstein, Percy Cohen, Norman Dennis, Ralf Dahrendorf, A.H. Halsey, David Lockwood, Cyril Smith, J.H. Smith, Asher Tropp and John Westergaard.
33. In contrast, for instance, to Durkheimian sociology, or Friedman's economics.
34. Dore's first advice to his research students - to me at least - was to go and read Ayer's *Language, Truth and Logic*.
35. Discussion, 10 January 1997.

REFERENCES

Abegglen, J. (1958), *The Japanese Factory: Aspects of Its Social Organization*, Glencoe IL: Free Press.

Albert, M. (1991), *Capitalisme Contre Capitalisme*, Paris: Editions du Seuil.

Bellah, R. (1957), *Tokugawa Religion*, Glencoe IL: Free Press.

Benedict, R. (1946), *The Chrysanthemum and the Sword: Patterns of Japanese Culture*, Boston: Houghton Mifflin.

Coase, R. (1984), 'The New Institutional Economics', in *Journal of Institutional and Theoretical Economics*, **140**, pp. 229-31.

Cole, R. (1978), 'The Late-Developer Hypothesis: an Evaluation of its Relevance for Japanese Employment Practices', in *Journal of Japanese Studies*, **4**(2), pp. 247-65.

Cole R. (1974), 'Review: British Factory-Japanese Factory', in *Contemporary Sociology*, **3**(5), pp. 389-92.

Crouch, C. and R. Dore (1990), 'Whatever Happened to Corporatism?', in C. Crouch and R. Dore (eds), *Corporatism and Accountability: Organized Interests in British Public Life*, Oxford: Clarendon Press.

Dahrendorf, R. (1995), *LSE: a History of the London School of Economics and Political Science*, Oxford: Oxford University Press.

Dore, R. (2000a), *Stock Market Capitalism, Welfare Capitalism: Japan and Germany Versus the Anglo-Saxons*, Oxford: Oxford University Press.

Dore, R. (2000b), 'Will Global Capitalism Be Anglo-Saxon Capitalism?', Address to International Industrial Relations Association 12th Congress, Tokyo, 31 May.

Dore, R. (1999), ' Preface' to new edition of *City Life in Japan*, London: Japan Library.

Dore, R. (1997a), 'Nihon to no hanseki' (My Half Century With Japan), in British Council (ed.), *Quality Britain '97.*
Dore, R. (1997b), 'The Argument of The Diploma Disease: a Summary' and 'Reflections on The Diploma Disease Twenty Years Later', in *Assessment in Education*, **4**(1), pp. 23–32 and 189–206.
Dore, R. (1997c), 'Preface' to new edition of *The Diploma Disease*, London: Institute of Education.
Dore, R. (1997d), *Nihon o tou: Nihon ni tou: zoku fufuku no shosō* (Asking About Japan, Asking to Japan: Faces of Discontent Sequel), Tokyo: Iwanami shoten.
Dore, R. (1996), 'Confucianism, Economic Growth and Social Development', in J. Kreiner (ed.), *The Impact of Traditional Thought on Present-Day Japan*, Munich: Iudicium-Verl.
Dore, R. (1995), 'Comment on the Kosai Paper' in Japan Foundation/Centre for Global Partnership (ed.), *The End of the Century: the Future in the Past*, Tokyo: Kodansha International.
Dore, R. (1994a), 'Otome and Frank Daniels', in I. Nish (ed.), *Britain and Japan: Biographical Portraits*, London: Japan Library.
Dore, R. (1994b), 'Incurable Unemployment: A Progressive Disease of Modern Societies?', *Political Quarterly*, **65**(3), pp. 285–301.
Dore, R. (1994c), 'Japanese Capitalism, Anglo-Saxon Capitalism: How Will the Darwinian Contest Turn Out?', in N. Campbell and F. Burton (eds), *Japanese Multinationals: Strategies and Management in the Global Kaisha*, London: Routledge.
Dore, R. (1994d), 'Why Visiting Sociologists Fail', in *World Development*, **22**(9), pp. 1425–36.
Dore, R. (1994e), *Nihon to no taiwa: fufuku no shosō* (Dialogue With Japan: Faces of Discontent), Tokyo: Iwanami shoten.
Dore, R. (1993), 'Rethinking Free Trade', in R. Morgan, J. Lorentzen, A. Leander and S. Guzzini (eds), *New Diplomacy in the Post-Cold War World: Essays for Susan Strange*, Basingstoke: Macmillan; and New York: St Martin's.
Dore, R. (1990a), *Will the 21st Century be the Age of Individualism?,* Tokyo: Simul.
Dore, R. (1990b), 'An Outsider's View', in K. Yamamura (ed.), *Japan's Economic Structure: Should it Change?*, Seattle: Society for Japanese Studies.
Dore, R. (1987a), *Taking Japan Seriously*, London: Athlone.
Dore, R. (1987b), 'Citizenship and Employment in an Age of High Technology', in *British Journal of Industrial Relations,* **25**(2), pp. 201–25.
Dore, R. (1986a), *Flexible Rigidities*, London: Athlone.
Dore, R. (1986b), 'Blackburn and Kishiwada: Proletarian Towns and Middle Class Towns', in T. Umesao, H. Smith II, T. Moriya and R. Ogawa (eds), *Japanese Civilization in the Modern World II: Cities and Urbanization*, Osaka: National Museum of Ethnology.
Dore, R. (1984), 'Technological Self-reliance: Sturdy Ideal of Self-serving Rhetoric?', in M. Fransman and K. King (eds), *Technological Capability in the Third World*, Basingstoke: Macmillan.
Dore, R. (1983a), 'Watashi no Nihon shakai kenkyū: hitotsu no chiteki jiden' (My Research on Japanese Society: an Intellectual Autobiography), in *The Hosei*, **10**(3), pp. 26–38.
Dore, R. (1983b), 'Goodwill and the Spirit of Market Capitalism', in *British Journal of Sociology*, **34**(4), pp. 459–82.
Dore, R. (1982), 'Adjustment in Progress: a Lancashire Town', in J. Bhagwati (ed.), *Import Competition and Response*, Chicago: NBER.

Dore, R. (1979), 'More About Late Development', in *Journal of Japanese Studies,* **5**(1), pp. 137–51.
Dore, R. (1978), *Shinohata: Portrait of a Japanese Village*, London: Allen Lane and Pantheon.
Dore, R. (1973; 1990), *British Factory-Japanese Factory,* London: Allen & Unwin.
Dore, R. (1967), 'Introduction', in R. Dore (ed.), *Aspects of Social Change in Modern Japan*, Princeton: Princeton University Press.
Dore, R. (1964), *Education in Tokugawa Japan*, London: Routledge & Kegan Paul.
Dore, R. (1961), 'Function and Cause', in *American Sociological Review*, **26**(6), pp. 843–53.
Dore, R. (1959), *Land Reform in Japan*, Oxford: Oxford University Press
Dore, R. (1958), *City Life in Japan: a Study of a Tokyo Ward*, London: Routledge & Kegan Paul.
Dore, R. and T. Ouchi (1971), 'Rural Origins of Japanese Fascism', in J.M. Marley (ed.), *Dilemmas of Growth in Prewar Japan*, Princeton: Princeton University Press.
Dower, J. (ed.) (1975), *Origins of the Modern Japanese State: Selected Writings of E.H. Norman*, New York: Pantheon.
Fukuyama, F. (1999), *The Great Disruption: Human Nature and the Reconstruction of Social Order*, London: Profile.
Gellner, E. (1988), *Plough, Sword and Book*, London: Collins Harvill.
Gerschenkron, A. (1962), *Economic Backwardness in Historical Perspective*, New York: Praeger.
Gordon, A. (1998), *The Wages of Affluence*, Cambridge MA: Harvard University Press.
Halsey, A.H. (1985), 'Provincials and Professionals: the British Post-War Sociologists', in M. Bulmer (ed.), *Essays on the History of British Sociological Research*, Cambridge: Cambridge University Press.
Hayashi, N. and P. Kornicki (eds) (1990), *Early Japanese Books in Cambridge University Library*, Cambridge: Cambridge University Press.
Hazama, H. (1974), *Igirisu no shakai to rōshi kankei* (British Society and Industrial Relations), Tokyo: Japan Institute of Labour.
Hirsch, F. (1977), *Social Limits to Growth*, London: Routledge & Kegan Paul.
Inagami, T. (1999), 'Shakai shinka, jukyō, kojin shugi: Dore no Nihon kenkyū 50 nen o furikaete' (Social Evolution, Confucianism and Individualism: Reflections on 50 Years of Dore's Japan Research), in Fukuoka UNESCO, *9th Japan Research International Seminar Proceedings*, Fukuoka.
Kawanishi, H. (1992), *Enterprise Unionism in Japan*, London: Kogan Page International.
Kumazawa, M. (1982), 'Shokuba shakai no sengoshi' (Postwar History of the Workplace Society), in S. Shimizu (ed.), *Sengo rodo kumiai undōshi ron* (Debates About the History of the Postwar Labour Movement), Tokyo: Nihon hyoronsha.
Leibenstein, H. (1966), 'Allocative Efficiency Versus X-Efficiency', in *American Economic Review,* June.
Lipset, S. (1996), *American Exceptionalism: A Double-Edged Sword*, New York: Norton.
Lynd, R. and H. Lynd (1929), *Middletown: a Study in Contemporary American Culture*, New York: Harcourt Brace.
Maurice, M., F. Sellier and J. Silvestre (1982; 1986), *The Social Foundations of Industrial Power: a Comparison of France and Germany*, Cambridge MA: MIT Press.

Riesman, D. (1950), *The Lonely Crowd: a Study of Changing American Character*, New Haven: Yale University Press.
Schmitter, P. (1979), 'Still the Century of Corporatism?' in P. Schmitter and G. Lehmbruch (eds), *Trends Toward Corporatist Intermediation*, London: Sage.
Shonfield, A. (1965), *Modern Capitalism*, London: Oxford University Press.
Sprott, W. (1952), 'Principia Sociologia', in *British Journal of Sociology*, **3**, pp. 203–21.
Useem, M. (1996), *Investor Capitalism*, New York: Basic Books.
Veblen, T. (1934), 'The Opportunity of Japan', in L. Binder *et al.* (eds), *Our Changing Order*, New York: Viking Press.
Veblen, T. (1915), *Imperial Germany and the Industrial Revolution*, New York: Macmillan.
Yanagihara, K. (1995), 'Nihon gakusha R. Dore no sengo 50 nen' (Postwar 50 Years of Scholar of Japan, R. Dore), in *Chuo koron*, July, pp. 218–48.
Young, M. (1958), *The Rise of the Meritocracy*, London: Thames and Hudson.

PART I

Technology-driven Social Evolution

1. Society and the individual*

Every Japanese, wrote Ruth Benedict, conceives himself as a 'debtor to the ages and the world'.[1] 'Every man', says another source, 'is a debtor to the world: to his parents; his schoolmaster; his friends and employers. He owes them his existence; his knowledge; his happiness and his daily bread'.[2] All his social acts must be guided and directed by an awareness of that indebtedness and of the duties towards others which it entails.

This ethic would have been explicitly acknowledged by the samurai of the Tokugawa period if he had read any of the books of moral exhortation which were written for him and if he in any way resembled the characters of contemporary fiction and drama. On his feudal lord he was quite clearly dependent for the rice income which he received as a hereditary retainer. To his ancestors and his immediate parents he was quite clearly indebted for maintaining the status of the family which allowed him to enjoy that position. That he should therefore strive to give loyal service to his lord and to maintain the honour of the family, thereby not letting down his forebears, were quite clearly duties of the highest priority. The peasant of the Tokugawa period probably did not have so easily available any such clear verbal forms for explaining to himself and to others why he should behave as he did. Nevertheless his state of dependence on others was just as real.

His was a closed society of limited opportunity and limited range of choice. [And a limited range of personal relations] – parent and child, elder brother and younger brother, mother-in-law and daughter-in-law, head of tenant household and head of landlord household, young man of 20 and any unrelated househead of 50 or more.... Such relations being small in number and of such a kind as to recur with great frequency, the appropriate behaviour they required was fairly minutely regulated. Most people had a clear idea, and within the same village an identical idea, of how a tenant should behave towards a landlord. These standards of proper conduct gained the greater compulsive force ... from the fact that throughout the life of each individual continuing to do what his forebears had done was the dominant feature of his activity. The son, working with his father, learned from him all he needed to know in order eventually to succeed to the headship of his family – when to

* From *City Life in Japan*, London: Routledge & Kegan Paul/Berkeley: University of California Press, 1958, pp. 374–93, last chapter slightly abridged.

plant the rice and how much fertilizer to apply, what neighbours should be taken what gifts at New Year, which gods were to be propitiated with what offerings, what was the correct approach to the landlord when asking him to take a reduced rent in years of bad harvest. Tradition was the more powerful in that it provided a clear answer for almost every situation.

[And there were] strong sanctions. Every family was, in plain fact, dependent on its neighbours. The right to irrigate its rice-fields at the time which should be determined by lot or by regular roster, the right to cut undergrowth as fertilizer and fodder from land held in common by the village or owned by a rich landlord, the co-operation of other villagers in protecting crops from nocturnal theft, their help at house building or re-roofing, at funerals or after a fire; all these were essential to the livelihood of the family.

In some villages where property was fairly equally distributed the reciprocity of rights and duties involved in relations between families was symmetrical. In others relations of dependence were closely associated with differences of status; branch families rendered to main families, and tenant families to landlord families, service and respect in return for protection and economic opportunity.

In either case the community, or powerful individuals within the community, could make life economically impossible for those who failed to observe the established proprieties governing relations between fellow-villagers. They could make life emotionally impossible too. It is impossible to ignore the fellow-villager one meets on the two-foot-wide paths between rice fields. And suddenly to meet with blank stares and hostility could be a source of extreme emotional discomfort for the individual accustomed to feeling the security of belonging to his village – to feeling assured that he is accepted by his fellow-villagers, that he will receive their gestures of respect or friendliness and can count on their sympathy and help in trouble.

If an individual was a part of his village, he was even more a part of his family. In a large household, living in a house with few rooms divided by flimsy partitions, no part of life was private. The individual shared according to his ability in the family's productive life, and he shared according to his status in the family's consumptive life. He shared in the family's recreations and in its joys and sorrows. His interests were his family's interests; his property was family property. If he offended against the rules of propriety governing his relations with other villagers his shame was his family's shame, for his honour was his family's honour, and the maintenance of that honour was a duty not simply to the other members of his immediate household, but also towards 'the family' which lived on though the individuals composing it changed, and to 'the ancestors' who had given the family the honoured status it enjoyed and whom the family united in honouring in rites at the family altar. If his actions consistently brought the family's good name into ill-repute, the family might reject him, for without its good name, without its good standing in the economic organization of the village, the family could not survive.

But his great-grandson, Mr Risookei, in modern Tokyo is a very different person and his life is lived under different conditions. His neighbours are simply people who live next-door and in whose economic or emotional life he shares as little as they in his. His employer is simply the man to whom for the moment he sells his labour. His livelihood depends on no one's goodwill; only on the fact that it continues to be in the interest of his employer to employ him, of his shopkeepers to serve him, and of his bank to maintain its reputation by safeguarding his savings. What employer he shall serve, which shop he shall patronize, how he shall spend his leisure time, whom he shall make his friends - these become questions which offer a conscious choice of alternatives. And, provided that his choices are not proscribed by the laws of the country, few people outside his immediate household will be concerned to show either approval or disapproval of his actions; perhaps only a small circle of workmates or neighbours, a circle which, small and constantly shifting with changes of job and of residence, is less important to his emotional well-being and has lesser power to influence his conduct by its expressions of approval and disapproval than was the case with the Tokugawa peasant and his fellow-villagers. 'The Risookei family' means little to such circles of acquaintances, and the fear that by exciting their disapproval he will bring dishonour on the good name of his family weighs little with Risookei himself.

Tradition, then, does not provide Mr Risookei with clear directions for leading his life or regulating his relations with his fellow-men; nor does his social environment provide pressures which serve to keep him moving in traditional grooves. His sources of direction are internal. It is a duty to *himself* to live up to the aims which he has set himself, and it is he who blames himself if he fails to achieve his ambitions to acquire wealth, or prestige, or saintliness, or power, or academic qualifications. It is his own conscience whose disapproval is excited if, in dealing with the manifold situations of choice which face him, he fails to live up to certain generalized standards of conduct which he has internalized.

But the 'inner-directed' individualist, Mr Risookei - or, to translate him into English, Mr Ideal Type - apart from being a very incomplete characterization, is not, it will have been abundantly clear from the rest of this book, typical of the citizens of Shitayama-cho. Life certainly is less closely regulated for the average Shitayama-cho citizen than it was for the Tokugawa peasant. Tradition supplies fewer guides to conduct. Many are imbued with a desire to do better than their fathers, rather than simply to 'preserve the family', its livelihood and its good name. Their need to retain the good opinion of others is less pressing, their moral controls are more internalized, their goals, their ambitions, their emotions and their responsibilities more individual. But at the same time, as discussions in previous chapters, of the family, of employment relations, and of neighbour relations have shown, this is only a question of degree; many are involved in stable relations of personal dependence on others whose good opinion and material support they value to the extent of allowing them to become the objects of their loyalty and the arbiters of their moral conduct. Many features of the system of social relations prevailing in the Tokugawa village are still preserved in the city. Mr Risookei is only an extrapolation; a carrying to extremes of certain trends in respect of which people in Shitayama-cho do differ from the Tokugawa villager. It will be the business of this final chapter to discuss some of these differences - differences in the nature of the principles by which conduct is guided and judged, and in the sanctions by which these are enforced.

EXPLICIT MORAL PRINCIPLES

Moral beliefs, attitudes and symbols have a dynamism of their own, and the more they are explicitly expressed in words the greater their entrenchment, the greater their power of independent survival. The ethical thinking of the modern city Japanese is strongly influenced by the fact that the system of social relations out of which the society of the Tokugawa period was built up - a system which was little questioned and which fitted the economic structure of that society - developed its own explicit ethic - just how explicit the size of a catalogue of popular moral treatises of the period would show.[3] This ethic persisted into the modern period and its strength was enhanced by wider diffusion through such means of mass communication as were available, in particular the school system. It was on this ethic that the citizens of Shitayama-cho were for the most part nurtured. It was an ethic which stressed dependence. In particular, as taught in the schools, the greatest stress was put on those vertical relations of dependence - of child on parents, servant on master, pupil on teacher, citizen on the Emperor and 'the authorities' in general - relations of dependence an adequate appreciation of which, and of the duties of obedience which they involved, was crucial to the authoritarian structure of government. But the ethic did not omit to stress horizontal interdependence also - as between neighbours, fellow-workers, fellow-pupils - and to teach the duty of maintaining harmonious relations of mutual support.

The circumstances of industrialization did not *enforce* any radical changes in the traditional ethic. Although the situation of the modern townsman *permitted* deviations from patterns of conduct which were obligatory in the village, it did not necessarily *demand* them. The son whose future no longer depended on eventual succession to his father in the family business or farm could defy his father, but there was no compelling reason why filial piety should not continue to be held a cardinal duty. The goodwill of neighbours may be of sufficiently minor importance for them to be safely ignored, but this does not prevent good neighbourliness from remaining a part of the definition of the upright man. Even where, in practice, all-out competition ruled rather than traditional co-operation - as between, say, school children taking entrance examinations, or rival tradesmen and manufacturers freed from the restraints of guild-regulated agreements - it was possible to justify the abandonment of one part of the traditional ethic (the duty of maintaining harmonious relations with one's fellows) in terms of another part (the duty of adding to the status, wealth or honour of one's family).

One modification was enforced in the traditional ethic by the emergence of Japan as a nation-state in competition with other nation-states. A new dimension of loyalty had to be added. The individual had to lose some of his individuality not only in his family, and in the slightly wider in-group of the people with whom he had *giri*-relations, but also in the nation. He had to develop a feeling of belonging to the nation, to take unto himself and make a part of himself the ambitions of 'Japan', to feel Japan's honour as his honour and Japan's shame as his shame….

The modern city Japanese was, thus, provided with standards of behaviour which were more generalized than those of the Tokugawa villager and hence more useful to him in the more varied circumstances and problems of his everyday life…. But the principles which were thus generalized and available to form a part of his conscience were those of the traditional ethic, abstractions of the duties implied in the sort of social relations which existed in the village, specifying broad loyalties to particular categories of persons. Principles of a more universalistic kind were not entirely lacking; hard work, courage, honesty and frugality were traditionally virtues. But, compared with the overwhelming importance attached to particularistic obligations towards persons, they were relatively little stressed.

However, partly as a result of institutional changes, partly as a result of the direct influence of foreign ideas, these and other newer principles of a universalistic kind have come to demand greater consideration in the moral scheme of things. Kindness and consideration to 'others', loyalty to principles and 'isms', the pursuit of truth, the frank expression of opinion, justice and equality before the law, the equality of the sexes, the duty of self-development, the right to seek happiness and self-fulfilment - these phrases enshrine principles of conduct which have acquired increasing importance. And frequently they clash with the older particularistic obligations. Some examples...:

A girl is due to marry the son of her father's business partner, but she decides she does not love him but someone else. Her father explains that it would be very awkward for him if the marriage did not take place. Would the modern Japanese applaud her if she sacrificed private feelings so that the family could behave as the *giri* norms prescribe? Or would they applaud her if she sought to assert her own individuality - what the new Constitution somewhat plagiaristically calls her 'right to life, liberty and the pursuit of happiness' - and sacrificed *giri* and filial piety in the process?...

Someone to whom you are indebted for past favours has a son who takes the entrance examination for a certain firm. A representative of the firm calls to ask you for a personal opinion of the son's qualities. You happen to know that he is an unreliable person. How would you answer the firm's enquiries? Do your best to see that he gets the job by finding some way of praising him? Avoid giving a direct answer? Or tell the truth that he is an unsuitable person?

The traditional type of Japanese moral dilemma has been the conflict of personal loyalties. Japanese moralists have always had to be ready with answers to such problems as: 'Which is the more important - loyalty or filial piety? What should one do when the interests of one's lord and the interests of one's parents are at variance?' But the sort of situations outlined above present dilemmas of a different kind, conflicts between, on the one hand, particularistic loyalties, and on the other either individual aspirations which it is held to be the right of everyone to hold, or generalized principles of conduct which are held to be applicable to all situations.

Most Japanese would recognize these situations as dilemmas; few, perhaps, would very sharply condemn the taking of either the one course or the other. Many would admit to confusion. But there is little doubt that the universalistic principles have gained ground as compared with the Japan of eighty years ago. The last question was, in fact, asked of a nation-wide sample of some 3000 Japanese in 1953 - 23 per cent said that they would do their best to get the son accepted by the firm, 48 per cent said that they would tell the truth about him. The investigators also asked a group of twenty-six 'experts' to forecast the results of the interviews. Twenty said that the former would be the most usual reply for a Japanese to make, and thirteen said that it would be 'most unusual' for a Japanese to say that one should tell the truth in such a situation.[4] The experts were intellectuals who, in Japan, tend to have a low estimation of their fellow countrymen (low, that is, by their own standards since they tend to be strongly opposed to the old particularistic morality). Nevertheless, this illustrates well the difficulty which any Japanese in these situations would have in knowing which course would secure the approval of the majority of his fellow countrymen.

TYPES OF MORAL SANCTION

These conflicts of moral standards are clearly related to changes in, and differences between, various types of sanctions. The distinction is sometimes made by American cultural anthropologists between shame-cultures and guilt-cultures, those, that is, in which the major moral sanction is the fear of being ridiculed and rejected by others, and those 'which inculcate absolute standards of morality and rely on man's developing a conscience'. Ruth Benedict, whose formulation this is, considers Japan to be a shame-culture. Shame is the root of virtue, and a virtuous man is one who 'knows shame'.[5] The general assumption of the cultural anthropologists (and one which springs in part from their wholly admirable purpose to counter narrow ethnocentrism by pointing to the relativity of culture and ethics) is that these mechanisms are selected more or less arbitrarily by different cultures from a vast range of human potentialities the bounds of which are only loosely determined by the limits of adaptability of the human organism.

A more suggestive formulation of the distinction between shame-control and guilt-control, and one which relates these to other features of social organization, is that of David Riesman. In *The Lonely Crowd* he suggests that shame-control is characteristic of all 'tradition-directed' cultures, and that guilt-control is only one aspect of the 'inner-direction' of the more individuated man typical of expanding and materially progressive societies in an area of free competition.[6] If this association between guilt-control and the early development of capitalism is valid for all societies and not merely for the West, one would expect the Japanese to have become gradually less sensitive to shame and more subject to feelings of guilt.

Not far from Shitayama-cho was a poster originating from the local Fire Services' propaganda department. It said simply 'Fires *(kaji)* bring shame *(haji)*'. Another notice nearby said, 'If you have a conscience *(ryooshin)* do not deposit rubbish here'. Perfect evidence, perhaps, of the transitional phase? But further reflection must lead to the conclusion that moral sanctions in Japan cannot be easily and satisfactorily dealt with in terms of any simple shame-guilt dichotomy. It will help first to make a list of some of the possible sanctions on behaviour which are important in Japan. An individual's choice of alternative courses of action may be influenced, consciously or unconsciously, by the desire to avoid,

1. Personal shame. The ridicule and disapproval of 'the world' which would follow deviations from an expected code of conduct. The extent of 'the world' will vary for the individual, from a narrow range of neighbours, friends, relatives and workmates, to, in the case of a politician or a film star, the whole nation.

2. Family or we-group shame. That is, to avoid bringing dishonour on his family, his school, his department, with, perhaps, in the back-ground the fear of being rejected by the group whose good name he has besmirched.
3. Punishment for breaking the law.
4. The displeasure of particular individuals resulting from failure to perform obligations towards those individuals.
5. The displeasure of particular individuals for failing in other respects to live up to certain standards of conduct which those individuals had enjoined on him.
6. The feeling of guilt which comes from failing to live up to standards which he has made his own.

In the Tokugawa village with its settled and commonly shared ways of life and standards of behaviour, the effect of all these sanctions generally coincided. The villager who was discovered secretly interfering with the weir at night in order to take into his own fields water which should properly go to his neighbour was personally ashamed to look his fellow villagers in the face the next day. The attitude of members of other branches of the family left him in no doubt that the honour of 'the family of the ancestors' was besmirched. He was punished according to the explicit rules of the village by having his own water ration reduced. He had to face the particular resentment of the neighbour from whose fields he diverted water, and the displeasure of his marriage go-between who had always taken an interest in him and was 'disappointed in him'. And probably, even before he was discovered, he had, as well as the fear of being found out, a feeling that he was 'doing wrong'.

For the modern city-dweller, these various sanctions still coincide in their effect over a wide area of conduct.... But their relative force has changed. The law has become clear and calculable and sharply defined in its scope; it is not represented by the paternalistic official with omnicompetent discretionary powers. Letting the family down is of lesser importance as 'the family' ceases to loom so large in the individual's consciousness. The importance of avoiding personal shame is in part maintained by the persistence of child-rearing habits of an earlier age when this sanction was a crucial one. Mothers do sometimes tell their children that 'people will laugh at' them, or they 'will be disliked' if they do such and such (although they equally often say that 'it is wrong' or 'naughty' *(ikenai)* to do such and such). For those who – as is possible in the towns – 'keep themselves to themselves' the fear of shame is of lesser importance. But, the majority do not keep themselves so aloof from neighbours, at least, and those who do are often motivated by an exaggerated fear of the neighbours' criticism to which greater intimacy might expose them. To start a fire to the danger of one's neighbours still, in the words of the poster, 'brings shame' and the culprit can only try to mitigate the wrath of his neighbours by making a full and abject apology. Fear of 'what the neighbours will think' weighs heavily on housewives, and the close quarters at which life is lived in a densely populated Japanese city exposes a very wide range of one's life to the neighbours' thoughts. Nevertheless, the force of this sanction is weakened in that the more mobile city dweller can always move to a new district and a new job - and, as the Japanese proverb has it, 'the traveller leaves his shame behind him'.

But most city dwellers are not continually moving on. Most are involved in a network of stable personal relations of the type which were described in an earlier chapter as *giri*-relations, and it is these, the relations of 'support and be supported', to which the fourth of our list of sanctions specifically applies.

[And the force of this particularistic kind of sanction can be greater than either guilt or shame. And, also, conscience itself] seems often to be less, in George Mead's terms, a generalized other as a specific other. That is to say that it is intimately connected with what we have listed as sanction *5*. 'I don't know what my mother will say when she finds out' is not very different from the typical expression of guilt: 'I don't know how to excuse myself to my dead mother' *(Shinda haha ni taishite mooshiwake ga nai*). Other expressions of guilt more familiar to the West are also frequently heard: 'I have done something wrong' (*Warui koto shimashita),* 'my conscience accuses me' *(ryooshin ga togameru* or *ki ga togameru),* 'I feel the pangs of conscience' *(ryooshin no kashaku wo kanjiru*). The idea of conscience as an innate guide which 'knows what is right and what is wrong' is not foreign to Japan. The modern word for conscience derives from Mencius, and Wang Yang Ming, who made conscience a central part of his philosophy, was not without Japanese followers. But the Neo-Confucianism orthodox in Tokugawa Japan had a different ethic. With its stress on obedience to superiors it saw knowledge of good and evil not as innate but as something taught by those superiors - taught in the history of Man by the sages of antiquity, and taught in the history of individual men by parents and teachers. The Christian who believes that his conscience is the voice of God within him feels that it is a duty to God to obey its dictates and that he has sinned in the sight of the Lord if he fails to do so. The Japanese who conceives of the voice of his conscience as the voice of his parents and teachers feels it to be a duty towards them to obey it, and if he fails to do so it is they whom he has let down. Even after their death his feelings of guilt may take the form of imagining how displeased these honoured parents and teachers would be, and his verbal expressions of that feeling may take the form 'I don't know how to excuse myself to...'. (In those who believe in ancestral spirits, these feelings may be related to the belief in the vindictiveness and malignancy of such spirits discussed earlier, much as Christian consciousness of sin is related to the hell-fires of a wrathful God.)

In comparative terms, conscience has certainly widened its scope in Japan since the Meiji period. But, to return to Riesman's thesis, whereas the development of a competitive capitalist society in the West was accompanied by a great expansion in the sphere of conscience, the development of less competitive and more regulated forms of capitalism in the more authoritarian Japanese atmosphere has given conscience less scope. The necessity of obeying superiors has restricted freedom to obey one's own conscience, and emphasis on the moral propriety of obeying superiors has made the following of one's own inner light appear reprehensible and presumptuous. The point at issue will become clearer if we put conscience back in a wider context as a characteristic of the 'individuated' man, and conclude with a brief discussion of the ways in which one can legitimately speak of increasing individuation in recent Japanese society.

THE INDIVIDUAL AND THE GROUP

The word 'individuation' will be used rather than 'individualism' to make clear that what is meant is a descriptive category for certain characteristics of behaviour and motivation, and not a consciously held politico-economic philosophy. It may be defined first of all by contrasting reference to what might be called 'collectivism', or, more ponderously if less ambiguously, 'collectivity-orientation'. For the individuated person, the things he wants most are things he wants for himself or for specific individual others, not for some group - some 'we' - to which he belongs. To realize his desires he relies on his own efforts, knowledge and skills rather than on the joint effort of his group. The things which make him glad or sad are primarily things which happen to himself (or to some individual others) rather than things which happen to a wider we-group of which he feels himself a member. He selects his opinions, beliefs and moral standards not simply to conform with his immediate social environment, but in the light of strongly held principles of right and wrong which he has internalized. The responsibility for his own actions he accepts as his own, and in his conduct he is guided by the dictates of his own conscience which would make him feel guilty if he deviated from the standards which he expects of himself, rather than by the fear that by departing from the standards of his group he will be accused of having let the group down. These various traits tend to be related; they may be summarized as reflecting the extent to which the individual 'identifies with' or 'merges self in' some wider group of which he is a member.

In this country the evaluative associations of the word 'individualism' are ambiguous: we are accustomed to speak approvingly of 'independence' when concentrating on the aspect of holding one's own opinions fearlessly regardless of the opinions of others, and disapprovingly of 'selfishness' when concentrating on the aspect of giving one's own aims and desires absolute priority. In pre-war Japan 'individualism' *(kojin-shugi* – a post-Meiji translation of the European word with similar referential denotation) had much the same pejorative ring as 'selfishness' *(riko-shugi).* Since the war phrases such as 'human rights' and the 'liberty of the individual' have been written into the constitution and gained such universal currency through the press and radio that a housewife in Shitayama-cho will condemn a husband who keeps a mistress on the grounds that it is an 'infringement of the wife's human rights'. The word *kojin-shugi* (individualism) was too thoroughly a 'bad' word to be easily purified, but other formerly emotionally neutral words which had been the exclusive preserve of metaphysicans – words like 'actor-ness' *(shutaisei,* i.e. being that in which resides the power of independent action) and 'self-direction' *(jishusei)* have been seized on as the slogans of the left-wing writers and educators, and even the counter-attack of the more conservative has generally taken the somewhat half-hearted form of stressing the responsibilities of freedom and the danger of confusing liberty with licence. These are changes in the values now upheld by the mass communication media. They may be dismissed as changes merely in the ideological superstructure, but they have undoubtedly given an extra stimulus to a long-term trend towards individuation in actual behaviour, a trend which, even before the war, despite the enshrinement of the traditional anti-individualist ethic in a position of unassailable supremacy, was nevertheless going forward concomitantly with changes in the structure of society....

Greater individuation there is, then, than in, say, the Tokugawa village, but still less than in Western societies. Some people still explain their conduct to themselves and to others as a 'duty to the family'. The solidarity of the ex-Tokyo Imperial University clique in the civil service is still spoken of as a menace to efficient government, employees of Mitsui may still avoid mixing socially with employees of Mitsubishi, and maintaining the ward's good name is still a motive which prompts people in Shitayama-cho to give donations for the Red Cross.

And this is not the whole story. Hitherto we have considered individuation only in contrast to 'collectivity-orientation'. In dealing with Japanese society a different polar opposite to individuation deserves equal attention – that, namely, in which the individual surrenders a part of himself not to a group of which he is a member, but to particular individuals whose leadership he accepts, with whose fortunes he identifies himself, on whose help he depends for securing his own advancement or happiness, on whose goodwill he depends for his emotional security, and on whose approval he depends for his self-respect. Sometimes, when groups are characterized by authoritarian leadership, it is not always possible to distinguish between the two types of non-individuation; to distinguish, that is, between behaviour which springs from self-identification with the family, and that which springs from personal submission to the househead; between identification with the fortunes of the family-atmosphere firm, and submission to the authority and protection of the employer....

Despite the depersonalization of employment relations with the increasing scale of modern industry, these types of relationship have not altogether lost their importance. It is the trade union boss, the foreman or the department chief who becomes the new patron. Dependence remains the keynote. 'A powerful backer will come to your aid and thus assure a favourable outcome' is the form in which shrine fortune-telling cards assure 'those engaged in disputes and conflicts' that they are bound to win.

Individuation can proceed, we have seen, working through the traditional patterns, in so far as personal relations become instrumentalized; a mere means to further individual ends - ... [with] inner individuation being only cloaked by the external forms of submission. But such individuation is an incomplete and stunted growth; by destroying trust it can only lead to moral anarchy.... Its logical dead end is the ruthless manipulations of T [a noted businessman/black-marketeer who was Shitayama-cho's richest citizen], corruption in the civil service, or the career of the fraudulent money-lender-university student who became the type case of '*après-guerre* youth' when he was found dead in his office, a bottle of poison in one hand, and on the wall a placard bearing his motto: 'What belongs to me is mine, and what belongs to others is legitimate game.'[7] It is understandable that 'individualism', of which these are often represented in Japan as the typical exemplars, should seem to many a destructive philosophy involving the negation of all responsibility, and that many voices have been raised in recent years to warn against the dangers of confusing liberty with licence, and to stress the responsibilities of freedom.

Democratic political institutions may be seen as a product of competitive individualistic capitalism, an adaptation of the individualistic ethic of the individuated man to the needs of co-existence in society. It can plausibly be asserted that it was economic individualism which laid the basis for the political emphasis on the importance of the individual which is of the essence of democracy.

But today the era of economic individualism is all but over. The later stages of capitalist development have brought a new kind of collectivism of a vaster and more impersonal kind than that of the medieval village - the collectivism of the giant industrial corporation, of State welfare services and nationalized industries, of shared fashions in clothes, enjoyments and values diffused by mass radio and television. In America where this trend has gone further than elsewhere, social scientists are beginning to mourn the disappearance of the 'inner-directed' man. His 'other-directed' supplanter, who depends increasingly on the goodwill and approval of his fellows for his emotional security and for his material well-being, values popularity above everything and develops a radar-like sensitivity to the values and standards of others which enable him to adapt chameleon-like in whatever environment he finds himself. If this is not a false prophecy of despair, and not a phenomenon specific to the American melting-pot situation, but a danger inherent in modern forms of economic organization, our only hope of avoiding the brave 1984 world of the novelists lies in the inertia of institutions, in the persistence of democratic forms of government after the type of character structure which created them has ceased to be the dominant type in our society.

The attempt has been made to transplant these institutions in Japan, in a society in which the older forms of collectivism have not disappeared, and in which the mechanisms which regulated industrial development have been imposed from above (having been borrowed from abroad) rather than worked out in the stress and conflict of clashing individual wills; a society which jumped from feudalism to the corporate stage of industrial capitalism and in which, as a consequence the individual entrepreneur has never had much scope to gain power, nor, with the continuance of the Tokugawa preference for advancement by learning and dependent service rather than by self-seeking money-making, has he had much chance to gain prestige as the admired type, the representative of the ethos of the society. (Even in districts like Shitayama-cho where the self-employed worker sets the pace and provides a model for the aspirations of employees, the typical self-employed worker is dependent on a big wholesaler or industrial firm, and it is to the university and a good job in the civil service or a large firm that most parents want to send their sons.) Now, forms of the new collectivism have arrived before the old ethic of dependence on the group and dependence on superiors has disappeared - large industrial corporations, government economic controls and welfare services, mass communication - new forms of dependence and new pressures to conformity.

The new collectivism is not inimical to some of the trends towards greater individuation [in, say] family relations and neighbour relations. But the economic dependence of the individual grows with the decreasing scope for economic activity outside large-scale industrial and commercial organizations.... Improving techniques of mass communication offer increasingly efficient means of fostering the trend exhibited in pre-war nationalism, towards a new kind of 'impersonal' dependence - emotional dependence on and identification with a vaster secondary group, be it nation, class or party, and its leaders. State social services increase this impersonal dependence at the material level....

Have democratic political forms much chance to grow in a society in which independence of thought and action are not established habits and established virtues - in which the open expression of differences of opinion and the acknowledgement of conflicts of interest are not expected or easily tolerated, nor the mechanisms developed for achieving compromise agreement by appeal to accepted generalized principles of justice and fair procedure? Can independence of thought and action become and remain established habits and virtues only in societies in which independence of economic activity is, or has been, the norm? Or can they become established simply by the influence of ideas and transplanted institutions - by the establishment of the forms of representative government and by the hypothetical devoted idealism of thousands of school-teachers - and in the teeth of the plain fact that the economic basis for some of the old forms of personal dependence still remain and new forms of impersonal dependence are growing in importance?

'It is a striking phenomenon', writes a Japanese sociologist in 1951, 'that today, when voices on all sides ring out with demands for "democratization" we should hear the words "liberalism" and "individualism" so infrequently. It may be argued that this is a reflection of a tendency to pin hopes for the future on a socialistic, rather than a capitalistic order. But if so we need to examine even more closely the spirit of dependence which seeks refuge and security in a socialistic order while avoiding the baptism of liberalism and individualism - while, that is to say, skipping over the process of individual reformation in the field of consciousness. In a typically Japanese way, the necessary revolution in individual attitudes - a revolution which is only possible through the self-awareness and effort of each individual - is being omitted.'[8]

The Westerner must guard against the fallacy of assuming (like the author quoted, together with most other Japanese intellectuals) that the stages of social development which Western countries have experienced are right and natural stages deviation from which is somehow unhealthy (for in the Westerner the historicist fallacy may become tinged with arrogance.) But it was difficult for someone who left Japan in 1951 to think other than in these terms of a nation whose leaders of opinion had decided that theirs was a 'backward country', a 'following-behind country', committed to imitating the development of the West now in its social and political as well as in its industrial forms. Japan had, owing to its peculiar circumstances, skipped a stage in the proper order of social development. The damage had to be repaired. It may be that 'the process of individual reformation in the field of consciousness' will be accomplished although all the omens are against it. It may be that the effort will be abandoned. One could hardly expect the period to last indefinitely in which the nation is prepared to take its values from, and measure its achievements by the yardstick of, other countries. (It did not, it will be remembered, last for very long in the Meiji period.) Eventually, a sensitive *amour-propre* may combine with entrenched interests to develop new goals of a different - a 'truly Japanese' - kind, and to create a new sort of society and a new sort of political regime in which the old forms of dependence are subtly combined with the new.

NOTES

1. *The Chrysanthemum and the Sword*, 1946, Ch. 5.
2. This succinct statement of the *on* doctrine derives from a recent advertisement of the Esso Petroleum Company (*Listener*, 23 September 1954, p. 494).
3. The *Kokusho Kaidai* (edited by Samura Hachiroo, 1926) lists 400 popular moral treatises published in printed editions before 1868.
4. Hayashi Chikio, 'Kokuminsei no Kenkyuu', in *Kyooiku Tookei*, August 1954, pp. 28-36.
5. *The Chrysanthemum and the Sword*, 1946, pp. 222-7.
6. *The Lonely Crowd*, 1950, Chs 1-2. My debt to this stimulating book will be apparent in other parts of this chapter.
7. Minami Hiroshi, *Nihonjin no Shinri*, 1953, pp. 34-6.
8. Iizuka Kooji, *Nihon no Seishinteki Fuudo*, 1952, p. 69.

2. On the possibility and desirability of a theory of modernization*

The verb 'modernize' has a valuable use for which it is not easy to find a substitute. The political leaders and intellectuals of most developing countries desire to transform their country. They wish to see transformations in their economy, usually in their political system and educational system; often, also, in family life and in religious and cultural matters. Usually, the model for their reforming efforts is some other country [or countries] more economically developed than their own....

Clearly, wholesale and rapid 'modernization' in this sense is a neat epitomization of the policy aims of the Meiji leaders of Japan in the 1870s, or Kemal Ataturk in Turkey in the 1920s, or of countless other political leaders since. This sense of 'modernization' may be paraphrased as follows: 'The transformation of the economic, political, legal, social or cultural life of a nation in accordance with models derived from other contemporary societies thought to be more "advanced".' It is a use of the word which implies nothing specific about the content of this transformation, its goals or its methods. There are as many forms of modernization as there are modernizing leaders.

There is a second, different, sense of the word which is particularly common in recent academic discussions. In this usage the deliberate transformations implied in the first sense are assimilated to the 'unengineered' transformations of societies like England and the USA during their periods of industrialization, all being seen as different examples of a single unitary historical process. This second sense may be paraphrased as: 'A process of social change, including and contemporaneous with industrialization, which has already been taking place for decades or centuries in the industrial societies and which is now starting to a greater or lesser degree in the developing societies.' As a convenient label one might call the latter sense of the word the 'intransitive' and the former the 'transitive' usage. That is to say: one can talk in the first sense of societies 'being modernized', not of societies 'modernizing', and in the second sense, vice versa....

* From Asiatic Research Centre, Korea University (ed.), *International Conference on the Problems of Modernization in Asia*, 1966, pp. 157–63; also Institute of Development Studies, Sussex University, *Communication* 38, 1969, slightly abridged.

The danger implicit in this second usage is that one is tempted to slip into such phrases as 'Modernization is a process which ...' - phrases which only make sense on the assumption that the concept is capable of *precise* definition. Thence arise attempts to arrive at such a precise definition by enumeration of the component elements of 'modernization'. Sometimes such a definition itself is graced with the title 'a theory of modernization'; sometimes the matter is pushed further and a real theory is built up which postulates the causal interrelations which link the various component elements of the process.... - an increase in the total or the per capita output of goods and services, a rising level of mass education, urbanization, a trend towards a nuclear family structure, an increasing functional specificity in organizational structures, an increasing tendency to allocate social roles on the basis of achievement rather than ascription, greater social mobility, bureaucratization, etc., etc.... Whatever the list, such attempts to define modernization (intransitive) run into a serious problem.

For an American - and it is chiefly in America that the word 'modernization' has recently been in vogue - it may be posed most sharply and crudely in the form: 'What to do about Russia?'... At least three distinct positions may be taken.

1. 'Modernization' means fundamentally a process which is an inevitable concomitant of industrialization. As such it has to be defined in terms only of those characteristics which history has empirically shown to be inevitably concomitant features. Since both Russia and America are to a high degree industrialized, the definition must be framed in sufficiently broad terms to enable one to say that both Russia and America have undergone a process of modernization. To give an example from the political field, one can, therefore, talk of an increasing degree of popular participation in politics or an increasing specificity of function in political structures as part of the process of modernization, but one cannot be more concrete about the forms of participation or specificity - to the extent, for instance, of including Western-style democracy as a part of the definition.
2. Russia and America [may be deemed] to represent different degrees of modernization or different types of partial modernization. Thus it might be asserted that Russia is less modernized than America and that inevitably, as time goes on, there will be an increase in political freedom, a greater scope for free market systems and hence a greater resemblance to the United States. Alternatively it may be argued that the convergence will come from both sides, and that as Russia gives greater scope for individual choice, the United States will see a gradually increasing bureaucratization of, and state control over, economic life. In either case, modernization is a single process which, in the long run (allowing for the

adjustment of lags in specific sectors), makes industrial societies alike in quite specific terms.

3. A third resolution of the problem is to abandon any assumption of inevitability and to import explicit value judgements into the definition of modernization. Thus, there can be a variety of forms of social change accompanying industrialization. Some are good and desirable; others are bad and undesirable. On this basis one can choose either to call the American model 'modernization' and the Russian 'partial modernization', 'failed modernization', a 'perversion of modernization', etc. Or, of course, *vice versa.*

[So you end up either being ethnocentric (solution 3) or speculatively futurological (solution 2) or condemned to making vacuous generalizations about highest common denominators like the following characterization of 'political modernization']:

An expanding degree of popular participation in politics: the development of the concept of citizenship; an increasing allocation of roles by achievement rather than by ascription; universalism in the law. All of which may be roughly summarised as increasing equality.

A greater magnitude and scope of government business; the rationalization and secularization of the political process; a greater degree of effectiveness in the implementing of governmental decisions - roughly summarized as an increased capacity of government.

An increase in the number and variety of political structures, in their functional specificity, in their complexity, and in the degree of their integration - for short, greater differentiation.

It is hard, in the framework of such concepts, even to pose the fundamental value questions, let alone the practical policy questions, which are the very stuff of politics in the developed as well as in the developing world. Granted that there is likely to be an increase in equality as industrialization proceeds, how much individual freedom has to be sacrificed to achieve it? Does the replacement of ascriptive by achievement norms, for instance, require that individuals should lose the freedom to will their property to family heirs? Is the sense of citizenship, resting on the institutionalization of political equality, compatible with the existence of great economic inequalities? And if not, what degree of inequality is tolerable? And if the sense of citizenship, and hence the legitimacy and hence the capacity of government, requires that economic inequalities should be kept within certain limits, how much should individuals' freedom to make profits, or to spend the profits they earn, be limited to that end?

And if one can ask how much freedom has to be sacrificed in the interests of equality, one can ask equally how much individual freedom has to be sacrificed in the interests of order. In the United States, for instance, unlike almost every other country in the world, it is not thought necessary in the interests of public order to deprive people of the freedom to buy lethal weapons without licence at any corner store, though it is thought necessary to deprive people of the freedom to belong to a communist party. In Russia, on the other hand, it is thought necessary to deprive people of the freedom to join any other party except the communist. And so on; it would be an endless catalogue which listed the ways in which the freedom of action of individuals has been limited in order to maintain the stability of a system of power.

Similarly, one may ask, how much freedom has to be, or ought to be, sacrificed for economic development? How much does state planning require the restriction of freedom of economic activity; the use of political power to mobilize labour in ways which restrict individuals' free use of their leisure; the restriction of the freedom to choose one's type of education in the interests of a planned direction of human resources? And so on.

This is the kind of problem that politics is really about. It is the kind of problem that tends to slip through the too-broad mesh of a 'theory of modernization'....

The final conclusion is, therefore, that for the leaders of countries in Asia or elsewhere who are trying to modernize, a theory of 'modernization' (intransitive) is unlikely to be very helpful, whichever of the three possible approaches is taken. I think it would be better for the social sciences in general, and for political science in particular, if the concept of 'modernization' in this intransitive sense ... were dropped from their vocabularies except as a broad label (like, say, 'low temperature physics') which defines a field of study – 'the social etc. changes accompanying industrialization'....

[So what should one do if one is] interested in the problems of the developing countries and subject to the nagging feeling that scholarship ought to be useful? My own answer would be a piecemeal empiricism which (a) takes the goals of a process of modernization from the goals actually held by modernizing leaders, (b) defines the problems in terms of adapting actual existing situations to those goals, and (c) seeks to elucidate these problems by building up a body of specific theoretical generalizations by means of *ad hoc* comparison of similar situations in history. These generalizations would be of the form: 'If such and such happens in circumstances defined as such and such, so and so is the likely result.'

'Take the goals actually held by modernizing leaders'? In practice one must make a choice. In some developing countries the goals of political leaders do not extend beyond maintaining their own power. Those who thus treat political power as a private possession may easily be eliminated from sympathy. Even those who exercise power with a sense of responsibility, however, may set a variety of objectives for the modernizing transformation of their country. Some aim only to acquire certain prestige-carrying symbols; a glittering airport, a steel mill, a seat on the Security Council. Some think in military terms of enhancing national power by acquiring a powerful army - and so on. Some scholars would select for sympathetic consideration only those sets of goals which gave a prominent place to the prevention of communism. My own predilection would be to take as a serious topic of study only the problems of those governments whose modernization plans revolve around the achievement of a level of economic growth which permits a continuous and general rise in levels of living. Economic growth is, after all, a precondition for many of the other changes commonly desired - the enrichment of cultural life, the development of education, even the expansion of governmental services which permits the specialization of governmental functions - and at the same time some of these changes, such as the development of education, are also preconditions for economic growth.

To narrow the problems of modernization to this particular focus does not mean that they thereby become technically economic. I am suggesting, in fact, that this is a focus eminently suitable for the inquiries of sociologists, psychologists, political scientists and all other workers in the social sciences. Take, for example, the question: 'in a world where technology does not have to be newly invented but can be systematically imported, is economic growth best achieved by giving free play to the individual profit-seeking enterprise of individuals in a market economy, or by the state taking command of the available investment resources and using them in accordance with a centrally directed plan; or in what sectors is the one appropriate and in what sectors the other?' This is a question which involves sociological considerations of such matters as the conditions determining the actual structure of motivations in individual entrepreneurs or bureaucrats, and political considerations of the forces influencing decisions in the planning process, and of the structural forms best adapted to various social and cultural conditions for carrying out planning decisions. The list of study topics of this kind can be extended indefinitely. In so far as the state is likely anyway to play an important role in economic development, at the very least in creating the infrastructure of communications and educational services, how can it acquire the authority necessary to mobilize investment resources and enforce its plans? How far ought, or can, opposition be simply repressed? As a factual question, at what point does repression destroy the possibility of achieving government by consent, by willing or grudging co-operation? As a value question, how much individual economic or political freedom is worth sacrificing in order to hasten the speed of economic growth? What is the role of ideology in maintaining the legitimacy of consent? How far can traditional local authority structures be utilized to mobilize consent for policies of economic modernization, and how far must they be destroyed and replaced by new organizations - political parties or bureaucratic structures? What is the relation between levels of literacy on the one hand, and the minimum degree of mass political participation required to maintain consensus on the other?

[For comparative studies tackling these questions, 'process models' as opposed to 'end-state models' can be useful.] In the nature of things, the countries seeking to modernize are more likely to learn something about the mechanisms of modernization from countries that have 'been modernized' (been transformed largely through the efforts of modernizing leaders) than from those whose economic and social development owed little to central political direction. Japan and Russia are obvious candidates as such process models already in a very advanced stage. No one country, however, is likely to offer a very satisfactory process model, and certainly not countries whose reforming efforts began many decades ago. The Japanese recipe for development, for instance, is not likely to be repeatable. Modern developing countries are not as ideologically isolated, they face a faster rate of population growth, they have available a much more advanced industrial technology than nineteenth-century Japan. They cannot maintain the legitimacy of the government and its modernization policies by a nationalism which is fed by a series of successful expansionist wars. They do not have the elements in the pre-modern social structure and cultural tradition which facilitated Japan's later development - and so on. That is why countries like India and China are more likely to be taken as process models for actual imitation. Although time has not shown conclusively the relative efficacy of their different recipes in terms of results; at least they are recipes worked out with reference to contemporary conditions.

More fruitful, however, than the study or imitation of single 'process models' as a whole is the comparative study of particular problems in a variety of societies. For example, many countries are seeking to raise productivity in their traditional agricultural sector. In Asia, especially, the villages are often dominated by landlords. Would a land reform, redistributing ownership to the tenants, facilitate the process of economic development?

To be fair, a good many of the social scientists concerned with problems of modernization do in practice tackle concrete problems such as these, in a manner similar to this. The two major points which I wish to make in this paper are: first, that the attempt to create, or to force discussion into the framework of, a general theory of (intransitive) modernization only muddies the waters of discussion; second, that explicitly to select for consideration the goal of economic development from among those actually held by modernizing leaders, and for sociologists and political scientists as well as economists to frame their questions with reference to it, serves both to clarify the issues at stake and, in the economy of academic resources, to make scholarship of use (if it can be of use) primarily to those people who - by my values at least - most deserve consideration.

3. Land reform and Japan's economic development: a reactionary thesis*

There is general agreement among the students of Japan's economic development that agriculture's contribution to the task of building a strong industrial base was a considerable one. It provided export earnings and import substitutes which helped in acquiring the machinery and raw materials which had to be bought abroad. It managed a steady expansion of the supply of staple foods which enabled a growing town population to be fed reasonably cheap food. It contributed through the land tax a substantial portion of the funds which provided the infrastructure of communications, government and education, and through the profits of the landlords some of the capital which developed especially the small industries. And it was in part a growth in productivity which made this 'squeeze' possible without such a drastic lowering of rural living standards as to cause uncontrollable political instability.

Was this in part because of, or in spite of, the nature of the land tenure system? It has by now become a truism that one important factor determining the productivity of agriculture is the system of property institutions under which land is owned and used. The question which naturally arises, therefore, is this: granted that agriculture made a substantial contribution to Japan's economic growth, was it the best that it could have made? Or is it possible that under a different land tenure system it could have done more?

This question, like all the other 'if' questions about human history, can only be answered by guesses derived from comparison with other countries. For such comparisons it is useful to have a typology. The one I suggest below has no particular merit except that it seems to be applicable to a variety of situations and is a handy basis for generalization.

The typology is little more than a distinction between two types of land reforms based on the kind of landlord whose power and property is affected. The key is therefore the definition of the two types of landlord. The first is typically one who acquires control of a territory by military conquest or by

* From *Developing Economies*, Special Issue, 1965, **3**(4), pp. 487–96; and T. Shanin (ed.), *Peasants and Peasant Societies*, Harmondsworth: Penguin, 1971, pp. 377–88, slightly abridged. Chapters 3 and 4 are a product of my year at the FAO, writing the UN's *Progress in Land Reform* (1966), in turn seven years after writing *Land Reform in Japan* (1959).

infeudation – being allocated territory by a warrior chief who thereby secures his allegiance. At first he is lord and master in every sense; he draws produce from the cultivator by virtue of his monopoly of violence; political control and economic exploitation are one and indivisible and there is no conceptual distinction between rents and taxes.

At a later stage of development the autonomy and arbitrariness of his political power may become circumscribed by the development of a central state authority. The central government may claim the sole right to tax and the former feudal magnate now only draws a rent. He may still, however, exercise political power in his hereditary fief by ascriptive right, though he may exercise it through delegates, he himself living in the central capital and only occasionally visiting his estates for supervisory or ceremonial purposes.

The second type of landlord is characteristically one who achieves his position by *economic* means within the framework of a system of established political order; not by warfare or that milder type of warfare that is politics. Sometimes he is a merchant, sometimes a thrifty farmer who acquires land from the improvidence or misfortunes of others, sometimes a money-lender. He may also exercise some political power, but it is power exercised through the framework of a system of government in which he has no ascriptive right, only the power of manipulation gained by virtue of his superior wealth. Such landlords have smaller estates than the first kind, and they generally live near the land they own. They may, in Marxist terms, act as the rural wing of the bourgeoisie, a conservative political force which gains advantages for itself from contacts with the urban politicians, and provides the latter with a necessary basis of support in protodemocratic systems. They are not necessarily obstacles to all economic progress and can in some cases serve as the agents of economic development.

The next distinction follows logically from the first. What will be called a Stage I redistribution is one which expropriates, or in some way drastically reduces the power of, Type I landlords. A Stage II land redistribution is one which expropriates or weakens the second type of landlord.

For some countries the classification seems clearly apposite. One can pinpoint the two distinct historical events representing the two stages of land reform. In Czechoslovakia, Yugoslavia and other countries of the old Austro-Hungarian Empire the land reforms which took place after the First World War were Stage I reforms; those which came after the Second World War were Stage II reforms. In Russia one may take the land redistribution following the revolution as the first stage, and collectivization, destroying the power of the *kulaks,* as the second. There are other countries such as England where there has been no first-stage reform and where the Type I landlords have never disappeared. Their local political power has been whittled away to the point where only in the more remote areas of rural Scotland can the scions of noble families, such as Lord Home, claim a parliamentary seat almost as a hereditary right. Their economic hold over the land remains, however, though it is in no sense different from that of the Type II landlords - those who acquired their land by economic means, often by investing in small estates the profits derived from industry and commerce. (Already by the sixteenth century it is difficult to separate the two types of landlords, as witness the historians' disputes about the rise or fall of the 'gentry' or the 'aristocracy'.)

France, by contrast, quite clearly had a Stage I redistribution in the celebrated events which took place in 1789, but in neither France nor England has a Stage II redistribution taken place. Instead, in both countries, the Type II landlords who supported the bourgeois regimes of the nineteenth century were forced, as their political power waned, to accept tenancy reforms which redistributed income without redistributing the ownership of land. In these countries, and in England especially, industrialization *before* population growth created serious pressure on the land and the ability of landlords to accept gradual reform (if only because they had already acquired substantial industrial interests too) has created a situation where the entrepreneurial tenant can be counted as a member of the prosperous middle class. In Ireland, on the other hand, greater population pressure, greater tenant distress and a more intransigent unwillingness of landlords to accept reform led, not to evolution, but to drastic changes which saw the virtual elimination of the Type I landlords in the space of a decade.

Again, there are countries where a first-stage land reform has only recently been carried out; India, for example, where the removal of the *jagadirs* and *zemindars* did not immediately affect the Type II landlords, and Iran where only the holders of whole villages were affected by the original land reform measure.

A new phenomenon in the modern world, however, is the accelerated spread of communications, education and political consciousness, one of the results of which is that the political demand for land reform can become irresistible in countries which are otherwise at a level of economic development at which, a century ago, effectively organized popular political demands of any kind would have been unthinkable. Hence the strong political pressure for a Stage II land reform in India, only a decade or so after the first. Hence the second wave of land reforms in Iran which is aimed, two years after the first, at the estates of the smaller landlords. Hence, too, countries where the land reform which has taken place has been in effect a telescoped Stage I plus Stage II operation, jumping from a structure of large 'feudal' holdings to atomized peasant proprietorship. Bolivia is an outstanding recent example.

If the reader still thinks that the typology has any validity he will have no doubt where to fit Japan into the picture. The Meiji Restoration and the creation of a centralized system of government dispossessed (though with handsome compensation) Japan's Type I landlords, the *daimyo.* They remained wealthy, but their wealth was no longer in landed property. They almost entirely lost local political influence and became a metropolitan aristocracy, and although they were granted, to be sure, a place in the political system in the House of Peers, at no time was the House of Peers at the centre of political power.

This fact in itself was of considerable importance for Japan's industrialization. Those who controlled policy after the Meiji Restoration were not landed gentlemen but members of a bureaucracy who depended for their income on their salaries, and on the less formal income channels provided by their more or less corrupt relations with the new industrial class. They had, therefore, no personal interest in protecting agricultural incomes at the cost of slowing the growth of industry. They could, and did, maintain a high level of taxation on agriculture. There is a marked contrast here with the situation in, say, England, where the landed aristocracy, with strong personal agricultural interests, maintained their political influence until a relatively advanced stage of industrial development. It was not until the middle of the nineteenth century that the repeal of the Corn Laws marked the final emergence to political supremacy of industrial interests. Similarly, in a good many Latin American countries today the continued political power of a traditional landlord class (fortified by those who have put urban wealth back into the purchase of landed estates and adopted traditional values) remains an obstacle to serious industrial development.

The removal of the *daimyo* left a clear field for the Type II landlords, those smaller village landlords who had been acquiring control over land by economic means in the latter half of the Tokugawa period. The first decades of the new regime saw an extension of their power; various factors, but especially the operation of the new tax system, increased the amount of land which such landlords controlled, from about 30 to about 45 per cent of the total. They remained the dominant economic and political influence in the countryside until Japan's Stage II land reform put them out of business in 1947–9.

No one can seriously doubt that the Stage I land reform represented by the dispossession of the *daimyo* was an essential pre-condition for Japan's development. The question whether or not the land tenure system after 1870 was the best one to promote that development resolves itself, therefore, into the question: could the Stage II land reform with advantage have come earlier? Supposing that the Meiji government had insisted that the certificates issued in the 1870s should always be given to the actual cultivator and that all other claims and liens should ignored or compensated for; and supposing that it had set rigid limits to the area of land which any family might subsequently acquire by purchase; supposing, in other words, that the Stage I and Stage II land reforms had been telescoped into one, thus establishing immediately a small peasant holding system; would the growth of agricultural productivity have been faster, agriculture's contribution to economic development in general greater?

There are some good grounds for answering 'no'. One might list them as follows:

1. These landlords were village landlords, themselves often farmers, with an understanding of agriculture and personal motives for improving their tenants' standards of husbandry. (Though rents were generally fixed rents, in produce, the tradition of rent reductions in years of bad harvest preserved elements of a share system.) Many of them, through experience as village headmen and contact with the *samurai* class, had developed Confucian ideas of paternal responsibility which meant that the economic interests were sometimes reinforced by a sense of moral duty to improve their tenants' production methods for the latter's own good. As a consequence they had the *motive* to use their economically-based political control of village society to improve agriculture.[1]
2. Second, they also were in a better position than other villagers to have the *knowledge* to do so. Being richer they had more leisure and travelled more. They brought their brides from further afield and consequently had wider kinship connexions. They could afford education and were sometimes the only literate members of their village. They were consequently in a better position to learn of superior methods practised elsewhere and to keep in touch with the national centres of technical innovation – as well as sometimes being inventors and experimenters themselves.
3. Many of the productive innovations in agriculture in this period required the creation of new formal organizations. Consolidated schemes for the reorganization of field sizes, irrigation and drainage systems certainly did. So did the creation of new marketing channels, of incentive-creating shows and competitions, of the primitive travelling-lecturer system of agricultural extension, and so on. Such organizations could be created much more easily in an authoritarian manner by use of the landlord's traditional power than they could have been if it had been necessary to persuade the majority of the villagers to come together to form such organizations on a footing of equality in a democratic manner.
4. The landlords' role as links in a communication system joining the villages to the centre of government was important for more than just the diffusion of agricultural improvements. They were interpreters of government policies without whom there might have been far more peasant uprisings and general political unrest than there in fact was. At the same

time their own political ambitions forced the creation of local government systems which could be gradually expanded to meet increasing demands for political participation, whereas if there had been no landlord class to make demands which were of a nature moderate enough to be acceptable with modifications to the ruling Tokyo oligarchy, concessions might have been delayed and really revolutionary forces built up which might have destroyed the whole structure of administration. The landlords were particularly important as interpreters of the government's educational policy and often played a leading part in the building and expansion of schools. As village landlords they sent their own children to the village schools, and hence had a direct interest in them. Even when they became absentees, for one or two generations they maintained close links with their village, and the desire to maintain the 'prestige of the house' in the village where the family land and graves were, prompted many of them not to begrudge taxes and contributions for village schools and public works.

5. The landlords commanded the 'agricultural surplus'. In their hands it was more effectively taxable. Moreover, many them used their wealth in productive ways - in the education of their children and in investment in food-processing and other local industries. If this wealth had not been squeezed out of the tenants it would have been used for direct consumption; the overall rate of savings would have been lower and economic development slower.
6. By analogy one might argue from situations such as Bolivia where a telescoped State I/Stage II land reform left the village without small landlords and without a structure of local leadership, and where there seems to have been not only no economic development but in fact a decline in production, and administrative anarchy.

As against these, one might set the following arguments for the contrary point of view:

1. The landlords may have brought new ideas and techniques to the villages, but this advantage was cancelled out by the well-known drawbacks of a tenancy system; the fact that tenants, with only insecure tenure, had no motive for carrying out improvements with long-term effects, and the fact that the burden of rents kept them so poor that they could not afford the kind of investment in, for instance, fertilizers, which was most capable of bringing big increases in production.
2. It is debatable whether the tradition-sanctioned authority of the landlords was a necessary condition for creating the organizational structure necessary to improve agricultural practices. The tradition of village co-

operation between equals is an old one in Japanese rural areas. There were villages, particularly in the commercially more developed areas of central Japan from Gifu to Hiroshima, where landlord influence was less strong and a more egalitarian type of village structure prevailed. These areas were not notably slow in developing the co-operative organization required for agricultural development, and there is no reason to suppose that the more authoritarian villages could not have adapted to more egalitarian forms if the influence of the landlords was removed - as in fact they did after 1950.

3. The landlords may have invested some of the income they squeezed out of their tenants in productive ways, but they also consumed conspicuously, to some extent in luxury imported goods. If there had been greater equality of village incomes there might not have been as much local investment in commerce and industry, but there would have been a quicker and wider diffusion of popular education. Many more villagers might have sent their children to school for, say, six years instead of four.
4. The pre-emption of local formal political authority by the landlords was a loss, not a gain, for agriculture. As soon as they were allowed representation in the national Diet their main interest was directed towards reducing their tax burden. This pressure on the national budget slowed the growth of agricultural research and extension services and of the developmental subsidy system. If the voice of the villages in the Diet had been the voice of practising farmers these things would not have been neglected.
5. The 'political stability' of the countryside ensured by the landlords' power was also a loss rather than a gain. If the demand for political participation had built up to revolutionary proportions before concessions were contemplated and a real revolution had taken place, there might earlier have emerged a democratic political system with a government really devoted to the cause of popular welfare.

It is impossible to reach any definite conclusions on this matter. On balance it seems difficult to believe, given the level of violence associated even with middle-class politics and even in the 1920s and 1930s, that a regime of any stability or any power to plan economic development could have emerged from a successful popular revolution at any time in the Meiji period. It equally seems difficult to believe that organizational and technical innovation in the villages could have proceeded as fast without the backing of traditional landlord authority. I am inclined to believe that economic development would have been slower if there had been a Stage II land reform at any time before, say, 1900.

But the situation was already different by 1920. By then most farmers were literate and more capable both of informing themselves individually about new agricultural methods and of forming the organizations necessary to put them into practice. (As Galbraith, 1963, has recently said, 'Nowhere in the world is there an illiterate peasantry that is progressive. Nowhere is there a literate peasantry that is not.') More important, if the landlord's traditional authority *had* been put to productive purposes in the Meiji period, this was only because that authority was *accepted* by the tenants. By 1920 tenants were beginning to lose their deferential submissiveness - as the growing number of disputes over rents and the formation of tenant unions testify. Hence, by this time, the advantages of landlord control had all but disappeared. Only the disadvantages of poor incentives and tenant poverty remained. A Stage II reform at any time after 1920 would probably have hastened economic development, as well as conducing to a more satisfactory internal political structure (more satisfactory by our present-day values) and possibly modifying Japanese external policies as well.

There are two further comments worth making on this issue. The first concerns the evaluative implications of the fact - if it is a fact - that the Meiji landlords contributed to the cause of Japanese economic development. Japanese historians are inclined to write of the landlord system in the Meiji period as a social evil. In part this is a back-projection into the past of judgements about recent situations, but in so far as this is not the case, what would they make of the assertion that on balance economic development took place more rapidly with landlords than it would have done without them?

One answer, which would probably be favoured by the majority, is that the assertion is wrong and that my summary of the balance between the two sets of arguments is at fault. There is, however, another answer. One can accept the assumption and still argue that a Stage II land reform was desirable at a very early stage. It may be granted that the landlords helped to hasten the pace of economic development, but this was done at the expense of miserable poverty on the part of tenants, and at the cost of preserving a system of social relations in the villages which was an affront to human dignity. It would have been better, it can be argued, to have improved the lot of the Meiji tenant even if this meant a slower pace of economic growth; even if it meant postponing the arrival of television sets in the villages from 1960 to 1980, to the generation of those tenants' great-grandchildren rather than their grandchildren. This is a perfectly valid argument. Economic growth is not the only end in life. Just how much sacrifice of personal welfare by the present generation is justified by how much improved welfare for future generations is a difficult value question which every development planner must face.

The second comment is this: none should try, without very drastic modifications, to draw from the history of Meiji Japan the conclusion that a small village landlord system is a beneficial factor in the initial stages of economic growth and seek to apply this as a 'lesson' to the situation of the developing countries today. It is inappropriate as a lesson from many points of view. The population growth rate in most of the developing countries is much higher than it was in Meiji Japan, thus adding a new dimension to the problem of rural development. Communications techniques have improved considerably, making less necessary the informal intermediate policy-interpreting function of the Meiji landlord. Many countries have less need to squeeze industrial capital out of the traditional agricultural sector, because of mineral revenues, foreign aid or the taxation of agricultural exports produced by capitalist plantations. Above all, the political revolution of the twentieth century - the new assumption that all governments ought to derive their power from electoral consent - together with the development of mass media in even poor countries, has created a political demand for land reform even in economies which are characterized by an almost wholly subsistence agriculture. What this means is that the traditional *acceptance* of landlord authority - a necessary condition for landlords to play the kind of useful role they played in Meiji Japan - has already been destroyed. Social relations in the villages have often reached a level of conflict similar to that of Japan in the 1920s, even though agricultural development may remain at Japan's 1870 level.

The trouble with these 'if' questions about history is not that one can rarely arrive at satisfying answers. Even if one gets an answer it is rare that one can draw any simple 'lessons' from it for the solution of contemporary problems. For if there are some senses in which the countries of the world are moving in different directions - the poor perhaps getting relatively poorer and rich relatively richer - there are other ways - in the accumulating stock of scientific knowledge and political ideas - in which the world as a whole moves on.

NOTE

1. The literature available in English reflects only a fraction of the information available in the works of Japanese scholars, but a good general idea of the development of agriculture in Japan, and in particular of the role of the landlords, may be gained from the following: Dore (1959), Dore (1960), Johnston (1962), Nakamura (1965), Ogura (1963), Ohkawa and Rosovsky (1960), Sawada (1965) and Smith (1956).

REFERENCES

Dore, R.P. (1959), 'The Japanese landlord: good or bad?', *J. Asian Studies,* **18**(2).

Dore, R.P. (1960), 'Agricultural improvement in Japan: 1870-1900', *Econ. Devel. Cult. Change,* October, Part 2.

Galbraith, J.K. (1963), *Economic Development in Perspective,* Harvard University Press.

Johnston, B.F. (1962), 'Agricultural development and economic transformation: a comparative study of the Japanese experience', *Food Res. Instit. Studies,* **3**(3).

Nakamura, J.I. (1965), 'The growth of Japanese agriculture: 1875–1920', in W.W. Lockwood (ed.), *The State and Economic Enterprise in Modern Japan,* Princeton University Press.

Ogura, T. (1963), *Agricultural Development in Modern Japan,* Japan FAO Association.

Ohkawa, M. and Rosovsky, H. (1960), 'The role of agriculture in modern Japanese economic development', *Econ. Devel. Cult. Change*, **9**(1), pp. 43–67.

Sawada, S. (1965), 'Innovation in Japanese agriculture', in W.W. Lockwood (ed.), *The State and Economic Enterprise in Modern Japan*, Japan FAO Association.

Smith, T.C. (1956), 'Landlords and rural capitalists in the modernization of Japan', *J. Econ. Hist.,* June.

4. Modern co-operatives in traditional communities*

There are parts of Africa, Oceania, Latin America and some of the fringe areas of Asia where the tenure of land remains in some sense communal. Either all or some of the land available to a group of people is seen as belonging to them collectively, or to a chief acting as in some sense the group's trustee.

Most colonial governments in such societies made it possible for individuals, or individual families, to get, either from their own or from some other land-owning group, secure, legally protected and heritable rights to particular parcels of land. In fact they generally tried to promote such a change. By and large, post-independence governments have not altered that policy.

There is, however, a common, not implausible and indeed attractive argument in favour of holding back the process of individualizing communal tenures. It runs as follows. The communal tenure of land provides a material basis for a take-off into co-operative or collective farming. The limitations of individual family smallholdings are everywhere increasingly apparent. Wherever agriculture is progressive and go-ahead, farmers are forming ever closer co-operative links. The bonds of community solidarity should not be destroyed but preserved, and gradually rationalized into modern co-operative forms. People who already are a group will take more easily to group farming than a collection of individualistic farmers.

The argument is not new. It was propounded by the Russian populists of the nineteenth century, who saw the traditional Russian village community, the *mir*, as a basis for modern co-operatives. The late developer, they argued, could skip all the intermediate stages of development. History is like a grandmother who scoops the marrow out of the bone for her youngest grandchild, letting the older grandchildren cut their fingers on splintered bones trying to get at theirs.[1]

Equally, the contrary view has a long history. Modern co-operative forms, it is urged, are the result of a long and painful transition from a communal to an individualistic and thence to a new collective stage: the process of

* From P. Worsley (ed.), *Two Blades of Grass: Rural Co-operatives in Agricultural Modernization*, Manchester: Manchester University Press, 1971, pp. 377–88, abridged.

development cannot so easily be short-circuited. This view was never put with more vigour and clarity than by Frederik Engels.

> All civilised peoples begin with the common ownership of the land. With all peoples who have passed a certain primitive stage in the course of the development of agriculture, this common ownership becomes a fetter on production. It is abolished, negated, and after a longer or shorter series of intermediate stages is transformed into private property. But as a higher stage of agricultural development, brought about by private property in land itself, private property in land becomes in its turn a fetter on production, as is the case today with both small and large ownership. The demand that it also be negated, that it should once again be transformed into common property, necessarily arises. But this demand does not mean the restoration of the old original common ownership, but the institution of a far higher and more developed form of possession in common which, far from being a hindrance to production, on the contrary for the first time frees production from all fetters and gives it the possibility of making full use of modern chemical discoveries and mechanical inventions.[2]

Though not everyone would agree with this particular evolutionary scheme of human history, many would accept the view that there is a sharp distinction to be made between traditional community forms and modern types of co-operation. Clauson, for instance, speaks of modern collective agriculture (in his terminology, based on 'tertiary' communal tenure) as 'fundamentally different in character' from the more primitive forms of communal tenures he describes, being 'based on conscious planning, the product ... of an advanced stage of human thought'.[3]

However, the fact that many countries have moved from early communal forms to modern collectivist forms through a stage of private property does not necessarily imply that all societies must. And if we have now to unlearn many of the things which our fathers taught us about the errors of the social evolutionists, most of us at least remain suspicious of glib characterizations about 'advanced' and 'less advanced' processes of thought. Without accepting every demonstration of the essential rationality of men in the simplest societies, without going all the way from the smugness of 'Your peasant, of course, takes a simple view of life' to the new-style bourgeois-baiting 'The bloody peasants are every bit as smart as you are, chum', one still asks for plausible criteria, plausible indices and plausible evidence before one is prepared to accept sweeping assertions about 'fundamental differences' between patterns of social relations in preliterate societies and those in our own.

[So the question remains: do traditional relations of solidarity help or hinder modern co-operatives? Clearly other factors like the actual economic benefits of co-operatives are crucial.] A cotton grower on the shores of Lake Victoria with only a co-operative ginnery nearby to take his cotton to is not relinquishing much when he sacrifices his right to market his own cotton, his right to set his own selling grades, even his right to choose the strains of cotton he will grow. But a farmer near a big city who grows miscellaneous vegetables would be relinquishing a wide degree of autonomy if he bound himself to a marketing co-operative; an Israeli immigrant who enters a *moshav* relinquishes much more, and a family which enters a full production collective very much more.

Similarly, the rewards prospectively to be gained by the sacrificing individual will vary. The cotton grower may gain a reduction in ginning costs, access to otherwise inaccessible markets, secure prices; the suburban vegetable grower only a marginal reduction in his marketing costs. Sometimes the gain will be cheap access to common facilities; often (all too often, perhaps) it will be privileged access to cheap government credit.

[So] the question may be rephrased as follows: for any given economic opportunity situation, and the given balance of perceived rewards over perceived sacrifices which a particular form of co-operation would offer in that situation, experience suggests that some groups of people will take more readily to co-operation and operate more viable co-operatives than others. Is it true that groups which still have the kind of 'primordial' solidarity which goes along with communal land tenure are, other things being equal, likely because of that solidarity to be among the more successful? Or is there such a 'fundamental difference' between that kind of traditional solidarity and the solidarity of a co-operative that there is no correlation at all? Or, indeed, is the correlation a negative one, traditional solidarity being a positive disadvantage for would-be organizers of co-operatives?

HOW SOLIDARY IS THE TRADITIONAL SOLIDARY COMMUNITY?

The first thought that occurs to one when reading of a good many societies is that there is indeed a fundamental difference; the difference being that the so-called traditional solidary societies, for all their communal tenures, simply are not very solidary. 'Primitive communism' is a myth, or at least by no means the universal accompaniment of a communal form of tenure.

Descriptions of African societies, for example, suggest that communal 'ownership' of land is often accompanied by highly individualistic exploitation of it. If individuals often work in common with friends, 'it is communal help given to an individual, not community work, still less sharing of a community product'.[4] And where, in a situation of balance between communal ownership and individual use, the density of the population increases, 'it is the individual usufruct feature rather than the communal one which predominates'.[5]

Again, even if communal labour is an important feature of these societies, the communal work groups do not always necessarily define a community, since the composition of the groups may shift according to the task....

Then again, the purpose of the co-operation is not always mutual assistance. Sometimes an essential subsidiary purpose is competitive display. It is reported of the Tiv that the big 'hoeing parties are called by senior women', and that 'if a woman calls a big hoeing party, supplying generous amounts of food and beer to all those who worked for her, she will be called "important woman" by them, the men of her compound and all her other neighbours for months afterwards'.[6] Similarly, in one district of Ethiopia, a clear distinction is made between strictly 'bread and butter' work exchanges, and the kind of 'potlatch' occasion when work is exchanged for lavish entertainment, and different words are used for the two kinds of occasion.[7]

[Another example:] in Mexico, when collective *ejidos* were created in the 1930s, there was little sense of returning to or reinforcing tradition. Instead the new measures were looked on as real innovations, urged by their proponents as necessary to 'create a collective conscience and drive away selfish individualism' and denounced by their opponents as essentially unrealistic because 'the Mexican peasant is essentially an individualist, and individual utilization of the land by him, without any control or discipline, is the method best suited to his psychological conditions and mentality'.[8]

AUTHORITY PATTERNS

... It is still true that in a good many parts of the world - particularly where, for instance, irrigation facilities are used in common - there are small village communities which maintain some kind of community control over land use, co-operate regularly in all matters of daily life and agricultural production and have the kind of cohesive group spirit - a sense of intimacy with each other and sharp differentiation from the world outside - of the kind which sociologists call variously community-like, affective and particularistic, family-like, *gemeinschaftlich*, primary, etc. In these cases, at least, there should be social bonds capable of being mobilized for modern forms of co-operation.

Not necessarily, however. There is another dimension which has to be considered besides that of cohesive solidarity, and that is the question of the type of traditional authority. Small traditional communities may be patriarchal or fraternal, despotic or egalitarian; status may be ascribed by birth or it may be achieved by skill or magic; differences in status may be marked by minimal forms of defence and command, or by the most elaborated and exaggerated of such forms. Communities of both types may show equal solidarity. Effective co-operation of a modern type, however, is rarely, if ever, successful under ascribed authoritarian leadership [as various examples, from the Gash delta of the Sudan,[9] and from Bolivia,[10] show].

INSTITUTIONALIZED SUSPICION

The field is being narrowed. Some traditional settlements are ruled out of the discussion because they lack cohesive solidarity; others which are cohesive are authoritarian. But there are some traditional communities which are both cohesive *and* egalitarian. [One particularly interesting example is a] co-operative in New Guinea.[11] Here the traditional social structure was clearly egalitarian. There was no institutionalization of factional rivalry. There was no institution of strong chieftainship. Leaders were chosen, not born - chosen for age, wisdom, experience or military prowess. In this context a new type of organization was developed. On the initiative of an illiterate ex-policeman with no knowledge of cost accounting and no position of inherited power, but only a shrewd business sense, considerable energy and an ability to communicate his enthusiasm and his vision of future prosperity, a group of five villages were persuaded to pool their savings to buy first one and then a second tractor. In time they developed a successful sweet-potato farm of nearly two thousand acres, producing crops to the value of £6000 a year and considerably increasing the income of the five hundred people who were, from time to time, engaged in working on it.

Already at the time it was studied, however, there were obvious questions to be asked concerning the viability of this venture in the long run. Several of its features are worth examining closely.

1. The venture undoubtedly depended for its success at the time it was studied on the fact that it utilized traditional community sentiments. Without the bonds of mutual trust which bound the members to each other, it would have collapsed. For instance, all the marketing transactions were handled by the energetic leader of the project, the ex-policeman, who made up for his illiteracy by a considerable shrewdness as well as initiative and persuasive power. Neither he nor his literate cousin, who acted as treasurer, kept proper accounts, nor did he make any clear distinction between the co-operative's funds and his own private spending money. Nevertheless, he appeared to live modestly and was not, apparently, the object of suspicion or resentment.

   Similarly, a sense of obligation to one's fellows seemed to be an effective driving force in the work organization. Absenteeism was not common, and once the morning meeting had been held and the work tasks allocated (the discussion might last for an hour) one overseer and two foremen were enough for a work-force of eighty people.

2. One implication of what has just been said is that there was no differentiation between the social community as an all-embracing group and the project as a functional organization. This is clearly illustrated in the wage system. There were slight variations in the wages paid, not just according to function in the project (the tractor drivers and foremen, of course, received more) but also according to status within the community - an extra bonus was given to the village officials even though they did the same work in the gardens as others.
3. The project was not, in other words, organized on a basis of exact reciprocity, guaranteeing to each a return exactly proportionate to his contribution. Thus, for instance, members of the village contributed various amounts to the collection when the tractor was bought, but they did not receive strictly proportionate repayments. Instead they recognized a vaguer claim to call on project money for emergency needs. Economic transactions within the project, in other words, were assimilated to the traditional patterns of gift exchange, with their much looser and longer-term criteria of reciprocity.

This, quite clearly, is not the particular form of rationality of modern economic man. An attempt to get the project to adopt a formal constitution, with carefully defined powers of general assemblies, elections of officers, formalized audit, etc., rapidly foundered on the people's illiteracy.

Nevertheless, such systems will eventually be needed. Modern forms of co-operative organization are based on institutionalized suspicion. They are predicated on a belief in original sin. Man, the assumption is, has an inevitable tendency to corruption. Therefore organizations must build in checks and balances such as the audit and the periodic re-election of officers. The modern co-operative does deserve, in fact, to be called a 'higher form' because it requires a rather sophisticated appreciation of the idea that this institutionalized suspicion in the long run benefits all, including those against whom it is directed. Thus the treasurer welcomes the audit - even though the audit makes sense only on the assumption that the treasurer might have been dishonest - because it clears him of suspicion. That justice should be done may be in the interest of the members; that it should be seen to be done is in the interest of the elected officials.

It can be predicted with fair certainty that the Erap mechanical farming project of New Guinea will sooner or later need these institutional checks, certainly if the organization is to grow. And if the checks of institutionalized suspicion are necessary, they will also be immensely difficult to create. Where personal bonds predominate the action of the auditor in calling for every document and scrutinizing every signature is not looked on simply as a following of the rules, fully legitimate and in the best interest of everyone, including the treasurer; it is seen as John X the auditor personally demonstrating, by the fact that he takes his duties seriously, his suspicions regarding the personal probity of James Y, the treasurer. And James Y is likely to be resentful. To be sure, such reactions are not unknown in the sophisticated co-operatives of modern Western societies - so much so that as soon as a co-operative can afford it, it impersonalizes the process by calling in an outside firm of accountants as auditors. Most governments which seek to promote agricultural co-operatives in developing societies provide a similar external auditing service and require that co-operatives use it. But the situation remains fraught with possibilities of friction and resentment. 'I intend it, Mr Chairman, as no reflection whatever on the officers of our co-operative when I suggest that in principle the auditors' report should be made available to every member of the co-operative' is not the kind of formulation which members of peasant societies are likely to be skilled in; nor is the disclaimer, insisting on the separation of institutionalized role relationships from total interpersonal relationships, likely to be easily believed. The necessary effort of imagination and of control of affect is not one which people in small rural communities anywhere get enough practice to acquire the habit of....

This, then, is the dilemma in which co-operatives are caught. Either the objective rules, with their suspicious assumptions of original sinfulness, are scrupulously applied - with the likelihood, given the diffusely personal nature of social relations in such societies and the principle that no quarrels are as fierce as family quarrels, of arousing such animosity between those who apply rules and those to whom they are applied that the organization is burst asunder - or else the rules are not scrupulously observed and the non-observance eventually becomes so flagrant that the losers in the game of influence withdraw from the co-operative or it founders in the factional struggle for advantage.

VALUABLE ELEMENTS OF TRADITION

The transition to modern, rationalized forms is an immensely difficult one; but, of course, it is not a complete transition, from all to nothing or from black to white. Modern co-operatives rest on a delicate balance between mutual trust and mutual suspicion, between disinterested sentiments of loyalty and self-interested calculation. The institutional checks on the honesty of officials must be confined to broad general checks: if there is not some trust the system becomes unworkable. In one region of Africa where co-operatives have suffered from official dishonesty, systems of minute checks have been planned. Co-operative officials had been known to steal half the content of a bag of fertilizer and substitute flour. A suggested solution was a system of seals on the fertilizer bags, plus a rule that co-operative officials should not open bags except in the presence of appointed delegates of the members. But are the delegates always going to insist on their rights to be present, even if the business of finding them whenever a bag has to be opened leads to a frequent waste of time and even if their insistence will inevitably be interpreted as a vote of non-confidence in the manager? It is unlikely. The only workable kinds of check, the only tolerable forms of institutionalized suspicion, are those which serve as periodic reminders of the sanctions against dishonesty and so help marginally to reinforce internalized sanctions, and marginally to reassure members who have a good deal of trust in their officials' honesty anyway....

[Trust and loyalty can also come from other sources than traditional community solidarity.] The workers of Rochdale would never have formed their organization on the basis solely of a perceived coincidence of individual self-interest. The sense of class solidarity, of being fellow workers embattled in a hostile environment, was an essential element in their motives.

THE POSSIBILITIES

These, then, are two elements of the traditional solidary community which need, in some measure, to be carried over into the modern co-operative - the sense of mutual trust between members, and the sense of loyalty to the group. The trick lies in retaining these elements while at the same time introducing the rationalized accounting methods which replace the loose reciprocity of gift exchanges by a strict apportionment of benefits to contributions, and (even more difficult) the devices of institutionalized suspicion which prevent the abuse of leadership powers. The trick is an immensely difficult one for the reasons noted. Not many marriages survive long after the wife starts insisting, for instance, that the husband should never break the seal of his wage packet except in her presence.

But this is not to say that the trick is impossible. Some marriages do survive the accepted institutionalization of suspicion, however contrary that may seem to the canons of affective personal relations, most particularly when both partners realize that their prospects outside their present marriage are grim. It is perhaps the same kind of circumstances which account for the fact that the trick has been managed in Japan. There co-operatives of a modern type have been built - and built successfully - on the basis of what, a hundred years ago, were traditional communities. The new accounting systems and auditing systems and systems of electing officers have been introduced according to models set by the central government, and by and large they work as intended. They were not introduced without friction, occasional charges of favouritism and corruption, factional and personal quarrels. But these were kept within bounds, largely perhaps because divorce was impossible. In the tight structure of Japanese agriculture, there was nowhere else to go; farming which depended on irrigation depended, *ipso facto*, on co-operation. If co-operation ceased, the water ceased to flow, the rice ceased to grow and people starved. [The co-operatives have also] been the only source of certain material advantages, since they were the channel of a good deal of government aid - credits, cheap supplies and preferential marketing arrangements.[12]...

And so we come back to our 'economic factors'. The transition from a traditional community to a modern associational co-operative is a difficult one, but it might be managed if the balance of material advantage derived from co-operation is favourable enough - if the losses to be expected if people stopped co-operating, or the gains to be anticipated if they co-operated more, are great enough - and if the other norms and values of the society (time discounts, evaluation of truthfulness, etc.) are sufficiently favourable to enable the co-operative to survive the difficult transitional period....

NOTES

1. See the view of N.C. Chernyshevsky, quoted in F. Venturi, *The Roots of Rebellion*, 1962, pp. 150-2.
2. Quoted from *Anti-Dühring* by D. Mitrany, *Marx Against the Peasant*, 1951, p. 30.
3. Sir Gerald Clauson, *Communal Land Tenure*, FAG, Rome, 1953, p. 23.
4. A. Gaitskell, *Report on Land Tenure and Land Use Problems in the Trust Territories of Tanganyika and Ruanda-Urundi*, FAO, Rome, 1959, pp. 12-13.
5. See P. Bohannan, *Tiv Farm and Settlement*, London, HMSO, 1954, p. 23.
6. *Ibid.*, p. 25.
7. H.S. Mann, *Pilot Field Study in Systems of Land Tenure: Landlord-Tenant Relations in Chore Mikitil Woreda*, 1964, pp. 49-50 (mimeograph).
8. Solomon Eckstein, 'Collective farming in Mexico', PhD thesis, Harvard, May 1961, p. 113.
9. Ali El Tom, *Land Reform and Associated Rural Institutions in the Republic of the Sudan*, Khartoum, 1961, p. 94 (mimeograph).
10. Ferragut, *op. cit.* p. 61.
11. Described in R.G. Crocombe and G.R. Hogbin, 'The Erap mechanical farming project', *New Guinea Research Institute Bulletin No. 1*, 1963.
12. It must also be said that Japanese rural communities did not start, a hundred years ago, from quite the same level of unsophisticated family-like community bonds as are common in many parts of the modern world. The organization of irrigation, for instance, was highly rationalized on a basis of fairly strict equation of contribution and benefits, and even literacy was fairly common.

5. Education and jobs: stages of development*

Elaborating theories of social evolution - series of 'stages' through which all societies are supposed to 'evolve' - was a favourite pursuit of nineteenth-century sociologists. Such theories are out of favour these days. They are associated with 'the idea of progress' which our nineteenth-century ancestors believed in, but which we are supposed to be too sophisticated to have any truck with. Nevertheless, schematizations of historical stages can be useful. The one that follows [and is shown in Table 5.1] is not intended to be universal, to indicate the pattern which all societies follow. As we shall see later, the salient characteristic of late developing societies is precisely that they do not go through all these stages. But in the more slowly developing societies of Europe a similar path of development can be traced.

The periods are meant to be the periods when certain patterns first appeared or became dominant, not periods to which they are *confined*. The fundamental point about this scheme is this: you cannot understand the way education for work changes without understanding changes in the way work itself is organized. The two sets of changes interact with each other, and one can even make out a good case for saying that the changes of work organization are 'primary', i.e. changes in that field more often cause changes in education than the other way round.

For a pure form of the first type of society, look at this account of how the *jajmani* (or *jejemani)* system used to work in Indian villages. Bailey[1] is describing a situation some time after the penetration of a money economy, but when the vast majority of the villagers were still subsistence farmers, getting their income from their own holdings. There was, however, already a specialist division of labour to some extent:

> The village employs three BRAHMINS, two BARBERS, a WASHERMAN, two HERDSMEN for cattle, a HERDSMAN for goats, a TEMPLEMAN, and two SWEEPERS....
>
> The BARBERS, BRAHMINS, WASHERMAN, TEMPLEMAN and SWEEPERS are paid by a tithe system *(jejemani)*. After the main harvest is gathered they receive from each

* From *Certification, Education and Work*, a course book for the Open University, with contributions from Angela Little, 1981, pp. 10–23, abridged.

Table 5.1 A schematization of social evolution

	Emergent or dominant forms of		
Type of society	Occupational selection	Occupational training	Making a living by
1 Feudal/tribal 'natural economies'	Inheritance	Informal family training	Self-sufficient family production, plus loosely reciprocal status-bound exchange
2 Proto-industrial	Inheritance plus sending to apprenticeship	Some general education: apprenticeship training as extension of family training	Sale of goods and labour services in the market
3 Early capitalist	Ditto, except that certain levels of general education may be required for entry to apprenticeship or institutional training	Formal institutional training either to supplement apprenticeship or before career entry	Sale of goods and labour services in the market
4 Bureaucratic (late capitalist and socialist)	Almost exclusively certificated through performance in general educational/vocational courses	Pre-career vocational training plus formal in-career training plus work experience	Entry into work organizations for careers

> house, which is in the system, a payment of paddy. Then, when their services are required, they get another payment, usually in rice. For the SWEEPERS this takes the form of a handful of cooked rice from each house each day. The TEMPLEMAN receives only the annual payment, since ordinarily he has no day-to-day activity for the different households. The HERDSMEN and the woman of the same caste-group who looks after goats are paid in paddy after the harvest, the amount from each household depending on the number of cattle it sends to the herd. The cowherds and the goatherd collect a handful of cooked rice every day from the houses whose cattle they take. (Bailey, 1957, pp. 95–7)

In this sort of society, both the jobs that people did *and* the income rights that attached to doing those jobs, were regulated by tradition. And training to do those jobs - both the subsistence farming that occupied the majority and the more specialized jobs - was a matter of learning-by-doing in the family.

Few people in our society could still be described as coming under what is called the feudal/tribal pattern in the first line of my evolutionary scheme. In this country, perhaps the Queen is the only almost pure case in which both who does the job and how much she is paid for doing it are regulated by tradition (even if it is tradition reinterpreted by Parliament). Even the hereditary landowning aristocracy, and their gamekeepers brought up to gamekeeping by gamekeeper fathers, though they are similar as far as job allocation and training is concerned, are already in the next stage in terms of the last column: their rents and their wages, respectively, are regulated by the market.

Two elements separate that first, feudal/tribal, pattern from the second, proto-industrial, stage. The first is the shift from traditional 'just wages' and 'just prices' to a society with markets in which the income one gets from doing a job depends on the market price of the goods one makes or the services one has to sell. The other is the growth of mobility. Not everybody follows the occupation of his father or her mother. Some carpenters and barbers and landowners and (in theory) all celibate priests, do not have children. A landowner might have several, but, in England where primogeniture was established, would keep the estate intact by passing it on to only one of them, the first born. So apprenticeship develops; children are sent to learn a trade from an established practitioner. Occupational *selection* is determined, in other words, by the accident of family connections, or the personal inclination of the child, or more often the whim of the parent. [As Stone records:]

> In 1758 Arthur Young's clerical father had no hesitation in apprenticing him against his will - at a cost of £400 - for a mercantile accountancy training for three years, instead of sending him to Oxford and into the Church, which he later claimed he would have preferred.[2]

The range of possible careers was much limited by a family's social and economic circumstance: occupational selection was structured by the class system. But (outside the Church), *training* was still very largely a matter of learning-on-the-job in a family enterprise. The only difference between hereditary transmission and apprenticeship was that apprentices went into someone else's family as quasi (and subordinate) family members. In [both England and Japan] indeed, it seems that even where children did follow the family calling, a kind of apprentice exchange was common. [An Italian visitor, writing in about 1500 said:]

> The want of affection in the English is strongly manifested towards their children: for after having kept them at home till they arrive at the age of 7 or 9 years at the utmost, they put them out, both males and females, to hard service in the houses of other people ... Few are born who are exempted from this fate, for everyone, however rich he may be, sends away his children into the houses of others, whilst he, in return, receives those of strangers into his own ... I, for my part, believe that they do it because they like to enjoy all their comforts themselves, and that they are better served by strangers than they would be by their own children.[3]

[Motives in Japan seem to have been a bit more respectable, judging from the following bathhouse conversation between two housewives:]

> 'Our eldest boy is a real trial. We don't know what to do with him. He's our only boy, for better or for worse, and we rather spoiled him and didn't send him out to service. We're regretting it now, though. It's no good being smart and clever if you don't know how to get out among strangers. He doesn't know a thing about making money. He only knows how to spend it.'
>
> 'Ah, well, they all have to go through that stage and sow their wild oats. We sent our second boy into service with the main family; we told him it would be good for him to live with strangers.'
>
> 'Did you? He must be a good boy to take it so well. You're right, unless they go out and eat somebody else's rice they've no conception of how other people think or feel. When you have people under you, for instance. Until you pinch yourself you don't understand how pinching hurts other people. Children who never go away from home don't know what hurts and itches mean.'[4]

FORMAL VOCATIONAL SCHOOLING

The shift to the next, my early capitalist, stage marks the beginning of intentionally vocational education within institutions outside the family: schools, colleges and universities. That shift, however, did *not* necessarily entail (though it later opened the way to) a change in the way people were *selected* for occupations. Take the case of doctors. It was still by being the son of a doctor, or by being apprenticed to one, that one got a foot on the medical ladder, but in the training for that occupational role, learning-on-the-job was supplemented by lectures and demonstration in medical schools.

[At first apprenticeship training was regulated by the various guilds, though primarily as to its length - seven years, usually - and the fee to be paid; it was a long time before the Guild of Barber-Surgeons, for example, tried to regulate what they should be taught.]

[As far as medicine was concerned,] the first change in this system, the first intervention of public authority, came with the granting of a Royal Charter to the London Guild in 1462, which was made conditional on the introduction of examinations for apprentices on completion of their seven-year training. 'The ignorance, negligence and stupidity of some barber-surgeons and the obvious consequences for the public were attributed to the want of the examination, correction and punishment by a due supervision.'[5] But although the Guild now examined before admitting to entry, the training of the apprentice was still entirely in the hands of the master barber-surgeon to whom the person was apprenticed. 'On-the-job' training remained the sole form of training available.

[Gradually formal lecturing on anatomy and the diagnosis and cure of diseases became more common.] There were appointments of medical lecturers at the universities, and the College of Physicians in London held special lectures. At one such course, at the beginning of the seventeenth century, Harvey announced his discovery of the circulation of the blood. But these activities played little part in the actual training of physicians or surgeons. By 1705, however, regular courses in anatomy for apprentice barber-surgeons were being organized in Edinburgh and a full-time instructor was employed by the town council. The courses were soon transferred to the University. Similar developments took place in Glasgow, though the link between surgeon practice and formalized teaching came much later in London, Oxford and Cambridge. It was during the eighteenth century also that the surgeons broke free of the barbers and formed their own separate association.

And so the pattern was established. With the accumulation of medical knowledge, the balance between theoretical knowledge - perhaps better described as systematized book knowledge - and learning-by-doing in apprenticeship steadily altered, and institutional training became a *necessary* supplement to apprenticeship. A local history of Blackburn describes a typical medical career of a much respected local doctor, John Grime:

> He was born in 1802 and was educated at Gomersall boarding school, where he remained for many years, and received the basis of a good education fitting for the medical profession, and served his term of years with Dr Cort, of this town, after which he removed to St George's Hospital, London, for the purpose of completing his medical education. Admitted in 1825, a member of the Royal College of Surgeons, he returned to his native town. In 1832, Blackburn was visited by the Asiatic Cholera, he exerted himself at that time, and his success was complete in giving medicine and advice to put a stop to its ravages, the incessant demand upon his skill increased in consequence.[6]

ENTRY BY PRE-CAREER QUALIFICATION

The next step within this early capitalist pattern was for the relative weight of institutional training and apprenticeship to change to the point at which the former became a *substitute* for the latter, with the learning-by-doing also being formalized and institutionalized in the hospital internship. This was an important step because it changed the mechanisms of occupational selection. It became possible to become a doctor, not by entering an apprenticeship, but by entering a medical school and passing the examinations which became the necessary *and* sufficient requirement for a licence to practice.

There is no doubt that in many fields this supplementation of learning-by-doing with formal systematic instruction - and even, perhaps, the practice of requiring pre-career qualifications before starting to learn-by-doing - was a great advance in efficiency. With the advance of science there was so much more to be learned. The general principles underlying the 'how-to' practices of particular trades became more clearly systematic and more essential for developing *new* techniques.

In this transition to formal institutional professional training, particularly in the engineering field, Britain lagged well behind Germany. The President of the Liverpool Engineering Society made the comparison explicit in 1913:

> Engineering is both an art and a science, and, in the past, development in the art has usually preceded the science of the subject, i.e. the practical man has produced the new engine or machine, and afterwards the science of the subject has been developed. This order is now being reversed, and the scientific treatment of the subject is preceding the development of the art of construction of the new machine. The development of the diesel is an example of this. Diesel investigated the problem from the scientific side before proceeding to have engines constructed, and he adopted the unusual course of writing a scientific treatise on the subject at the time his trial engine was under construction. This method of investigating the scientific aspect of the problem before beginning the constructional part has the great advantage that it, in general, saves a great deal of money, which under the older system had to be spent in making costly trial and error experiments.
>
> We in this country, have, in the past, attached greater training in the art than in the science of engineering, and in consequence we have not been so well fitted as the Germans to develop those branches of engineering which are more dependent on scientific knowledge.[7]

BUREAUCRATIZATION

To return [to the historical scheme and] to the medical field: finally, in 1947, in Britain came the transition to the last stage - the bureaucratic stage - in our model with the National Health Service (NHS) and the transfer of most doctors to salaried status. John Grime, in Blackburn at the time of the Asiatic cholera, was selling medical services in the open market. Doubtless his illuminated scroll from the Royal College of Surgeons helped to inspire confidence and draw patients in the first place. But according to that report it was his *performance,* his skill in handling the cholera which made his reputation and brought him local fame and a large practice. (Though not, the author went on to say, wealth, because he was too kindly to collect money from the poor.) Success as a practitioner, in other words, depended on how well he learned his trade as apprentice and at St George's, and how well he applied his knowledge in practice.

With the final, bureaucratization, phase this changes. Doctors, once they are licensed to practise, now receive salaried positions. There is still a market element in their income in the shape of the capitation fee – a part of their salaries which depends on the number of patients registered as under their care. But basically their income is fixed and, once they are over the qualifying hurdle, assured.

That change potentially makes a difference to the relation between schooling and work. It means that, from the viewpoint of pure self-interest, the important thing for the modern aspirant doctor is to get that qualification which assures him a position in the system. (No effective law prevented John Grime from selling medical services in the 1820s even if the Royal College had not admitted him.) It also makes it *less* important for his income that he has mastered the substantive knowledge his profession requires. Put in terms of our earlier taxonomy of types of schooling this means that from the point of view of self-interest alone there is a shift in the relative importance of learning to *do* and learning in order to *get* jobs. With this move there is the attendant danger that mere ritualism, a concern simply to 'get by', sets in.

Becker's study of medical students in Kansas is a subtle analysis of how ritualism can set in.[8] His students were highly intelligent and often quite idealistic about their chosen career. As their overload of learning began to oppress them through their first year's study, a few retained enough of their idealism to pick and choose what they would concentrate on, according to whether it seemed likely to be useful to them later as doctors. [But the majority, came to be predominantly concerned with 'what would come up in the exam'.]

However, in the case of doctors, there are several other motives which can effectively supplement self-interest in helping to keep medical education relevant and medical students concerned with the substance and usefulness of what they learn. As Becker's students moved on to clinical work in direct contact with actual medical problems, they again became concerned with the more functional aspects of their work. In medicine, the desire to do a good job as an end in itself is reinforced by the fact that, in a personal-service profession, the obligation of honest and conscientious service becomes a direct personal obligation to individual patients. Again, because of the profession's history of self-regulation and ideology of public service, the esteem of one's professional peers, and hence self-esteem, are likely to be more dependent on a reputation for performance rather than on symbols of worldly 'success' like the size of one's car or yacht.

It should also be said that the effectiveness of the older mechanism of the 'judgement of the market' as a means of keeping professional practitioners up to the mark and of giving them individual incentives to get effectively trained was always qualified by the limited ability of the public to assess performance. It is easier for customers to judge the competence of a carpenter by his products than to assess the expertise of a doctor by his diagnoses, because the professional knowledge of the doctor is so much more complex and arcane to the layman (apart from the fact that, as the old joke has it, doctors can bury their mistakes.) Bernard Shaw, arguing earlier in this century for a salaried bureaucratized medical profession, pointed out that the market incentive system gave doctors every reason to keep people sick; a salary system gave them the incentive to keep people well so that they would have less work to do for the same pay. Ivan Illich, who believes that all professionals are engaged in a conspiracy against the public, argues that even in a salaried system doctors still use their professional authority to persuade people that they are sick, simply for the sheer joy of exercising that authority.[9]

These dangers of ritualization of the qualifying process are much greater in the case of some other professions - for example personnel management, for which entrants go on executive development programmes which:

> range from short 'exposure' to prolonged residency, during which a host of issues and techniques bearing on 'human relations' and macro-economic policy problems are covered, with excursions in between into 'systems analysis' and 'sensitivity training'. The latter is designed to make managers more interpersonally 'competent' and to modify their behaviour so that their peers and subordinates will experience a heightened sense of 'self-actualization'.

- to quote Ivan Berg's description, with ironic quotation marks, in his *Education and Jobs: the great training robbery*.[10] The reason why these business courses are more open to irony than medical education is because the latter is concerned with a cumulating body of scientific knowledge within which there is a high degree of consensus as to what is true and what is not, and where the frontiers of discovery currently are. Personnel management, by contrast, is a field for the elaboration of theories which are as much evaluative (this is a state of relations one *ought* to aim at) as positivistic (this is how technically you achieve this state of relations) and hence necessarily more subjective. Second, efficient performance in a doctor is much easier to measure than efficient performance in a personnel manager. Hence, in personnel management, the possibilities of elaborating word-spinning rituals to make ever-higher levels of 'qualification' of no substantive value become much greater.

[All of which suggests that one should take a long hard and sceptical look at the role of professional bodies in limiting entry to keep up the price of their services, in making claims to ethical standards of public service, in pretensions to intellectual superiority, etc.]

GENERAL EDUCATION

[In the evolution of the four-stage model, there is a] complementary change in the role of general education ... of very great importance. In the early capitalist pattern 'general education achievement' joins 'entering apprenticeship' as a selecting mechanism; in the bureaucratic phase, it replaces it. This requires some explanation.

The first concern of the General Medical Council (the usual shortened title of the body established as a result of the 1858 Act) was with the general educational standards of doctors. There were far too many 'rude mechanicals' among provincial GPs. No longer should a doctor be able to take any Tom, Dick or Harry as an apprentice. Students, it recommended, must be registered, and a prerequisite for such registration was that 'they had passed an examination in Arts at a standard accepted by the Council'.[11]

This 'acceptable standard' has steadily risen. [But not because of an increasing concern to get 'men and women of culture'.] You may have heard stories of the medical schools which require three As at GCE A level for entry. The relevance of the A-level subjects required is usually obvious (e.g. biology, chemistry, physics), but why should *standards* be so high? Is it that the study of medicine actually requires that degree of mastery of foundation learning in specific subject matter? Or is it that medicine, being a high-prestige subject, has many applicants and the selectors can take the 'best'? In what sense are students with three As thought to be the 'best'? Surely it is because their achievements in specific A levels are seen as proxy measures of their underlying 'general ability', a promise to the university teachers that they will be quick learners and a joy to teach; a promise to the medical profession that their intelligence will shine through in their subsequent dealings with the public and so uphold the profession's good name. Whether the 'best' students in that sense make the best doctors or whether personal qualities might not be just as important as intellectual ones is a matter of frequent controversy, reflected in the decisions of some medical schools to alter their admission criteria.

But the general practice remains unaltered. A-level achievement tests are generally used by universities not only as indications of whether the student knows enough biology, say, to understand anatomy lectures, but *also* as proxy measures of general ability. Sometimes the ability-measure use overrides all questions of relevance. See, for example, what the *Compendium of University Entrance Requirements* (1979) says about 'technical subjects' - the subjects one would have thought highly relevant to the engineering life, but which are generally reputed to be reserved for the less intelligent bands of the ability spectrum. 'Technical subjects, such as ... Engineering Workshop Theory and Practice either are not acceptable at all, or even though passed at A level, may only be counted as O levels' even for entry to university engineering faculties.

[In Britain this deliberate use of general educational qualifications as a proxy measure for intellectual ability started in the nineteenth century, with the Indian and then the home civil service giving the lead. Arguing for such a change in the Commons, Macaulay got off the memorable line:]

> If the Ptolemaic system were taught at Cambridge, instead of the Newtonian, the senior wrangler would nevertheless be in general a superior man to the wooden spoon. If instead of learning Greek, we learned the Cherokee, the man who understood the Cherokee best who made the most correct and melodious Cherokee verses - who comprehended most accurately the effect of the Cherokee particles - would generally be a superior man to him who was destitute of these accomplishments.[12]

Britain, of course, was not particularly innovative in this respect. The Chinese had been doing the same thing for twelve hundred years.

NOTES

1. F.G. Bailey, *Caste and the Economic Frontier*, Manchester, Manchester UP, 1957, pp. 95–7.
2. L. Stone, *The Family, Sex and Marriage in England, 1500-1800*, London, Weidenfeld and Nicholson, 1977, p. 447.
3. *Ibid.*, p. 108.
4. Shikitei Samba, *Ukiyo-buro*, quoted in R. Dore, *Education in Tokugawa Japan*, London, Routledge, 1963, p. 268.
5. R.S. Roberts, 'Medical education and the medical corporation' in F.N.L. Poynter, *The Evolution of Medical Education in England*, London, Pitman Medical, 1966, p. 71.
6. P.A. White, *Blackburn As It Is*, Blackburn, 1852.
7. G.W. Roderick and M.D. Stephens, *Scientific and Technical Education in 19th Century England*, Newton Abbot, David and Charles, 1913, p. 95.
8. H.S. Becker, B. Geer, E.C. Hughes and A.L. Strauss, *Boys in White: Student Culture in Medical School*, Chicago, Chicago University Press, 1961.
9. I. Illich, *Medical Nemesis*, London, Calder and Boyars, 1974.
10. Harmondsworth, Penguin Books, 1970, p. 85.
11. Roberts, *op. cit.*, p. 197.
12. Quoted in P.J.Wiles, 'The correlation between education and earnings; the external-test-not-content hypothesis', *Higher Education*, **3**(1), pp. 43–58.

6. Unions in a technologically mature society*

Fifteen years ago when I was writing about differences between British and Japanese industrial relations, it seemed to me that there was more evidence of British practices coming to resemble Japanese practices than *vice versa*.[1] William Brown[2] [has recently described some of the changes which seem to suggest that this might indeed be happening - more enterprise specific training, plant bargaining, multi-union negotiating committees, single-union agreements, increased importance of 'ability to pay' as criterion in wage negotiations, increased use of job-evaluation schemes designed for internal consistency rather than external market reference, increasing use of devices to secure 'employee involvement' etc.]

Most secular trends in industrial societies can be in some way linked with the one undeniably unidirectional and cumulative trend of the modern period - the growth of scientific knowledge and the ever-increasing sophistication and productiveness of applied technology. The link in this case seems to me a double one.

First of all, the rapid cheapening of the technologies of transport and communication has the effect of (a) intensifying international trade competition, and (b) intensifying the demonstration effect and so increasing the pressure on governments whose voters' standard of living is falling behind that of other countries. It is no wonder that 'competitiveness' has become the buzz-word of the decade in both Britain and the USA - and ten years ago nobody was quite sure whether the correct noun was 'competitiveness' or 'competitivity'.

That competitive pressure to raise productivity can be intensified from time to time by particular events - in Britain by the sharp 1980–81 recession, in Japan by the sudden recent rise of the yen - but it has been - and as long as we continue to maintain a basically free trade economy for a long time will be - slowly increasing all the time as the container ships have got bigger, the satellites and optical fibres more efficient, and air-freight trade has grown as a proportion of total trade. (It is now, apparently, over a quarter of the foreign trade of the United States.)

* Extracts from a paper delivered to the International Industrial Relations Association (IIRA) International Conference, Tokyo 1988; figure originally in *Taking Japan Seriously*, p. 153.

The second effect is the change in the nature of work which follows the change in technology. International competition does not only intensify; it changes, also, in form. The acceleration in the rate of product innovation and the increasing complexity of the products traded, mean that success in the competition depends not only on low prices, but increasingly on the non-price factors of innovation, quality, performance, reliability and after-service. And quality is not something easily secured by the external-monitoring, coercive supervision and monetary incentives of Taylorite methods of control over work. It requires some kind of inner commitment to doing good work - professionalism in the sense that good performance becomes a condition for self-respect.

The transition from the classical paradigm to the alternative paradigm in the pioneer industrial countries is accelerated by direct diffusion from the original home of the alternative paradigm - Japan. A recent *Business Week* special number on quality in American manufacturing[3] makes it clear that adoption of the Japanese practice of replacing external inspection by a responsibility system of the kind which has become standard in Japan - each worker being responsible for the testing and certification of his own work - is the crucial breakthrough in developing new patterns of employment - and new standards of quality.

This is not to say that the Japanese employment system is going to be adopted lock, stock and barrel by the older industrial countries. In more individualistic societies the ideology of enterprise loyalty is not going to be easily reproduced, nor the claims of personal and family life so easily sacrificed to the requirements of work life. And, in Britain at least, it is ironic that these trends away from 'market-oriented' employment systems towards 'organization-oriented' employment systems take place under a government which is dedicated to the restoration of market forces, and is even trying to introduce market principles into the civil service, Britain's originally most 'organization-oriented' organization. The principles of career employment are being flouted, with accelerated promotions and the bringing in of outsiders from the business world breaking seniority rules and drastically altering the career expectations of lifelong employees - with quite disastrous effects, one might add, on civil service morale.

In countries where there is less automatic deference to organizational superiors than there is in Japan, the alternative paradigm will develop in a different form. As is suggested in Figure 6.1,[4] the most likely adaptation to all the influences which flow from technological development and greater affluence - adaptation to the erosion of the traditional sanction of poverty, to the erosion of automatic coercive 'feudal' deference, to the increased importance of human as compared with physical capital, to the increasing divorce of ownership and control in industry, etc. - is further movement in the

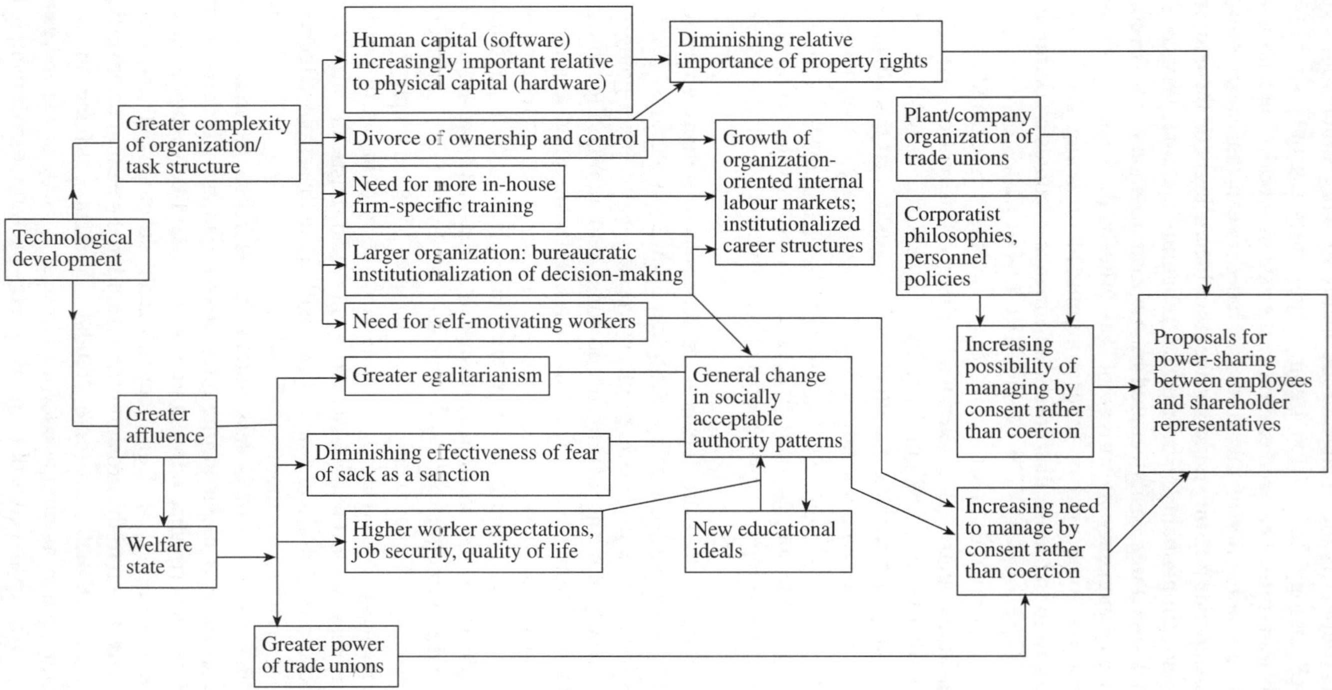

Figure 6.1 Industrial democracy and job restructuring

direction already set by the Scandinavian countries and Germany - towards greater industrial democracy. European firms will continue to be very different in atmosphere from Japanese firms (and British firms from Swedish firms, for that matter). What they will have in common is that they will give those who work in them (in them, not for them) some sense of a community in which they have membership - and that the sense of identification with the firms which this implies will be stronger than the class identification postulated by the classical paradigm.

THE WITHERING AWAY OF THE CORPORATION?

That is all very well, the reader might say, and plausible if we are talking about the Toyotas, the IBMs, the Rhone-Poulencs, the AEGs, the British Oxygens of the industrial world. But surely the changes in technology which are bringing about the transformation of the employment systems of large corporations in the older industrial countries, are also causing the disintegration of the large corporation itself. Henceforth small is going to be more and more beautiful.

One element of the classical paradigm was the assumption that economies of scale, in a large number of industries, were inexorably making the large corporation responsible for a larger and larger share of employment. The statistical trends in employment, by size of enterprise or plant, seemed to confirm this in most countries - until the 1970s. Thereafter the trend seems to have been reversed. …

One obvious source of these changes is the progress of automation - the progressive substitution of machines for simple routine manual and mental tasks in manufacturing, and the steady displacement of manufacturing labour into service occupations where establishment sizes are likely to be smaller - the standard story of the 'tertiarization' of the economy.

A second source is the working out of the core-periphery distinction referred to in discussing British changes. As firms are more concerned to 'bind' their valued workers to them by income and security and career promotion privileges, they also become more selective in choosing whom they think it worthwhile to bind.

There are, however, two different types of peripheralization. On the one hand is the relegation to inferior work conditions of part-time and temporary workers who do the unskilled or semi-skilled fetching and carrying, the simpler assembly line jobs, together with the contracting out of security, cleaning and canteen services to be performed by small firms which may also offer less secure and less well-paid conditions of employment. This is the distinction between primary and secondary labour markets familiar from the labour segmentation literature. …

The other part of 'peripheralization' is the resort to outside contracting for a wide range of services - training, design, management consultancy, marketing, data-processing, machine-maintenance - which have hitherto been provided in-house. This is partly, in a world plagued by stagflation, a response to the end of the high-growth period - an attempt to reduce fixed costs and thereby gain in flexibility. But it is also, probably, a response to the increasing technical complexity and hence human capital cost of the services which industry needs, so that only the largest firms can achieve economies of scale if they try to provide them in-house.

The viability of the outside contracting alternative depends in part on the development of stable contracting relationships, in many ways intermediate between 'market' and 'hierarchy', of a kind which Stinchcombe has recently interestingly analysed.[5] There are similar developments in the sub-contracting of manufacturing - an increasing tendency to develop 'preferential supplier', 'tied supplier' systems, particularly in those branches of manufacture where quality and timely deliveries are of the greatest importance. (Another trend on which direct Japanese influence is clearly traceable.) These developments, again, would imply a reduction in the average size of firm.

In the United States the end-product of these trends is sometimes spoken of as the 'hollow corporation' - the major corporation as simply the planner and authoritative coordinator of a wide range of activities through relationships which are neither the 'hierarchy' of vertical integration, nor the unstable links of market contracting. Some suggest that the change will be widespread and spectacular. Sabel and Piore, who speak of a 'second industrial divide',[6] see the pattern of the future exemplified not only in such 'hollow' or, in their phrase 'solar' firms, but also in the regional agglomerations of small and medium enterprises integrated (with local governmental help) by numerous links of competition and co-operation - as in Tuscany and Emilia-Romagna, the 'Third Italy', or the area near Salzburg or parts of Baden-Württemburg.

Once again, the technological dimension is crucial. They see the viability of a new era of 'flexible specialization' as depending not only on the social inventions of new types of stable contracting ties, but also on the electronic revolution. The adaptation of computers to process control, together with the differentiation and specialization of consumer demand is seen as having a dramatic effect on economies of scale.

Putting all this together, then, what is likely to be the effect of 'technological maturity' on the scale and distribution of union membership? Global generalizations are clearly dangerous if one is discussing societies as diverse as Norway with a 65 per cent union density rate and the USA or France with rates around 20 per cent; countries like Britain or Sweden with a single trade union centre, countries like Germany where the central organizations divide by function and countries like Italy or France or Japan where they divide by ideological allegiance. Abandoning discretion, one might, however, hazard the following speculations.

1. An increasing proportion of more educated workers may become self-employed or employees in small, quasi-family type, probably profit-sharing, firms providing business services, but still a large proportion of the work force (including the more educated workers) will continue to be employed by large private sector corporations or the public sector.
2. The importance of the latter, in spite of recent waves of privatization and attempts to realize 'small government', is unlikely to diminish, and so is the propensity of public service workers to join unions.
3. The shift to the 'alternative paradigm' in the private sector may mean not a shift towards the 'enterprise union' pattern but sometimes towards a 'no-union' pattern. Union density rates are, at any rate, unlikely to increase in the private sector.
4. The greater difficulty of organizing workers in the small and medium enterprises which draw from the secondary labour market means that union membership will be increasingly confined to the more privileged sectors of employment - unions of labour aristocrats rather than of the underprivileged.

To repeat: there is no reason to expect any generalization about the role of unions to hold over *all* technologically mature societies. Technology may be an important determinant; it is not an overwhelming and unique one. Think, for instance, of the diversity of the experience of, say, France, the USA and Japan in the heyday of smokestack industrialization.

Part of that diversity is explicable as an effect of the timing of industrialization, the late development effect; for example, the fact that Japan's industrialization really got under way *after* the development of power sources like gasoline engines and electric motors, which did not involve the scale economies of the steam engine, and so favoured the competitive power of the small family firm against the large factory. Other sources of diversity lie in cultural traditions (attitudes towards authority, general levels of inter-personal trust, intensities of nationalist feeling, etc.) or the idiosyncratic effect of historical incident - institutional upheaval in the aftermath of revolution, war, or defeat or the influence of outstanding union leaders.

So the best one can do by way of generalization is to list some of the tendencies which, other things being equal, might be expected to follow directly from the changes in work and industrial organization which new technologies seem bound to entail - with all due allowance for the fact that other things are likely to be far from equal and sometimes work to counteract those tendencies entirely.

1. One can expect the role of unions and collective bargaining in wage determination to diminish, because of a growth of 'person-related' elements, as opposed to 'job-related' elements in wages and salaries which are less amenable to collective regulation. …
2. Income inequalities are likely to increase, and the role of unions in spreading the gains in productivity brought by new technologies is likely to diminish. …
3. The erosion of the 'classical paradigm' implies, not necessarily the end of ideology, but at least the end of the particular kind of socialist ideology which has animated the union movement of Europe and Latin America and Japan and (intermittently and partially) the United States … The available substitute ideologies seem unlikely to be as powerful as a source of solidarity, or of militancy, or of political influence. They are more likely to be concerned with the reduction of inequalities within the system, and with resistance to bureaucratic authority – perhaps Poland's Solidarity will prove to have been more like the model of future union militancy in the capitalist countries than is generally imagined.
4. The tendency of recent decades in a number of countries for militancy to be more characteristic of public sector than of private sector workers will probably become more pronounced. The switch to the 'alternative paradigm' is not easy in the public sector. The sense of 'participative membership in the organization' can be stimulated in private sector firms by the real circumstances of competition in the market, profit-sharing schemes and the like, by the cultivation of an atmosphere of open participative friendliness[7] which blurs the nature of authority relations and makes for a compliance which is not merely coerced. But in the large public sector bureaucracy nothing similar is available to compensate for the secular decline in deference as industrial societies 'use up' the legacy of pre-industrial status systems, and nothing similar to modify the perception of adversarial employer–employee relations except a shared spirit of public service. That can work at professional levels, but is difficult to mobilize for the rank and file. And if the unions of government workers are linked to parties opposed to the government in power, that difficulty is compounded.

   Other factors can make that difficulty even greater: (a) the public sector contains large numbers of the intellectual proletariat – particularly workers in health and education and social welfare services who have intelligence, and high levels of education, but low incomes relative to those of the private sector and (b) the squeeze on government revenue, as the steady secular expansion of the functions of government takes government spending to the limits of a democratic electorate's taxability, is likely to mean poor relative pay for public sector workers and copious sources of dissatisfaction.

5. Technological maturity, increasing complexity and sophistication of our technology mean increasing economic interdependence, and hence increasing power of relatively small groups of workers to hold society up to ransom - the electric power workers are a commonly cited example, or the air traffic controllers, protagonists in a notable American confrontation in the early 1980s. A key question is whether that potential power - generally in the public sector - will be allied with the militancy just spoken of. The likelihood is that it will not be; the public sector workers most prone to ideological commitment are for the most part the least powerful.
6. Given all the trends of change listed earlier it is unlikely that many national union organizations will become strong enough in future to claim a role as 'social partners' in the concertation of macroeconomic policy such as that achieved by unions in Scandinavia or Austria in the 1960s and 1970s, or in Australia in the 1980s. Where regular mechanisms for consultations have been established, as in the countries mentioned, they may well persist, but where such institutions do not yet exist, there seem few countries - certainly not Japan - where they are likely to be created anew, unless it is specifically as a co-ordinating forum for public sector bargaining.
7. Unions in some countries may face a decline in the calibre of their leadership. A technologically mature society is likely to be a meritocracy with much greater equality of educational opportunities than the societies of the past. Many union leaders of previous decades came from poor families, left school early and gained for themselves the education they needed - and were inspired to do so by the ideology of the 'classical paradigm'. Nowadays, for people of their ability, the road is open to positions of power and prestige in the establishment itself. …

CONCLUSION

If there is a common theme in these speculations it is that the way our societies seem to be moving as a result of changes in technology seems more likely to weaken and fragment, rather than to strengthen, labour unions. Once again, though, the importance of variations in national traditions and national institutions cannot be overemphasized. For all the similarities in the *tendencies* set up by changes in the material - and social - technologies we use, Japanese unions in the year 2000 will still look more like Japanese unions today than like British unions in the year 2000. And vice versa.

NOTES

1. Ronald Dore, *British Factory-Japanese Factory*, California, University of California Press, 1973.
2. William Brown, 'The changing role of trade unions in the management of labour', *British Journal of Industrial Relations* 214, ii, July 1986.
3. *Business Week*, 8 June 1987.
4. [In good Weberian tradition, the only exogenous variables in Table 6.1 are technology and philosophies. The figure is reproduced from *Taking Japan Seriously*, p. 153.]
5. A.L. Stinchcombe, 'Contracts as hierarchical documents', in A.L. Stinchcombe and C.A. Heimer, *Organisation Theory and Project Management; Administering Uncertainty in Norwegian Offshore Oil*, Oslo, Norwegian University Press, 1985.
6. Michael J. Piore and Charles F. Sabel, *The Second Industrial Divide*, New York, Basic Books, 1984.
7. Colin Crouch, 'The future prospects for trade unions in Western Europe', *Political Quarterly*, Jan–March, 1986.

7. Philosophies of history*

CYCLICAL REPETITION OR EVOLUTION

'Philosophies of history' may sound slightly pretentious. Most of us manage to live our daily lives without one, and so indeed do most historians who nevertheless succeed in providing fine analytical descriptions of particular concrete events and societies. The philosophy of history, one might think, is something one can safely leave to interested specialists.

However, not so. Most of us do in fact have, however unconsciously, some kind of philosophy of history. That unconscious view of history tends in some way or other to colour our perceptions of social and political issues, be they matters of education policy, policies towards crime, the danger of war or the possibilities of strengthening the United Nations. Perhaps it has to do with basic personality tendencies towards gloomy pessimism or cheerful optimism; at any rate most people are, one might say instinctively, history-as-decline theorists, history-as-cycles theorists or history-as-evolution theorists.

For example, one frequently hears people in Britain describe Thatcherism as a reaction against the excessive egalitarianism of Labour governments and predict that sooner or later there will be an egalitarian reaction against the excesses of pure marketism under the Thatcher regime. Or one hears people

* From *Japan, Internationalism and the UN*, London: Routledge, 1997, Chapter 1, pp. 3–15, slightly abridged. This is taken from a book originally written for a Japanese audience as a polemical contribution to Japanese debates about foreign policy in the aftermath of the Gulf War and the controversy about whether the Japanese army should have played a part in that, and subsequently in the UN's Somalia operation. With the title *Kō shiyō to ieru Nihon* (The Japan That Can Say 'Let's Do This'), its intent was to counter the diffuse chauvinism of a previous best-seller, Ishihara and Morita's *The Japan That Can Say 'No!'* ('No!' to the United States, that is). Its message for the Japanese establishment was that the best way to secure a position of respect and even prestige in the world was to frame a foreign policy which promoted not merely Japan's immediate economic and security interests, but also mankind's long-term 'project' (the only viably long-term alternative to annihilation) of building an international 'rule of law' system. (It also had a message for Japan's peaceniks, namely that they should abandon their over-our-dead-bodies opposition to changing the Constitution. Instead of declaring that Japan would have no army and maintaining the absurd pretence that it actually had none, revision could be a good move which opened the way for a real 'peace constitution' which restricted the use of armed force to self-defence and genuinely internationalist purposes.) The English translation from which this chapter – a potted history of the development of mankind's long-term 'project' – is drawn was published together with comments on the argument from nine Japanese writers as a contribution to an understanding of the emotional and political mainsprings of Japan's foreign policy.

saying the history of education is a story of alternation between periods of authoritarian emphasis on disciplined instruction and periods of permissive freedom and now we are at a turning point.

Economists are frequently cycle theorists. Those who study business cycles are primarily interested in uncovering the mechanisms which cause the transition from boom to recession and are not often concerned with the question whether *this* recession *now* differs structurally from the recession fifteen years ago. The followers of Kondratieff are even more extreme in their belief that one can discern, as a result of successive waves of introduction of new technology, long-term 50–60 year cycles in the economy. They assume, in other words, that capitalism 'as a system' has basically remained unchanged for two hundred years.

Before the industrial revolution, in the seventeenth and eighteenth centuries cyclical theorists predominated among philosophers of history. Among the most explicit, Vico and Condorcet are the most famous. In the Far East, the Confucianists who saw history as a succession of periods of Ji and Ran - of stable order and disorder - and the popular Buddhism, well expressed by the author of the opening words of the Gempei ballad: 'the bell of Gion tolls out the message: the potentates of today are the broken men of tomorrow' - these too were cyclical theorists. In recent times Arnold Toynbee won fame and popularity in the United States and Japan - less so in his own country - for his panoramic vision of the rise and fall of successive civilizations.

The cyclical theorist sees human societies as passing through time, but with no particular direction. Both the theorists of decline and the theorists of evolution would disagree. In its vaguest form the history-as-decline view expresses itself in the complaints of the disgruntled old, forever reminiscing about the good old days of their youth, and muttering about 'the way young people nowadays ...'. But, until the middle-ages, it was in many societies an explicit doctrine of revealed truth. The age of Yao and Shun in China, Eden, the High Plain of Heaven of Japanese mythology, the Grecian Golden Age - the original human society was an ideal paradise created by the Gods. The appearance of original sin, the growing strength of baser instincts - since then it is all a story of continuous decline.

Equally insistent on the notion of a 'direction' in history, but giving it a very different evaluation, are the social evolutionists; or one should rather say the theorists of social progress. 'Progress' and 'evolution' need to be distinguished. The former means movement in a *desirable* direction whereas 'evolution', in principle, contains no evaluative overtones and simply means 'proceeding in a given direction as a result of determinate mechanisms'. In practice, of course, most of the nineteenth-century thinkers described as social evolutionists - Hegel, Kant, Spencer, Morgan, Marx - all had a firm belief that mankind was steadily progressing - or at least, in the case of Marx, if not steadily at least through the leaps of revolution.

In the twentieth century, having seen two world wars costing tens of millions of lives; having seen the rise of a Nazi Germany which elevated genocide to the status of national policy, we are not so sure about progress. From the simple believers in ineradicable original sin to more complex theorists of the essential nature of science, men and women, disappointed in Man, have come to reject the optimistic nineteenth-century theorists as naïve victims of wishful thinking; and those who deny progress for the most part are likely also to deny evolution. History is more likely to be seen as meaningless; a continuous directionless flux in which elements of progress mix with elements of reaction.

THE VARIOUS DIMENSIONS OF SOCIAL EVOLUTION

I believe that is mistaken. I would summarize my own view of history as follows.

Proposition 1

Toynbee is right that most of recorded history is the story of the rise and fall of civilizations. It often happened that when a civilization disintegrated the knowledge that its members had accumulated - their material inventions like water-wheels or their social inventions like the secret vote - became completely lost. Much had to be reinvented by succeeding civilizations. It took about a thousand years before Renaissance Italy could get back to the level of Rome at its peak.

Proposition 2

Since the Renaissance, however, and especially since the scientific revolution of the seventeenth century and the industrial revolution which followed, the means of recording, accumulating and diffusing technological knowledge have fundamentally changed and - short of a nuclear war which threatens the very existence of mankind - it is hard to think of the possibility of this rapidly accumulating stock of knowledge being lost.

Proposition 3

It is precisely this accumulation of knowledge and technology which conditions the evolution of society. By 'condition' I do not mean 'determine'. The accumulation of material and social techniques serves to enlarge the scope of human choice. Different countries, different people, make different choices. However, human nature and human drives are not all that heterogeneous. Hence, when choosing from the menu of 'possibly usable alternatives' offered by the accumulated technology, human groups - individuals, business firms and states - tend to make choices which are not all that diverse. It is this which gives a fair degree of universality to the 'directioned' nature of history. Consider, by way of illustration, the way in which countries of the Third World seek to 'modernize' - to become like the 'advanced' industrial countries; or Eda Saburo, the leader of Japan's Socialist Party in the 1960s, setting his targets for Japan: 'an American standard of living, the Welfare State of a Sweden, the culture of a France'.

Let me give some examples of the similarity in choices among 'usable alternatives' - of the way, that is, in which the accumulation of technology conditions but does not determine social structure.

Mankind (or at least that part of Mankind which lives in Europe, America and Japan) has accumulated the technology necessary for making splendid television sets. In some respects the organization for using that technology - the business firm - is everywhere very much the same. The machines used, the layout of the workplace, the staging of the productive process most obviously, but also organizational structure, the division of labour among production workers, foremen, drivers, researchers and developers, telephone operators and directors, even the accounting methods and the organigrams of the production department and the sales department look very much alike in Germany, in China, America or Japan. But, nevertheless, in some dimensions of very great importance to society - whether the labour market is in continuous flux or there is something like lifetime employment; the wage differentials corresponding to different roles in the division of labour, the balance of rights between the shareholders who provide capital and the workers who provide labour; whether the business firm is generally viewed as a kind of community or as a piece of property of the shareholders - in all these things there can be very wide differences amongst societies. That is one example of the way in which technology constrains but does not completely determine social outcomes.

There are some who believe that eventually social institutions will be so conditioned by the need to make efficient use of technology that the world will become more or less homogenized. It is certainly not difficult to believe. One of the important consequences of technological advance is the spectacular cheapening of transport and communication of the last forty years. The markets for raw materials, the markets for manufactured products, especially electrical and electronic products and automobiles, even markets for insurance, education and medical services have been very largely internationalized. One consequence is that, within individual countries, the conflict between those who gain from foreign trade and those who seek protection has grown fiercer. It may be that the protectionists will gain the upper hand and the process will slow down, but the prospects are that this process of the internationalization of markets, continuously spurred by further developments in communication and transport, will continue at a growing pace.

In most kinds of markets it seems as if it is not American-style capitalism with its emphasis on individual freedom and self-realization, but Japanese style capitalism with its emphasis on group co-operation and the setting of common (national or industry-wide) objectives which has the competitive edge - not the capitalism which emphasizes short-term gains, but that which seeks market dominance over the longer term. In any open market competition, as a result of processes of natural selection, the most efficient system, that is to say the Japanese system, should become dominant, and thus become the universal world system. At least that seems like a plausible argument.

Unlike biological natural selection, moreover, which operates through the single mechanism of genetic inheritance, the natural selection processes of social institutions involve a dual mechanism. One is, indeed, the perishing of weak organizations and the survival of stronger ones. The other is revitalization - raising the efficiency of existing organizations through adaptive learning. One can see both mechanisms at work in the American automobile industry. On the one hand, while American automobile manufacturers are closing factories at a fast rate the investments of Japanese companies are opening new ones. But at the same time, the American and British firms remaining in the industry are rushing to adopt Japanese-style quality circles, total quality control, and just-in-time manufacturing methods; they are building security into their labour contracts, creating employee councils, and establishing stable relations with their suppliers. Things have even got to the point where the great success-story hero Iacocca is being criticized for the size of his salary.

Nevertheless, it would be a mistake to jump to the conclusion that, because of what has happened in the last ten years, by the year 2030 the whole world will have converged on Japanese type capitalism. Quite apart from the possibility of a surge in nationalist protectionism the Japanese people's own value system might change. They might begin to value individual freedom and self-assertion more than the satisfactions of group co-operation; the number of Japanese who feel more admiration for an Iacocca-type hero than for the austere, ascetic industrialist of the older Japanese generation, like Doko,[1] may increase. As a consequence the efficiency of Japanese style organizations may diminish. All of which is to say that one must never forget that the choices people make among the 'usable alternatives' are inevitably infused with judgements of value.

TECHNOLOGY AND VALUES

Proposition 4

But are values not, themselves, partly formed by technology? In the Japan of a hundred years ago when the technologies of agriculture and of industry were best adapted to family production, words like 'the ancestors', the *ie* (the family, 'the house of ...' as in 'the House of Windsor'), 'the ways of the family', the *yome-san* (the imported bride of the eldest son, mistress-to-be of the household) were common everyday words, and duties towards the *ie* were at the core of everyday ethics. But as technology has vastly outgrown the ability of small family units to cope and large corporations have come to dominate the economy, both the vocabulary and the reality have changed. These words are rarely heard in today's society of dependent employees. This is but one illustration of the way in which technology influences values and ethical systems, and how changes in the one have a direct causal relationship with changes in the other.

In broad terms one can say the following: there is a distinct pattern in the *degree* to which social institutions are subject to the constraints of technology. Most closely constrained is the division of labour in the production process: next most closely constrained is the legal property structure which facilitates that division of labour. Next in the ever-widening circles of constraint come the family system and the education system, while least directly influenced of all are the value system, religion and the arts.

This is not to say that religion and the arts are uninfluenced by the accumulation of technology. Marxists have a clear and simple story about this: religion and the arts are simply part of the super-structure which maintains the hegemony of the ruling class by justifying the unequal distribution of wealth and power entailed by the production system and the property system. (The myth that an American can become an Iacocca; the message shared both by Christianity and by Salvationist Buddhism that it is the poor that are privileged in the after life.) But highly mobile fluid industrial societies lose their homogeneity; neither state nor church have the power to impose narrow ideas of justice and morality on the whole society. There are other mechanisms much more important than the efforts of the ruling class to maintain their position which link, on the one hand the accumulation of technology, and on the other the directions of change in morality, ideology and the arts. One might suggest two.

(a)

As the Analects say: 'When clothing and food suffice, then can Men come to know the *li*' – that all embracing concept, variously translated as rites, as propriety, as ethics. As technological advance brings greater affluence there is a steady increase in the number of specialists in the *li* - professional artists and musicians, professional teachers of philosophy or of the history of thought. With the improvement of communications and transport these specialists increasingly go to study in other countries, go to international congresses. There they mix with fellow specialists whose education has been conditioned by different social systems and different cultural traditions. They come to form a kind of international professional quasi-community. One sees in formation a kind of global professional culture divorced from the cultural traditions of particular states or ethnic groups. This process is most advanced in fields where language is not important and there is a high degree of commercialization of the products the specialists produce - in fashion and advertising for instance. It is at its weakest in fields like philosophy where language is all important and even the most famous can sell only a few thousand books. But even among philosophers, for instance, there is, today, a similarity in the topics they tackle, their methods, and their criteria of truth, whether they be in China or Germany or the United States, which would have been unthinkable a hundred years ago.

(b)

In affluent societies the struggle for survival becomes less severe. The 'coming to know *li* when clothing and food suffice' phenomenon affects the ordinary citizen too. Just think how our world of birth control and anaesthetics, a world of lifespans approaching eighty years in which children grow up with little confrontation with death, differs from the world of a hundred years ago when most people who reached the age of twenty had had the experience of seeing brothers and sisters dying before their eyes, and often in great pain. It would be strange if there were not some general change in sensibilities. The cruel atrocities inflicted by Wellington's troops in the Peninsular War at the beginning of the nineteenth century were not reproduced on the same scale in any of Britain's subsequent wars. It is unlikely that Japan's Self Defence Forces could be persuaded to behave with the same ruthlessness as their grandfathers showed when they 'moved into' China fifty years ago.

THE CUMULATION OF SOCIAL TECHNOLOGY

Proposition 5

Along with a tendency towards more 'tender' sensibilities there is also an accumulation of social technology. It may not be so obvious as accumulation of material technology, but it should not be underestimated. Consider the proliferation of regulations - the difference between the first publication in

Japan of the 'Compendium of the Six Laws' and the mass of publications one finds in Japanese bookstalls today – the Six Laws for Agriculture, the Six Laws for Education, the Six Laws for Small and Medium Industries and all the rest. It is not simply a matter of quantitative change, but also of progress in quality – the reduction in ambiguity, the specification of various alternative contingencies, the diversification of administrative devices. 'You call that Progress!' is the likely response, not only of anarchists but also of the free marketist followers of Hayek, Friedman and Thatcher. But they are surely wrong. No one in his right mind would maintain that every bit of these accumulated social technologies contributes either to efficiency or to human happiness. But it is equally undeniable that over the last century, in the production of public goods like health and education systems and defence, and in the maintenance of order, and in the concern for fairness, and hence for the minimization of conflict, there has been a steady process of social invention.

THE FORMATION OF INTERNATIONAL PROFESSIONAL QUASI-COMMUNITIES

Proposition 6

The increasing density of administration and (provided that the pursuit of self-interest by the administrators can be kept under control) its increasing efficiency is not confined to individual countries. There has been a vast growth of international organizations and international administration. It was only 70 years ago, in the early 1920s, that Nitobe Inazo and Maeda Tamon went to what was then, for Japanese, the strange and distant town of Geneva to become the first Japanese members of an international organization. Today, the number of Japanese in international organizations are counted in their hundreds, and soon in their thousands, and two of the United Nations organizations are headed by Japanese nationals. These organizations provide the focal point for many of what are called international professional quasi-communities. Meteorologists, experts in infectious diseases, maritime administrators, members of voluntary organizations dealing with refugees, environmentalists – all create their own trans-national organizations and develop common value systems.

INTERNATIONAL LAW

Proposition 7

One of the most important of these professional quasi-communities is that of the lawyers and international relations experts with the International Court of Justice as their focal point. There is a slow development of a consensus about the universal principles of justice - principles transcending the traditional value systems of individual countries - to be applied in the settlement of cross-border disputes, between individuals, between business firms, and between countries. It is the slow development of this consensus which is creating the basis for global order, for international rule by law.

GLEAMS OF THE EMERGENCE OF 'WORLD GOVERNMENT'

Proposition 8

Within individual countries there is one indispensable condition for judges to do their job of objectively adjudicating disputes and reaching acceptable decisions as to who is right and who is wrong, who wins who loses. It is the existence of a police force capable of intervening when disputes reach the level of violence and capable of ensuring, if necessary by physical coercion, that the judgments of courts are carried out - the existence of a policing system which forestalls violence before it happens and discourages anybody from taking judgments lightly. The realization that this principle, demonstrated in the history of every individual country, means, when applied to international affairs, that dispute resolution needs not merely an international court and an international law but also an international policing system - that realization has been steadily growing among political leaders since the nineteenth century. That much is evidenced in the uncertain steps towards such a goal which the world has produced - the Hague Convention of 1899, the founding of the League of Nations and, in 1945, the creation of the Security Council of the United Nations.[2]

THE EVOLUTION OF CONSCIOUSNESS

Proposition 9

I wrote 'that realization has been steadily growing'. It is not too difficult to predict that it will grow further for there is a clear inter-relationship between this growing realization and the trends of change discussed above, rooted in the accumulation of technological knowledge - and of the capital goods in which that knowledge is embodied. Both are products of the evolution of human society.

THE ODD POPULARITY OF CYCLICAL THEORIES

I like not to consider myself a particularly dogmatic person, but the above propositions about social evolution seem to me so patently obvious, that it is odd that there can still be cyclical theorists in the world and that, indeed, their books, not mine, should become best sellers. A good example is Paul Kennedy's *Rise and Fall of Great Powers*.[3] His account of the rise and fall of hegemonic powers, especially his description of the rise and decline of the Pax Brittanica and the Pax Americana in the last two centuries is persuasive and backed by a wealth of historical detail, as one would expect from such an able analytical historian. But the conclusion seems to be that there is an invariably repeated pattern. To maintain its power the hegemonic country inevitably runs down its economic strength; eventually it is overtaken by a more vigorous power riding on the strength of a more vital economy and the locus of hegemony shifts. The suggestion is that this is a kind of historical law many times repeated in the past and bound to be repeated in the future.

It is not surprising that the book elicited great interest in both the United States and Japan. 'So America's problems are not temporary troubles, but signs of a secular decline. So where is the next hegemonic power coming from? Which is the most likely candidate, if not Japan?' With dire anxiety on one side of the Pacific and happy cheerfulness on the other it became a popular theme of the intellectual and the not-so-intellectual magazines; earnest articles discussed the exact scenarios through which the law that economic power must eventually turn itself into military power would be enacted, and the form that an eventual Pax Japonica might take.

What the Kennedy thesis, in its usual interpretation, ignores is the process of secular evolution in international affairs. Think back to the time when Britain was establishing its hegenomy, to 1863, for instance, when a British fleet shelled Kagoshima in retaliation for the murder of an Englishman. Until the turn of the century, in Asia and in Africa, it was possible for Britain to send warships and troops anywhere to protect - and advance - its interests, provided it avoided frontal confrontations with other great powers. Today, the United States, with a destructive power thousands of times greater than Britain ever possessed, gave sufficient importance to 'international opinion' to deem it prudent to get the support of the Security Council before it sought to move against Iraq. America did, for reasons which world opinion could see as having a certain grain of justification, move unilaterally against Granada in 1983 and against Panama in 1989, but it did not venture to attack Cuba, its enemy neighbour for thirty years. There, it was not only world opinion, but also the existence of another superpower, the Soviet Union which provided an important constraint - a constraint which no longer applied at the time of the Gulf War. Think also of the ending of the Gulf War. It is said that the reactions provoked by the CNN's world-wide broadcasts showing fleeing Iraqi soldiers being mercilessly gunned down by American planes, were one factor in the decision to cease fire - one more illustration of the link between technology and formation of 'world opinion'. We have come a long way from the London *Times* printing the first dispatches from the Crimean War in 1855 or even from the days when news of the Japanese troops' rape of Nanking gradually crept out through primitive film taken by American missionaries. Nowadays, the formation of a first-reaction world opinion takes twenty-four hours.

There are other ways in which hegemonic countries become less able effectively to deploy military force. One factor is the ability of even small countries to acquire weapons of a destructiveness unthinkable half a century ago and, if cornered, to inflict unacceptable damage even on a hegemonic power. Another is the way in which the Western ideology of nationalism and ethnic self-determination has spread throughout the world. Both Vietnam and Afghanistan show that the attempt to maintain colonial rule by military strength - albeit nominally through 'aid' to a local independent government - is no longer an easy proposition.

Given these secular changes in the conditions for exercising hegemonic power it is hard to see how anyone can still hold to the notion that there are unchanging historical laws which govern the rise and fall of great powers.

EVALUATING EVOLUTION

The reader - let us imagine a reader who might call himself Mr Realist - might well answer as follows: All right, Mr Idealist, let us for the moment accept your evolutionary argument and let us accept your definition of the way the world is going in the long term towards a situation in which there is either a peaceful settlement of disputes through a body like the Security Council or, if it is necessary, to use military force to deal with transgressors against the international rules, in which a monopoly of that coercive force is held by such an international organization. But that is a state of affairs belonging to the far, far distant future; something whose shape one can only dimly perceive way over the horizon. Look at the world today. Look at the way nationalism is flaring up in violent manifestations all over the world. Do you really believe that in the near future nation-states are going to do what the Japanese *daimyo* did in 1870 when they surrendered their sovereignty and military independence to the central government? Do you think that nation-states are going to give up their sovereignty in military matters in favour of an international organization? Are they going to accept national emasculation? An independent army is the quintessential symbol of national sovereignty. It will take centuries of your kind of evolution before states are prepared to give it up. That will only happen when the integration of the world's economies, when the erosion of national sovereignty in favour of international organization, has proceeded in the non-military dimensions to a far greater degree than is forseeable in the near future.

Meanwhile, until that happens, the only way in which any kind of semblance of international order can be maintained among armed nation-states is either through the traditional mechanisms of the balance of power or through the co-ordinating control of a hegemon. That is why one should, for instance, welcome the thinking behind the Pentagon's long-term strategy document which was leaked to the press in March 1992 – the document which said that, as the only remaining superpower 'the United States must accept its role in the maintenance of international order and ensure that it is always prepared to act alone when co-ordinated international action is not possible or there is an urgent need for a speedy response'.[4] What is wrong with that? Particularly since the same document goes on to say that the United States must 'take full account of the interests of the other advanced industrial countries' when acting alone. Otherwise there would be a danger of 'upsetting' the existing political and economic order.

Just think back to history, Mr Realist might continue. The unification of China under the first Han emperor, of Britain and of France – the creation of unified kingdoms where once power was decentralized among endlessly warring fiefs. Or think back to the two-and-a-half centuries of peaceful order created by the Tokugawa, bringing an end to the sixteenth-century internecine wars. Every time the pattern is the same – the centralizing force – king, emperor, shogun – is someone who has won out over his rivals in the struggle for power. He wins out, but, recognizing that the feudal barons still have the power to 'upset the political and economic order' he accepts that he cannot wield his supreme power in an arbitrary way. He asks for their co-operation. The famous Magna Carta was exactly that; an agreement on the rule by which King and barons would constrain each others' power. From this bargaining emerges organizations – parliaments – to set and enforce the rules, and out of these grows the rule of law and the institutions of democracy.

If this is the common pattern in the creation of individual nation-states why should the future creation of a global state proceed any differently? And what would be wrong with that anyway? A lot would be wrong with it, replies Mr Idealist. Your 'realism' is not only over-pessimistic; it also overlooks important aspects of history. First of all, unification through the power of single hegemon is not by any means the invariate pattern. Think of the establishment of the Meiji Government in Japan. It was a coalition of four powerful fiefs which overthrew the existing hegemon and supported the creation of a formally absolute imperial government subsequently transformed over a couple of decades into a constitutional monarchy.

Nor should one overlook the development of technology. A lot has happened in the four hundred years that separates us from the battle of Sekigahara which confirmed Tokugawa supremacy, and it is not only that the muskets the Portugese introduced to Japan have given way to the hydrogen bomb. In the time it took for the great Lord Maeda to march post-haste from his castle town in Kanazawa to meet Hideyoshi in Osaka, Secretary of State James Baker could make several trips between Washington and Jerusalem and have long conversations on the plane with a dozen other foreign secretaries while on the way.

Nor should one overlook the evolution of ideas, the evolution of Man. At the time of the battle of Sekigahara, in the reign of Louis XIV, the world did not contain people who called themselves 'pacifists'. There was no such concept as 'the rule of law'. One should not overlook the importance of the existence of a growing number of people who can think beyond the duty of loyalty to nation-state with military force as its expression. If you are fond of history, continues Mr Idealist, what about this for a historical fact? In 1946 the United States Congress passed a resolution the sense of which was that American military forces which, it was anticipated, would be assigned to duty with the United Nations as a result of the progressive implementation of Chapter 7 of the UN Charter, could be committed to United Nations peace enforcement activities by a simple vote of the UN Security Council, without the need for any further reference to Congress.

Do you not find that astonishing? The contrast with the self-assertive world-management stance of contemporary American policy could hardly be more marked. You could, I suppose, put it down to the euphoric generosity of a nation that had just won a major war. But, continues Mr Idealist, I think that would be wrong. At the end of World War II, the world really had evolved to the point at which the establishment of some kind of collective security mechanism, depending on the conciliar mechanisms prescribed in the United Nations Charter, had reached the realm of realistic possibility. For a brief while there were real and active efforts to create the necessary institutions. But, with the intensification of mistrust between the USA and the USSR these efforts came to an end. Everything that has happened to the United Nations since - from its early efforts at peace-keeping operations to its work to reduce infant mortality in Africa - has been conditioned by that Cold War. Now that the world has been released from the shackles of the Cold War, why can we not take up once again those efforts to create a real collective security system? Far better that than to wait for the long-term evolution of American hegemony.

To summarize the position taken in this book in one sentence: if only Mr Idealist and Mr Realist would co-operate, then it should be possible not simply to sit back and watch what Mr Realist calls a 'natural process' but to take positive efforts to influence that evolution and bring it closer to Mr Idealist's ideals [by, that is, actively organizing the taming of America – a suitable role and a suitable policy goal, the book argues, for Japan].

NOTES

1. Doko Toshio (1896–1988), a forceful-leader type industrialist, famous for turning around failing companies, as a business leader, and, at the end of his life, as chairman of a committee to reform government. Also for the austerity of his personal life and his breakfasting on a single grilled sardine.
2. [I cannot resist one hindsight comment as I ruefully re-read this 1992, pre-Somalia, statement of faith. The remarkably honest November 1999 United Nations report on the Srebrenica disaster is another small step towards that same goal with its admission that international policing has to be something more than the interposition of neutral forces. It was sad that in the same year there had also to be such a huge step backwards when the Serbia–Kosovo bombing, with its total disregard for any practical consequences for humans, gave 'humanitarian intervention' such a bad name.]
3. P. Kennedy, *The Rise and Fall of Great Powers*, London, Unwin Hyman, 1988.
4. *Asahi Shimbun*, 9 March 1992.

8. A note about technological determinism*

I've always assumed that among sociologists 'technological determinist' was a term of abuse, and that declaring myself to be one has had an element of trailing my coat, of teasing the orthodox (even though I mean it only in the qualified sense that I've explained in Chapter 7). But I wonder how out-of-date my notion that technological determinism is still seen as hopelessly naïve has become. Everybody now seems to be a technological determinist. Perhaps it's a new kind of millennial bug. The 'knowledge economy' will totally transform our lives. IT is the revolutionary beginning of a new age, and so on.

Are we going to eat information, clothe and house ourselves in knowledge? To be sure, the advertising industry and the stockbroking industry are expanding their share of GNP by leaps and bounds. But how will the availability of a new means of communication - the shift from telephone, mail and fax to the internet for the transmission of (some kinds of) information, business orders, designs or whatever - transform the production of beer or houses or insurance so fundamentally? To be sure, the pace of technological innovation has been accelerating in recent decades (just count the decade-by-decade increase in patent registrations in the United States), and that acceleration does change the nature of business competition quite considerably. But the quantum leap of the IT revolution? I don't buy it.

One can see how in the stock market the internet hype which produces the absurd capital values of dot.com companies is driven by a combination of gullible crazies and rational speculators (those who believe that they will be able to tell the difference between a minor correction and the beginning of a panic slide and so get out in time when the bubble bursts). But the new technological determinism has affected social scientists too. Take, for instance, the fascinating conversation between Anthony Giddens and Will Hutton in their new book *On the Edge* (Jonathan Cape, 2000). Hutton takes the sceptical line, which seems to me sensible. But Giddens is a quantum leap man. All very puzzling.

* Personal note, March 2000.

PART II

And Late Development

9. The modernizer as a special case: Japanese factory legislation, 1882–1911*

The 'modernizer' is a special species of the genus 'innovator' and one which only in the last century has appeared in large numbers on the human scene. There have, to be sure, been groups and individuals at many moments in world history who would qualify under the definition of the modernizer which I propose to use: 'one who seeks the transformation of his own society or segments of it in imitation of models drawn from another country or countries'. Those Japanese court officials of the seventh century who tried to remould their country on the model of T'ang China are a case in point, and one could probably find many examples on the fringes of the great empires of the past. But it is only in the last century of Western colonialism and rapid technological change that this has become a world-wide phenomenon. It is also only in the last century that the doctrine of human progress has achieved such implicit world-wide acceptance that the imitated models have been seen not simply as 'superior' but also as 'more advanced' – further ahead, that is, in some imputed scale of linear progressive development. The consciousness of backwardness, the concept of underdevelopment, are relatively new.

The backward late-developer has obvious advantages which have been discussed by writers as diverse as Leon Trotsky, Thorstein Veblen, and Alexander Gerschenkron. The steam engine does not have to be invented twice. But the modernizer of a late-developing nation suffers from certain psychological disabilities too. In a world of competitive nation-states his modernizing zeal is likely to be highly correlated with – he himself is likely to claim that it is a function of – patriotism. And patriotism requires pride in country. So the admission that his country is backward which justifies his modernizing efforts has to be reconciled somehow with the defiant assertion that in some respects his country is superior. And the more wholesale the modernizing reforms his intelligence commends to him, the more difficult the reconciliation can become. The problem can take on a peculiarly personal poignancy for intellectuals and politicians in frequent contact with foreigners from the 'advanced' countries. Their national identity becomes a salient part

* From *Comparative Studies in Society and History*, 1969, **11**(4), pp. 433–50, slightly abridged.

of their self-identity if only because they are likely to be treated abroad in a categorical fashion, as representatives of their country rather than as individuals, so that some kind of pride in nation becomes a necessary condition for elementary individual self-respect. And the greater the cultural or racial distance between the modernizer's own society and those Western societies where industrialism began, the more this is likely to be the case, because the more he is likely in his personal contacts to be treated in terms of his national category. Thus the dilemma was more acute for Japanese than for Russians in the late nineteenth century, is more acute for Indians than for Latin Americans today.

The search for some indigenous source of pride is likely to take a religious or ethical form. Ruritania perhaps did not invent the submarine, but she has a higher faith and purer morals than those who did. The claim is more easily sustained in countries with an ancient literate culture than in those which lacked written traditions before the advent of the West and where philosophies of negritude or consciencism or *African* socialism tend to lack both clear definition and real popular roots. Where it *is* easy, however, because the cultural tradition is a rich one and the popular roots deep, the modernizer has to do a difficult balancing act.[1] He may see a little backward-looking nationalist obscurantism as an instrumentally useful integrating device. He may even find it personally appealing. But he can never be sure that he can keep it sufficiently under control for it not to hamper his modernizing efforts. Cow-protectionist nativism in India might not have grown to its present strength if Indian intellectuals had not in the past shown a tolerant and expedient indulgence towards claims that India possessed a spiritual superiority which outweighed the West's advantage in techniques. And Prince Ito, who with some misgivings gave his support to the resanctification of the Emperor and of the ethic of loyalty and filial piety in Japan in the 1880s, was perhaps lucky not to live to see where Japan would be taken in the 1940s by the tiger his successors failed to ride.

The present paper will seek to trace the nuances which this 'modernizer's dilemma' gave to the debates within Japan in the last decades of the nineteenth and the first decades of [the twentieth] century over one proposed piece of legislative innovation – the first national Factory Act.

THE BACKGROUND OF WESTERNIZATION

Legislation for 'the regulation and protection of factory labourers' (to quote the first draft bill) was not widely mooted until after the initial surge of institutional renovation during the first two decades of the Meiji period. Those decades, roughly 1870 to 1890, were years in which the modernizers dominated the Japanese political and intellectual worlds. 'Modernizers', of course, is a blanket term for a number of diverse categories, diverse in their concerns, in their choice of models and in the degree and nature of their enthusiasm. There were the light-weight fashionable xenophiles who interlarded their conversation with foreign words, flaunted their derbies and their watch-chains and bought horsehair sofas for their houses. There were those who read the translations of Mill and Rousseau, were genuinely moved by the vision they saw, and became the intellectuals of the opposition, urging the French, American, and British models of modernity on a government increasingly attracted to the Prussian. There were the Christians, many of whom found more or less viable means of remaining Confucian samurai too. There were the businessmen, concerned with creating a framework for enterprise and willing to believe that the whole complex of Western individualistic social institutions was part of that framework. And there were the civil servants who had studied abroad or who worked in Tokyo beside foreign advisers. They took the principle that Japan was to be modernized for granted and got on with planning the details of the new institutions to be created with copious reference to every foreign example they could lay hands on. It was thanks to them that by 1890 Japan had acquired a new school system, a new judiciary, a new system of local government, a new army and navy, a new banking system, a new commercial code, a new criminal code, the draft of a new civil code and a carefully devised political constitution.

The traditionalists put up little opposition, once the suppression of the Satsuma rebellion in 1877 finally induced resignation in those whose interest in resisting the modern world sprang from resentment at the loss of privileged positions in the old regime. There remained the ideological resistance of those who were unwilling to abandon the Confucian values of their fathers and those whose nationalist spirit was offended by the un-Japanese excesses of the fashionable xenophiles. Few of them opposed the new legal institutions in principle. They were concerned, rather, with the modification of the content of the new codes and systems in matters most nearly touching on the central values they wished to uphold; this they did with some success, gradually modifying the ethical content of primary school teaching and delaying the enactment of the civil code for six years until they could bring its family provisions into closer harmony with the traditions of the Japanese family system. They owed their success in part to the fact that the modernizers had also grown older, more concerned about challenges to their authority, more alarmed by the spread of liberal ideas, and therefore had reason to welcome a reassertion of the Confucian ethical system, in which individualism was equated with selfishness and the challenge to constituted authority was condemned as neglect of the categorical imperatives of loyalty and filial piety.

I have said that the traditionalists did not oppose in principle the creation of a whole new legal, political, and educational system on basically Western lines. For this there was one particular reason [to convince foreigners that Japan was modern and 'civilized' enough to deserve revision of the 'Unequal Treaties' which had been forced on Japan in the 1850s. After 1893 and the revision of the treaties, these 'expendiency' arguments had lost their force.] It was therefore largely in terms of its probable concrete consequences that the factory legislation was debated when drafts were submitted to public discussion, first in 1896–7, then in 1902, and finally in 1909–11. Nevertheless, the reflexes of twenty years of modernizing reform were not so easily lost. It was impossible for the measure not to be treated in part as yet another example of the modernizer's borrowed innovation.

And, indeed, there was some justification for doing so. The Factory Law which was finally enacted in 1911 was not a result of interest group pressure. The civil servant who piloted the law through the Diet committees remarked two years later that there was a difference between the course of factory legislation in Japan and the West. In Japan, right to the end, it was chiefly government officials and scholars who favoured and promoted the measure against the coolness or opposition of industrialists and politicians. There were no representations from the workers or worker organizations, nor did the matter ever become a party issue.[2] His observation is more or less valid if one includes a few radical journalists in the category of 'scholars' and if one excepts an 1898 petition in support of the measure by the Association for the Foundation of a Labour Union, a short-lived body with fewer than three thousand members[3]...

[However,] this was before the days when charges of 'social dumping' and of unfair exploitation of cheap labour gave industrial legislation any window-dressing value. It was a reform, therefore, which had low priority, and its promoters faced a long uphill struggle before, nearly thirty years later, the bill became law. The main chronological landmarks of those thirty years are set out below. The following analysis of the terms of discourse in which the debates were conducted draws chiefly on the minutes of the Higher Councils of 1896 and 1898, and on the Diet debates of 1910–11.

Chronological Outline[4]

1882 Research begun within Ministry of Agriculture and Commerce.
1887 Drafts completed of two laws regulating, respectively, conditions of labour for employees and for apprentices; these were not published.
1890 In response to public outcry over conditions in the Takashima coal mine, Mining Regulations were enacted which contained some compensation provisions and other protective controls.
1891 Chambers of Commerce circulated with a proposal for factory

legislation in general terms and asked for opinions; almost no support for legislation.

1896 General proposals circulated to prefectural governments; majority in favour.

1896 These proposals debated by newly formed Higher Council for Agriculture Commerce and Industry. Considerable opposition from industrialists on the Council.

1898 A draft Factory Law circulated to Chambers of Commerce and debated by an enlarged Higher Council for Agriculture, Commerce, and Industry. To apply to factories with fifty or more workers, banning labour of children under ten, limiting to ten hours a day the labour of those under fourteen, requiring educational provision for employed children under fourteen who had not finished schooling, requiring two days a month holiday, and payment for industrial injuries. Also requiring official registration of employees and imposing penalties for seducing away the labour of other employers. Higher Council amended by removing the registration of employees, extending the maximum daily hours for those under fourteen to twelve and applying the same restrictions to women.

1899 This revised draft generally approved when circulated to prefectural governors. Change of government prevented legislation.

1902 New bill drafted and circulated to Chambers of Commerce and to prefectures. Application now to all factories employing thirty or more workers. Minimum age raised to eleven, but exceptions to be made permitting employment of younger children for a further ten years. Maximum working day for women and children under sixteen, twelve hours, but fourteen to fifteen hours to be permitted exceptionally for further ten years. Night work for women and those under sixteen banned (except where shift working made it unavoidable!). Bill never presented to Diet.

1909 New bill published and eventually presented to Diet. Now applied to all factories employing steam power or otherwise dangerous. Minimum age of employment, twelve, but exemptions for younger children for next ten years. Hours and night work provisions as in 1902. Opposition particularly strong from textile manufacturers. Bill withdrawn.

1910 More detailed bill circulated to Chambers of Commerce, prefectures and employers' federations. Further revisions made by a special committee chaired by the leading industrialist, Shibusawa, in the light of their replies.

1911 Bill presented to the Diet. To apply to factories employing ten or more workers. Minimum age twelve (though some temporary, some permanent, exceptions for ten to eleven-year-olds). Twelve-hour maximum for women and children under fifteen, but exceptionally two-hour extensions for the next fifteen years. No night work for women and minors, though exceptionally permitted for next fifteen years. In passage through the Diet amended by restriction to factories employing fifteen or more workers, and enforcement postponed for a further five years.

THE HISTORICIST ARGUMENT

I have already quoted the civil servant's estimate of his predecessor's assumptions when they began their first preliminary research. The social institutions of an industrial society must come with its material techniques. There are, however, two different ways of arriving at this conclusion. The first is the 'historicist' argument that the social consequences of technological change are likely to be the same in every society and will require the same counter-measures to deal with them. The second is the 'package deal' argument. If Japan is to be a 'civilized country' she must have all the hallmarks of civilization. It was particularly their implicit or explicit use of the second argument which opened the reformers to attack as 'slavish imitators' of the West. Let us first, however, consider the uses and implications of the historicist argument.

What is striking about the historicist argument is the way in which it was implicitly accepted both by the proponents of the reform and by its opponents. The characterization 'advanced countries' (*senshinkoku*) and 'backward' (or 'following behind') countries (*koshinkoku*) is used with little self-consciousness as an established distinction. Soeda Juichi, one of the ablest of the second generation of civil servants, a man who had studied in London and Heidelberg, then head of the Treasury and later a banker and newspaper chairman, spoke in the following vein in support of factory legislation in the committee of 1896. 'The advanced countries have recognized the need for legislation for four reasons: bad conditions weaken the health of children and potential mothers, hence of a country's soldiers and hence of her defensive power; bad conditions breed epidemic diseases; the promiscuous mixing of the young of both sexes leads to moral deterioration; resentment against maltreatment leads to labour problems, and generalized social conflict. 'The advanced countries,' he said, 'have all recognized the need for legislation on these grounds.' I am not saying that just because other countries have certain laws then we must necessarily have them too. I am saying that these problems are beginning to appear in Japan.'[5] And, as his colleague Kaneko Kentaro, a Harvard graduate and later a Minister and negotiator of the Portsmouth Peace Treaty, added later in the debate, Japan had the chance to forestall difficulties which must inevitably arise. In England factory legislation had been under discussion for seventy years, but England did not get down to enacting laws soon enough. Hence the particularly 'sad and pitiful' history of British industrialization. Japan can learn from this. 'It is the advantage of the backward country that it can reflect on the history of the advanced countries and avoid their mistakes.'[6]

The opponents of the measure did not need to deny the historicist premise. They could delay rather than oppose: 'an excellent idea in principle, but not yet'. Thus, Okura Kihachiro, one of the most successful of the many-sided entrepreneurs of the nineteenth century: [He agreed] in principle with the need for protection of workers... 'But it is important to adapt to time and place. If one were to bring laws from European countries where industry began centuries ago, and apply them straight away in this island country of the Orient where industry is just about to get underway I think the consequences might be dangerous.'[7] It is noticeable, too, that when Chambers of Commerce and prefectural governments gave their comments on the 1902 draft bill there was almost no overt rejection of such legislation in principle. The normal expression of opposition was 'the time is not yet ripe'.[8] This formula, in fact *(jiki-sosho),* remains in modern Japan the standard cliché for expressing opposition to reform proposals. It is not only a matter of Japanese politeness ('you are not entirely a fool, only mistaken in your timing') but also a recognition of the inevitability of progress along what is implicitly assumed to be a linear path of development.

The line of development is often assumed, too, to be open-ended ... - a rising path of gradual progress as opposed to a single jump to modernity - [so] that interim half measures can also be justified. So the Minister could say, when introducing the 1911 bill to the Diet, that 'compared with European countries which, as you all know, as regards hours of work and other matters are extremely advanced, the present measure may be considered an extremely inadequate one, but nevertheless it would be impossible at present to introduce European-type measures immediately into our country'.[9]

In addition to the 'too soon' argument, however, the opposition did sometimes employ two other kinds of argument ... - first, that far from there being any inevitability about Japan's 'following behind', Japan can import from the West only the good things, leaving the bad things alone. Second, it is argued that Japanese cultural traditions being different from those of Europe, social phenomena which are inevitable consequences of technological development in Europe may not be inevitable consequences of those same technological innovations in Japan.

The former argument is well exemplified by Okura, the industrialist quoted earlier. 'Japanese civilization is still only skin-deep. We have taken over many good ideas and institutions from Europe, but a lot of bad ones too' - notably, he went on, strikes.[10] The implication is that strikes were not simply an inevitable consequence of the industrial situation but just as much an imported artefact as a lathe. And, indeed, the fact that the word he used for 'strike' was 'sutoraiki' is *prima facie* evidence that he was partially right. (It will be impossible for us ever again to test the thesis that the structural situation of modern industry leads inevitably to the *invention* of the technique of the strike …)

A good deal more is made of the second argument. Japanese traditions and the Japanese people are different (and, it is often implied, superior) so that the same industrial troubles are not likely to arise. The same Okura argued that 'Japanese workers are a good bit smarter than European workers, it seems to me. They are literate and they know what's what'. Consequently, 'if there is any deviation from proper procedure they immediately come up with a complaint'. Moreover, they have organizations and they hire lawyers. The universities are producing a superfluity of unemployed lawyers some of whom go around the construction sites touting for work. Nowadays it is the employer rather than the employees who needs protection. …

But the most common form of the 'Japan is different' argument dwelt on the superior ethical quality of the relation between master and man in Japan.[11] The tradition of benevolence and loyalty, the employer's assumption of a protective responsibility for his workers, operated and could continue to operate to mitigate the evils of industrialization.[12] A factory law was not only unnecessary; by coldly specifying rights and duties it might, to use the phrase by which the summaries of Chamber of Commerce comments on the 1902 draft normally epitomize such arguments, 'be destructive of the fine traditions which are peculiar to our country'.[13]

The argument comes in for a certain amount of scorn from the more uncompromising supporters of the law. There may be something of a family atmosphere in the smaller workshops, but in the big textile factories, the paper mills, the iron foundries? 'Can one talk of a family relationship between employer and employee when they don't even know each other by sight?'[14] On one occasion, Kaneko Kentaro, though not speaking directly to this point, suggested that paternalism, of a modern kind rationally adapted to large industry, was by no means natural to Japan but *also* something which Japan had to learn from the West. He illustrated what he meant by describing the idyllic situation which prevailed in a one-factory town not far from Manchester. The owner was the grandson of the founder, and most of his workers were third-generation employees. He contributes largely to the upkeep of a hospital, a local school, and a church where every Sunday 'he goes to worship with his workers since all are equal in Christ'. He opens his grounds to them for an annual fete when the gardens are at their prettiest, and the way in which he retains his people's affection in a near-feudal relationship is clearly evident in the way the workers touch their caps to him and in the kindly words he addresses to their children when he meets them in the street.[15]

A good many of the proponents of legislation, however, approached this particular argument with rather more circumspection. … To disparage it would be to seem to sell Japan short, and this they could ill afford to do when they were vulnerable to the charge of unqualified admiration of the West.

Thus one of those who made the point that family relations were impossible in large factories prefaced his remarks by saying that 'to be sure I don't suppose that factory employers in our country are cruel to their workers in the way that foreign employers are, but it can be that the workers get bad treatment even without any intention of cruelty'.[16] Similarly, Kaneko, who used the example of the Manchester feudal employer to admonish his countrymen, started off his speech by disclaiming that he was either a unilateral defender of the workers or 'one of those who, *like the Anglo-Saxon races,* believes that the poor and inferior are simply there to be used for the profit of the capitalist'.[17]

Many others were careful not to deny the premise of superior Japanese traditions, only to qualify their importance. Thus Soeda Juichi, summing up for the government at the end of the 1896 debate and apparently somewhat shocked by the strength of the industrialists' opposition, was careful to point out that he was not making any wholesale condemnation. He agrees that there are examples of employers who show 'the traditional humanity of the Japanese people, the altruism which shows kind consideration of one's inferiors; in a word, benevolence'. But these were not average employers.[18] Another argued that such benevolence might indeed now be general and there would be few problems as long as industry remained in the hands of the 'present generation of warm-blooded men brought up in the traditional Japanese education'. But 'we are now importing Western education and if one looks at the customs of Europe, as the notion of mere capitalists, of the power of capital, gathers strength, and the single-minded concentration on profits, then we shall lose the traditions we were brought up in and eventually we must face it that there will be a tendency for the blood to run colder in people's veins'.[19] Others argue … [that] there might soon be Western factory owners operating on Japanese soil and they could not be trusted to be restrained by the traditional Japanese ethic in default of legal regulation.[20]

THE 'TRAPPINGS OF CIVILIZATION'

[Much of the debate was not about real problems as inevitable consequences of industrialization, but concentrated on the 'imitation of the West' problem. Thus] Oka, the chief of the Industrial Bureau ... wrote with feeling in 1913:

> The importation of the ideas and institutions of the West which began with the Meiji Restoration swept into the remotest corner of society, leaving almost nothing unchanged. Since the proposals for factory legislation first saw the light of day in 1882 at a time when the tide of so-called Westernization was at its peak, and since

> the regulations proposed threatened considerably to restrain the freedom of management in industry, those who had reasons on those grounds of interest to dislike the bill, sought to bury it not once but a hundred times with the charge that it was 'blind imitation of the West'. Even those who did not go as far as this would comb through the provisions of the bill to see if any were mere 'fair copies of the West'. For the promoters of the measure, to counter prejudices of this kind by careful detailed explanation was, for ten and more years, a constant object of their endeavour, a recurrent theme to which they returned time and time again.[21]

The law's promoters perhaps had the more difficulty in fighting this particular battle in that the desire to keep up with the Western Joneses did in fact play a part, albeit an unacknowledged one, in their motives, as some of their less guarded phrases made clear. Thus Oka himself, the author of this *cri de coeur* remarked in the Diet in reply to a critic who saw the bill as a weak-kneed measure more designed to protect employers than workers, that indeed it was not an ideal law or something 'that, *vis-à-vis* the advanced nations, we can *be proud of*'.[22]

Generally, however, it was only in occasional unguarded moments that such remarks were let slip. As Oka indicated, the proponents of the measure were on the defensive in this regard and consciously avoided putting the matter in the perspective of a simple attempt to acquire the 'trappings of civilization'. With perhaps some resort to hair-splitting distinctions it is possible to discern four techniques of argument which they used to this end.

The first was simply to deny that a concern for foreigners' *opinions* played any part in their motives. Kaneko, for example, in a speech in 1896, did this obliquely by referring with scorn to an action which had been so motivated – a ban recently imposed by the city authorities on the building of factory chimneys in Kyoto. It appears that a bath-house proprietor had erected a large brick chimney in the Higashiyama district of Kyoto, and foreigners had complained of it as an eyesore which ruined the beauty of the old city. The city authorities had reacted by banning chimneys altogether. Some control over industrial location was in fact needed, said Kaneko, but not of such a sweeping or ill-motivated kind.[23]

A second technique was to stress the originality of the Japanese measure and to deny that it was intended as a mere copy of the West. This was not easy since all the provisions of the Japanese bill had precursors elsewhere. Soeda Juichi got round this difficulty in 1896 first by pointing to *other* measures where Japan could claim real originality and secondly by claiming that Japan could gain distinction by being *ahead* of other countries, by being the first country to avoid the mistakes of the West and solve the problems of industrialism before they actually arose.

> It is no good just bringing 'translated legislation' here to the Orient. I am absolutely against this. It's somewhat of a digression but I may even say that I think we made

> a mistake in our local government system in this regard. I am pretty much of a conservative and I am wholly against legislation by translation. Now if you look at the Industrial Bank Law, for example, you will find that there is absolutely nothing in it derived from foreign examples.[24]

And again:

> It is my hope, as a scholar, that we shall be able to avoid repeating the mistakes of the advanced countries, and gain the honour of finding a fine and complete solution to these problems in our country. I don't think Japan need feel faint-hearted in this endeavour. As Count Shibusawa knows, the Americans, for example, have still not properly solved the problem of creating a National Bank. Yet we in Japan, with the help of Count Shibusawa and others, managed to solve it quite early. ... We are faced again with an academic problem which gives us an opportunity for work which will redound to the honour of our capitalists and of our country.[25]

The third technique has already been noted. The measure's proponents were willing to concede the moral superiority of Japanese traditions, both by direct praise thereof and by disparagement of the mistakes that foreigners had made or of the cold rapacity of their national characters. Thus they could offer some solace to wounded *amour-propre,* some consolation for the indignity of admitting that Japan had to learn from the West.

The fourth technique has been demonstrated in Soeda's speech just quoted: 'It is my hope as a scholar ...', 'We are faced with an academic problem ...' The debate was taken out of the simple Japan = pupil: Western nations = teachers context and moved to a different frame of reference. Japan was one of a number of countries faced with certain common problems. She could solve them by reference to principles evolved by *scholars,* members of an international community evolving doctrines of universal validity, doctrines to which no country had a proprietary claim. Thus the phrase, 'it is now the accepted opinion among scholars that ...'[26] is used several times in the debate to clinch an argument. That the scholars in question were mostly Western was not relevant. There were Japanese scholars who echoed or improved on their opinions. And scholarship, in any case, was without country.

In part the use of this technique involves assimilating the doctrines of social scientists to those of natural scientists; the social technique of the factory act must be assimilated to the material technique of the steam engine, seeing both as examples of universal principles to which no country can claim patent rights. It is a cliché of the students of cultural diffusion that techniques are more readily absorbed than are values. The techniques of Western medicine may run into trouble, in Ceylon or China, for example, because traditional medical lore is often closely integrated into a whole world view and also represents a means of livelihood to traditional practitioners whose interests are threatened. But opposition to the electric light on the grounds that it is an offence against national pride to show interest in foreign inventions is not a common feature of the modern underdeveloped world.[27] Hence the more the modernizing reformer can represent principles of public policy as analogous to principles of electricity - the more he can represent his reforms as being a matter of techniques - the easier his task can become. He has a natural tendency towards scientistic positivism; it is in his interest to slur over the difference between fact and value.

In this case, however, the debates took place in an intellectual climate in which the distinction between fact and value was not conventionally made. ... In Tokugawa Japan ... Confucianism was all-embracing, as all-embracing as modern Marxist-Leninist-Maoism. The Confucian scholar was entitled to pronounce not only on matters of fact but also, even more especially, on matters of value.

The high prestige of the scholar in the Confucian tradition - a prestige which depended in part on this fusion of the priestly with the scholarly role - was another special feature of Japan's development not commonly duplicated elsewhere. There is, to be sure, something inherent in the situation of the late-developer which adds to the importance of the scholar and his scholarship. The nation must advance by absorbing knowledge from abroad rather than by independent invention; the foreign *expert* is welcomed; the returned *student,* the bearer of knowledge, occupies a strategic position. But the authority of scholarship might not often assume quite the proportions that it did in Japan where it could borrow from the traditional authority which had always attached to the role of the scholar. Both these considerations suggest that the appeal to universal principles of scholarship might not always be as helpful to the modernizer's cause as it was in Japan.

SENTIMENT AND INTEREST

[A lot of the 'blind and demeaning imitation' charges came tongue-in-cheek - on grounds of pure self-interest - from industrialists whose fortunes were founded on imitation.] The *real* traditionalists, those to whom the charge of 'demeaning imitation of the West' would have come naturally, were antipathetic to modern industry as a whole and rather in favour of state regulation of working conditions. The line of thought represented by Lord Shaftesbury in England was present in Japan, despite the differences between Confucianism and High Toryism and despite the distortions of the late developer's situation. Thus, in 1888, it was the journal *Nihonjin,* the main mouthpiece of the traditionalists' call for a return to Confucian morality, which exposed the plight of the Takashima miners and prompted the first attempt at state intervention. This criss-crossing of the three lines of division, the first in terms of interest, the second in terms of generalized xenophobia/xenophilia, and the third in terms of specific sentiments of sympathy or indifference to the plight of the factory workers, consequently blunted the force of the arguments from national pride and made the tasks of the reformers somewhat easier.

Certainly the reader should not gain the impression that the considerations dwelt on here dominated the debates, even those parts of them which considered the general principle of whether or not legislation was desirable. Most of the discussion revolved around other aspects of the question. Humanitarian appeals, usually muted, but sometimes of impassioned eloquence, to save the workers from poverty, misery, and disease, were met with the arguments that the facts were wrong, that even if they were not, the conditions of factory workers were better than they had been in the villages beforehand, and that in any case some sacrifices had to be made by somebody for the advance of Japan. If children were kept out of factories they would starve; in any case they were only doing play-work, and it was having a healthy beneficial effect in stimulating a spirit of industry within them. The argument that the Japanese nation could ill afford to ruin the health of its people and in particular of its soldiers was met by the counter-argument that Japan's present need was to boost exports and that industrial production would fall disastrously if industry were restricted. And this in turn was met by the arguments that employers would lose in the long run from the wastage of healthy labour power; that Japanese industry was grossly over-manned compared with its European counterparts; that shorter hours combined with higher performance could mean more production and lower costs. The argument that there were good and bad employers and that the law would only aim to bring the worst closer to the level of the average, was challenged on the grounds that trained men were not available to staff an adequate inspectorate and that meanwhile the law would do harm in the best factories by putting what was a moral relationship between master and man on a footing of clearly specified rights and duties, thus leading to endless disputes. That the main objections to the draft law sprang not from nationalist pride but from employers' fears of a fall in their profits cannot be doubted, and it can plausibly be argued[28] that the law only eventually became possible after heavier industry which employed skilled male adults had developed to the point at which its representatives carried greater weight in business circles than did the employers of female labour in textiles and other light industry. The former were willing to override the opposition of the latter because they had much less to lose from factory regulation and something to gain by improving the image of the capitalist in Japanese society.

Nevertheless, it seems highly probable that their vulnerability to charges that they lacked a proper national pride and excessively admired the West blunted the reforming drive of those who favoured the bill either from humanitarian motives or from a concern for national welfare as a means to national power. I have tried to chart some of the ambivalences which sprang from [that] consciousness. [The reformers'] strongest card lay in their appeal to a body of knowledge and a body of historical experience which was the property of no nation, but something universally valid for all mankind. They were skilful in its use, but not quite skilful enough to conceal the fact that while the principle of electricity might be the universal property of mankind, along with the social techniques of government inspection, building licences, minimum age regulation and the like, the decision whether or not to use these techniques is not a technical one. And it is in the field of values that national pride is most jealous to preserve national autonomy.

NOTES

1. As Mary Matossian puts it in an excellent survey of the ways in which the modernizer's dilemma is resolved in explicit ideologies: 'If the intellectual is to lead the masses of an industrially backward country in the undertaking of great endeavours, he must provide them with incitement balanced by comfort, with self-criticism balanced by self-justification.' 'Ideologies of Delayed Industrialization', *Economic Development and Cultural Change,* **6**(iii), April 1958, p. 218.
2. Oka Minoru, *Kojoho-ron*, 1913, p. 99.
3. Kazahaya Yasoji, *Nihon shakai-seisaku-shi,* 4th edn, 1938, p. 135.
4. General accounts of the history of legislation may be found in Oka Minoru, *Kojoho-ron*, 1913, Kazahaya Yasoji, *Nihon shakai-seisaku-shi,* 4th edn, 1938, Numata Inajiro, 'Rodoho' in Ukai Nobushige *et al.*, (eds), *Koza Nihon kindai-ho hattatsu-shi*, Vol. 5, 1958.
5. Nosho Koto Kaigi, *Giji sokkiroku,* Vol. 1, 1961, reprinted in Obama Ritei (ed.), *Meiji bunka shiryo sosho*, p. 38.
6. *Ibid.*, p. 50.
7. Noshoko Koto Kaigi, *Sokkiroku*, p. 46.
8. Noshomusho, *Komukyoku, kojoho-an yoryo ni taisuru ikensho tekiyo shu*, 1904.
9. Committee debate of 16 February 1911. Teikoku Gikai, *Gijiroku*, p. 184.
10. Noshoko Koto Kaigi, *Sokkiroku*, p. 46.
11. In part using these same debates B.K. Marshall has recently offered a succinct analysis of the Japanese business ideology, *Capitalism and Nationalism in Pre-War Japan*, Stanford, 1967.
12. See, for example, the speech of Tanabe Kumaichi in the Diet, February 5 1911, *Gijiroku,* p. 5.
13. Komukyoku, Noshomusho, *Kojo hoan horyo ni taisuru ikensho tekiyo shu.*
14. Noshoko Koto Kaigi, *Sokkiroku*, p. 194.
15. Noshoko Koto Kaigi, *Sokkiroku* p. 53.
16. *Ibid.*, p. 93.
17. *Ibid.*, p. 50.
18. *Ibid.*, p. 54.
19. *Ibid.*, p. 56; the speaker was Masuda Ko.

20. Soeda Juichi, *ibid.*, p. 40. Noshoko Koto Kaigi, *Sokkiroku*, pp. 92, 93, 100.
21. *Kojoho-ron*, p. 164.
22. Committee debate of 16 February 1911, *Gijiroku*, p. 7.
23. Noshokoko Koto Kaigi, *Sokkiroku*, p. 51.
24. *Ibid.*, p. 55.
25. *Ibid.*, p. 55. There is a piquant element of the *argumentum ad hominem* in these remarks. Shibusawa had, in these debates, spoken against the factory law proposals.
26. See *ibid.*, pp. 24, 28, 29.
27. It was, though, of early and extreme Ghandiism. See Mary Matossian, *op. cit.*, p. 224.
28. As it has been by Kazahaya Yasoji, *op. cit.,* pp. 138–42.

10. Late development*

> 'The basic principle of the nineteenth-century British private enterprise economy was to buy in the cheapest market and to sell in the dearest. For the employer to buy labour in the cheapest market implied buying it at the lowest rate per unit of output; i.e. to buy the cheapest labour at the highest productivity. Conversely, for the worker to sell his labour in the dearest market meant logically to sell it at the highest minimum price for the minimum unit of output.'[1]

To be sure, as Hobsbawm goes on to point out, this principle underlying all contemporary theorizing about the industrial situation was not completely assimilated by workers and employers 'as the rule of the game' until towards the end of the century, in the final stages of the Great Depression. Earlier it had been modified in practice by custom and convention - by notions of 'a fair day's work for a fair day's wage', of the need to provide a subsistence minimum, of a 'proper' skilled/unskilled differential, of paternalistic obligation, and of the duty of faithful service. But already by the middle of the century the 'new model' of unionism had developed all kinds of devices which assumed the dominance of market principles and were designed to improve the bargaining power of workers acting collectively in the market - restrictions on entry into the trade, unemployment benefits, emigration benefits, allowances which rationalized older tramping systems and helped workers to move from labour-surplus areas to labour-scarce areas, and so on. And by mid-century, the experience of market fluctuations was sufficiently ingrained for both employers and workmen often to prefer a shorter hiring period to a long one, so as to keep open their options for driving a better bargain if the market situation should change.[2]

Was there, then, no British employer who saw himself faced with the same problems as the innovating Japanese employers described in the last chapter, and none who sought to solve them by similar devices, similarly deviating from strict market principles? Far from it. At certain periods there were loud complaints of shortage of skilled workers; there were constant denunciations of the instability and unreliability of the work force. A number of individual 'progressive employers' reacted to such problems by experimenting with institutional devices very similar to those which became standard in Japan. But

* From *British Factory-Japanese Factory*, London: Allen and Unwin/Berkeley: University of California Press, 1973, chapter 15, pp. 404–20, abridged.

there were never *enough* of them to make any impact on the system as a whole - until, as Chapter 13 has suggested, the last decade.

The early tentative moves in this direction were of several kinds. There were, to begin with, 'traditional paternalists' [like the] Quaker Bright family in Rochdale.[3] And already, before the end of the eighteenth century, there was a beginning of non-discretionary rule-bound enterprise welfare. Boulton and Watt, for example, the makers of steam engines, as well as pioneering apprentice schemes, taking their workers on outings and 'looking after' senior and experienced workers with special wage increments, also set up a contributory sickness insurance fund for their workers[4] - a move towards welfare 'as of right' rather than from benevolence. Robert Owen's paternalism ... was also very much rule-prescribed as well as discretionary; his famous system of aggregating and rewarding good conduct marks was an example.

Owen's emphasis on rewards was one of his outstanding deviationist features. The part of tradition that most employers retained and codified was the stern paternalism of swingeing disciplinary regulations, the point of which for some employers was that they offered a means of reducing wages. Rewards tended to become assimilated into a contractual system of incentive payments little different from piecework. But other enterprises did retain systems of rewards and bonuses which were intended to have symbolic as well as material importance, and to bind men to the company 'by as many ties as possible' - the railways for instance.[5] Other means of stabilization ... included long-term contracts,[6] mutual non-poaching agreements between companies and even, in 1840, a suggestion for legislation to establish a registry of servants somewhat similar to that proposed in the early drafts of the Japanese Factory Law.[7] The railways, which required skilled and responsible workmen and were not so bound by the fixed-price-for-equal-skills traditions of older trades, developed *de facto* seniority systems of promotion[8] and even of wage increments within grades. They frequently housed their workers too, as, of course, did many other employers.[9] At the end of the century some of the gas companies, jolted out of their complacency by a wave of labour troubles, tried to outbid the unions with co-partnership schemes.[10]

But most of these embryonic trends were aborted. Boulton and Watt's successors swept away the insurance scheme as part of their moves to rationalize the business. [Admit such things a rewards for long service, said a railway manager in 1868, and] pay 'will cease to be measured by the natural relations of supply and demand, and will be raised from time to time upon conventional feelings to a standard more than the market value of the services rendered'.[11]

In Japan a sufficient number of firms in a sufficiently dominant position deviated far enough from market principles of employment to form a 'critical mass' capable of changing the character of the system as a whole. In Britain, on the other hand, the deviants were few and of feeble influence: the market principle won. Let us list some of the factors which explain that difference. The relevant time-periods considered are roughly Japan from 1880 to 1930 and Britain in the first three-quarters of the nineteenth century.[12]

RELEVANT DIFFERENCES

1. In contrast to the Confucian ideology discussed in the last chapter, the ideology of market individualism was already deeply entrenched in Britain *before* industrialization began. It was the Communist Manifesto, echoing the words of Carlyle a decade earlier, which made famous the phrase 'cash nexus' to describe the only thing that remained to bind employer and employee, but already, half a century before that, Adam Smith was speaking most naturally of labour as a commodity like any other commodity, differing only in that the long-term effect of its price on supply was *more* long-term than for most other commodities since it operated through the Malthusian checks on the one hand, and earlier marriage and healthier breeding on the other ...

The difference in prevailing ideologies between the two countries correlates clearly with differences in pre-industrial economic organization. Agriculture and handicrafts remained in Japan a family affair to which the Confucian ideology was well adapted: British agriculture was already largely organized on a capitalist basis with a thriving market in free wage labour well before industrialization began. It is not surprising that the market principle became deeply entrenched, not only in the theories of Scottish economists, but also in the everyday expectations and assumptions of those who bought and sold labour.

2. A more specific aspect of the last point is the very wide spread of the putting-out system in British industry before and in the early days of the industrial revolution. The piecework pattern of payment survived its transformation into a factory system and this doubtless helps explain the prevalence of this form of wage payment - so much the purest expression of the market principle that Marx saw it as the system best suited to capitalism.[13] Putting-out manufacturing was not so highly developed in nineteenth-century Japan. Above all there is no gradual transition to factory production. The new factories brought in new technology and new organization, very often in quite different locations from the cottage industry areas.

3. A *laissez-faire* market economy is an individualistic economy. Once the bonds of fief, of manor, of guild and corporation are loosened, the political and the economic community are separated. Economically the individual is atomistically alone in the national market. 'The free man', said the Revd Joseph Townsend, in the famous pamphlet in which he spoke of hunger as the necessary, peaceable and silent stimulus to useful labour, 'should be left to his

own judgement and discretion'.[14] If he cannot survive it is to the politically defined community that he turns, not to the enterprise, for the new enterprise is not a politico-economic unit as the old guild was; it is an economic enterprise *tout court*. The survival of an interventionist philosophy in the political sphere (for the victory of *laissez-faire* thinking was never complete in England)[15] in fact facilitated the adoption of impersonal market individualism in the economic sphere proper. The Speenhamland system forcefully illustrated both the new assumption that securing a subsistence minimum was not the business of the employer but of the local political community, and also the fact that the political community was prepared to accept these responsibilities ...

Hence, unlike the much more 'cellular' society of Japan at the turn of the century where charity and paternalistic duty were expected to begin at home among one's own employees and subordinates, in Britain discussion of the duty of the higher classes to the lower had already shifted onto the plane of national politics centring around Poor Laws and Factory Acts, hospitals, and later, state pension schemes. Not local, but national collectivist solutions were sought to the problem of insecurity and misery. The Owenite impulse was carried forward to the search not for new management styles but to legislative solutions; the thought that welfare and security were the state's job absolved employers from action and left their consciences clean.

4. The battles fought at this political level over the development of social legislation not only changed Britain, they also, when conjoined with other similar battles fought in Europe and America, changed the world. The fact that Japan started industrialization 'late' is all important. Ideologies are not confined within frontiers. There are such things as world 'norms' concerning the range of employment relations which are feasible and desirable. Nowadays these norms are codified in conventions and resolutions of the International Labour Organization. In the nineteenth century they were much more diffusely defined, but still real, as the slow progress of the abolition of slavery demonstrated. These norms were very different in the first decade of this century when Japan's industrial institutions were taking shape from what they had been in Britain's industrial infancy a century earlier.

Over-schematizing one might summarize as follows. Free market principles of employment have a natural appeal to employers in a world where unions do not exist or are prohibited by law. They become less attractive to employers when trade unions win their right to exist and so severely limit the employer's bargaining superiority. But by the time this happened in Britain, by the time employers began to have material incentives for seeking alternatives, the existing market principles were so firmly entrenched - and so reinforced by the pattern of trade unionism itself - that change was difficult. Employers had, in any case, lost their power unilaterally to change institutions without the co-operation of the unions.

Japanese employers, on the other hand, could see the writing more clearly on the wall. The inevitability of strikes and class conflict is occasionally predicted - though not always accepted - in the debates over factory legislation in the last decade of the nineteenth century. A decade and a half later there was little doubt as to what was in store. By 1922, when employment relations were still in a fluid state, international respectability required Japan to give trade unions an accepted place in the political firmament by allowing them to choose a representative to attend the Conference of the ILO. Japanese employers, therefore, knew that they had to live with unions at an early stage; they were able to adjust to that future prospect by institutional innovations *before* the unions became so strong that their options were foreclosed - while they still had a large measure of control over the situation.

5. Universal primary schooling was a late development in the history of British industrialization. Japan, by contrast, had probably 90 per cent of its boys attending standardized and reasonably efficient primary schools at the beginning of this century, at a time when there were still fewer than eighty factories employing more than five hundred workers. Preferential employment of young school leavers was an option open to early Japanese industrialists more clearly than to their earlier English counterparts. It is not surprising that they should have taken it. All questions of literacy and numeracy apart, the schools had disciplined the new generation to habits of timekeeping and steady application which their parents often lacked. The schools provided convenient recruiting grounds where teachers' reports, school records and later the firm's own dexterity and intelligence tests could *select* recruits and make sure that the big firms like Mitsubishi which pioneered school-leaver recruitment could cream off each age group. 'Creaming-off' was possible because, although there was a shortage of skilled workers and of girl school-leavers willing to enter textile factories, there was never a shortage of boy school-leavers, and the big firms from an early stage offered better employment prospects and so could attract the cream.

6. The differential development of industry and education is part of the late-development effect. Late-developing societies generally find it easier to build a modern educational system than to build a modern manufacturing industry. One might also consider it as typical of the late-development syndrome that Japan developed a modern industry *without* the slow penetration of capitalist wage relationships in agriculture which preceded Britain's industrial revolution. Japan's agriculture has remained a structure of *family* holdings employing little wage labour. Add to the picture: (a) primogeniture inheritance, (b) the fact that, with the average size of holding down to two acres, the available land was already filled up, and (c) the fact that improved public health and nutrition enhanced the survival chances of children. More families had surviving, non-inheriting younger sons. The opportunities for younger sons to

be adopted into existing land-holding families which lacked heirs also diminished. Younger sons, therefore, were increasingly marked out from childhood as destined to leave the village. They came on the market at the end of their schooling conditioned to look not for a few years' work with the hope of returning to the village, but for a career - and ready to accept low wages for the guarantee of good prospects. The fact that the culture of the Japanese peasant family in which they grew up was already a quite economically rational one, calculating to *long* time horizons, reinforced these preferences.

7. Another likely reason why Japanese employers were more prone than their earlier British counterparts to be attracted to the idea of recruiting youngsters is because they were more likely to have to do their own training anyway. Late-developing Japan imported the latest nineteenth-century and twentieth-century techniques into a society where traditional artisan skills resembled those of sixteenth- or seventeenth-century Europe. Japan had to make a technological leap - whereas Britain made a shuffling technological advance. The smooth progression from the artisan skills of eighteenth-century Britain to the factory engineering skills of the next century is reflected in the continuity of apprenticeship systems and modes of skill certification throughout the transition from guilds to unions. New inventions came gradually and in penny packages. ...

8. Another difference explains why - quite apart from the problems of initial introduction of new techniques - worker-to-worker transmission of techniques through informal apprenticeship systems was less adequate in Japan than in Britain to satisfy the demands of industry: Japanese industry expanded faster than Britain's.

9. Just as important, perhaps, is the fact that Japanese industry grew more steadily.[16] The cycles of boom and slump were not so lengthy; the troughs not so deep, their effect in tempering optimism about the prospects of long-term growth not so devastating. Japan, like all follower countries, knew better where she was going. The present of the more advanced countries offered an image of her future.

Let us twist some of these strands together. The Japanese employer had reasons for recruiting young school-leavers and training them that the British manufacturer hadn't - their easy availability, their cheapness, their disciplined willingness to learn, and the fact that, because of the technological leap and the faster rate of growth, the market could not provide for his needs so that he would have to do his own training anyway. His experience of steadier growth made him more optimistic about the future: he could calculate that if he invested in training and devised schemes to keep his workers in order to recoup his investment, market conditions would be likely to *allow* him to keep them fully occupied. Seniority scales and other long-term incentives followed naturally - and were that much easier to afford since the young workers, competing for entry into the firms which offered good prospects, were hirable at such low initial wages.

10. There is another possible factor in the willingness to pay seniority premiums and to spend money on welfare facilities, etc. The Japanese engineering industry started late, with more advanced capital-intensive technology than the early British industry, using expensive imported machines. It is probable - though there are no decisive figures to prove it - that labour costs represented a smaller proportion of total costs for the average Japanese manufacturer than for the average British manufacturer at a comparable stage of development - despite some evidence that machines were lavishly over-manned.[17] A 5 per cent increase in labour costs would therefore have less serious implications for the health of the business.

11. A further aspect of cost structure: leaving plant idle is more serious the higher the ratio of the loss incurred by leaving capital unutilized to the saving from not paying the wages of the worker who would otherwise have worked it. Hence absenteeism and high turnover were more seriously costly to the heavily capitalized Japanese employer who bought his machines from high-wage foreign countries and employed cheaper local labour. Hence a stronger incentive for him to find ways of 'stabilizing' even semi-skilled machine-minding workers.

12. The late starter begins with advanced production technology. He is also likely to start with advanced organizational technology. Another important difference - remarked on by Japanese contemporaries as a reason why Japan could develop more orderly employment practices - was that whereas the owner-managed firm predominated in the British economy until an advanced stage, Japan was dominated by corporate organizations from the very beginning - and as the last chapter showed it was they which were responsible for the crucial innovations in the employment field. Some of these corporate organizations were state organizations where concern for profits was minimal: others were parts of the large Zaibatsu empires which increasingly dominated the private sector. The relevant features of these corporate organizations, as compared with owner-managed firms, were:

a. Their greater security of prospects, obvious in government enterprises, and in the Zaibatsu firms a consequence of their oligopolistic position in internal markets, the size of their financial resources, and their political influence. This security conduced to more long-term calculations of the costs and benefits of employment policies.
b. Their greater size - a necessary precondition for successfully operating a career structure for manual workers.
c. Their bureaucratic management structure - in the private firms no less than in the government enterprises partly because the former were

modelled on the latter. The fact that the recruitment and promotion patterns which provided the career structure for managers were highly elaborated and entrenched at an early stage (unlike the nineteenth-century British pattern of market recruitment or family recruitment of managers) made it easier to extend those patterns to manual workers.

13. The dualism which developed in Japan's sponsored industrialization between the large bureaucratic capital-intensive firms which benefited from state sponsorship and the small private firms which did not, reflected a difference in capacity to pay which - as soon as trade union organization started - made enterprise unions, which could push each employer to the limit of his capacity to pay, a natural form of organization. Since the development of lifetime employment patterns preceded the development of effective trade unions, the enterprise form was the natural one anyway. The electrician in one firm who does not expect to be in the labour market again, has no great interest in the wages paid to electricians in other firms. A nineteenth-century Birmingham moulder who never knew when he would be stood off and looking to another small foundry for employment had every interest in the local market.

Another difference relevant to the pattern of trade unionism: British unions were created and achieved definite organizational shape at a time when they were anathema to employers; they therefore *had* to meet off the factory premises - often with secret society rituals. In the postwar period, when the Japanese union took shape, no employer dared question the unions' right to exist. They could organize openly on the premises. This also helped to make them workshop-based. And, as has been pointed out several times before, the enterprise-based union serves very much to reinforce the whole employment system.

LATE AND LATER DEVELOPMENT

All these differences between Britain and Japan in particular can be generalized as differences between early developers and late developers in general - as part of a general late capitalist development syndrome. In fact, the later development takes place the more pronounced these late-starter characteristics are likely to be, the more marked the late-development effect in industrial relations. The later industrialization begins:

- the less likely (see Gerschenkron on the psychology of backwardness[18]) that it will be dominated by a *laissez-faire* philosophy, the more likely that the state will play a predominant role;

- the less chance of any repetition of the slow evolution of putting-out systems into factory systems or of a slow transformation of peasant into capitalist agriculture preceding industrialization;
- the more likely the development of school systems is to precede the development of a substantial manufacturing sector;
- the bigger the technological leap from traditional skills to those required by the new technology imported from the advanced countries;
- the bigger the organizational leap; the more likely industry is to *begin* with rationalized bureaucratic forms of organization including specialist personnel managers operating objective recruitment and promotion schemes - the more so if, as is likely, the state plays a direct role in the industrialization process through state corporations or partnership schemes;
- the more the norms diffused to the late starter from the industrialized countries are likely to stress the rights of trade unions and workers and the need to treat workers as human beings, not as mere sellers of a commodity called labour. Corporations in the contemporary late-starter countries, sending their personnel officers to business schools in Europe and America, *begin* industrialization under the influence of human relations theories and Y-theories, and theories about the virtues of consultation with workshop representatives;
- the more secure the big firms (because the state cannot afford to let them collapse) and the more plan-oriented the management (partly as a result of the absorption of advanced-country business techniques) and the longer the time horizon for the cost–benefit calculation of personnel policies;
- the sharper the dualism between the big firm sector characterized above and the small firm sector, the more privileged the big sector workers, the more their unions are concerned with job security, and the more likely plant or enterprise-based organization.

It is not hard to find evidence for some of these propositions in the contemporary developing world. [See Chapter 16: ed.] Equally, one might find confirmation in the history of European industrialization. Germany, a later starter than Britain, has always had more organization-oriented, less market-oriented forms of employment than Britain. [See Chapter 6: ed.]

THE PATTERN OF CAUSATION

In this chapter we have been concerned not with those features of the Japanese and British systems which seem clearly to owe a lot to the inertia of behaviour - different kinds of authority relations and different patterns of work group formation, for example - but with certain kinds of formal institutional innovations which were generally adopted in Japan and not generally adopted in England - and with the reasons for the difference. Attitudes and values, it was suggested at the end of the last chapter, clearly had something to do with it. First, the attitudes and values of workers in Japan probably made the innovations more likely to have their desired effect than they would have been if British workers were involved. Second, the attitudes and values and explicit ethic of Japanese employers was more congenial to those innovations; the institutions concerned seemed more in keeping with their basic sense of propriety than they would have done to their British counterparts.

The present suggestion is that other factors also counted. These innovations were more likely to have *profitable* results for Japanese manufacturers at the turn of the century than for British manufacturers earlier for reasons quite beside the specifically national cultural predispositions of the workforce. These are reasons which have to do: (a) with the different structure of economic opportunities and constraints which the late development situation presents, and (b) with differences in values - in the way people perceive and define their advantages - which derive not from differences in national character but from situational differences (e.g. being a graduate employee manager rather than a classical entrepreneur, or being a primary school graduate rather than an illiterate migrant from rural areas); these situational differences being *also* a consequence of the difference between early and late industrialization.

It is hard to say how *much* causal weight to attach to the different factors. A seniority wage system was both consonant with Japanese conceptions of age hierarchy, and also a rational means for employers to get the most out of their workers at least cost. Supposing there had not been such a neat coincidence? What about features that were culturally and ideologically congenial but not advantageous - or the other way around? Which consideration would have won?

Marxists and neo-classical economists ought in principle to agree that of course material interests would have won. In practice, the majority of economists on whom I have tried these ideas appear very reluctant to give up their assumption that the British market-oriented system is somehow 'normal' and the Japanese a curious deviation to be ascribed wholly to very special 'cultural factors'. Probably this is because the notion of a specific late-development effect casts doubt on the validity of all universal models either of economic growth or of rational labour market behaviour; it is just more comfortable to take it as self-evident that the Japanese are peculiar. ...

NOTES

1. E.J. Hobsbawm, 'Custom, wages and work-load', in A. Briggs and J. Saville, *Essays in Labour History,* 1960, p. 113. Also in E.J.H., *Labouring Men,* 1964.
2. *Ibid.*, p. 121. Recall, also, the modern reluctance to put verbal agreements in writing. One imagines, though, that as, with experience, people began to recognize the pattern of the trade cycle, there ought to have emerged a preference for long-term contracts by workers at the peaks and by employers at the troughs of the cycles.
3. R. Bendix, *Work and Authority in Industry,* Harper Torchbook edn., 1963, p. 49.
4. Eric Roll, *An Experiment in Industrial Organization,* 1930, reprinted 1968.
5. P.W. Kingsford, *Victorian Railwaymen,* 1970, p. 28.
6. *Ibid.*, p. 191.
7. Kingsford, *op. cit.*, p.11.
8. *Ibid.*, p. 145.
9. S. Pollard, *The Genesis of Modern Management*, 1965, p. 200.
10. E.J. Hobsbawm, 'British gas workers 1873–1914', in *Labouring Men,* 1964, p. 171.
11. Kingsford, *op. cit.*, p. 145.
12. No strictly comparable phasing is possible, of course, since Japan did *not* repeat Britain's history. Some of the obvious growth indicators of levels of industrialization do not move together. Britain, for example, had less than 40% of employed males in agriculture well before the end of the eighteenth century. In Japan that point was reached in the 1930s, by which time Japan had nearly 10% of employed males in the metal trades, a point which Britain did not reach until after 1850. Textile workers made up 24% of the total labour force in Britain according to the 1856 census. They never reached 10% in Japan.
13. E.J. Hobsbawm, 'Custom, wages and work load', p. 131.
14. *A Dissertation on the Poor Laws by a Well-wisher of Mankind*, 1786, quoted in R. Bendix, *Work and Authority in Industry*, Harper Torchbook edn, 1963, p. 74.
15. For helping to sort out my ideas on this score I am indebted to Barry Supple and to his 'Legislation and virtue: an essayon working-class self-help and the state in the early nineteenth century' (mimeo).
16. In only 12 of the 35 years 1886 to 1920 did the number of registered factory workers in Japan decline over the previous year; the declines were small and only once, when a fall of some 18% was spread over the period 1890 93 did they continue for more than one year (K. Okawa *et al.*, *Nihon keizai no seichōritsu*, 1955, pp. 83–5). Comparable British indexes are hard to find, but to take one easily to hand: in 19 of the 35 years from 1855 to 1889 the recorded production of iron ore fell below the previous year's total. This included three periods when the decline continued for three successive years, and the five-year decline of the Great Depression – a fall of 27% from 1882 to 1887 (Mitchell and Deane, *Abstract of British Historical Statistics*, reprinted 1971, p. 129). For other indicators of the amplitude of the British trade cycle – including the estimate of a 50% fall from peak to trough in the depression of the early 1840s, see W.W. Rostow, *The British Economy of the Nineteenth Century,* 1948, p. 44.
17. David Landes, 'Japan and Europe', in W.W. Lockwood (ed.), *The State and Economic Enterprise in Japan,* 1965, p. 117.
18. A. Gerschenkron, *Economic Backwardness in Historical Perspective*, Praeger paperback, 1965. The essay of that title.

11. The late-development effect in schooling and education*

It is time for some general propositions. I will offer three. Other things being equal (we'll consider what things later), the later development starts (i.e. the later the point in world history that a country starts on a modernization drive):

- the more widely education certificates are used for occupational selection;
- the faster the rate of qualification inflation; and
- the more examination-oriented schooling becomes at the expense of genuine education.

Let us look at each of these in turn.

. . . THE MORE JOBS DEPEND ON QUALIFICATIONS

Chapter 3 has already tried to show how and why educational qualifications counted for more in Japan than in Britain. To be sure, 'late development' is not the only factor. Britain's non-reliance on formal qualifications was extreme, even among early developers, partly, presumably, because Britain has never since Cromwell experienced the sort of modernizing spurt which in Napoleonic France created the Grandes Ecoles, or at least established them in such a position that they soon acquired very important qualifying functions for government and industry. But the 'late-development effect' is clear. Certificates undoubtedly counted for more in Sri Lanka in the 1950s than for, say, Japan in the 1910s; more for Kenya in the 1960s than for Sri Lanka in the 1950s. It is easy enough to explain why. Part of it is the later developer's need to catch up fast - by importing knowledge and skills in formal educational packages. The most important part is the general tendency of the late developer to import the *latest* technology from the metropolitan models -

* From *The Diploma Disease: Education, Qualification and Development*, London: Allen & Unwin, 1975, Chapter 6, pp. 72-83, abridged. Previous chapters have described in turn the relation between developments in schooling and the occupational structure [on lines elaborated for Europe in Chapter 5] in Britain, Japan, Sri Lanka and Kenya.

social as well as machine technology. And, as a piece of social technology, the device of making even more refined and universal use of educational certificates for job allocation is becoming – as we saw *à propos* of Britain in Chapter 3 – more and more 'perfected' every year. Thus, Sri Lanka, earlier in the century, followed then current British practice in providing apprenticeship/mid-career-training routes into accountancy and engineering. Kenya, starting later, did not, but instead adopted the degree-entry practices which were just becoming formalized in Britain.

But it is time to look at that 'other things being equal' clause. Some other factors do over-ride the tendencies just described. There are a few odd corners, even in what is conventionally thought of as the developing world, where a man's ability to make his way in the world does depend a good deal less than in most on the educational qualifications he carries. Hong Kong is such – though decreasingly so. It is one of the few places where industrialization has been the product of the same sort of small-scale entrepreneurship as laid the basis for Europe's (especially Britain's) industrialization. Most men's income and status have depended on what they actually know and can do – on their skills and their push and intelligence more than on the pieces of paper they have been able to show potential employers. Hong Kong does not have the same sharp dualistic division between a highly desirable modern sector and an impoverished, despised, traditional sector typical of most developing countries. There is, rather, a steady graduation in enterprise size and modernity and considerable movement along the gradient.

The reasons for this are complex. It is partly because Hong Kong *does* have an unusually high quotient of clever, innovating businessmen who were capable of expanding tiny family workshops into larger, wage-employing viable firms. Another reason is because, as a colony, with a government which was solely concerned to hold the ring, state employment – given the small range of government services and the absence of state enterprises – has played a small part in total employment and so been less influential than in most developing countries in setting the general patterns. Even Hong Kong is changing now, however. Government employment is expanding. The big multinational corporations which always did tend to recruit by certificate are more firmly entrenched and have expanded their recruiting needs; more and more of the home-bred Chinese enterprises have grown big enough to have specialized personnel managers and to adopt the 'rational', 'modern' methods of recruitment by qualification.

In countries where big organizations – the state or large corporations – have dominated the industrialization/modernization process from the beginning, and where thrusting small-scale entrepreneurs have been lacking, or even positively discouraged by harassing licensing restrictions, the division between the traditional and the modern sector is sharper and the importance of educational qualifications correspondingly greater. Of the total working-age (15 to 59) population of Senegal, about 6 per cent are in jobs secured by social security provisions – modern sector jobs within the purview of the labour inspector. Of these nearly a half are government or public sector enterprise jobs, and of the rest a large proportion are in big rationalized French-owned firms which set minimum education standards for nearly all jobs. In Tanzania the corresponding figures are about 6 per cent in modern sector jobs (in establishments employing more than ten workers) of whom (1970) 58 per cent are in government or in parastatal corporations. A glance at Tanzanian newspaper job advertisements will show how finely graduated the correspondence between jobs and educational levels has become. A parastatal printing corporation wants a proof-reader: 'Form 6 leaver with good passes in Swahili and English'; a Security Officer: 'at least Standard Seven'; a Costing Clerk Grade II: 'at least Form 2 leavers'. It is not a bad generalization that the almightiness of the certificate varies in direct proportion to the predominance of the state in the development process. Weber made insistence on qualifications part of his classical definition of bureaucracy as an ideal type – and for very good reasons; certificates are objective; governments need, among other things, standards of impersonal judgement which protect them against charges of corrupt favouritism.

The other feature of countries like Senegal or Tanzania is the cliff-like nature of the separation of the modern sector from the traditional one. The twilight zone of what it is now fashionable to call the 'informal sector' – the roadside and empty-lot mechanics who will weld on a Bournville cocoa tin to mend the exhaust pipe of the civil servant's Mercedes, the leather workers making handmade bags for the tourist trade, the furniture-makers, the men who collect empty Essolube cans from the garages twice a day and have them processed into serviceable oil lamps by sunset – this twilight zone is small in total size, and its tiny enterprises, which are mostly family affairs offering little wage employment, rarely show much prospect of expanding into modern enterprises, particularly in those African countries where the people who have in the past shown entrepreneurial skills (the Asians in East Africa, the Lebanese in Senegal) are coming under increasingly nationalist restrictions of their activities.

Hence the 'informal sector', the 'transitional zone', is *not* in fact a transitional zone for individuals. It is not a means by which one moves from rural traditionalism into the modern sector by easy stages. Its entrepreneurs have little hope of achieving the life-style or the prestige of the modern-sector managers: its workers are not likely to graduate to more secure, better paid jobs in big firms. They are working in the twilight sector precisely *because* they have failed to get jobs in the modern-sector firm – and their chances of doing so are likely to diminish rather than increase as the new jobs which do become available are snapped up by their educationally better qualified juniors. Where the informal sector is that small and insignificant, then, it does not offer a route up the cliff-face from the traditional to the modern sector. The only way to make that transition is by the cable cars of the educational system.

But, of course, the tendency for government to play a leading role in the development process is *also* something which tends to increase the later development starts – because of the greater weight of the elite's sense of 'backwardness' among the motive forces for development, as Gerschenkron argued *à propos* of the successive generations of European development.[1] Likewise the tendency for dualism to be more exacerbated the later development starts is another part of the 'late-development effect'. (First, there is a greater technological gap between the traditional economy and the current generation of techniques available for import; second, in so far as the living standards of the modern sector are pulled up by the influences of rich country standards, the higher the latter go the greater the gap is likely to be. The Japanese Emperor in the 1890s required only imported horses and a locally made carriage. President Kenyatta needs a Benz or a Lincoln.)

So both these factors can be assumed to be subsumed in the proposition that later developers are more bemused by qualifications. That leaves three things as independent sources of variation:

(i) the presence or absence of people with thrusting entrepreneurial talents *à la* Hong Kong;
(ii) the presence or absence of the political will deliberately to counter the forces leading to dualism and qualificationism – *à la* China;
(iii) the economic and strategic circumstances which may limit the scope of these last two factors. It may be, for instance, that even if Senegal were peopled by Chinese, its poverty of resources, geographical position, and the entrenched nature of French influence would leave so little room for manoeuvre that things would still not be too different.

. . . THE FASTER THE RATE OF QUALIFICATION INFLATION

Qualification inflation results from a faster growth of the school system than of the number of modern-sector job opportunities. Our proposition can therefore be translated either: the later development starts, the slower the rate of creation of modern-sector job opportunities; or, the later development starts, the faster the growth of school enrolments.

The first proposition is unlikely to be true [in spite of greater capital-intensity etc. of later industrialization]. It is the second proposition which is the crucial one: school enrolments grow faster - so much faster as to counteract any tendency there *might* be for job opportunities to grow faster too: hence an imbalance which grows at a faster rate in later starters. Compare the figures for our four countries (Table 11.1):

Table 11.1 Growth in secondary enrolments (% p.a.)

Britain	1864-93	3%
Japan	1900-10	8%
Sri Lanka	1950-60	14%
Kenya	1960-70	20%

Sources: Taunton Commission, *Schools Inquiry Commission Report*, 1868, Vol. I. Appx VI; Bryce Commission, *Royal Commission on Secondary Education*, 1895, Vol. I. para. 52 and Vol. IX; Japan: Ministry of Education, *Gakusei Kyujunenshi*, 1964; UNESCO, Statistical Yearbook, 1963, 1971. British figures are for seven sample counties only; endowed and proprietary schools only.

The first reason why this should be so is fairly obvious. It follows from the first of our three propositions. The greater the degree of credentialism, the more the schools are the *only* channel of social mobility; the more complete the absence of any route up the cliff to the modern sector except the educational cable car. Studies of educational aspirations in Malaysia show that there is a smaller proportion of children hoping to press on to the university among the Chinese, who are supposed to be ambitious, persistent and energetic, than among the Malays who are supposed to have rather smaller doses of these qualities. The reason, clearly, is that, for the Malays who dominate the bureaucratized government (and, through government, expatriate big business) sectors of the economy, certificates really count; for the Chinese Malaysians whose opportunities lie in the small business sector, they have less value.[2]

A second part of the explanation is that the later development starts, the more firmly implanted in the international consensus is the idea (still highly controversial in Britain as late as 1870) that it is a proper, indeed essential function of the state to provide for its citizens' education ... [Providing] schooling and the hope, however fallacious, of escape into the modern sector, is often easier than, say, carrying out a land reform or otherwise redistributing resources in ways that might make life in rural areas more productive and more tolerable. Third, the later development starts, the worse the dualism is likely to be - the greater the modern-sector/traditional-sector differential in income, power and prestige; the greater the attractions of trying to scale the cliff … [especially] where population growth, or the initial disequalizing effects of economic growth, have actually worsened living standards in rural areas.

Also, fourth, later developers have better means of communication available; hence the late developer's villages are more integrated into the polity and more subjected to demonstration effect. Tokyo, where all the university graduates were, was a pretty remote place for the vast majority of Japanese villagers in the 1890s; a place on the end of a telegraph line, described in the newspapers which came three days late. A good proportion of Kenya's contemporary villagers have seen Nairobi on a television screen. And they are more likely to see access to that modern sector as feasible as well as desirable because, fifth, the later development starts, the more the meritocratic ideal of equality of opportunity is entrenched in the international consensus; the more likely, therefore, an integrated school system providing subsidies, scholarships, etc., for poor children to reach the top – given, sixth, the additional factor that the 'sense of backwardness' is likely to be greater, greater also the urge to catch up, greater the premium placed on efficiency; greater therefore the arguments for meritocracy as a means of mobilizing all the talents. What these last four factors all combined to produce, therefore, is a *greater intensity of popular demand* for education, particularly for schooling at the sort of levels at which valid job certificates are thought to be produced.

One could argue, finally, that the later the timing of development, the less a government is likely to be able to resist that demand – because the more deeply the democratic notion that governments should be responsive to popular will is likely to be built into the system.

However, *some* governments, for some time at least, can resist – which brings us to the first variable one has in mind when one puts the 'other things being equal' qualification to the proposition that qualification inflation is worse in later developers. Tanzania, for example, can still make some claim to be the manpower planners' dream land. In the planner's ideal world, qualification-escalation just is not allowed to exist. He will allow expansion up to 100 per cent enrolment in a basic primary open-access span of education which is not presumed by anyone to confer any job rights in the modern sector. Beyond that he seeks to fix for all time what he has assumed to be the 'correct' equations between qualification levels and job requirements …

Tanzania still operates such a system. The budget for Form 2 leavers, Form 4 leavers, Form 6 leavers and university graduates is set for some years ahead, and the government declares its firm intention of allowing just that many and no more into the secondary schools – however strong the mounting pressure for more secondary places as the number of children reaching the end of primary increases annually and each individual child's chance of getting to a public secondary school correspondingly diminishes. Even in Tanzania, however, the state has not been able to prevent the growth of a 'spill-over' private secondary sector, a growth which was accelerating in the more prosperous areas in the mid-1970s.

In Kenya next door, as the last chapter described, the government has all but given up attempts, even within the public sector, to dam the flood at the secondary entrance stage, and is in fact abandoning any attempt to do so at the tertiary stage. The most obvious explanation of the difference lies in the contrast between the collectivity-oriented philosophy of Tanzania's leaders and the individualistic philosophy of Kenya's, but other features of the political structure also play a part – the degree of federalism, for instance, and the dependence of governments on popular election.

India, the authentic home of the BA bus conductor, famous for its 60000 unemployed graduate engineers – many of them already with master's degrees – is a good example of the importance of those latter features. Every responsible Indian who writes on problems of his country's education deplores the unbridled expansion of higher education of unemployables when 60 per cent of the population still either never reach or fail to finish primary school. But in India control over education is decentralized to the state level. Schools and colleges are one of the most tangible ways of winning the electorate's favour.[3]

The problem is not new in India. Already at the beginning of the century, the headlong expansion of higher education was sufficiently widely recognized to be a problem that legislative controls were introduced. Nothing better illustrates the marvellous Canute-like hubris of the British Raj than Lord Curzon's confidence that he had settled the problem once and for all. It is worth recalling his words before the legislative council. If he had not acted, he said:

> ... the rush of immature striplings to our India universities, not to learn but to earn, would have continued till it became an avalanche ultimately bringing the entire educational fabric to the ground – colleges might have been left to multiply without regard to any criterion either of necessity or merit; the examination curse would have tightened its grip on the rising generation; standards would have sunk lower and lower; the output would have steadily swollen in volume, at the cost of all that education ought to mean; and one day India would have awakened to the fact that she had, for years, been bartering her intellectual heritage for the proverbial mess of pottage.[4]

All that, he claimed, he had stopped. Once and for all. In 1904.

[One other important variable affecting the role of qualification has already been discussed in the preceding chapters: the degree and type of social stratification. In some 'older' societies with long-established status systems, the 'lower orders' have been conditioned for generations to see themselves as 'naturally' condemned to underdog status. If the only primary school available is one which peters out after the third grade, they are not much upset; they do not bewail the foreclosing of chances of mobility they have hardly conceived of. By contrast, in African societies which had little stratification before they were colonized (even in the kingdom of Buganda or the emirates of northern Nigeria there was little elaborated hereditary *cultural* differentiation between the upper and lower strata) the 'modern sector' is equally new to everyone. No particular group is seen as having a preternatural right and everyone is free to compete. One can hardly imagine a Ministry of Education *anywhere* in the modern world setting out, as the Taunton Commission did in Britain in the 1860s,[5] to calculate the number of 'upper and middle class school-children' as a means of estimating the requirements for secondary education.]

Finally there may well be cultural differences, also, which override the 'late-development effect'. Cultural differences can affect the vigour of the competitive impulse; the extent to which peoples easily 'take to' the new pursuit of qualifications of status and of 'place' in the modern world. Quite apart from between-country comparisons, compare the reputations, for example, of the Masai and Kikuyu within Kenya, or of the Hausa and the Ibo within Nigeria. Another dimension of cultural difference is in the importance attached to education as such – the intrinsic prestige traditionally accorded to 'learning' and the 'scholar'...

. . . THE MORE SCHOOLING EQUALS EXAM-TAKING

The mechanisms of this third proposition are obvious. They follow from the last point. If it is to get certificates that people go to school ... then the more the schooling process itself is likely to revolve around certification.

Once that process begins it has inbuilt mechanisms that make it self-reinforcing. The more consciously children are sent to school to get certificates and the greater the demand for schooling for that purpose, the greater the number of primary schools geared up to prepare children for secondary entry, the tougher the competition, the more primary schools' and teachers' performance is measured by their proportion of secondary entrance 'successes'. The greater, therefore, the teachers' emphasis on teaching for the examination, sticking to the syllabus, concentrating on learning to remember rather than to understand, showing extra attention to the bright boys who have a chance of making it; in short, demonstrating in all they do, *their* concept of exam results as the be-all and end-all of schooling – and consequently the more the qualification-orientation of the *children* and their parents is reinforced, which in turn reinforces those tendencies in teachers, and so on.

There are three other factors which make the situation worse in later developers. The first is another facet of dualism. Schools themselves belong to the 'modern sector'. Their buildings and furniture are patterned after imported designs if not actually imported. The contracts and modes of payment of teachers follow the conventions of the civil service and the factories, not of traditional rural areas. The rhythms of the school conform to the imported seven-day week, not to the moon phases of local calendars. And, most important of all, the knowledge and attitude content of what they purvey is remote from the context of village experience. In other words, the gap between the culture of the school and the culture of the home is likely to be greater, the more pronounced the dualism of the country's development pattern - which is itself a function of late development. Japanese schoolchildren in the 1890s learned about steam engines which perhaps only one person in their family had ever seen; they learned about Benjamin Franklin, and public libraries. But at least more effort was made to relate them to village life than was done for the children in, say, Jamaica's schools in the 1930s (see V.S. Naipaul's hilarious account of the writing of formal compositions on family holidays at the seaside; Naipaul, *A House for Mr Biswas*, 1961, p. 322). The point is, at any rate, that the more remote school work is from daily experience, the more easily it becomes a mere ritual, a merely instrumentalized means of getting marks.

Second, because of the tremendous pressure to expand school enrolments on exiguous budgets, schools are poorly equipped. Qualification-orientation obviously gets worse if there *are* no laboratories and libraries even to provide the opportunity of developing discovery methods of learning, if there *are* no alternatives to chalk and talk, memorization and testing.

Finally, in the later developers the birth of a school system and the development of a qualification-based occupational system are likely to be simultaneous. The very concept of 'school' and of formal education entered the society in recent times as part of the package of 'modernity' brought by the imperialist powers. By contrast, most of the older industrial countries have formal pedagogical traditions (and some educational institutes) dating back to pre-industrial times *before* educational certificates acquired bread-and-butter value - dating back, in other words, to the time when learning was thought to be about getting *knowledge* or wisdom, to make a man respected or holy or righteous or rich. These older traditions still persist in the older countries. They serve to maintain the fiction that education is about moral and intellectual uplift and enrichment. And such fictions *are* important. What men define as real is real in its consequences. The fictions *do* serve as a countervailing force to weaken tendencies towards qualification-orientation, particularly when they are boldly reasserted by rebellious students demanding the end of examinations, and urging that universities should stop prostituting themselves by subserviently acting as graders of human material for the capitalist system (even if they do falter and fall into confusion when any university teacher offers to take them at their word and abolish all degree *certificates* as well as examinations). In later developing societies, where all except the very first generation of purely soul-saving mission schools (and even some of those) had selection/credentialling functions, these useful countervailing fictions, having no roots in any local past, are harder to establish and sustain. The pursuit of certificates can be even more naked and unashamed.

This aspect of the late development effect is perhaps even more subject to 'other things being equal' qualifications. There are other things besides cultural gaps which lead to bookish ritualism in schooling. When Britain was being modernized by the importation of Renaissance culture, it may have been partly the cultural gap which made the classical learning of the Elizabethan grammar schools such a ritualized product, but it was sheer inertia which kept it in such a desiccated state for another three centuries.

But setting aside all questions of the truth of *general* propositions of the kind 'the later development starts, the more ...', one thing we can assert with confidence. In the Third World today the importance of qualifications is greater than in the advanced industrial countries. Educational systems are more likely to be geared to qualification-getting, and the consequences for the society and its pattern of development are likely to be even more deplorable than in our society.

Here ends the diagnosis. The next five chapters look at possible solutions.

NOTES

1. A. Gerschenkron, *Economic Backwardness in Historical Perspective,* 1965.
2. Malaysia Ministry of Education, Planning and Research Division, *Preliminary Report on a Study of Opinions About Education and Society*, 1972.
3. L. Rudolph and S. Rudolph (eds), *Education and Politics in India: Studies in Organization, Society and Policy*, 1972.
4. Quoted in V. Mazumdar, *Education and Social Change*, Simla, Indian Institute for Advanced Study, 1972, p. 6.
5. *Inquiry*, Vol. 1. Appendix 2.

12. Technological self-reliance: sturdy ideal or self-serving rhetoric?*

GLOSSARY

For the purposes of this paper, words are used as follows:

Transfer of technology By 'transfer of technology to developing countries' I understand 'getting knowledge that is only in some foreigners' heads into the heads of one's own nationals'. The learning process may well be largely accomplished by buying and studying some piece of imported capital equipment in which the new knowledge is embodied, as when the Japanese government bought its first Jacquard loom, and had its craftsmen dismantle and assemble it time after time until they had learned its technology and could then begin to think about devising or buying or stealing the technology of making it. And nowadays it may be a sensible shortcut to import both machine and its original devisors in some form of joint venture. But it is entirely possible for technology to be transferred as blueprints or as images in someone's head.

Buying technology involves buying (a) the right to be taught the technology, (b) exemption from claims under patent laws, and also, though not *necessarily*, also, (c) hardware embodying the technology, although that is often the most sensible shortcut.

[The common phrase 'independent technological capacity' needs breaking down into **independent technology learning capacity** and **independent technology creating capacity**, hereafter 'learning capacity' and 'creation capacity' *tout court*.] The first is what the Japanese showed they had by the time they could put their Jacquard loom back together again blindfold; the second was what they had when they worked out which of its metal parts they could safely substitute with wood. One sometimes needs, also, the separate concept – **independent world technology reconnaissance capacity**; the information-gathering network that can survey what is available in the world,

* From M. Fransman and K. King (eds), *Technological Capability in the Third World*, Basingstoke: Macmillan, 1984, pp. 65–80, abridged. Written after a three month spell at the Institute of Economic Growth, Delhi University, and immediately before joining the Technical Change Centre.

detect new developments, judge what is worthwhile buying and learning in detail. Unless otherwise specified I include that in learning capacity, the other part of which is, of course, the theoretical sophistication to understand what is going on in new technology.

Nationalism A pretty horrible emotion (in all its forms throughout the declension: I am a patriot; you are a nationalist; he is a bloody chauvinist). But some people's nationalism is more forgivable than others. The asymmetry in GATT, allowing protectionism to poor countries and denying it to richer countries seems to me an 'inequity' justified by the objective of reducing international income disparities. For the same reason, the nationalism I would deplore in a rich country I find more condonable in developing countries. Along with other pretty distasteful things, like India's Madamolatry and other cults of the personality, it may provide absolutely necessary cement for growth strategies in which the state (claiming to represent the nation) has to play a central role. This not only sounds, but is, condescending, perhaps. Well, if apologizing is any help, I apologize.

SRACI syndrome or self-reliance-as-categorical-imperative syndrome: a condition that requires attention when there is evidence that it inhibits healthy growth; usually the result initially of an excessively high nationalism content in the political bloodstream, but sustained by various self-equilibrating mechanisms to be discussed later. Its main symptom is excessive regard for creation capacity and contempt for learning capacity. The expression of the SRACI syndrome in British industry is sometimes lampooned as the NIH syndrome: 'not invented here'. At the conferences on Development Alternatives which look forward to the day when some blacksmith in Bihar will produce a genuine Third World Alternative to the bicycle, NIH can be elevated to the status of high principle. Thus the Monrovian Declaration of the Organization for African Unity, 'the transfer of technology' is a term that 'should be stricken from the International vocabulary'.[1]

PROPOSITIONS

1. Learning capacity needs a dash of humility; creation capacity needs a dash of hubris. Still halfway-rational nationalism can promote both in the mix required (Gershenkron and the advantages of backwardness in the right hands); emotional nationalism inhibits the first and promotes hypertrophy of the second - hence the SRACI syndrome.
2. Most developing countries need a certain amount of creation capacity from the very beginning of industrialization. It may be that, by now, the Intermediate Technology Development Group can take care of most of

their 'appropriate to factor endowments' problems (there must by now be as little payoff in a search for a new winnowing machine as there is for a new corkscrew); 'appropriate to local environment' problems may well require some invention - adapting a standard blast-furnace to local lignite, a canning process to local fruits, a waterjet loom to temperatures far higher than where they have been hitherto used, etc.

3. But, for a long, long while (a while that gets longer and longer for the later developers; it will be longer for Korea than it was for Japan, and longer for Malaysia than it will be for Korea), *learning capacity is overwhelmingly more important than creation capacity*. Japan, for the best part of a century, put nearly all its effort - with due teeth-gritting humility - into learning. They tolerated, though with much discomfort, the stereotype that resulted - 'clever imitators these Japs but nothing more'. Creation was reserved for marginal adaptation. But now they have got to the frontiers, and it has become central. In 1979, one quarter of all foreign patents registered in the US were registered by the Japanese as, during the 1970s, they climbed ahead, first of the British, then of the Germans, Swedes and Swiss.

   They are still paying more for their earlier learning than they are yet earning from their newer venture into teaching, but the balance of payments on *new* technology contracts became favourable in 1973. Between 1950 and 1978, during which time the Japanese bought the bulk of the new knowledge produced in the West between 1940 and 1978 (including the big wartime production), they paid out to foreigners - in royalties, outright purchase, returns on equity participation, etc. - $9 billion. Putting that sum in constant 1978 dollars would increase it, but would not bring it near the $60 billion-odd which was spent on R&D by the USA alone in the single year of 1978.

4. Developing countries differ enormously in their present, and short-term potential, learning capacity. This is partly a question of size: 0.05 per cent of Senegal's manpower compared with 0.05 per cent of India's manpower is as a platoon to a battalion. But it is also a question of:

   (a) intellectual sophistication - again technological skill levels in India are vastly superior to those in any African and most Latin American countries;
   (b) international contacts to create a technology intelligence network for efficient worldwide technological reconnaissance - again, India's brain-drained diaspora is a great potential resource, still utilized only through informal contacts;
   (c) honesty - how far one can trust in the, let us call nationalism in this case, 'patriotism' of one's technologists - how far, when they are

> supposed to be negotiating with foreign multinationals on behalf of the country or of a 'national' firm, one can trust them to be honestly negotiating with them and not getting into bed with them.

Given the enormous range of difference in these dimensions, any generalized prescriptions for 'developing countries' are practically worthless.

5. The open-economy strategy versus delinked self-reliance debate [often called the ISI vs. EOI debate - import-substitution industrialization versus export-oriented industrialization] and the technological dependency/self-reliance debates, are different debates. Delinking, minimization of foreign trade (the minimum necessary for imports of capital goods and technology) *plus* a vigorous policy of building learning capacity and using it for large-scale technology imports, is a perfectly viable development strategy if your learning capacity is really good enough and your economy is big and resource-endowed enough ..., [but in practice] there does seem to be a correlation between the positions countries take in the two debates. Self-sufficiency in trade and the cult of self-reliance in technology *tend* to go together.

THE INDIAN CASE

India is a splendid example. India needs much more attention in the technology debate because it is the one country where self-reliance is actually being practised, where there is a well-developed industrial base, and a substantial cadre of highly trained and very bright people to contribute (interchangeably) to her learning capacity and her creation capacity.

What follows are a few impressions picked up in a few weeks in India while engaged on other things. If some of the emotionalism which attends many economic debates in India - and none more markedly than those concerned with matters of self-reliance - has rubbed off onto my feelings in the matter, I apologize in advance. My thesis is as follows:

1. India has too many desperately poor people multiplying far too rapidly for Indians to be content with the sort of growth rates they are getting. They spell, in fact, mounting disaster.
2. Faster growth could come (a) from exports of manufactures, (b) from making high-cost manufacturers (both state and private), now guaranteed all modern comforts by their monopoly positions, bestir themselves to create a bit of learning capacity and so seek ways of becoming more efficient (and, if they have export potential) even world competitive.

3. Such policies are inhibited (a) by the self-interest of the monopolists, aided and abetted by (b) the research scientists in government, and (c) the politicians and intellectuals who have the gall, from the vantage point of their homes in the more salubrious parts of Delhi and Calcutta and Bombay, to mix their fanciful rhetoric about self-reliance with the most moving expressions of their deep concern for 'the weaker sections' of society.

To begin, then, with growth: 1980–81 was a good year in India. Growth more than compensated for the bad year of declining output that preceded it. Over the two years taken together GNP rose by 2 per cent (industrial output by 4 per cent). Population, meanwhile, increased by 4 per cent.

K.N. Raj is no alarmist and no enemy of self-reliance, but he could not find much ground for hope at the Indian Statistical Institute's anniversary celebration of the Mahalanobis legacy.[2] The Mahalanobis scenario of self-reliance should have had India half-industrialized by now. Instead, the same 74 per cent of the work force is in agriculture as when he was drafting his first plans. Landless agricultural labourers numbered 31 million in 1961, 55 million in the 1981 census. Growth has been confined to limited areas. 'Over at least one half of the country, the rate of growth of agricultural output has lagged significantly behind the rate of growth of agricultural population.' Raj speaks of an actual decommercialization of agriculture and lower living standards over large parts of the country. There are reports from many districts of agricultural wages remaining roughly what they were in the 1960s – while the industrial worker consumer price index went (1960–80) from 100 to 439.

Inexorable population growth absorbing most of the increase in production has meant that 'there could not have been any significant increase in the demand for manufactured consumer goods'. The small-domestic-demand depressant of industrial growth is, as Raj puts it, not Keynesian, to be cured by fiscal or monetary tuning, nor curable by income redistribution. It is for real: 'of a more structural nature, connected with the rate of growth of agricultural output and of population.'

That is the problem. No prospects of significant fertility decline. A vast increase in the labour force over the next fifteen years already born anyway. More potential mothers reaching the age of eighteen than at any time in history. India just cannot do with economic growth rates of 2–4 per cent. Given her endowments of resources and skill, and the elapsed time for accumulating experience (TATA's steel mill at Jamshedpur started in the same year as Japan's first at Yawata), there is no reason why it should not have been India rather than Brazil and Korea that is beginning to export cars and ships and manage growth rates of 6–10 per cent.

So what has gone wrong? It is not only restricted domestic demand. Raj relates how Mahalanobis expected - reasonably - that once the infrastructure of basic capital goods industries was created, industrial growth would accelerate. In fact it has slowed - lower now than in the 1960s: the inevitable slowdown as the import-substituting industrialization programme of replacing imports comes to an end, not being compensated by new sources of expansion - certainly not foreign trade. India's foreign trade is about half South Korea's, a country with 5 per cent of its population. The change in trade structures of the two countries is striking (Table 12.1):

Table 12.1 Composition of exports (%)

	Primary products	Textiles/ clothing	Machinery/ transport equipment	Other
India 1960	55	35	1	9
India 1977	44	20	6	30
Korea 1960	86	8	–	6
Korea 1977	15	32	17	36

And the slow down has happened *in spite of* a steady increase in investment. Gross savings rose, from 9.5 percent of GDP at the beginning of the 1950s to 22 per cent in the late 1970s, and investment in industrial plant more or less proportionately - a very respectable rate indeed. *But* the industrial plant that these savings financed became steadily more costly (prices rose faster than the general price level) and less productive. Why? Raj suggests, in addition to increased energy costs, 'underutilization of capacity, inefficient plant utilization and poor technology built into the existing capital stock'.

All too plausible if the visitor to India only looks around him. But the 'poor technology' needs to be divided into two categories. The envelopes whose surface-coating is so poor that one's pen tears holes, the block-pad made with a perforator with so many teeth missing that every page tears like a Rorschach test, the filing-cards of such wastefully thick lamination that one wonders what rough handling library readers must mete out to their catalogues - all these things might possibly be the result of 'making do' with antiquated equipment lovingly maintained with improvised spare parts, eschewing re-equipment in the interests of saving national capital resources for more basic essentials like steel mills and atom bombs. All very laudable: hurrah for the informal sector.

But the second kind of 'poor technology' is very different. A car called the Ambassador is an early 1960s Morris Oxford: design, technology and tools imported originally for a joint venture, bequeathed subsequently to a wholly Indian firm. At some point in the 1960s India could say: 'import substitution in cars has now taken place'. Period. Have the production engineers at the Ambassador car factory been out there on the shop floor, not just keeping the plant in tiptop museum piece condition, but wondering how they can improve the manufacturing process to get costs down? Have they been staying on after 5 p.m. in the evening working on projects for a design modification? Have they been scouring the trade press, buying foreign cars for dissection, searching avidly for cheap ways of buying or stealing other people's innovations to make the Ambassador better and cheaper? If they have, it is strange that there should be no sign of these efforts in the product which continues to trickle out of the factory, year after year, unchanged, I am told, in shape or performance, as gas-guzzling and polluting as any early 1960s car ever was, the only change being the steadily rising price.

And why should they be doing all those enthusiastic improvement things anyway? Answer: for all the same mysterious reasons as a group of engineers and managers in TELCO, one of the firms in the TATA group with a very particular ethos, *have* done all those things, have kept to world-competitive efficiency levels in trucks and buses, and by virtue of these efforts displaced Leyland entirely in South East Asian markets - reasons that (again I rely on hearsay) have something to do with self-actualization, liking efficiency for its own sake, feeling part of a group that can be proud of itself, etc. Certainly, if those motives are *not* present among Ambassadors engineers, it is hard to see how they can have any other incentives: certainly not financial ones. Complete protection against foreign competition, an *x*-years waiting-list of customers, controlled cost-plus pricing allowing for steady increases in wages in real as well as money terms. Stay on after 5 p.m. working on some improvement project? You must be joking.

To move from anecdote to scholarship, an analysis of the accounts of Indian companies shows clearly, apparently, that the monopoly firms have high profits and low growth, the firms in oligopoly industries have lower profits but higher growth.[3]

If the reader senses a certain moralistic judgement here - TELCO engineers good, Ambassador engineers bad - it is partly because I do value productiveness and innovativeness and being keen on one's work as intrinsic values; partly also because I cannot forget that figure of 55 million village labourers with steadily diminishing work opportunities, and believe that only a generalization of TELCO behaviour can stave off disaster for them.

THE PRIVILEGED SELF-RELIANTS

So the first group of beneficiaries from self-reliance are the managers and engineers of the protected industries. They can sit back and relax. 'We have *achieved* self-sufficiency in automobiles.'

The system allows them, also, to be generous to their friends. They can, though sometimes the government takes a bit of persuading, mollify the unions with wage increases. They can afford to pay high prices for their steel. So the feathers work through the bedding of the whole organized sector. With labour markets, in particular, insulated from supply/demand pressures coming from the informal and agricultural sectors, the organized sector as a whole can absorb the bulk of the income increase that the economy generates. The privileged island grows more privileged: quite apart from the flesh pots of middle-class Bombay, a recent thesis calculates the wage of the unskilled labourer in the Bhilai steel plant at 5 to 7 times the wage of agricultural labourers in the fields around the plant.[4] Smart union leaders can sell job opportunities in the organized sector for the price of several months' wages.[5]

This state of affairs persists - Ambassador manufacturers can even pose as paragons of self-reliant industrialization - very largely because of the miasma of self-reliance rhetoric, academic and governmental, which encourages them in their complacency. The sources of this rhetoric are, I suspect, very varied. I say 'I suspect' because what follows should be read as provocative hypothesis, being based on hearsay and inference from hearsay rather than systematic enquiry. I trust that it will, however, serve to open up the issue.

One source of the rhetoric, to begin with, is doubtless all those employed in public sector R&D and government scientific laboratories - or, more exactly, the people who administer them and speechify about them, rather than those who actually do the work. Of course, creating new technology is more exciting than scouting it out, copying it, learning it from elsewhere. And even if you do not feel confident about actually being able to create it, it is much better for your prestige if people *think* that is what you are doing. So, naturally, most of the talk about independent technological capacities sounds like talk about creation capacity not about learning capacity.

Moreover, the creation of new technology involves experiments, large budgets for equipment, the building of project empires: learning may only involve literature searches, study tours, the chance to be involved in the design of new industrial projects.

It is small wonder that the scientific community is thoroughly in favour of building creation capacity. Apparently there are some in government who wonder whether such an emphasis is necessarily in the national interest. In the science and technology chapter of the Sixth Plan, the scientists who presumably wrote it clearly felt under some pressure and wrote defensively about the current emphasis in government on cost-effectiveness, and aversion to taking big financial risks, which 'carried the danger of erosion of the spirit of self-reliance and indigenous effort'.

I am sure there are some scientists and technologists to whom this means that engineers building a cement plant, say, should do everything they can to figure out for themselves the best technology to use, and rely on foreign consultants only when necessary - and not to tell them things they could find out themselves by more assiduous search ... But to many others it means that Indians should use their creative capacity to create what the Delhi wits would call a really Hindu cement technology.

In point of fact, to stick with cement for a moment, a good deal of imaginative work at the Cement Research Institute in Delhi is going on. A pair of researchers (one of them since brain-drained to Illinois) have published over the last year three papers in *World Cement Technology*, one reporting detailed studies of the properties of pozzolano cement using power-station waste fly-ash (capable of adding up to 20 per cent to the existing cement production capacity very cheaply), one reporting tests of locally available mineralizing additives which would allow a 10 per cent reduction in kiln temperature, and another suggesting the use of lignin waste from Indian paper factories to thin the feed slurry, reduce its moisture content and save 4 kWh a ton from the drying process. There is no doubt about the quality of the creation capacity displayed (even if it does seem to be all done in the laboratory, not centred in the coal face of the production process). But, at the same time, the *learning* job of keeping up with mainstream cement plant technology - with all the energy-saving and capital cost-saving developments of the last ten years - simply has not been done. Krupp-Polysium have had to be brought in to do a turn-key job for Coromandel's new cement plant, and the Modi Group, after two years persuading the government that self-reliance was not possible, have finally negotiated permission to get Blue Circle as consultants (jointly with an Indian firm) for the construction of theirs. (It will take six years from first plans to completion.) Meanwhile it is the Korean firm, Hyundai, which is competing with Blue Circle and Krupp-Polysium for plant construction orders and which has won the contract to build an up-to-date plant in Indonesia.

One can see pretty clearly the pattern of interests which should have prompted the government scientific establishment (which presumably wrote the science and technology chapter) to take the defensive line in the Plan quote above. But why should a leading civil servant and intellectual like Hakser quote these lines and endorse their sentiment with such warm approval: 'Self-reliance must be at the very heart of science and technology planning.'?[6] The question is a little like asking why every Indian intellectual has to be in favour of socialism: it is part of the ambient intellectual climate. But it is possible, I think, to separate out several distinct discrete strands.

1. One is a purely cognitive matter of economic conceptualization. Economists have not all absorbed the fact that technological change is far more dynamic than it ever was, obsolescence faster (and it is *not* just a matter of micro-electronics, and the fact that international competition over very large areas is now competition in product type and quality, not price competition for standard products). Raj quotes Mahalanobis as thinking that once India had created its basic industries, it would enjoy enormous advantages of lower costs for capital goods. But that was not to foresee, for example, the very great cost reductions that have been made in steelmaking and cement-making technology in the last ten years. Cement can now be produced more cheaply from the big dry-process plants with energy-saving precalciners which make most of Japan's cement, even counting the high capital charges, than it can in most of the fully depreciated older and smaller wet-process Indian plants. The fact that so much of Japan's capacity is in newer processes is largely a function of her high levels of investment leading to a more recent average vintage of capital, and one can hardly blame India's slow rate of investment on the cement industry. But some of the developments of the last ten years do lend themselves to incorporation in retro-fitted modifications to upgrade existing plant. How far the engineers of India's cement plants have been active in learning about these techniques, and seeking ways to take advantage of them, I cannot say. All I do know is that the Indian economists who have told me of the cement industry, its supply and political corruption problems, and suggested that the *only* thing needed was simply to increase capacity, are missing an important dimension. 'We have mastered cement technology', is their assumption – the way Mahalanobis thought one did generally with capital goods.
2. A second strain is the real difficulty of turning the situation around. Apart from the vested-interest situation, the sheer difficulty of changing the incentive pattern is admittedly considerable. A steady removal of protection, and exposure to the stresses of international competition is the obvious way of making firms improve their competitiveness, but for an industry as far behind international levels as Ambassador cars, the time scale for becoming internationally competitive would have to be a long one. A schedule of decreasing tariffs with the firm promise – or, rather, threat – of zero tariffs imports in, say, ten years' time, would seem to be a possibility, but I am told by a senior bureaucrat who thinks along these lines that the Ministry of Finance sternly sets its face against such schemes. Tariffs are revenue, and it is unsound to tie up your options in revenue sources far in advance. Such is the importance attached to forcing industry into world competitiveness.
3. There may also be in this a touch of the Brahmin economist's contempt

for industry. Agricultural economics flourishes. Agricultural economists rub shoulders easily with Jat and Rajput farmers. Economic historians turn over every clod of agrarian history. But commercial history? Studying the doings of those *low caste* Bania fellows? Of Marwaris?

4. Another element, perhaps, is a certain self-denying asceticism. Indian intellectuals really are a bit more moral than the intellectuals of most other developing countries, and many, I think, particularly those who have lived abroad, take a certain pride in the fact they do not go lusting after the latest Toyota and Mercedes, and are content to bump along in an Ambassador as the price of their country's following a decent, egalitarian and self-respecting development path. It is a (very, very modified) form of Ghandiism one can sympathize with, even if it has consequences that are far from egalitarian.
5. And, finally, nationalism, of course. It is not only that scientists want to think of themselves as creators not learners; every patriotic Indian wants to think his scientists creative. But that is a less important part of it than the xenophobic part. The brave posture of scorning any help from foreigners (from the foreign multinationals who have the property rights in a lot of the technology) is appealing. In reality it takes more patriotism *and* self-confidence to grit your teeth in all humility, negotiate with the multinationals, drive an intelligent bargain and be damned to those who impugn your integrity. But it is easier and more comfortable to be purer and to have no truck with foreign devils. And the academic economist can empathize with an engineer who feels that way ...

I hope I have made my case that when talking of an independent technological capacity, India's situation requires more attention to learning capacity and less to creation capacity. I have tried to guess at the forces that sustain an ideology that overwhelmingly favours the latter over the former, which ideology both justifies and reinforces policies and practices that seem inappropriate ...

NOTES

1. OAU, *What Kind of Africa in the Year 2000*, 1979, p. 21.
2. K.N. Raj, 'Problems of plan implementation: resource mobilisation', *Mainstream*, 26 January 1982, pp. 24–8.
3. N.S. Siddharthan, 'Industrial stagnation: a study', *Mainstream*, 26 December 1981.
4. A. Saha, *Cultural Influences on Industrial Productivity: India and Japan* (Karaghpur, Indian Institute of Technology).
5. V. Ramaswamy, *The Textile Workers of Coimbatore*, Delhi, Oxford University Press, forthcoming.
6. P.N. Hakser, 'Reflections on science and technology in the Sixth Five Year Plan', *Man and Development*, **III**(3), September 1981.

13. Shinohata: epilogue*

I work nowadays in an Institute of Development Studies. Its business is to pursue knowledge which might be useful to the countries of the Third World which are trying to 'develop'. It was once thought that someone like myself who had spent several years contemplating what has happened in Japan over the last century might have some novel perspectives on the matter. I am not sure that I do, but living among people who are constantly talking about 'development' does prompt certain thoughts about Shinohata which I might otherwise not have had.

To start with, there is that strain in modern development thinking which grows out of a much older 'where are the snows of yesteryear?' kind of romanticism. See what a mess our crass materialism has made of our society: the pollution, the decline of the family, the drugs, the loss of purpose, the loss of simpler, purer pleasures. Let the poor countries learn from our horrible example and seek some *alternative* pattern of development. When Chou En-lai suggests that the Chinese would be happy to remain bicycle-riders for ever, many of our philosophers of 'true development' (car-owners to a man) heartily applaud the appearance of a man of vision.

Such a view would be almost entirely incomprehensible in Shinohata. I say 'almost' because there *are* parents who worry slightly that their spoiled children are thriftless and wasteful, have lost a 'sense of the preciousness of things'. But that is the last dying kick of the puritan ethic, not a romanticization of the simple life in the style of our zero-growthers. Shinohata's citizens are too close to their past poverty for that. They revel in their new-found comforts, and I entirely sympathize.

To be sure, Shinohata was in many respects a much more exciting and exotic village for an outsider to visit in 1955 than twenty years later. There were more colourful characters around; they got drunk more often; people seemed more impulsive and passionate. I doubt if Shinohata will ever again produce an incident as suitable for a Fernandel farce as it did the day the fire brigade went fishing. And doubtless, outside observers apart, Shinohata farmers looked forward, then, to their shrine festivals and drinking parties with much keener anticipation than they do to their far more frequent outings today. Doubtless, too, they felt greater warmth and security and kinship with more of

* From *Shinohata*, London: Allen Lane, 1978, pp. 312–18.

their fellow villagers than they do today, and I am sure there was great satisfaction in accomplishing the lengthy and laborious task of making their own soya sauce, even if it tasted ghastly compared with the bottled product of modern chemical expertise they buy today. But with all that went the long hours of sheer hard grinding toil needed to maintain even an austere standard of living; the work-horse resignation of the young bride combining housework and farmwork under her mother-in-law's unremitting discipline, the anxieties that often attended the business of keeping up dutiful neighbour relations in the imprisoning village community which circumscribed social relations far more conclusively than they do today. For these things Shinohata people have no regret. Even less - for 1955 was already a period of considerable comfort compared with 1935 and *a fortiori* compared with 1905 - do they have regrets for the days when the sanction for not working, or not saving against the bad seasons, was real gnawing hunger; not having food in the house for days at a time.

Nothing that I have seen and heard in Shinohata has made me doubt the virtues of economic growth. It has made me doubt the current prescriptions for getting it, however. Fifteen years ago those who spoke and wrote about development took it for granted that the only obvious way to a general rise in living levels was industrialization - learning to make those additional things besides food which make for a comfortable style of living and acquiring the capital equipment to make them by machines and inanimate energy rather than by human toil. Nowadays industrialization has become almost a dirty word. Probably the majority of writers, at least the academic writers, on development who concern themselves with industrialization are less interested in promoting it than in highlighting its ill-consequences - the way it creates income inequalities, invites the domination of multinational corporations, etc. Rural development, by contrast, is thought to be an excellent thing: the number one priority which all the international agencies want to back.

Of course there is a lot of sense in giving rural development high priority. Japanese farmers did not take long to acquire the idea of 'improvement'. They have been diligent in their husbandry, cautiously willing to experiment, quick to seize an opportunity of making two blades of grass grow where only one grew before. If their output had not kept up with the growth of the Japanese population - and if the silk they produced had not financed a lot of Japanese capital imports - Japan's industrialization would have been much slower. Nowadays they get more than twice as much rice off each acre as they did a hundred years ago. But the chief factor responsible for that is their enormous use of chemicals made in highly capital-intensive factories. Nor is it the increase in their *own* productivity which makes them so well off today, but rather the way the Japanese economic and political systems allow them to share in the great leaps in productivity made by industry. And the reason why those leaps have been possible in the last twenty years is because of the foundations laid in the 1890s and the 1900s.

Those foundations were laid only because the Japanese did not act according to what have today become the prescriptions of enlightened development strategy: they put the bulk of the savings the Japanese economy was capable of making into industrial investment, not into agriculture. Moreover a lot of the industrial projects backed by government money at that time would certainly never have got off the ground if they had been judged by the sort of cost–benefit project appraisal methods used today. It took the Japanese a long time to learn to use their first steel plant in a way that made it anything like profitable by international standards. But industrialization was their goal and costly learning was the only way of getting there. And in the end it paid off. It was not, perhaps, the pay-off which the designers of the strategy intended. They wanted to make *Japan* strong and powerful, a force to make the nations tremble. They succeeded only in making *the Japanese* comfortably well-off. Although Shinohata people were solidly behind the original intentions, in retrospect they seem to prefer the actual outcome.

But it took a long time – some eighty or ninety years – from the laying of those foundations, and the squeezing of the farmers that made it possible, to the pay-off in the 1960s and 1970s. I believe that the reason why so-called development theory today is in such an emotion-laden mess, the reason why the rate of slogan-obsolescence among its practitioners seems to be constantly accelerating ('take-off to sustained growth', 'balanced social and economic development', 'employment-oriented strategy', 'redistribution with growth', 'poverty-focused planning', 'basic needs strategy', etc., following, one after the other, with bewildering rapidity), is that people cannot – or believe they cannot – afford to wait. The traditional growth strategy with a heavy emphasis on industrialization has, we are told, 'failed'. Failed in what? Failed to transform agrarian Sri Lanka or Ghana into an affluent industrial state in fifteen years? Failed, in the absence of industrialization, to raise the living standards of the Sri Lankan or Ghanaian peasants? The perception of failure seems chiefly to be a function of the unrealism of the original expectations. What is not entirely certain is whether the disappointed expectations are only those of the people who make the running in the International Development Conference Community, people whose enthusiasm for international equality is stronger than their sense of history, or whether there is also a strong sense of frustrated expectations among the poor of the developing countries themselves.

There are some good reasons why the poor in developing countries should feel such frustration, why they should be unwilling to wait as patiently for the millennium as the people of Shinohata waited. Nowadays political leaders in most countries (much less so in countries animated by a strong nationalistic drive like China) claim that the purpose of development *is* popular welfare rather than national strength. They make promises. Unlike the authoritarian leaders of an earlier Japan when the world was younger and still allowed for the possibility of benevolent autocracies, they *need* to make promises to stay in power. Another difference is that better communications, the shrinking of the globe, make life-styles - and income levels - in the modern sectors of the developing countries much more like those of the rich countries than they used to be. Accra is much more like London today than Tokyo was like New York or Paris in 1900. And so internal disparities within the developing countries - between the alien life-styles of the modern sector rich and the peasant poor - become that much more glaring, and glaringly at variance with the rhetoric of equality and socialism which many of the developing countries today profess.

So there are *some* good reasons for thinking that Japan's history is not going to repeat itself very closely elsewhere, and that it is not politically realistic to expect the peasant masses of the Third World (except perhaps the Chinese peasant masses) to wait as long for the fruits of 'development' as the Japanese have waited. What I am not certain about, however, is how far the now widespread belief that 'traditional growth strategies' are 'bankrupt' and 'have failed' is a reasoned response to these political realities, how far it springs instead from the impatience of idealistic development theorists in the rich world who know about compound interest rates in principle, but could never accept intuitively how long the long haul of industrialization has to be.

Whatever the reasons, the doctrines of 'poverty-focused planning' and a 'basic needs approach' nowadays dominate the development field. The emphasis is on immediate improvements in diets and standards of health care, the provision of clean water, decent housing and basic schooling for all. Suppose that this had been the dominant doctrine in Japan in the later nineteenth century. It is a subject that I have often speculated on; most specifically in print some ten years ago when I tried to work out what would have happened if the postwar land reform had been carried out in the 1880s.[1] For a variety of reasons, having to do with the way new technology spread, the pattern of rural marketing organization, the sources of investment funds, the relations between political stability and the propensity to invest etc., I concluded that a land reform at any time after 1920 would probably have hastened the rate of growth; a land reform - and a shift to more egalitarian patterns of consumption - before 1900 would very probably have slowed it. Quite probably, too, to come back to 'basic needs strategies', massive state expenditure on health, water and education, or shorter hours and better safety standards in factories, would have slowed the rate of capital accumulation. The people of Shinohata might only be getting to their first black-and-white TV sets today, rather than being on the second generation in colour.

And would that have been a bad thing? I just do not know. What the jargon calls intergenerational distribution problems are among the most intractable problems of social policy. I know, personally, the present generation of Shinohata people. As I write this the Yamamoto grandson who is staying with us here in England has just come home from the expensive English Language School in Brighton which, thanks to the non-consumption of the generations of the 1870s and 1900s, his policeman father can now afford to send him to. It is real flesh-and-blood friends of mine whom I would be wishing poorer if I said that the more egalitarian growth strategy would have been better, and shadowy great-grandfather figures of the past whom I would be wishing a little extra comfort - which one imagines (for their presumed degree of subjective frustration is one element in one's judgement of others' situations) they probably would not in any case have seen themselves as entitled to expect. It is not surprising that my instinct is to decide in favour of the former and to conclude that Japan made the right choice.

And I suspect the advocates of a 'basic needs strategy' today judge by the same criteria; they too weight the balance in favour of the flesh-and-blood people they know, the people with yaws and bilharzia they see in the Third World villages today, not their shadowy competitors, the generations as yet unborn (and in spite of the fact that, with present population growth rates, the latter are likely to have worse yaws and worse bilharzia if the rate of capital accumulation is not increased).

And in fact, I suppose, nobody ever does choose otherwise and vote against the present generation and in favour of the insubstantial wraiths of the future, as long as they are thinking in the individual utility terms of welfare economics. When political leaders do give their vote to the unborn generations in effect, it is not primarily in individual welfare terms that the choice is made. They see themselves, rather, as servants of some abstract entity, as working for the Nation, or for History. The people of Shinohata know all about politicians who think like that. On the whole they have seen enough of them, and prefer their more welfare-oriented and vote-oriented successors who hold power today. It is one of the ironies of history, though, that they owe their colour television sets as much to the former as to the latter.

NOTES

1. See 'Land Reform and Japan's Economic Development: a Reactionary Thesis', in T. Shanin (ed.), *Peasants and Peasant Societies* (Penguin Modern Sociology Readings), Harmondsworth, 1971, pp. 377–58 [Chapter 3 in this book]. Also *Land Reform in Japan,* London, OUP, 1958.

PART III

But Culture Does Matter, Too

14. Individualism: its growth and future*

In my last lecture I spoke of a market-as-second-best view typically held by British social democrats - the view that on most of [the issues discussed] the community option was in principle to be preferred to the individualistic one, but the price ... - in bureaucracy and inefficiency - was just too high. I distinguished between that and what I called the Thatcherite position which is that on most of these issues the individualistic option is intrinsically preferable.

THE ECONOMIC DETERMINISM STORY

But the point I wish to make here is that on all the issues I have listed we do, in our modern societies, see ourselves as having real choices, often painful choices, between individualistic and collectivistic solutions. They are issues we can get passionate about, and they are issues on which elections can be won or lost. But there is a view that, although we may seem to have a free choice, the outcomes of all these debates are in fact determined; the level of individualism in a society, the level of self-seeking, emotional ungroupishness, self-reliance or antiauthoritarianism - to use the sub-categories of individualism which I introduced in my previous lecture - are in fact given by history.

The argument is a little more specific than the general philosophical arguments for determinism and the nature of the illusion of free will. That argument is about sequential causation - the thesis that every event has a set of ascertainable causes preceding it in time. The historians' argument about the rise of individualism involves a different set of basic principles - what one might call system compatibility. It is an argument about what institutions - what recurring patterns of rule-bound behaviour - can readily coexist with what other institutions, given two major constraints. The first is the constraint

* Extracted from *Will The 21st Century Be The Age of Individualism?*, Tokyo: Simul, 1990, pp. 43-82. Originally from the second of three Ishizaka Lectures given in Tokyo in 1989. The final section on 'who admires whom' makes one realize how long a decade can be. Perhaps the former PM Nakasone's discussion of the growth of *kenbei kanjō* (dislike of America) in the January 2000 issue of *Chūō Kōron* provides a basis for reflection of what the next decade might bring.

of logical compatibility: the 'ought' rules - the 'thou shalt do this' rules - of one institution should not contradict the 'ought' rules of another.

Think of the trouble it caused in China - and recently again still causes - to have on the one hand a family system based on an ethic of filial piety - an emphasis on the duty of honouring one's parents as exceeding any other duty and, on the other hand, a political system in which every citizen supposedly had an obligation to denounce the political misdemeanours of every other citizen, no matter how closely related by kinship ties they might be. The clear intention of China's rulers, in the 1950s and 1960s, was to restore compatibility of the family and political systems by changing the family system. That proved extremely difficult and in the late 1970s and 1980s the political system was changed instead. It looks, since the Tiananmen Square incident, as if the pendulum has, however temporarily, swung back the other way.

The other constraint is the straining in the human mind, or in the human heart, for emotional as well as logical consistency. People feel uncomfortable - what the psychologist, Festinger, labelled 'cognitive dissonance' is set up[1] - if they are expected to act according to one set of values in one sphere and a different set in another.

The assumption of some such constraint was made by all those people on Japan's Ad Hoc Education Commission who argued that, if Japan was to have innovative and creative Nobel-prize-winning scientists, it had to have a school system and an occupational system which encouraged individual self-assertion. People could not be expected to be conformists at school and at home - taking care not to think differently from everybody else - and suddenly non-conformist in their laboratories, breaking through established and accepted paradigms to carry science forward.

So what, on the basis of these assumptions - that institutions must be logically compatible and that human beings seek to avoid cognitive dissonance - do historians have to say about the rise of individualism? Predominantly that it was caused by economic change, and that that economic change was very largely a function of technological change.

[An example is to be found in] a very fine study written in 1930 by the Belgian historian Mark Bloch[2] [which details the processes by which in eighteenth-century France the development of educational techniques led to the end of communal grazing and private property enclosures.] ...

The writings of historians and sociologists abound with attempts to spell out this social transition in general terms. From status to contract, from mechanical to organic solidarity, from *gemeinschaft* to *gesellshaft*, traditional versus modern society. [Take for] example Riesman's formulation[3] of the last dichotomy ... [Societies in which people have] little scope - or expectation of scope - to make conscious choices and shape [their] own destiny, [are transformed by] technological innovation; innovation partly in material technology, partly in social - organizational - technology. For example, the growth of stable government and the establishment of law and order, comes partly from improved methods of warfare, better roads, better grain storage, and partly from better organization - rules of order for conducting business at meetings, systems of audit, standardization of weights and measures and other inventions.

[But the crucial factor in the expansion of individual choice is the rise in productivity due to innovations in agriculture and crafts. The restraints on land ownership] ... guild restrictions, traditional status obligations which do not allow efficient use of new technology finally give way. They may be commuted into rents. More of total production enters into the market, cash economy. Hence, again, more scope to innovate, to make choices.

Growth also means more exchange over wider areas. More goods move. People move with them. They see ways of life different from those to which they are accustomed, yet close enough that they can imagine themselves adopting them. They begin to develop what Lerner calls empathy,[4] that capacity for imagining oneself as an occupant of other roles which is a precondition for seeing oneself as capable of, as offered opportunities for, making choices.

The development of literacy expands the capacity for empathy: it promotes objective self-awareness; it makes role models available from other places. It makes them available from other times, too, when the growth of literacy is accompanied by the growth of a curious, reflective leisure class ...

The story is familiar and highly plausible. Individualism developed pre-eminently in societies in which there were (a) mobility, (b) literacy, and (c) a large segment of the population producing, in family enterprises, for fluctuating markets which required continuous management decisions, acts of choice, on the part of at least one person in each family.

Veblen put it as succinctly as anyone could when he spoke of 'the system of handicraft and petty trade' producing in Britain the 'animus of democratic equity and non-interference, self-help and local autonomy' which slowly changed British monarchy and oligarchy into democracy.[5]

THE MORAL INNOVATION STORY

That is what one might call the economic determinism story - or even the technological determinism story - and it is still the favourite story among social scientists. The notion pithily expressed by Marx in the phrase 'existence determines consciousness' has much persuasive power. There are, however, two other alternative stories; the moral innovation story and the national character story.

The moral innovation story in effect reverses Marx's dictum: 'Consciousness determines existence.' It is the stance often adopted by those writing in the comparative religion tradition. There are great prophetic religious innovators - or perhaps, innovative movements of thought which are then crystallized in the teachings of a charismatic religious figure in the way the ideas of Essenes come to be embodied in and known to history as the teachings of Christ. These charismatic leaders change the world by giving men and women new conceptions of themselves.

To choose one representative author again, Louis Dumont's account of the rise of individualism in the West is rather like that.[6] [He attributes a large role to Christianity-promoting individualism in the Roman Empire, losing it in the Middle Ages, and recovering its original impetus with the Reformation when individualism became] this-worldly, not other-worldly as it had been hitherto; the basis for an operative practical morality, very much as Max Weber described it in his famous essay on *Protestantism and the Spirit of Capitalism.*

Not many of those who tell the moral innovation story offer it as an exclusive account of social change.... And likewise, few of those who tell the economic or technological determinism story would deny the importance of crystallizing ideas. Without the separation of the concepts of state and civil society, and the idea of the social contract and the doctrines of human rights, the English and American and French Revolutions would never have been what they were, nor would the pattern of individualistic capitalism have developed in quite the same way.

And, without the doctrines of monetarist economics and the philosophical elaborations of von Hayek and Milton Friedman it is doubtful whether the developments of the last decade, the movement towards greater individualism which I discussed in my last lecture, would have been quite what they were. In practice, in other words, the difference between the economic determinist story and the moral innovator story usually becomes a difference in emphasis, a difference in the evaluation of the relative importance of different events in a causal chain.

THE NATIONAL CHARACTER STORY

But the national character story is somewhat different. This suggests that different societies have different inherent characteristics, or, more explicitly, that different populations have different personality tendencies. It suggests, further, that these are of a relatively enduring kind, and that they play a big part in shaping both the institutions and the idiosyncratic behaviour of what remain today very different societies in spite of having very similar economic organization and social institutions, using similar technology, having similar laws of property, electoral systems, commercial codes, laws governing marriage and divorce, similarly structured educational systems.

This is not a view which will come as a surprise to Japanese readers, given the proliferation of works in recent years devoted to *Nihonjinron* - the analysis of what it is to be a Japanese. Most such works take it for granted that the difference between Japan and Europe as feudal societies was as great as, and in the same dimensions as, the differences which are discernible today. And there is evidence for the view. As frequently observed - by Marc Bloch, for instance[7] - European feudalism was already much more individualistic. The relationship between lord and vassal was much more overtly contractual.

A German or a British knight could cheerfully hold land in fief from two lords and owe separate, limited, and not usually conflicting, obligations under each arrangement: a Japanese *samurai* held an unlimited and unilateral obligation to a single lord. The notion of individual rights established by a contract freely entered by individual choice was already well established in Europe's feudal society: it was alien to Japan's. What we see here are differences in enduring national traditions.

Indeed, Alan Macfarlane sees similar differences in national traditions *within* European feudalism. His book on the origins of English individualism denies that it was a fifteenth- or sixteenth-century product of the Renaissance and Reformation, and the erosion of the bonds of peasant community by the growth of markets and the use of money. England in 1250 was already a much more individualistic society than the rest of Europe; there were developed markets for land and labour, considerable mobility, a distinction between farm and family, rational accounting. The Englishman stood alone. 'Symbolized and shaped by his ego-centered kinship system he stood in the centre of his world.'[8]

And in the degree to which their modern capitalism is based on individualistic assumptions, the Englishman, or rather Englishmen and Americans, do still rather stand alone, with Japan at the most extremely differentiated opposite pole. Take, for example, the extent to which those who own a majority block of shares in a company expect to exercise control over it. The American and the British view - recently highlighted in Japan by the arrival of Mr Boone Pickens as a holder of Koito's shares - is that the rights of ownership should be unconstrained. The owner of a company should be able to sell it to someone else as easily as he can sell a racehorse or a house. The Japanese view - or at least the view dominant in Japan - is that a company is primarily a community of people, and its owners ought to accept the obligation to act in the best interests of those people, not solely in their own self-interest.

And one behavioural symptom of the difference is that, although there are similar stock markets and similar take-over rules in all four countries, hostile take-overs occur frequently in individualistic Britain and America, a good deal less frequently in Germany and Italy, and almost never in Japan.

INDIVIDUALISM AND MODERNITY: THE REALM OF IDEAS

Differences between Japan and European countries which can be reasonably interpreted in an individual versus group dimension are so obvious that it is not surprising that individualism has been a key term in Japanese debates over the last century between 'modernizers' and 'national essence' conservatives. On the one side were those who argued that progress required Japan not only to take over the technology and the major functional social institutions of the West, but also to undergo a similar 'Westernizing' transformation of values. On the other were those who argued that it was essential to preserve the Japaneseness of Japan, not only for reasons of identity and pride, but because Japanese values were just intrinsically superior. [The 'preservers' reached their apotheosis in the late 1930s: the 'modernizers' in the late 1940s: now a large proportion of the authors of the extensive *Nihonjinron* literature on the Japanese national character see its anti-individualistic stress on harmony as a dominant characteristic and] are inclined to think that Japan is not really the worse off for that [characteristic], particularly now that its economic performance excites unconcealed American envy, and even about Japanese society, there are Americans prepared to write books with titles like *Japan as Number One*.[9]

DEFINING JAPANESE DISTINCTIVENESS

But … what *are* the differences between the Japanese modal social character and that of, say, the United States, with respect to individualism. Let us try to get behind some of the stereotypes of groupishness common in the West, pieced together from images of employees singing the company song and doing physical jerks every morning, or of motley mixed-age groups of tourists in a foreign airport trotting behind a flag-carrying tour leader.

One interesting contribution … from a younger Japanese professor of management, Mito, a member of the liberated postwar generation. He describes how:

> Japanese intellectuals, that is to say those who consider themselves to have some

> knowledge of Western scholarship and culture, usually claim and are conceded by others, to have some understanding of, and to practice, individualism. But I have long been doubtful. I had observed how nearly all the Japanese professor intellectuals I know never offered an opinion without first gauging its effects on others, would quite shamelessly say different things to different people. 'Some individualism! Some democracy!' I had rather scornfully thought, and took a certain pride in thinking that I could do a little better than that myself.[10]

But when he went to study English at a language school in an English seaside town, he began to have second thoughts. He went sightseeing with a mixed group of German and Icelandic students and as they were uninhibitedly expressing their own opinions and wishes, he found himself all too naturally playing the mediator role, completely suppressing his own views and wishes - and automatically assuming that another Japanese present would do the same - in order to harmonize the conflicting individualisms of the others. [He is led to reflect on the linguistic manifestations of this difference: the uses of 'yes', '*hai*' and '*ee*'; the invariate 'I' and 'you' versus personal pronouns varying with the person spoken to; the frequent use by the other students of the word 'because', unyielding assertions of being in the right.]

What does all this mean in terms of behaviour? Stronger attachments to the family; a stronger identification of school-children with the classroom group, a stronger *aisha-seishin* - love of company - on the part of employees. In fact a rather different basic model of the employment relation - what one might call a career-contract model involving the open-ended merging of the individual in the group, in contrast to the job-contract model [of] Britain and America, ... less like a marriage and more like a passing affair.

So much for the identification/sense of belonging part of groupishness. But groups have structures, statuses which can be, more or less, hierarchically ranked, normative rules which govern behaviour. [Cf. Johnson and Ouchi's interesting study of differences in group structure and organizational behaviour between Japanese and American firms in California.[11]]

In the Japanese companies there was more flow of information upwards from below: the top man is not an issuer of orders, but a facilitator of decisions - by general consensus. There is a sensitive concern for the personal welfare of all members of the group. Americans take the functional meaning of differences in rank more seriously: the top man with his top pay has got to take the top burden of decision-making: he does not expect his subordinates to work out their differences into compromises first.

'Americans will disagree with their bosses rarely but violently; the Japanese often, but politely'[12] - because no particular emotional strain is attached to frank disagreement with a superior. Americans are potential contestants with their bosses, the fundamental deference of Japanese to *their* bosses can be taken for granted.

HIERARCHY AND SOLIDARITY; DEFERENCE AND GROUPISHNESS

As compared with Americans, that is to say, Japanese are not only more identified with their company, they are also more deferential to their superiors. Which is the more important characteristic? How do the two relate?

Hierarchy and group solidarity are never easy to disentangle. Note, for example, that polite language in Japan, very much like the use of *vous* or *Lei* or *Sie* as opposed to *tu* or *du* … is used in both dimensions … - to show respect to a status superior … or at the beginning of an acquaintance with a status equal…. Familiar forms can be used, as in Europe today (or among seventeenth-century Quakers) as a means of asserting an egalitarian, authority-rejecting attitude to life in general.

The ['modernizer'] Japanese social scientists … of the postwar enlightenment have generally had no doubts about the relative roles of hierarchy and group solidarity in Japan. Lack of individualism they identify with lack of rights. Rights are what subordinates have progressively, throughout Western history, wrested from their superiors by collective action: it is hierarchy which is the prime enemy of Japanese individualism. Or, put another way: it is contract which holds together societies of free individuals. Japanese society is characterized by an extreme looseness of the notion of contract. Modernization is a process of the shift from status to contract. The looseness of contract is a reflection of the continuing, unmodernized strength of the status principle.

So it is that when older Japanese social scientists pick out a single key principle for the characterization of what differentiates Japan from other industrial societies, it is usually something which stresses hierarchy, authority, status. Professor Nakane's 'vertical society',[13] Professor Doi's stress on *amae*[14] are examples. Younger writers are more likely to take as their starting question not, as their seniors did, 'What's wrong with Japan?' but 'What's so good about Japan? Why is it so successful?' Hence, (for groupism does not have such a bad international press as authoritarianism) they are more likely to put the emphasis on lateral ties. Professor Hamaguchi's 'contextualism' is an example.[15]

But is 'authoritarianism' the right word? Even the older writers - Professor Kawashima, for example, who used the term 'patriarchalism' - did not seem to be saying the typical Japanese exploitative superior was authoritarian in the way the pre-war Germany was described by writers like Erich Fromm as authoritarian.[16] There is a paradox here. It is precisely because the principle of hierarchy is so well respected in Japan that superiors do not *have* to behave in an authoritarian way…

In some … societies authority can only be maintained by stern, unapproachable aloofness, perhaps only by people who have appropriately commanding personalities. This is much less the case in Japan - which is one reason why there can be a very high seniority element in promotions ...

[But] one should not assume that hierarchy is an essential precondition for lateral group solidarity in Japan: more egalitarian and equally solidary groups are also found ... Many producers guilds and village communities have long operated effectively with systems of rotating or elected leaders ... Japan of the late Tokugawa period was far from deficient in rebellious reformers who were disloyal to their feudal lord in pursuit of what they saw as the greater duty of their loyalty to the fief. Groupishness does seem to me to be a separate structural principle in its own right, not to be subsumed under hierarchy.

But do groupishness and deference exhaust the elements in the differences between Japan and other countries? ... It seems to me that affection, affectivity to be more pompous, is an important and neglected aspect of the matter. One might see a general Japanese propensity to personalize, and to introduce affect into, social relations, as being in contrast with the determination of, say, Englishmen, to keep a lot of specific functional relations on an impersonal, affectively-neutral basis.

The pattern of trading relations between major manufacturing firms and their sub-contractors (between *parent* firms - *oya kigyo* is the telling Japanese phrase, though no ownership ties are implied - and their *shitauke* suppliers) seems often, in Japan to be more like a personal than what is thought of in the West as a business relationship - much more a matter involving social contacts and give-and-take long-term reciprocity....

These different dimensions of difference ... correspond, at least partially, to the different dimensions of individualism which I offered in my first lecture. The acceptance of hierarchy corresponds with my first type - anti-authoritarianism and its particular manifestation, anti-statism....

As for the second type of individualism, self-reliance, the willingness to tie up one's future in a lifelong employment contract ... stands in direct contrast. My third definition of individualism - what I called 'emotional ungroupishness' contrasts with the high affectivity-loading of personal relations ... And as for self-seeking, the fourth definition, although one can never prove these quantitative assertions, one could cite endless incidents to show that the balance between individual self-enrichment and group loyalty tilts more towards the latter in Japan.

COMPATIBLE OR CONFLICTING STORIES?

To point to the enduring nature of character differences between national groups is not necessarily to say that the economic determinism story is false. It may just be that modal social characters are not so responsive in the short term as many of the theories discussed earlier suggest. But the long term can be very long indeed.

Macfarlane's guess about the English, for instance, follows Montesquieu whom he thinks was right in speculating that the British derived their individualistic political system, their land and inheritance laws from the Germanic tribes as Tacitus described them.[17] And as for what made the *Germans* different, at that point even Marx who had an explanation for everything gave up and ranked the Germanic, along with the Asiatic mode of production and that of classical antiquity, as just one of three undetermined pre-feudal alternatives.

There is, of course, still no clear disproof of what our nineteenth-century ancestors would have taken as axiomatic - namely that national character is 'in the blood'. There is nothing inherently implausible in the idea that differences in gene pools and the dominance of different temperamental traits contribute to national differences, even if only racists take much comfort from the thought.

But since we know that almost any human genotype can adapt to almost any human culture it is brought up in from infancy, genetic determination may not explain very much of the variance - certainly not among populations as racially mixed as European ones, though it may have more relevance to differences between more clearly racially differentiated populations.

But suppose that the modified economic determinist view is basically right - changes in economic structure do cause change in modal social character, but only very slowly. That offers an alternative to the 'in the blood' explanation of the enduring differences between Japan and the West - what may be called the [cultural lag aspect and the cultural reinvention aspect of the late development explanation. As a result of the late nineteenth-century changes in the economy,] structures did begin to change; 1910 Japanese were a good deal more individualistic than 1810 Japanese, but the trend did not last. The groupishness and deference and affectivity appropriate to a feudal society, though beginning to be eroded during the competitive interlude, were still there to be creatively reinstitutionalized in the modern corporation - to which they were, and remain, eminently appropriate. The question, then – a question to be taken up in the last lecture – is whether the corporate capitalism which the West now shares with Japan will lead to the decline of individualism in the West, too.

A FOURTH STORY: THE CULTURAL DIFFUSION STORY

I made something like the last point about late development 30 years ago, but ended with the question: is it possible, as far as individualism is concerned, that what the economic infrastructure cannot do by repeating the [slow, evolutionary] historical processes of Europe, the demonstration effect might do instead? Will Western values just be imported? Can they alter daily life and basic ethical principles as they have undoubtedly altered the intellectual and artistic life of high culture?[18]

The underlying hypothesis ... assumes that the characteristics of population groups of superior power and prestige tend to be admired by, and imitated by, population groups of lesser power and prestige. And no one going to Japan for the first time in 1950, as I did, would have any doubt [who admired whom ...]

Now I have become more sceptical. There is no longer in Japan the same universal admiration for the American way of life. The 'Japan that can say no' has some very harsh things to say about the United States. And the period of American cultural/ideological dominance - like the period of early competitive small-firm capitalism at the beginning of the century - was just too short to have lasting effects ...

Certainly, such clues as one can gather from attitude surveys do not indicate any clear rise in individualism.[19] ... And yet, today, in 1989, 'internationalization' is a word on everyone's lips. Popular journalism is constantly discovering signs of a rapid crumbling of the traditional order. It seems to me, however, that in the individualism dimension the signs are distinctly mixed. Hierarchy seems if anything reinforced in Japan as the trade unions seem increasingly unable to strike for higher wages. But on the other hand a lot of voters did abandon their established hierarchical attachments to LDP politicians in the elections of the summer 1989.

As for self-reliance, there is reportedly a growth in self-reliant self-employment; more labour mobility, more people prepared to look outside the big organizations for a livelihood. Emotional self-sufficiency? The drier, *shiraketa,* youth are supposed to be distinctly self-sufficient....

Japan is changing, but so is the rest of the industrial world and it is the implication of those changes for individualism that I want to consider in my last lecture.

NOTES

1. L. Festinger, *A Theory of Cognitive Dissonance,* Stanford, Stanford UP, 1957.
2. 'La lutte pour lindividualisme agraire dans la France du XVIII siecle', *Annales d'histoire economique et sociale,* 1930, translated as *La fine della comunita e la nastier dell'individualism agrario,* Milano, Jaca Book, 1979. References here are to the Italian edition.
3. David Riesman with Nathan Glazer and Reuel Denny, *The Lonely Crowd: A Study of the Changing American Character,* New Haven, Conn., Yale University Press, 1950.
4. D. Lerner, *The Passing of Traditional Society: Modernizing the Middle East,* Glencoe, Illinois, Free Press, 1958.

5. T. Veblen, *Imperial Germany and the Industrial Revolution,* New York, Viking, 1939, pp. 100–101.
6. Louis Dumont, *From Mandeville to Marx: the Genesis and Triumph of Economic Ideology,* Chicago, Chicago University Press, 1977.
7. Marc Bloch, *Feudal Society,* Chicago, University of Chicago Press, 1961.
8. A. Macfarlane, *The Origins of English Individualism,* Cambridge, Cambridge University Press, 1978.
9. Ezra Vogel, *Japan as Number One*, Cambridge, Harvard University Press and Bellknap, 1979.
10. T. Mito, *Kō to Shi*, Miraisha, 1976, p. 81.
11. R.T. Johnson and W.G. Ouchi, 'Made in America (under Japanese management)', *Harvard Business Review*, Sept.-Oct. 1974.
12. *Ibid.*, p. 63.
13. C. Nakane, *Japanese Society*, Berkeley, University of California Press, 1970.
14. T. Doi, *The Anatomy of Dependence*, Tokyo and New York, Kodansha International, 1973.
15. *'Kanjinshugi'*. See E. Hamaguchi, 'Nihon bummei no kihonteki seikaku', in *Hikaku Bummei*, Vol. 2, 1986.
16. E. Fromm, *Fear of Freedom*, New York, Holt, Rinehart and Winston, 1941.
17. *Op. cit.*, p. 170.
18. *City Life in Japan*, London, Routledge, Kegan Paul and Berkeley, University of California Press, 1958. [See Chapter 1 of this volume.]
19. Tokei Suri Kenkyujo, *Kokuminsei no kenkyu: daihakkai zenkoku chosa. (A study of national character; The 8th nation-wide survey)*, November 1989.

15. Authority, hierarchy and community*

HOW TO EXPLAIN: HISTORY, IDEAS, TRADITIONS

The reader should have a fairly good idea, by now, of the differences in authority styles that we are talking about. I think it likely that he will agree that: (a) the differences fit in with, seem like logical consequences of, the difference between the purely contractualist 'Company Law' model firm and the 'Community' model firm as set out in Chapter 3; and (b) it is not intuitively surprising that the Japanese Community type should have superior competitive power.

Once again one has to ask how much of the difference is 'national character' - genes which nobody can do much about, or culture shaped by institutions which change slowly only over generations - and how much is to be attributed to contemporary sustaining institutions? Let us begin with the former, with culture in fact, because there is nothing very useful I can say about genes. [Figure 15.1] makes clear the implicit framework of explanation I'm using. The 'cultural factors' are, in effect, the precipitate of history, the flows of causal influence shown by the A arrows.

The pattern of quiet authority, unassertive leadership and acceptance of hierarchy has by no means always been the dominant pattern in Japan. In the period of turbulent feudalism from the eleventh to the end of the sixteenth century, the military rulers of Japan - or of their respective parts of it - were rather different men, even if they were not exactly as they appear in the historical fiction which is still favourite reading for Japanese managers. Their style of leadership - dominant, awe-inspiring, thrusting and predatory - was the kind of leadership equally characteristic of feudal Europe, though in Japan too, as in Europe, most admired when combined with warm personal concern for the loyal followers. But between modern Japan and that period of

* Extracted from *Taking Japan Seriously: A Confucian Perspective on Leading Economic Issues*, Stanford: Stanford University Press, 1986, Chapter 5, pp. 91-9. As part of an attempt to sort out differences in authority relations in Japan and Britain, and to compare them with the status/contract dichotomy, I try to unbundle the notion of 'cultural factors'. In the first paragraph, the terms Company Law firm and Community firm contrast between firms where 'managerial agents of shareholder principals buy and sell their labour' [nowadays 'human resources]-type of firm, and 'managers as elders of employee community work to keep shareholders happy much as they treat other outsiders like their suppliers'-type.

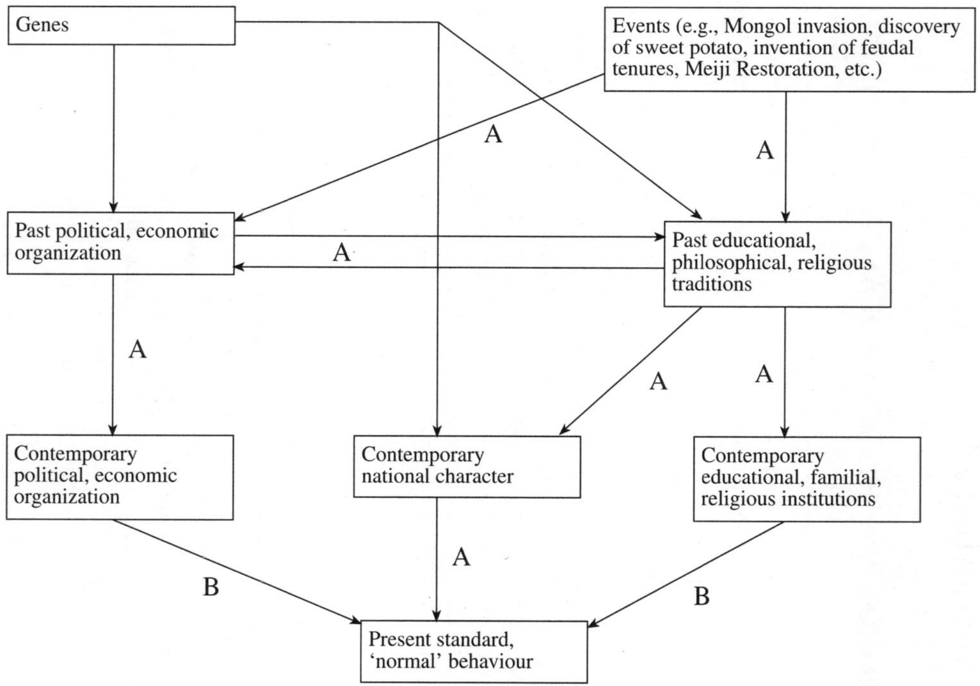

Figure 15.1 Culture and causal influences

uncentralized anarchic feudalism intervened the Tokugawa period - two-and-a-half centuries of gentling peace. It was a period which saw a steady growth of bureaucracy in the classical rationalizing manner which so fascinated Max Weber: a gradual formalization of career patterns, careful division of responsibility, recording of precedents, filing of archives and so on. The major offices of state remained hereditary, but the actual exercise of power - largely confined to keeping law and order and collecting taxes - was in the hands of the increasingly precedent-bound, rule-bound bureaucracy.

That experience must surely have given the Japanese the basis for a very different paradigm of authority from that which history has given the British. Britain, too, saw the end of its civil wars in the seventeenth century. But Britain substituted for martial warfare the verbal warfare of politics. Politics has been the sphere *par excellence* in which we have preserved the styles of leadership and domination appropriate to an aristocratic military society. Politics has kept alive our admiration above all for strength in leadership - for bulldogs and iron ladies - while at the same time keeping alive our distrust of all those who exercise authority. Britons have become accustomed to hearing those in authority continuously denounced by their rivals for their predatory intentions or their incompetence or both, if never before so frequently and so intimately as in this television age. Tokugawa Japan, by contrast, was an administered society with no open politics. Interest conflicts were largely resolved by intrigue, cabals, persuasion and periodically cleansed corruption. The appearance of absolutism was preserved. As in the Austria described in Musil's *Man Without Qualities,* the illusion was maintained that all decisions represented the will of the appropriate competent authority, and only occasionally and desperately was there anyone to challenge the official doctrine that that will was always exercised with benevolence.

To be sure, those challenges rose to a crescendo in the middle of the nineteenth century, and the Meiji Restoration ushered in an era of Western politics, Western-style public denunciation of authority. But for the whole period since, the dominant pattern has been of a quasi-permanent opposition group denouncing - from outside - the authority of a quasi-permanent group of insiders which possesses a superior claim in legitimacy. The British pattern - leaders of equal stature, equal claims to legitimacy, denouncing *each other's* predatory abuse of authority - has never been established. 'Benevolence', a notion appropriate only to authorities whose legitimacy does not depend wholly on elections, is still a relevant concept.

THE ROLE OF IDEAS

And, to return to the Tokugawa period, there is some basis for the view that, as military regimes in peasant societies go, there actually *was* a little more benevolence about than is common. If so, then some credit must be given to the Confucianism which, predominantly in the interpretation given by the Sung scholars of China, became the dominant ideology of Tokugawa Japan and the core of the educational system which it gradually created. In a Western society which starts from a jaundiced, 'original-sin', view of human nature, Acton's assessment of the inevitable corruption of power seems naturally to follow. As a system of power-control, democracy becomes the only possible form of government, though the worst, because government anyway brings out the worst in men.

By contrast, in a society which starts from the premise of original virtue, as Confucian societies did, it is possible for things to be different, especially since Confucian writings devote not as much time, it is true, but some time, to underlining the duties of benevolence in rulers as well as the duties of obedient loyalty in subordinates. They promise - though naturally emperors and shoguns did not dwell on the fact - that a ruler who fails in benevolence will very properly be overthrown by popular revolt, for if the people are so oppressed that they rise in rebellion then this will be proof that the mandate of heaven has been withdrawn. The word usually translated as benevolence, of course, does not mean welfare paternalism, but rather a general sense of responsibility for others and for the social order, an abstention from greed, concern for the interests and dignity of subjects, a concern for justice, tempered with the optimistic faith which puts more reliance on the judicious use of rewards than on punishments.

Two things follow from the dominance of such an ideology in a society, especially if it is embodied in texts which form the mainstay of that society's educational system. First, with all due respect to the human capacity for hypocrisy and to the duty of sociologists to be cynical, some people *must* be induced by internalized norms of conscience to be more responsible in the exercise of power than they otherwise would be. Second, given the expectation on the part of subordinates of the *possibility* of power being exercised with benevolence, benevolence actually becomes an efficient strategy for the retention of power. In such a society, a little benevolence can go a long way to evoke trust, much further than in a society where expectations are lower and suspicion of power more deeply ingrained. One can see this revealed in the patterns of revolt. For all that it was a gentler society than, say, feudal Iran or feudal Ethiopia, or feudal Britain, Tokugawa Japan was still a long way from being a model Confucian society. Authority was sometimes blatantly predatory. Some feudal lords were grasping and rapacious, their tax exactions harsh. And the peasants frequently rebelled. But the rebellions were always protest rebellions, based on the Confucian premise that rulers could be and *ought to be,* benevolent, and that a desperate life-risking protest might call them back to the path of virtue – as sometimes it did if only, in most cases, through the wholly unpredictable intervention of higher authority. It is a long way from John Ball and the egalitarian assertions of his peasant revolt, with its nostalgia for the golden age when Adam delved and Eve span and no one was set up in authority over his fellows, and with its view of political authority as mere property and of all property as theft.

In modern industry this difference in backgrounds counts. A Japanese manager finds that a little 'benevolence' goes a long way. Trust his subordinates and they may well trust him. A British manager has to go further, to overcome a suspicion of authority in general, which is often reinforced by class antagonism and sometimes, even, by John-Ball-like utopian beliefs in the possibility of abolishing managerial authority altogether and substituting workers' control.

SUSTAINING INSTITUTIONS: COMPETENCE

So much for some of the historical differences which may explain the different bases of authority in the two societies. More interesting are the contemporary factors – the B arrows in Figure 15.1 – features of the organization of the firms themselves, and of the society which surrounds them, which serve to sustain authority patterns of such a different cast in Britain and Japan.

So far we have managed to conduct the discussion without making a distinction of some importance. It is a distinction between what one would be tempted in Britain to call intra-class and inter-class authority patterns. It is a distinction which really applies only to what I shall henceforth call 'bureaucratic organizations', of which examples are BP, the police, the civil service, ICI, universities, the armed forces in Britain, and practically any medium-large business firm as well as all public-sector organizations in Japan. The 'bureaucratic organization' is a sub-species of – or, if you like, a more 'evolved' form of – the 'organization-oriented type' defined in Chapter 2. For our purposes (and we may ignore most of the billions of scholarly words expended on 'bureaucracy' since Max Weber discussed it) its defining characteristics are:

1. They get employees young, for careers.
2. Career tracks are fairly predictable; certain rules define the 'hedges' on either side of each track: the best and the least you can look forward to. These usually involve age constraints: e.g. the minimum age for Under-Secretary is 38; managers get appointed to the board between the ages of 51 and 53, etc.

3. Career tracks are different for different types or grades of entrance: graduate administrator; graduate technician; clerk; technician; labourer.
4. The highest career track a person can aspire to is determined by his educational qualification.
5. The exigencies of fitting a finite number of people to a wide and changing variety of jobs, puts a premium on 'generalists': generalist administrators, generalist craftsmen, whose career progression requires them frequently to change department (and *learn* a new field of expertise) in order to edge one rank higher.

So, to go back to our distinction, which applies in Japan most clearly to bureaucratic organizations, we have on the one hand authority relations between seniors and juniors on the *same* career track, and, on the other, authority relations between those on a higher and those on a lower career track, between brigadier and lieutenant, as opposed to between brigadier and corporal. Where that distinction can be made (i.e. in bureaucratic organizations which *have* notional career tracks) it is generally the case that within-career-track authority patterns are more easily sustained both in Britain and in Japan. For all I know there may still be civil-servant Principals who address Under-Secretaries as 'Sir or Madam'. Perhaps not, but even if such overt deference has faded away in the last 20 years, few senior civil servants in Britain have reason to feel that, if they are not constantly firm and vigilant, defiance of their authority might break out among their juniors at any minute. Their relation with the clerks and secretaries, however, may be more problematic, and require more positive self-assertion.

So the fact that, in Japan, not just a few grand firms like ICI and BP, but almost every firm with hundreds rather than tens of employees *is* a bureaucratic organization in the sense outlined above, helps considerably with intra-career-track relations – the 'juniors disagreeing with seniors frequently and politely' syndrome. In a business firm in Britain with an emphasis on occupational specialization and a 'best man for the job irrespective of age' ideology, the most obvious rival for a computer manager's job is the person with whom he is expected mostly closely to co-operate – the deputy computer manager. And if there are any doubts at all about the confidence the managing director puts in the computer manager, that can be a recipe for trouble. Where, on the other hand, as in the bureaucratic organization, managers are generalists who expect to spiral upwards through successive postings in different departments, and everyone knows that it is unheard of to reach the rank of Assistant Secretary, say, or – in a Japanese firm – Department Director, before the age of *x, expectations* are limited, and consequently personal defeat and frustration reduced; rivalrous competition is narrowed to a band of approximate age-mates. No junior seems to be saying 'I can do your job better than you can. Why don't you make way for me?' because the *system* makes such a pretension ridiculous.

[The essay continues with a discussion of the way on which authority relations within organizations between those on higher and those on lower career tracks are sustained by the rigorously meritocratic nature of the Japanese educational system, and the way it affects the perceptions of competence - and probably the substantive competence also - of those on higher career tracks.]

16. Industrial relations in Japan and elsewhere*

[One] part of the 'late-development effect' thesis argues that market-oriented patterns of industrial unions and industry-wide wage setting will not get established or if established will lose their importance. [This] would seem to be true (though the law can *sometimes* 'fossilize' such patterns established in the early stages and prevent their disappearance). The other part of the hypothesis – that these will give place to an enterprise union/enterprise bargaining structure – is, however, wrong, or only half true. It overlooks another 'late-development' principle: the later deliberate industrialization/modernization starts, the greater the role of the state.

[It has been much greater] in determining the *outcomes* of bargaining – in the three countries with weaker trade unions than in Britain, where the institutionalized strength of trade unions has destroyed the incomes policies of both major political parties in turn, or in Japan, where the union movement is, according to one's point of view, strong enough for the government not to have had the courage to try an incomes policy or weak enough for no such policy to have been necessary.

But state action and national-level negotiation and agitation are not everything. The bargaining process also shifts in part from the industrial to the plant or enterprise level, and in Sri Lanka and Mexico, where big firm unions can negotiate substantially higher-than-average wages, that part is the bigger part. And in so far as plant bargaining does assume greater importance, the reasons seem to be those one would expect. In a dualistic structure, the unions of the big firms, which have everything to gain by going it alone, are likely to do so. The expansion of the subject matter of bargaining (to embrace not just

* Extracted from A. Craig (ed.), *Japan: a Comparative View*, Princeton: Princeton University Press, 1979, pp. 324–70. *British Factory-Japanese Factory* developed the notion (see Chapter 10) that many of differences in the structure of corporations and industrial relations in the two countries could be ascribed to the fact that Japan was a late developer, beginning its industrialization at a point much later in world history than Britain. Thence arose the question: so are other late developers more like Japan than like Britain? Do even later developers have even more pronounced Japanese-like characteristics? Three research officers spent the best part of a year respectively in Mexico, Sri Lanka and Senegal finding out. Two of them could have produced their own books on their countries, but got involved in other things before they had finished. This paper was based on their notes and my own visits.

wages and hours but a wide range of other matters too: welfare provisions, working conditions, grievance procedures, discipline) means that agreements can be made only at the plant or enterprise level. Labour immobility makes recruitment into the firm a major concern replacing the traditional concern with regulating the numbers entering a craft to prevent any 'flooding of the market.' And in so far as there is leeway in wage bargaining by state regulation, it comes from manipulating a structure of wages and job categories specific to the organization, which can only be bargained over within the organization.

The answer to the second question about unions - whether or not they are accepted by employers as an inevitable and legitimate part of their factory's organizational structure - [is fairly clear]. No large firm manager in any of the countries sees a no-union option as open to him. Small firm owners in Mexico and Sri Lanka do see themselves as having such an option (not so easily in Senegal, where the law prescribes the election of delegates, though some may simply ignore the law). But a Mexican small-firm owner is likely to prefer to take out insurance against a genuinely militant union by inviting the local CTM official [official of the establishment union which had been part of the dominant PRI party since the 1930s] to organize his factory. And even a Ceylonese works manager who was determined not to have a union in his factory of 120 engineering workers (a determination which he said came from his bitter personal experiences as an engineer in one of the state corporations best known for being riven by the struggles of competing unions) nevertheless claimed that his workers' welfare society and its committee effectively did all the representational jobs that needed doing. Few people any more, in other words, are prepared to say flatly, 'I am running this firm, it's my job to manage, they can just take it or leave it'.

[The] *degree* to which unions are accepted, showed a wide range. In Monterey, Mexico, a union official claimed that in the 1930s employers were frightened of unions: 'despite the fact that our ideas were based on a Christian humanism. Little by little the ideology of the employers changed, thanks to the diffusion of the papal encyclicals and the influence of the unions. Now... the workers are no longer considered the "work force" but as heads of families. The company and union have gradually formed themselves into a team, and little by little, the company has acquired a disposition toward change which the union has accelerated.'

In a match company in Sri Lanka, there is a whole-factory *daily* production bonus depending on total output, and the managers happily delegate to the union the responsibility of disciplining all those who are not 'pulling their weight' - [not much more than] a revival of widespread early industrial practices of indirect hiring through labour contractors.

[Both are very different from factories where the] assumption is, on the union side, that the duty of worker solidarity vis-à-vis managers far overrides any *shared* interests workers and managers might have in, for instance, preventing theft or violence or shoddy workmanship in the factory; on the manager's side that the workers are naturally concerned to get as much money for as little work as possible and will 'get away with' anything they are allowed to get away with. This, roughly, is the situation in some of the state corporations in Sri Lanka; unions exhibit a general syndrome of militancy. ([In] the steel corporation, for instance, when one department lacked essential raw materials the union delegates insisted on their right to be idle and it took over a month before they were persuaded to agree to transfer to work in other departments.)

In part this reflects the genuineness of class feeling in Sri Lanka between the anglicized managerial class and the Sinhala-speaking underclass. Britain transmitted the most extreme form of its class divisions to Sri Lanka - the military form with its division between a hereditary officer caste and the 'other ranks' living in quite separate social worlds - and the institutional traces of that legacy are still apparent in the state corporations today. Although practices are gradually changing, managers are still referred to as 'officers' and have their own 'officers' clubs' in some corporations; disciplinary sanctions involve 'charge-sheeting' in court-martial style, and so on. Add to this the ideological input, the fact that egalitarian ideals (originating, perhaps, in another part of British traditions) are stronger in Sri Lanka than in the other countries. The demand from some unions for *flat-rate* production bonuses to replace bonuses proportional to salary may be seen as an example of this, as is the widespread resentment of the gap between workers' and managers' salaries - much more marked than in, say, Mexico, where the actual pay differentials are a good deal greater.

There are two other factors in Sri Lanka. First, competition for members between rival unions can easily lead to demonstrative 'we *really defend* our members, right or wrong' activity. Second, no union leader or worker can easily be convinced that his prosperity depends on the corporation's prosperity, because he knows that the corporation's 'prosperity' depends not on how hard he works but on how readily the state allows price increases or subsidizes the corporation's losses - particularly when he deals with managers who are equally happy to keep things ticking at a ritualistic level of activity, as if they thought that somehow or other their status as university graduates gives them a prebendary *right* to a state pension in the form of a corporation salary.

That situation can be changed, however, even within the context just described. Dynamic top management in one corporation altered the work habits and sense of pride of junior managers and altered the attitudes of the union - initially because of top managers' skill in dealing with them (conceding for instance, the egalitarian flat rate bonus scheme), increasingly as the corporation began to gain a national reputation for its successes because they came to feel 'involved'. They were willing to accept that some dismissals were justified (and dismissals were, in fact, far more frequent than in other corporations) and willing to accept changes in work arrangements to enhance productivity - even though this corporation too, had several unions competing for members.

There are many intermediate positions but ... no apparent correlation between (a) the actual power a union has, (b) the managers' wish to involve the union in decision-making, and (c) the co-operativeness of the union. This is largely because *most* of the powers that unions possess have either been given to them by the law or won in their *own* interests, not voluntarily given by managers in the interest of efficiency through involvement. The control which most Mexican plant unions exercise over recruitment (and which some of Sri Lanka's unions are increasingly pressing for, and getting) is a right won by workers concerned with jobs for their sons, not a planned devolution of powers; so also is the control which many Mexican unions exercise, to a greater or lesser degree, over promotion.

The Monterey firms are most interesting in this regard. Here the ideology of union involvement is strongest. Managers point out that even the security guards are in the union, and that they do not choose lawyers to be personnel managers - both pieces of evidence that they do not have a 'confrontational' view of union–management relations. But in practice the union shares less in decision-making than in other companies where 'confrontation' is expected. Union officials take part in productivity committees, and there is an effective system of department grievance committees - which in effect sanction disciplinary action and can in theory act as a brake on work intensification - in which the unions play a major role. But they do not have control over recruitment and promotions as unions do in many other firms. Managers explain that the grant of such powers would corrupt union leaders. The fact remains that the union accepts a wide range of managerial authority as unchallengeable and as such in the Mexican context would justifiably be considered weak.

So it would in a Japanese context. One can find many Japanese unions which were just as deferential to management authority and had carved out just as small a share of power as the Monterey 'white' unions, but many of the large Japanese firms do have unions which, while holding the same ideology of partnership and absence of confrontation as the Monterey unions, and leaving a wide range of production decisions to the unchallenged authority of managers, nevertheless combine with this the bargaining toughness over wages of the stronger Mexican or Sri Lankan unions.

Some of the circumstances which have made this possible, and conversely the circumstances which determine in the three societies studied the emergence of something different from the pure type 'organization-oriented' model which one might have generalized out of the Japanese example, will have become clear in the foregoing discussion.

The relative unimportance in Japan (as compared with later developers) of the state and the courts in the regulation of industrial relations; … the relative unimportance of state enterprise; …. the absence in Japan (as compared particularly with Sri Lanka, and even with Mexico) of inherited class divisions - with clear cultural, status-group divisions between classes. [On the last point] compare, for instance, the remark of a Japanese manager in Mexico:

> University graduates are a problem. They expect 4 000 pesos a month immediately after they graduate - and they can get it. They expect a room of their own and a personal secretary. They put *licenciado* or *ingeniero* on their calling cards. Can you imagine a Japanese graduate doing that? And Japanese graduates, anyway, only start at 3 000 pesos - in a country where the average wage level is much much higher. It seems that in Mexico, when you graduate from a university you move into a different social class - and nobody questions the justice of these wage differentials.

Perhaps, also, Japan's long pre-industrial tradition of bureaucratic legalism (compare the arbitrary *caudillismo* of Mexican local government traditions) has predisposed Japanese workers more effectively to accepting the legitimacy of institutional rules (rather than seeing *all* social outcomes as the result of power inequalities) and hence toward co-operating to make them work. Again, the same Japanese manager, after he had given me a long explanation of their hiring rules - a ban on rehiring, not more than one person from the same family, and so on:

> No, I'm afraid I can't give you a copy of these rules. They aren't properly set out anywhere. I agree with you that it's very important that they should be. As a matter of fact I've drafted a set of rules once or twice. But my Mexican colleagues have been all against it, and I've had to drop the idea. They say: you're right that if you set out the rules clearly you constrain the workers. But you also constrain management too. You limit our powers of discretion. So the rules are all unwritten. It does have advantages. You can be more humane, for instance. You can show *ninjo* 'human sympathy' to a worker off sick. Social security guarantees him 60 per cent of his wage, but he might have several children and be sick for a couple of months. If he's a good worker, there's nothing to stop us making up his wage.
>
> Resentments if you do it for some and not others? Well, to start with, people keep these things secret. Then there's a basic difference between countries like England or Japan, where there's a basic spirit of equality and here where there isn't. People here don't think they have a *right* to equal treatment.

Also one might invoke a general syndrome of deference to authority which may well be more strongly institutionalized in Japan and more salient a part of the 'modal personality' than in the other three countries, and which may explain, therefore, a greater willingness to accept unquestioningly the authority of managers in some spheres. Once again our Japanese manager, this time on the difference between Japan's Confucianism and the 'deformed kind of Catholicism' of modern Mexico:

> How does it show itself concretely? Well, I'll give you examples. A man comes late; you ask him why. In Japan he would say: 'I'm sorry, I'll try to do better tomorrow.' He may not in fact do better and you know he may not, but at least he admits he's in the wrong. But here they'll say, well, yes, as a fact I'll admit my lateness - but I left home at the same time as usual. It was the bus. It's not my fault.
>
> Or, say, production over the month is down to 80 per cent. You call the factory manager and ask him why. A Japanese factory manager would say: 'yes, I'm sorry, my powers of command have not been adequate to cope. The actual circumstances were such and such.' But here it's, 'Well, it's not my fault. I did my job properly. The materials we got this month were defective. Four per cent of the work-force left; the personnel manager didn't get us the replacements soon enough.

Finally, one must, again, come back to the strong strain of 'groupishness' in Japanese culture - the greater propensity which Japanese seem to show, as compared certainly with the three nationalities considered here, to merge themselves in a group and to work together for collective rather than individual goals. This cannot fail to have predisposed Japanese unions more easily to integration, or co-optation, within the structure of the enterprise:

> Yes, I've thought a lot about that. The first reason, I think, is that the Mexicans are 'dry' [*dorai,* emotionally uninvolved and calculating, as opposed to *uetto,* susceptible to sentimental considerations]. Then, I think, Mexicans don't think 10 or 20 years ahead; they're more likely to be seduced by the prospect of 500 pesos extra now than by their prospects of advancement in 10 years' time. Third, in Japan the whole social system - and I mean the organization of the firm as well as of the society - protects a man and gives him security and a place. Here there is no security: people feel they have only themselves to rely on. Fourth, there is no orderly progression by promotion. That's all because of personal loyalties. For example, if someone is hired on the recommendation of the chief accountant and he goes to work in the personnel office, then in Japan his chief loyalty would be to the personnel manager and the accountant would expect that to be the case. But here no. His first loyalty is to the accountant. That sort of thing destroys the system. It means that you can only trust people of your own group. If a Mexican were to take over from me, you would see all the top jobs change - to bring in his own people. So - to get back to the mobility thing - if you're a factory manager, you've no *calculable* prospects of becoming a director or chairman; you're a factory manager, and if somebody offers you an extra 1 000 pesos to be a factory manager somewhere else, you'll take it.
>
> Finally, another thing is that there's no sense of the firm being a public organization which belongs to everybody. In our firm [Matsushita], as you know, the original founder is still alive, but it's not really *his* firm in the way that Mexican firms *belong* to their owners. So there isn't any sense of loyalty to the firm. Well, that's an overstatement; there is some, but the sense of loyalty to individuals - to

oneself or one's family - is stronger. Take what happens to profits. In Japan a large proportion of profits are retained - they go to the *firm.* In Mexico, by contrast, all the profits are taken out as dividends by the owners. I suppose you could say that the Japanese system is semi-socialistic.

THE USES OF COMPARISON

... Several points emerge about the general model of the late-development pattern. The first is that the original formulation very much underestimated the role of the state in shaping employment systems. Here, clearly, is an important difference between late and later development. The later that development takes place, for a wide variety of reasons, the more likely the state is to play a predominant role in the development process and the wider the conception of the state's 'proper sphere of competence' in the 'international consensus' is likely to be.

A second reflection [concerns] the diversity of the *modes of diffusion* of institutional forms. The original model assumed several forms of international diffusion of norms and organizational forms, but only at the upper levels. Governments enact legislation under the inspiration of the ILO [etc. ...]. The interesting diffusion mechanism which I had overlooked, however, is the moulding of *workers' expectations* by influences from richer countries. These expectations, once established, may *force* certain policies on managers because the cost of disappointing these expectations (in low morale, non-cooperation, etc.) becomes too great. For example, in all three countries, we found the assumption that a man was hard done by if he stayed at the same wage rate in the same job for seven or eight years; we found the assumption that people had a *right* to job security; we found the assumption that every renewal of a collective agreement should bring an *additional* benefit to the workers as part of the general progress of society.

How did expectations such as these - expectations hardly common among British workers, say, twenty years ago - get implanted? And, how *much* has the diffusion of organizational forms and norms to answer for? The infrastructure/superstructure question is usually an insoluble and generally an unprofitable one. In the original formulation the hypothesis about a late-development organization-oriented pattern laid more stress on the 'logic of the situation' in late developers: the technological gap, the pattern of industrial ownership, the prerequisites of training. In fact, the more one thinks about the three countries, the more the direct diffusion of ideas - values, attitudes, knowledge about organizational forms seen as good in themselves - seems to be the more important factor.

The last point to be made about the general model is that there is a great deal which *neither* diffusion *nor* the 'logic of the situation' explains - a great deal which has to be ascribed to local cultural traditions, particular intellectual influences, 'national character'. The individualism/groupishness dimension is one which crops up incessantly in comparisons of Japan with anywhere else. The different nature of racial and class divisions in the five societies considered here clearly reflects itself in managers' choices of organizational forms, in the quality of the relationship between superiors and inferiors, the sentiments those relations invoke. The presence or absence of a strong religious-moralistic middle-class left-wing tradition in Sri Lanka clearly affects the character of its trade-union movement compared with that of Mexico. And so on.

... And so, from general features and general preconditions explaining them, one inevitably moves back to more particular features and conditions - from late development *tout court* to development at a particular historical juncture which never repeats itself.

But, all the same, there is enough which repeats itself in rough outline for the exercise of making and breaking hypotheses to be worthwhile. Whether those hypotheses about 'trends' and 'forces' are confirmed or falsified, one can learn something. If comparison with Japan prompts managers or trade unionists in Mexico or Senegal to see in their wage systems a career-providing personal wage system 'struggling to get out' of an 'equal pay for equal work' framework, then they might start questioning all those principles in a new way. Irrespective of whether they choose to go along with the trend, or to dig in their heels and stick to equal pay for equal work principles, they might at least be doing consciously what formerly they were doing only by inertia. By my lights, at least, any increase in rationality is a good thing.

17. The importance of educational traditions: Japan and elsewhere*

It is some time now since the economists decided that education was too important to be left to the educationalists. Numerous studies of the rate of return to educational investment have been published in the last decade and a half, mostly concerned to demonstrate - with increasing technical sophistication, introducing time lags and discount rates and shadow prices - that investment in education by the individual pays off in enhanced lifetime earnings, and investment in education by society pays off in enhanced rates of economic growth. The chief thing wrong with all this literature is that it suffers from the sin of misplaced aggregation. To an economist one pupil-year of education is a pupil-year, is a pupil-year. It is the numbers that count, because it is only the numbers that can be counted. It is always mildly flattering to see oneself quoted, but nowadays, when I pick up a book on education and development and take that furtive look at the bibliography to make sure the author has shown due awareness of my own modest contribution to the field, I do so more with apprehension than with pleasurable anticipation. As like as not, a book I once wrote on education in Tokugawa Japan will be quoted for one thing and one thing only: R. Dore estimates (or sometimes calculates; or sometimes, baldly, 'states') that in 1870, 40 to 50 per cent of Japanese boys and 10 to 15 per cent of girls were attending school. Apart from the fact that when I recently had occasion to go over these estimates, I found it hard to follow the logic of the reasoning which led to this guess, I have come to realize in recent years that the fault was as much mine as my readers' for putting so much emphasis on the *amount* of education that went on in Japan in the mid-nineteenth century. It is the *kind* of education that went on which deserves greater attention.

EDUCATION AND QUALIFICATION

Let us begin with a very simplified, ideal-typical distinction between the

* From *Pacific Affairs,* 1972, **45**(4), pp. 491–507, abridged. This is a revised version of a paper originally given as the Hume Memorial Lecture at Yale University in April, 1971. It was largely prompted by spending some time as a member of an ILO World Employment Mission to Sri Lanka at the time of the JVP 'Youth Insurgency', to which it refers. The ideas were later embodied in *The Diploma Disease.*

business of education and the business of qualification. Education involves changing people; it depends on awakening, and sustaining by a continuous process of partial satisfaction and further stimulation, curiosity and the desire for self-development, the desire to understand, the desire to achieve, and the desire to master. Qualification, by contrast, is a process of instrumental learning, learning which involves the passive absorption of ready-made answers in order to become qualified, certificated, and entitled to a job, a salary and a social status. Education results from the desire to learn; qualification results from the desire to be certified as having learnt. Education is learning as an end in itself or as a means to action; qualification is the merely instrumental *use* of learning, not to do, but just to be.

The distinction is of course oversimplified, [but nevertheless real]. Consider, for instance, the following, the gist of a conversation with a teacher of civics in Sri Lanka. I had asked her about the content of her teaching to her sixteen year-old classes. Her answer was exclusively in terms of the national examination taken at the age of 16.

> *What sort of topics do you discuss in the classroom?*
> Well, there are four parts to it really. You have to do six questions, one from each part. The first is about the departments of government; then the second is about democracy and feudalism and totalitarianism; the third is the government of Ceylon – Parliament, local government and so on. And the fourth is about British government, the Commonwealth and the United Nations. The United Nations is practically compulsory. There is a question on it every year.
> *No, I didn't mean the examination; I meant: do you discuss practical questions of current affairs in the classes? For example the new constitution? There was a lot of news in the paper yesterday about the abolition of the Senate. Would you discuss that?*
> The Senate, yes. Last year, for instance, there was a question about whether the Senate had fulfilled its role as envisaged by the Soulbury Commission.
> *With diminishing hope I pressed a little further. 'No, I meant whether you ever go outside the actual teaching for the examination and talk about things that are going on in the country.'*
> 'Oh no,' said the teacher, 'with students of that age I don't think it would be possible. You see they have no clear picture.'

LATE DEVELOPMENT

I would like to offer three propositions. First, in late-developing societies schools and universities are more likely to be qualification-oriented than education-oriented. One might even go so far as to suggest a more precise proposition – namely that the *later* industrialization and modernization starts the *more* qualification-oriented the schools are likely to become. Second, educational investment which is investment in qualification-producing institutions may hinder rather than promote economic growth. But third, the extent to which these propositions apply is very much dependent on each country's cultural and educational traditions. These traditions do have importance.

[... In post-independence Sri Lanka there had been an] enormous expansion of the school and educational system. Very real strides were made to guarantee equality of educational opportunity with a quite generous system of bursaries and scholarships. The trouble was, first, that the vastly expanded system remained geared to its original [colonial-period] purpose - the production of an administrative elite. Second, the shortage of job opportunities at all administrative levels led to increasingly tougher standards, and an accelerating spiral of disappointment and frustration. [... And] the expansion of the system has tended to exaggerate the qualification-orientation of the schools. At all levels, the expansion in numbers has intensified the struggle to pass the various qualifying examinations - at grade 8 to proceed to grade 9, at grade 10 to proceed to grade 11 and at grade 12 to proceed to the university - with quite disastrous results. Three decades ago eight years of education were enough to guarantee a secure, if humble, white-collar job. Two decades ago ten years of education were enough. A decade ago twelve years gave one a good chance of success. Now the country suffers from a disastrous surfeit of educated unemployed, disqualified by the aspirations they have absorbed in the school system, from returning to the farming and artisan occupations of their fathers. Since the job/applicant ratio is still slightly better for university graduates than for middle-school leavers, the pressure to push on ever higher up the qualifying scale intensifies. Repetition rates steadily rise. Only a third of those who reach grade 11 manage to do so straight from grade 10; a half have taken the qualifying examination twice in successive years, the rest have taken it three times or more....

That the school system, subjected to such pressures, should have become arid ritualistic qualification-factories, unable to concern themselves with the business of education, is hardly surprising. The poverty of the schools, the lack of adequate equipment and libraries, exacerbates the situation. Even physics in some schools must be taught up to university entrance level without benefit of laboratories, even of textbooks. Where schooling consists simply of copying and memorizing what the teacher writes on the blackboard, there is precious little opportunity for autonomous self-initiated learning. It is small wonder, in such circumstances, that the mind of the civics teacher quoted earlier should, despite her obvious intelligence and seriousness, have become totally imprisoned within the confines of an examination syllabus. Education in such schools seems at best to dull intellectual appetites, at worst to induce a mood of resentful, rebellious philistinism. In the same school as the civics teacher's, a group of boys taking their grade 10 qualifying examination for the second time with little hope of success, celebrated the end of the examination and the prospect of their inglorious drop-out from the system, by collecting all the maps they could find on classroom walls and burning them. In the same school one of the most promising science students was said, in the dormitories, to be telling his fellow-pupils that they were fools to waste their time on homework. Soon the revolution would come and it would all be unnecessary. Nothing in the whole educational experience of that intelligent child had given him the idea that the laws of thermodynamics had any significance at all except as something to be learned in order to get on in the system; they would have no relevance in the post-revolutionary society. Only a week after I met that boy several thousands of boys and girls of his generation were, indeed, hurling themselves suicidally against police posts. The tragedy of the situation lies not only in the loss of young lives, but also in the untutored naïvety of the slogans for which they are dying, reflecting the poverty of the education they have received. The older generation, which must bear part of the responsibility for qualifying them without educating them, is clearly bewildered. How can it be, asked the Ceylon *Daily Mirror* in an editorial, in the flowery nineteenth-century English which remains the norm in Ceylonese journalism, that 'the clusters of clean young men whom we thought were being groomed to be scholars with their bundles of books and earnest looks now prowl menacingly around; firearms in their hands and murder in their eyes'.

WHY WAS JAPAN'S PROBLEM LESS SERIOUS?

The problems of a qualification-oriented school system, prevented by the overwhelming salience of its qualifying functions from concerning itself with education, while not often so extreme as in Ceylon, are widely shared by other late-developing countries. How was it that Japan largely escaped these problems – the twin problems of the educated unemployed explosion, and the erosion of intellectual energies and entrepreneurial initiatives by a qualification-oriented ritualism in education?

One answer is that, as far as the first half of the problem is concerned, Japan did not entirely escape. A good deal of distress was caused by the friction attending the adjustment process of qualification-escalation. The unemployed graduate problem of the late 1920s played some role – probably not a decisive role – in the social conflict which only ended with the emergence to dominance of the military when the rebellious young were finally 'co-opted' by their seniors and mobilized for the development of Manchuria.

As for the second part of the problem, one crucial difference between Japan and the majority of today's late developers is that Japan was never colonized. Her modern educational system was not built around a framework originally devised to train the subordinate local members of a colonial administration. Moreover, the main framework of Japan's modern institutions was created *before* the pattern of pre-career qualification fully established itself in Japan. It was not until 1890 that a degree from the Faculty of Law at Tokyo University became the only route into the bureaucracy. By then the ethos of a development-oriented, change-oriented administration was well established. The 'good students,' the play-it-safe academic high-achievers, even though they did begin to give the bureaucracy a bad name for legalistic formalism by the 1930s and 1940s, were nevertheless partially socialized into the more dynamic performance-oriented traditions established by their predecessors. Similarly, the major industrial organizations had been established by men who had learned without necessarily seeking to be qualified; men who had often first conceived of the job they wanted to do and then gone abroad to learn it, long before industry settled down into its bureaucratic mould and the qualification routes of entry became formalized. These men not only established the ethos of Japanese industry, they also laid the basis for a dynamic of growth which prevented the unemployed-graduate phenomenon from being too serious and so prevented the struggle for ever-better qualifications (and the consequent examination-orientation of the curriculum) from becoming too serious.

It was equally important that the groundwork of primary education was fully established before there was much growth of middle-school higher education. In the 1890s when more than 80 per cent of boys were in primary schools, less than 5 per cent of them could be accommodated in secondary schools. The one-in-sixteen (or higher) selection ratio made it easier for the schools to concentrate on the general education of the fifteen rather than on the examination preparation of the small number who might aspire to be the one who would proceed to the secondary level – much easier than it is in those contemporary developing societies where the ratios are often more like 50 per cent in primary schools and 20 per cent in secondary. (Partly because of their class-structure and highly unequal income distribution, partly because of the educational planners' doctrines of concentrating initially on the training of middle and higher level manpower.) The fact that the chances of proceeding to higher education were, for the first twenty or thirty years of the life of the new primary system, considered rare and only for the exceptional child, meant that the rural primary school could be seen not as an escape-hatch out of agriculture, nor as the first step on the qualification ladder, but as a place where farmers' children went to become better farmers and citizens. And that tradition of primary education had time to get entrenched before the modern rat-race took hold.

TRADITIONS AND THEIR SURVIVAL

Still another factor was responsible for preventing the schools from being converted into qualification factories – Japan's educational traditions. The fact that Japan had a well-established educational system in the Tokugawa period, well before the drive to modernity began, was important not only because of the numbers of people made literate but because these schools established in Japanese culture a particular pedagogical tradition, a particular view of the purpose of education, and of the nature of the school as an institution.

In all industrial societies, the school and university system has become the major mechanism of occupational selection and social placement. The pre-industrial societies which have had well developed school systems have (like Tokugawa Japan or like England, or even the American colonies in the late eighteenth century) been stratified societies where there was little social mobility, and where such mobility as occurred depended on one's skill as an artisan, as a farmer, as a political manipulator, on one's sharpness as a merchant, and not on one's possession of educational qualifications. The schools and universities had a clearer class character and were not primarily mechanisms of social placement, since social status was for the most part hereditarily ascribed. Their function was to make of the gentry better gentry, to make merchants into better (morally and intellectually) merchants. Hirose Tanso, a Confucian scholar who ran a flourishing school in Kyushu in the 1840s, put the matter succinctly when he said, with a sidelong glance at the Chinese examination system which *did* give power to the qualified, that Tokugawa Japan had to accept the fact that the right to rule resided with the old established families. 'Therefore,' he said, 'since it is difficult to do away with the old established families, there is no alternative but to educate the children of the upper families so that they will lean toward the good, reject evil, and be of benefit to the country.'[1]

To be sure, the actual methods of teaching were formalistic and ritualistic in the extreme. There was nothing very exciting for a Japanese child in being made to rote-learn the Confucian classics for many years before he was allowed to discuss what those classics might mean. But the ablest minds survived this treatment, and with their appetite for learning relatively undulled. The teaching was ritualistic, but it was not instrumental. The child was told: this hurts me more than it hurts you, but it is necessary because at the end of it you will be a better person, better able to be 'of benefit to your country'. The teacher did not say: it is necessary because it is the only way you can get your qualification; learn only this and you will be able to collapse exhausted on the bottom step of an incremental salary-scale escalator in the comfortable knowledge that no further effort is required to move up. Even for the farmers and artisans of Japanese society, to learn to read and write and count was instrumental only in the sense that it enabled them to do their inherited job better, not in the sense that it enabled them to get a better job. It was also, as in the contemporary Protestant societies of Europe, a means of self-development, a means of acquiring the status of a fully participant citizen in one's community.

My thesis is that the pre-industrial establishment of this tradition of schooling as a means of self-development, of education as an end in itself, acted to mitigate what might otherwise have been the socially debilitating effects of introducing a qualification-oriented modern school system. It made it possible to establish schools in the villages which gave every farmer's children the opportunity for general education, without making them too proud to get their feet wet and their hands dirty. Not many societies have managed to develop, as Japan did, the tradition of the literate, diary-keeping peasant, keeping his diary as a means of self-monitoring, self-admonition and self-development, a means of practising Confucius' prescription 'every day to reflect three times'. There is an illustrative passage in a little book of moral uplift published in English in 1910 by the Japanese Ministry of Agriculture and Commerce. It is called *The Rural Life in Japan* and one of its stories concerns an exemplary headman near the city of Hiroshima. It was his idea that all the farmers should keep domestic fowls. For three years, he studied the best method of raising eggs. His zeal and patience gradually influenced the people, so that four hundred houses out of six hundred have come to keep chickens, with the result of producing 560 000 eggs, and of gaining 12 000 yen from their sale. 'The Savings Club' of the same village is said to have deposited twenty-five hundred yen in two months, since its organization. Masao Sasaki, the headman, together with his people, are now giving their united effort to this auxiliary industry with the object of prevailing upon the remaining two hundred houses to keep fowls. Not only the production of the best eggs, but the finding of good markets and the use of the profit for the benefit of the village, are being studied in the spirit of mutual help. The wholesome influence has told even upon the children, to such an extent that one nurse girl, sixteen years old, who has been entrusted with eleven chickens, has given so much attention to them as to give a name to each chicken and even keep a diary for them. Her interest has proved profitable, for she obtained 1 500 eggs from eleven chickens. The headman examined her eight months' diary and found it advisable to make copies and distribute them among the villagers. She was widely praised and recently married to a farmer of the middle class.

Perhaps one can see best of all the strength of these educational traditions in the fact that they survive even in the heart of the modern qualification rat-race itself. The business of preparing students in cram schools and by correspondence courses for the university entrance examinations is one of

Japan's most flourishing, multi-billion yen industries. One of its typical products is a monthly magazine called, significantly, *Snow and Firefly Days* - after the legendary Chinese peasant whose love of learning was such that he studied under the most unpromising conditions - in winter by the moonlight reflected in the snow, in summer by the glow of caged fireflies. Its April 1971 issue (published of course, in the first week of March - yet another indication of the Japanese keenness to get ahead of themselves) provides for a mere 75 cents a fascinating 350 pages. They are filled for the most part with descriptions of the types of qualifications offered at Japan's 600-odd universities, with reports on impending changes in entrance-examination styles, with tips and hints on how to cut corners, and how effectively to plan one's campaign. But through odd interstices of these anxiety-ridden contents, the older educational traditions shine through. There is, for example, an article on a well-known nineteenth-century diary by a Buddhist recluse entitled *How to Read, and How to Savor, the Tsure Zure-Gusa;* there are articles on Laos and biochemical warfare and women's lib, and there is a series of letters from high-school readers for a column (entitled 'In Search of Myself') the first of which begins by quoting the Socratic aphorism that the beginning of wisdom is to know what you don't know, and ends with his own aphorism that: 'the important thing is not whether I am making progress, but whether I am facing forward.'

I would not like to seem to suggest that the survival into the modern period of something of the attitudes towards learning and things of the mind, of the cultural definition of schools and the purpose of education, prevalent in Tokugawa Japan is the sole explanation of the vitality of Japanese intellectual culture and of the enterprise and serious-mindedness which the Japanese today show in the application of intelligence to practical problems in industry or in the framing of both political and social institutions. Schools, and what goes on in them, are only partial expressions of a cultural tradition, as well as being only one of the mechanisms which sustain it and transmit it from generation to generation. But they are an important mechanism, and I venture to think that Japan would be a different society, intellectually, morally and materially poorer, today if the Confucian scholars of the Tokugawa period had not endowed modern Japan with a tradition of schooling, with a cultural definition of 'school' which was concerned with the business of education rather than of qualification.

NOTES

1. *Ugen,* in *Nihon Keibai Sosho,* Vol. 32, p. 105.

18. Confucianism, economic growth and social development*

My starting point - and surely the starting point of anyone invited to tackle my theme - is a simple correlation. If one looks at the countries east of the Malacca Straits - or east of Suez, for that matter - all of those economies which can be described as 'of Confucian culture' have experienced sustained periods of rapid economic growth - at rates of 10 per cent a year or more -and all the other countries have not, though among them the two which have large populations of 'Confucian' origin - Thailand and Malaysia - have done better than the others. The contrast seems clear; the correlation seems too good to be ascribed to chance. One is moved to postulate some common ingredient, some causal x, which accounts for the correlation.

It is clear that x is not some characteristic of *political systems* since the striking thing about the correlation is that the 'sustained growth' countries have included North Korea in the 1960s and China in the 1980s, both under systems of government self-described as Communist, as well as the free market economy of colonial Hong Kong, and the more or less free market economies of Japan, South Korea, and Taiwan. That is not to say, of course, that political systems have been irrelevant. Far from it. The realization of whatever it is which constitutes the growth potential of these societies clearly requires certain political preconditions. 'Peace, good government and the regular collection of taxes' was Adam Smith's recipe for economic growth, and clearly their absence has inhibited development in East Asia over long periods of time. China did not see much economic growth when it was a divided, war-torn arena for the rivalries of competing warlords and foreign powers, nor when it was the arena for a battle between rival Communist Party factions unleashed by a megalomaniac Mao. And the discipline which was married with economic dynamism in North Korea in the 1960s seems to have turned in on itself and bred stagnation in the 1970s. Just as a growth hormone requires certain environmental conditions in its environment if it is to produce the desired growth effect - the animal has to be fed properly, in other words -

* From J. Kreiner (ed.), *The Impact of Traditional Thought on Present-Day Japan*, Munich: Iudicium-Verl., 1996, pp. 17–30, abridged.

so the *x*, whatever it is, requires an appropriate political environment if it is to result in economic growth.

But what is that *x*? Western intellectuals of a hundred years ago - even of fifty years ago - would have had few doubts. They would have assumed as a matter of course that the *x* these societies had in common was some set of biological characteristics of the Mongolian race that their populations form part of. When an American missionary, Gulick, suggested eighty years ago (in his book *The Evolution of the Japanese*)[1] that there was an essential unity in human nature and that the differences between Japan and Europe were differences in stages of social evolution, not ineluctable and permanent differences of race, he did so as one proposing a new and surprising idea.

The experience of the last half-century, however, has fundamentally altered our perceptions of race as a factor explaining national differences. Two things are overwhelmingly responsible. The first was the Nazi use of race as an instrument of nationalism which resulted, on the one hand, in the intellectual absurdity of claiming to discriminate between Aryan and non-Aryan in the racial melting pot of Europe, and, on the other, in the moral horror of genocide. The second factor was the emergence of a consensus among Americans that they must try to construct an integrated and, if possible, harmonious society out of a population in which the visible marks of racial difference - skin colour, especially - correlated highly with occupation and social status. An insistence on the equal potential, equal value, of all racially distinguishable population gene pools became an essential part of that consensus.

So it is to cultural differences that we now look for our *x*....

But two more preliminaries first. Discussions of this kind are bound, in the end, to be comparative. One would not, for instance, speak of low levels of self-assertion in East Asian societies if one did not know of other societies with higher levels of self-assertion. The existence of an implicit standard of reference - usually my own home culture - has to be borne in mind in assessing what I shall have to say.

Second, when I speak of certain East Asian societies as Confucian, or post-Confucian, or of their culture as a Confucian culture, I do not intend to convey either that those societies were *moulded* according to the doctrines of Confucius or his interpreters, or that large parts of their populations would willingly describe themselves as adherents of those doctrines, any more than when I describe Britain as a Christian or post-Christian society I mean either that the Church was the predominant force shaping England, or that the British people frequently go to Church. By Confucian culture I intend something like the following: 'a core complex of values, beliefs and customs which have characterized the dominant sectors (classes/regions) of the society, and which have been directly or indirectly validated or endorsed or reinforced by reference to people, traditions or scriptures which have explicitly called themselves Confucian.'

In that loose sense, then, what characteristics do the East Asian societies have in common, which one would think might well be related to economic growth? This is by now a well-ploughed field; in one of the pioneer books on Asian economic growth, *The Eastasia Edge*, Roy Hofheinz and Kent Calder, had many interesting things to say about it seven or eight years ago. Here, I limit myself to a few remarks on four characteristics which seem to me important: first, a generalized syndrome of dutifulness, second, acceptance of hierarchy, third, a particular form of elite consciousness, and, fourth, a faith in rationality.

DUTIFULNESS

By dutifulness, I mean something which could be put in its crudest form as follows. Try asking people: why are we born into this world? Is it to try to find happiness or is it to fulfil our duties? In Confucian societies more people than in America or in Europe would be likely to say 'duty' – if they would give you any answer at all, that is. Or at least more people *behave* as if 'duty' is the answer they ought to give. More people, in other words, are likely to feel guilty about not keeping promises or not turning up for work; more people are likely to feel uncomfortable if they cannot reciprocate favours they have received; more drivers perform conscientiously the prescribed maintenance tasks on their cars; more people are likely to sacrifice their own convenience in order to look after aged parents; more people are likely to constrain their own behaviour in order not to be a nuisance to their neighbours; more people are likely to stay within the bonds of an emotionally barren marriage because it would seem selfish to do otherwise. My evidence of this is, I must confess, imperfect. But I believe that statistics of family composition, divorce rates, factory absenteeism rates, or statistics showing the proportion of trains arriving on time would lend some support to my suppositions.

[Dutifulness was summed up in explicit Confucian writings as one of] the governing virtues of the five basic relationships out of which the web of society was woven.... All the emphasis, naturally, was on the duties of subordinates in these dyadic relations – except in the case of the one of the five which concerned a relationship between status equals – trust between friends and business associates.

But that is not to say that the duties of superordinates were neglected by any means. The duty of rulers to deal benevolently and justly with their subjects, their duty to be scrupulous in making distinctions between the world of the public and the world of the private – between their own self-interest and the interest of the nation which was put in their charge - was a duty they in their turn owed to Heaven just as much as their subjects owed a duty of loyalty and obedience to them. And those reponsibilities were mirrored, the Confucian scholars like those of Tokugawa Japan taught, by the responsibilities of heads of families and heads of fiefs.

One needs to remind the reader of the comparison point. One would not be so struck by this emphasis on duties if it were not in such marked contrast with so much Western philosophical thought - a point one hardly needs to labour on the second centenary of the Declaration of the Rights of Man. The story of the early Meiji translators of Rousseau and Mill having problems in finding a Japanese word to translate the French *droit*, the English *right*, is a familiar one.[2]

... What relevance might this have to economic growth? In listing earlier some of the behavioural manifestations of dutifulness I have already given a partial answer. The conscientious learning and the conscientious performance of jobs is an obvious ingredient in economic efficiency. But (sooner or later an essay on this theme has to pay *some* passing respect to the ghost of Max Weber[3]) might that very conscientiousness not be inimical to the capitalist spirit of innovation and entrepreneurship? Might it not simply imply a conscientious adherence to tradition? Not for nothing has the Confucian heritage been invoked until recently as the dominant factor actually *inhibiting* the economic development of China - not least by Weber himself.[4]

I suppose the most obvious answer to that is as follows. What preoccupied Weber was the *original* process of entrepreneurial innovation; the first breaking of the crust of custom. That may, indeed, have needed religious innovators imbued with a sense of their own rightness. But the post-Confucian states of East Asia have all come late to industrialization. They have been follower countries for whom the *object* of industrialization was taken for granted, in which the status of the industrial innovator was assured. All that was needed was conscientious pursuit of the means. And the thrusting capacity to innovate apart, some of the other characteristics of the Weberian entrepreneur supposedly responsible for the origins of modern capitalism, were indeed those of dutifulness - the ascetic self-denial which made capital accumulation possible, the hard work - and also, very much a characteristic of East Asian societies, the sense of a duty towards the family and one's descendants as a powerful motivator of economic activity.

That aspect of dutifulness perhaps needs rather more elaboration. Because work itself is seen as a fulfilment of duty - a performance of the role appropriate to one's *bun*, one's position in society - it should not be entirely self-interested ... It will be a long time ahead in the evolution of Chinese, or even of Japanese, capitalism before a captain of industry - or rather a captain of finance - gives the sort of public address that Mr Boesky reportedly gave to the graduating students of Stanford Business School in the months before he was sent off to jail: 'Greed? What is wrong with greed? It is greed which makes the wheels of the economy spin.'

HIERARCHY

That tendency to award a higher degree of moral approval to work on behalf of group rather than of self, clearly has a lot to do with the capacity for co-operation within organizations. So also does the willingness to accept hierarchy. (Again, don't forget the point of reference; I mean 'greater willingness than Europeans or Americans to accept hierarchy', though that too needs qualifying by pointing out the differences among *them*. Dutchmen and Germans seem able to accept organizational subordination without feeling demeaned and obliged to assert themselves to prove their manliness - or feminist modernity - more easily than Anglo-Saxons.)

Indeed, the two characteristics - groupishness and the acceptance of hierarchy - are clearly related, just as their opposites - individualism and egalitarianism - have always been close brothers in the evolution of European thought.

The way in which the explicit ethics of neo-Confucianism reinforced this acceptance of hierarchy has already been discussed. And in these respects the ethics faithfully reflected characteristics of behaviour. The rituals of daily life - the bows of subordinates to superiors, the self-effacing ways women were required to maneouvre their bodies when they entered rooms, the conventions which governed who could look directly at whom, who stood up when who entered the room - all reinforced the ever-present consciousness of hierarchy. So did speech conventions, more especially in Japan and Korea, where it is still impossible for two people to converse with each other without consciously, if implicitly, adopting the convention that A is the superior of B, or B of A, or that they are on a footing of equality.

Modern societies, in the conceptual schemes of the modernization theorists of the 1960s, were societies in which the principle of ascription gives way to the principle of achievement. In the West this erosion of the importance attached to ascribed status was assumed to imply automatically an increase in equality - certainly equality of opportunity, and, since now only graded differences of wealth and power and cultural achievement differentiated people, greater equality of condition too. In the post-Confucian societies, the abandonment of traditional forms of birth-ascription has been more rapid than in some of the older, more slowly-evolving societies of Europe. In Italian villages, for instance, signori landowners and ex-landowners still address former tenants in what would in Japan be called a *yobisute* fashion - without polite prefix or suffix – and refer to them as 'their' *contadini*. In Japan, by contrast, the erosion of the status privileges attaching to samurai ancestry proceeded quite rapidly. It did nothing to secure preferment for entry to the university faculties which led to the major power positions in society after the mid-1880s. It disappeared from the *koseki* family registers in 1917. And I was told the other day that the priests in Tama-gun began giving posthumous names with *in* rather than with *koji* endings not only to samurai families but to anybody who would pay for it well before World War II.

But in the Confucian societies, the erosion of ascription as a social principle has not implied the disappearance of the principle of *hierarchy* – of the idea that everybody, in the organizational context of each particular moment, has his proper *bun*, his proper role to play. The principles for the *allocation* of status have changed, but the importance attaching to status has been preserved. There is no better illustration of this than the Japanese Liberal Democratic Party which has adopted the *nenko-joretsu* practices, the seniority-plus-merit promotion system, of business firms. No one may be chairman of a Diet Committee until he has been elected four times, or a cabinet minster before surviving five elections, and so on. Seniority is one of the most egalitarian of all principles of status allocation; it rewards everyone who faithfully plays out his subordinate roles with enough dutiful patience.

The advantages of this acceptance of hierarchy for running modern organizations are considerable, though in the 1950s and 1960s when scholars were busy explaining why Confucianism was the explanation for the economic backwardness of East Asia, it was the *dis*advantages that were more commonly stressed. Among them, chiefly, that organizations could not make optimal use of differences of ability if they were constrained by seniority rules and prevented from appointing able young men to senior positions. Second, that the dominance of older people led inevitably to organizational sclerosis. What counters these tendencies (in Japanese organizations at least, and I think the same thing might apply in other parts of Asia) are the following features:

1. The care taken to secure relatively homogeneous ability levels in each grade of the organization by careful selection using chiefly the criterion of education performance. Where the *tsubu ga sorotte iru* – where all the grains are of much the same size – the likelihood that seniority rules put very able juniors under incompetent seniors is much reduced.
2. Seniority reduces the stakes at play in interpersonal competition [one competes only for slightly faster promotion than one's age-mates], and thereby enhances co-operation in pursuit of the organization's goals.
3. The traditional insistence on the duties of benevolent leadership from superordinates (a) leads to a stress on training one's juniors and so ensures efficient transmission of the accumulated experiential wisdom of the

organization – i.e. makes organizations efficient learning mechanisms, (b) mitigates any tendencies to be jealous of the superior energy, brains or imagination of one's subordinates; the seniority rules prevent them from threatening one's position directly, and as their leader and trainer, one can share in the credit their work gains for one's department within the organization.

THE CHARACTER OF ELITES

The principle of ascription, I have just suggested, has rapidly given way, in East Asian societies, to principles of achievement, without much altering the tendency for organizations to gravitate towards a bureaucratic form. And I suggested further that one of the reasons for the smoothness of transition was that the allocation of status depended on the hallowed traditional (and one *could* say Confucian; certainly more Confucian than Christian) principle of seniority. But it also depended on another criterion, if not of equal antiquity – the principle we nowadays call meritocracy, the allocation of status according to intellectual achievement. It was hereditary family status which decided who had a chance to become a *si dafu* in China, a *yangban* official in Korea, or a *bugyo* in Tokugawa Japan. But who *actually* filled those positions was determined for most of recent history in China and Korea, [in China, the *kakyo* examination system goes back to the Han dynasty] and even [in Japan as it] became a more literate and civilized society in the Tokugawa period, by competitive success in school examinations. Small wonder that when modern universities and civil services come to be created in East Asia, the principle of recruitment by examination competition becomes more readily and thoroughly applied than in any Western societies with the exception of France, and, in recent years, the countries of eastern Europe. [Hence also the most intense examination competition, with all its problems of cram schools etc.]

The efficiency advantages – especially for a pattern of industrialization in which the state bureaucracy and large bureaucratic firms are destined to play a major role – are considerable. Whatever doubts one may have about the use of examination performance in maths or social studies as a means of predicting who will be capable of learning to be a good sales manager or road network planner or personnel officer, the experience of companies all over the world is that the correlations between school performance and work performance are too high to be ignored. Consequently, the examination sorting system does roughly ensure that the positions in society which wield the most decision-making power and control the largest units of resources are held by the most intelligent people. The second efficiency advantage lies in the way the system confers legitimacy on those who are selected for high-status positions. They come to be defined by the society as people who 'deserve' the power they wield - perhaps in part by virtue of their good fortune in being born bright, but also in part because of their efforts, because they have been careful to develop and not squander the talents they were born with.

There is another aspect of traditional practices.... In the Confucian tradition - in sharp contrast to the Christian tradition - intellectual excellence and moral excellence are expected to go hand in hand. In Europe, schools looked after the head; the church looked after the heart. In East Asia the school's competence extended to both head and heart. One trained the head on a curriculum the essential core of which was the corpus of *moral* classics - Zhu Xi's Four Books. [That makes it] easier for the meritocratic elite to claim competence in the sphere of the 'ought' as well as in the sphere of the 'is'. Their student movements - 4 May, the Korean student protest, the Ampo demonstrations in Japan in 1960, Tiananmen Square - claim a fierce *moral* authority; as future *responsible* elites they claim to speak for the nation.

One can also expect, as a result of this tradition, to find fairly strong internalized mechanisms to keep bureaucratic corruption in check, a relatively high level of conscientiousness about work efficiency among officials, and a relatively high level of willingness to co-operate with state initiatives on the part of private businessmen. There remains a good deal of controversy as to how far these characteristics of their bureaucracies were responsible for rapid economic growth in South Korea and Taiwan. Hitherto, [there has been] a profound belief in the sovereign interpretations of most of the economists who have written on the subject, but the consensus seems to be shifting towards the view that the role of state leadership, in the administration of trade controls, credit controls and technology import controls has been far too important to be ignored.[5]

RATIONALITY

By this I mean 'rationality of means' - 'scientific rationality' one might even call it. I do not mean rationality in the sense of deriving all one's values and objectives from some basic all-embracing principles, nor 'economic rationality' in the sense of setting one's objectives solely in terms of income or wealth or growth maximization. I mean the tendency always to try to be clear about what one's objectives are, the tendency to separate arguments about the value of different objectives from arguments about the ways of achieving them, the capacity to evaluate alternatives by imaginative forecasting of their respective consequences, and the willingness to follow those consequences into a quite long-term future - not infrequently the future of one's grandchildren, and not just the next five years.

Fukuzawa Yukichi could be scornful about what Confucian scholars meant in practice by *kakubutsu-kyuri*,[6] (the method of philosophical inquiry endorsed by the Sung scholars – the investigation of things and inquiry into the principles behind them), but the fact is that while Europe, by the mid-nineteenth century, was well ahead of East Asia in elite science and in practical technology, there was nothing in the central religious traditions of the Christian societies which endorsed the idea that knowledge was to be acquired by the application of logic to empirical observation. Indeed, the authority of scriptural revelation was such that the proponents of science, and the proponents of many practical applications of science, had frequently to fight *against* the authority of the church. By contrast, the Confucian tradition did endorse in principle what scientists did, and there is little record in East Asia of opposition to scientific ideas or to the importation of new technology which was either organized by the self-avowed defenders of Confucian tradition, or which borrowed Confucian texts or concepts by way of justification. The glorification of intuition as opposed to reason, *à la* zen priest, has remained a minority strain.

To be sure, in the political sphere, and in informal group leadership of a *hara-gei* type (domination by gut intuition), there has been resistance to bureaucratic rationalization – a determination on the part of those who hold power to keep it unconstrained, to insist on rule by men rather than rule by law. But that resistance has been weaker than, say, in the Anglo-Saxon societies where the mystique of 'leadership' has held much more dominant sway. The difference in the power balance as between bureaucrats and politicians is symptomatic of the difference. In the Anglo-Saxon societies, politicians actually rule and do not just reign. Theorists talk of the separation of the legislative and the executive power in Western democracies, but their politicians like to see themselves as people who both make the rules and determine how to apply them.

The result is a greater predictability in the more bureaucratized East Asian societies which is probably good for social and economic efficiency. A recent article, for instance, compares the legal treatment of fatal traffic accidents in the USA and Japan. There is much less expenditure of social resources on the settlement of damage claims in Japan; a much higher proportion of cases is settled out of court. But the amounts paid in out-of-court settlements approximate closely the awards made in cases which are carried out to a legal conclusion – which is not the case in the USA.[7] The conclusion is that the much greater codification and transparency of the rules which judges use in Japan – as compared with the jury-influenced settlements in the United States – provide a much higher level of predictability in the law which encourages out-of-court settlement.

The other consequence of the 'rationality' syndrome which deserves noting is the tendency to calculate consequences to the long term. There is a famous saying by a former British prime minister to the effect that 'a week is a long time in politics'. Chance your arm, the message is; if you make the wrong decision, people will have forgotten in a few days and next time you will have a chance to make a better decision. In a regime of discretion all decisions are one-off decisions, and there is no great need to think of the long term. In a bureaucratic regime built on precedents, a rule formulated for today's decision can have consequences that reverberate into the future. The growth orientation and long-term investment behaviour of Japanese and Korean firms, the savings behaviour of Japanese and Korean households, must surely be linked to this, and what I called the 'rationality' as well as to the 'dutifulness' syndromes.

SOCIAL DEVELOPMENT

Here you are, the reader may say, offering this hymn of praise of Confucianism, and lauding its contribution to economic development, without a word about *social* development. What about the repressive aspects of East Asian societies: the denial of individual liberties, the right to be different, the right, even, of free speech? What about Tiananmen Square? What about the conformity, the newspaper self-censorship, the lack of much open public debate in so-called democratic Japan?

That *is* another story. This paper was not intended to give any overall evaluation of Confucianism, to say whether one should count it a good thing or a bad thing. It simply set out to assess how much the characteristics of East Asian societies which might loosely be called Confucian characteristics may have contributed to the economic growth of those societies. But if evaluation *is* called for, I do take it as axiomatic that growth in GNP is a good thing. (I can suspend disbelief long enough to accept the market valuations on which GNP accounting are based for want of any alternative. Economic growth can be taken as a proxy measure of economic development - something that by and large makes societies better.) That is certainly not the only thing that determines the quality of life in any society, but on those other aspects there is much less unanimity. One man's good society can be for another man a heartless state of anarchy or a suffocating regime of repression.

This is not the place to embark on discussion of what constitutes a good society. I close, however, with one not irrelevant thought. Given characteristics of the post-Confucian East Asian societies such as those described above, what, as they mature as industrial societies, are likely to be their distinguishing characteristics - as societies and as polities - as compared with the older industrial societies? That is a question which requires a book rather than a paragraph, so let me give it two sentences. As their technology gets more complex all capitalist democracies seem to me likely to face severe crises of social cohesion as market forces exacerbate inequalities - ability-based inequalities - thus reversing the trends of the last hundred years towards a reduction of property-based inequalities. Less individualistic societies might well be better placed to deal with that crisis than the more individualistic ones.

NOTES

1. Sidney Gulick, *The Evolution of the Japanese: Social and Psychic*, New York, F.H. Revell, 1903.
2. See e.g., Carmen Blacker, *The Japanese Enlightenment: a Study of the Writings of Fukuzawa Yukichi*, Cambridge University Press, 1964.
3. *The Protestant Ethic and the Spirit of Capitalism*, London, Allen & Unwin, 1967.
4. See Hans Gerth's translation of Weber's writings on China: *The Religion of Chin: Confucianism and Taoism*, Glencoe, Ill., Free Press, 1951.
5. See, especially, Robert Wade, *Governing the Market*, Princeton, Princeton University Press, 1990.
6. See Carmen Blacker, *op. cit.*
7. J.M. Ramseyer and M. Nakazato, 'The Rational Litigant; Settlement Amounts and Verdict Rates in Japan,' *Journal of Legal Studies*, **18**, June 1988, pp. 263-91.

19. In what ways a Japanese 'system'?*

Among social scientists a favourite way of characterizing much of what has been described above is to say that economic transactions in Japan are, as compared with other societies, much more commonly 'embedded' in face-to-face social relations. But note that this is not at all the Polanyi type of social embeddedness, the disentangling of which he sees as the pre-condition for the emergence of modern market capitalism.[1] Polanyi was talking about what sociologists call ascribed social relations - those one is more or less born into, between uncle and nephew in an extended family or neighbours in the same village, for example. The social relations in which Japanese economic transactions are embedded are, in contrast, achieved - membership in the firm, for instance, through selection tests designed to make sure that each set of new employees starts off on its appropriate career track as a relatively ability-homogeneous group. As a sub-contractor, one has to work one's way through Categories C and B before one gets to be a Category A supplier of Toyota. The greater tendency of Japanese associations to develop community-like characteristics is part of this more general syndrome of the tendency for economic transactions to be 'embedded' in this kind of (achieved) social relationship.

But to be more systematic about it, it seems useful to distinguish between two different mechanisms which create the system-ness of Japan's economic system - institutional interlock and motivational congruence.

INSTITUTIONAL INTERLOCK

The most obvious way in which the institutions of any country's capitalist

* From *Market Capitalism, Welfare Capitalism: Japan and Germany Versus the Anglo-Saxons,* Oxford University Press, 2000, pp. 45–8. This passage concludes the chapter in which I enumerate four distinctive characteristics of the Japanese economy as 'firms which on the "stakeholder", employee-favouring/shareholder-favouring dimension lean heavily towards employees: second, relational trading [as opposed to impersonal spot market trading], third, a greater tilt towards co-operation in the co-operation/competition balance among competitors, and, finally, a strong role for government as producer of public goods and umpire arbitrating clashes of private interests, in matters where Anglo-Saxon countries would leave the market to sort things out.' [p. 51]. Earlier 'systems' articles include 'The Distinctiveness of Japan' in Crouch and Streeck (eds), 1996, 1997, and 'Asian Crisis and the Future of the Japanese Model', 1998.

system may be described as a system, is through the jigsaw-puzzle-like 'fitting' of one institutional practice with another. Take, for example, the three salient features of the Japanese system:

(i) lifelong rather than highly mobile employment relationship;
(ii) long-term, obligated customer-market rather than auction-market mobile, supplier relations;
(iii) patient, long-term committed rather than short-term-returns-sensitive, equity capital and the consequent absence of take-overs.

Some of the obvious interconnecting 'fits', already hinted at above, are:

(i) Supplier relations can more easily rest in part on verbal understandings and trust because the assembler's purchasing manager, as a lifelong member of the firm who identifies with it, can commit not just himself but the firm. Although he is likely to move on to something else at his next posting, his successor will see himself as bound by promises his predecessor gave, and his predecessor will still be around in the firm to give his version of what those promises might have been. Lifetime employees have a strong and shared interest in the firm's reputation.
(ii) Wage differentials between the high-prestige, high market-power, leading firms in an industry and lesser supplier firms – the 'premium wage' paid in top firms – is made legitimate by the selection processes that go along with lifetime employment. Because first jobs are start-of-career jobs, you aim for the best firms. Top firms can therefore select the best workers, and invest a great deal in recruitment selection (in explicit budgeting terms more than on training) because they are recruiting for very long tenures.
(iii) And the length of tenures and the nature of the internal promotion system motivate individuals to train themselves: the top firms recruit the best learners and so maintain their top status and market power vis-à-vis subcontractors.
(iv) People who have committed their working lives to a particular firm, are more prone to take a long-term view, to have a low time-discount. The firm's future is their future – an important pre-condition for the long-termism which informs both the supplier relations and stable shareholding.
(v) Managers who have to watch their share prices in volatile stock markets to avoid take-overs cannot afford to keep underemployed workers on their books through recessions. The cross-shareholdings, committed capital and the absence of take-overs are, therefore, preconditions for lifetime employment.

(vi) Maintaining the cross-shareholdings may involve sacrificing gains available from investing in something with higher returns, in order to retain the long-term business relationship with the issuing firm. That long-term interest is more likely to be appreciated by lifetime managers. Lifetime employment was thus a precondition for the initial creation of the cross-shareholdings and of the conventions which surround them.

There is, also, of course, institutional interlock between economic and not primarily economic institutions – the structure of the family and employment institutions, for example. The distinctness of male and female roles in the marriage relationship, and in society generally, determines the acceptability of the sharp difference between the terms and conditions under which young unmarried and older married women are usually hired, and the 'male as breadwinner' assumption affects the acceptability of the lifetime distribution of male wages. It may well be, also, that the first-generation industrial workers from farm families were attracted into initially-low-wage career employment patterns which gave an assured future to their eldest sons who inherited the farm because their families accepted the need to 'set younger sons up for life'.

MOTIVATIONAL CONGRUENCE

But there is another mechanism which can make for coherence in social systems. It could be called, on the analogy of 'cognitive dissonance', 'motivational sonance' – the consistency of the motivating maximands which lie behind behaviour over a wide range of social/economic situations. Is there in all these institutional practices described, a similarity in the values which seem to be maximized, in the moral constraints that seem to be obeyed, which would make it plausible to say: well; it's just that people brought up in Japanese families and schools are largely predisposed to behave in this way, and to take happily to this kind of institutional practice, whereas people brought up in British or American schools and families are predisposed to behave differently and to fit into different kinds of institution? (Japanese or Americans, on average, that is to say. There is no need to postulate that no one brought up in America could fit happily into a Japanese-type firm, or that no Japanese could fit into the individualistic short-term life of a British company. The normal-curve distribution of behavioural predispositions spreads around the median in both societies. It is just that the median is in a different point on the various scales/dimensions involved.[2])

The following three seem to me the chief ones.

1. Anglo-Saxons behave in ways designed to keep their options open – to

keep their freedom to change jobs and loyalties, to shift investments, as soon as ever the prospect of advantage offers. Japanese are much more willing to foreclose their options by making long-term commitments from which, they accept, they can only with great difficulty disengage themselves.

2. In making their choices, Anglo-Saxons give greater weight to their own immediate welfare or that of their family or personal friends. Japanese are much more likely, by virtue of their long-term commitments, to have diffuse obligations to promote the welfare of others – the other members of the firms they have joined, their partners in long-term trading relationships, etc. Put starkly, this is a difference in the selfishness/altruism dimension.
3. The third difference, rather more often made into an explicit cultural norm than the other two, is in the 'productivist' dimension already elaborated in the previous chapter.

The multiple factors which might make, or manifestly are making, these dispositions change and, in changing, change the institutions which in turn mould the dispositions – how they change, with the effect, seemingly of 'financializing' the 'system', are the subject of the rest of the book. They range from unwilled social evolutionary changes in class structure, in the distribution of material and social capital, to changing interest-group objectives based on changing perceptions of self-interest, ideological influences, technological change, and globalization. They cover the whole gamut of, to adopt Runciman's useful basic classification:[3] modes of coercion, modes of persuasion and modes of production.

NOTES

1. Karl Polanyi, *The Great Transformation*, New York, Rinchart, 1944.
2. On the tedious methodological question of why I prefer to talk of 'behavioural dispositions' rather than of 'culture', see Ronald Dore, 'The distinctiveness of Japan' in Colin Crouch and Wolfgang Streeck (eds), *Political Economy of Modern Capitalism*, London, Sage, 1997.
3. W.G. Runciman, *A Treatise on Social Theory*, Cambridge, CUP, three vols, 1983–97.

20. Unity and diversity in world culture*

Why does culture matter to the student of international order? In what sense does the prospect that the world might be getting more culturally homogeneous (Westernized, modernized) have implications for the possibilities of sustaining an international order?

In at least three possible senses. First, there is the view that 'a' culture is 'all of a piece', is shaped by 'certain primary structuring ideas' which determine the 'general cast' of the religions, art styles, social structures, and political systems (including relations with outsiders) which that culture can spontaneously create, or can enduringly tolerate if it happens that they are imposed from outside. According to this view, Chinese or Hindu or Islamic cultures are each *in their substantive content* incapable of integration within a system of international order which has grown out of a different, Judaeo-Greco-Roman culture. The obstacles are at two levels.

First, at a purely cognitive level, there is not always enough similarity between cultures in their basic ways of conceptualizing ... such Western concepts as 'contract', 'law', 'responsibility', etc. Second, different cultures embody different value-systems and moral injunctions. Other cultures do not place the same relative valuations on order, peace, national (or ethnic, or regional, or ecclesiastical) self-assertion, neighbourly co-operation and so forth, as each other or as the West does.

The third sense in which cultural differences affect the possibility of international order has, unlike the other two, nothing much to do with the *substantive content* of cultures. The rules of order in a society of states - that agreements should be obeyed, that envoys should be immune, etc. - rest on some sort of perception of the inevitability of continuing intercourse, some sense that the society of states requires moral commitment to certain basic

* From H. Bull and A. Watson (eds), *Expansion of International Society*, Oxford, Clarendon Press, 1984, pp. 407–24, abridged. This paper was the result of my participation in a seminar organized over several years by Bull and Watson, which resulted in the book. In a letter to *Prospect* I sought to temper Huntington's enthusiastic adoption of his 'second generation nativist reaction' [in a *Prospect* article summarizing *The Clash of Civilizations and the Remaking of the World Order*, New York: Simon and Schuster, 1996] by pointing out that there were third and fourth generations, too.

rules because it is a community and there is no alternative to that community continuing to exist - neither the alternative of withdrawal of self, nor that of elimination by genocide of other. The society of states, that is to say, requires the existence of some sort of moral community, some degree of Kantian reciprocity and ability to take the role of the other which at minimum rules out the contemplation of genocide - at the very least it requires some such sense of community among those who act on behalf of states, and, if order is to be enduring, potentially also among the populations they represent. The sort of 'fellow feeling', the sense that the other person is of one's 'own kind', necessary for that minimal sense of moral community can be inhibited by a variety of things - most clearly, perhaps, by the fact that people have different skin colours or facial bone structures, but also by the perception that they have different tastes and faiths and values and table manners - different cultures. Greater similarity in these respects, therefore, on whatever substantive pattern the convergence takes place, enhances the possibilities of fellow-feeling, and hence the observance of the rules which sustain international order.

For handy reference we might call these three postulated mechanisms the cognitive dissonance mechanism, the value-clash mechanism, and the fellow-feeling mechanism. My first point is that the fellow-feeling mechanism is the most important of the three.

COGNITIVE DISSONANCE

Let us look at the cognitive dissonance mechanism first. Most of the supposed examples of the working of this mechanism turn out on examination to be something else. Take, for example, the supposed difference between Americans and Japanese with respect to the notion of 'contract'. To be sure, mistaken *expectations* of other people's behaviour (a form of cognition, certainly) are a potent source of conflict - as the story of almost any British strike shows, and international affairs perhaps more acutely. But they do not necessarily depend on misunderstandings of each other's concepts. Such well-known differences in behaviour as that between Americans and Japanese with respect to contracts are well known and discounted for. Japanese *expect* Americans to behave like Shylocks. They *understand* that 'contract' means something different from *keiyaku* - only too well.

And the identity of understanding is even more complete with respect to international contracts - treaties. The sophisticated apprehension of the meaning of 'law', 'contract', 'treaty' is in any society a minority accomplishment. There is much to be said for the view that the international system is a relatively autonomous one which socializes its own participants, whether they be Nigerian diplomats or Argentinian, and rarely encounters cognitive obstacles to the absorption of its basic terms of discourse.

It is certainly in terms of that universal conceptual currency, not in terms of concepts unique to their shared Confucian culture, that China and Japan have conducted their bilateral diplomatic relations in the course of this century. A recent study of how 'the inscrutable have negotiated with the inscrutable' over the last thirty years[1] makes this clear. The special features are primarily a matter of occasional use of claims to a 'special relationship' analogous to that used in Anglo-American relations. That is to say, fellow-feeling mechanisms, not cognitive dissonance/sonance mechanisms, are involved.

INCOMPATIBLE VALUES

As for the second mechanism, the value-clash mechanism, clearly differences in the dominant value priorities of states can exacerbate conflicts between them. In principle it need not. Provided there is no cognitive dissonance, provided the difference in values is clear, it can be taken account of as merely affecting the weightings of each side in conflicts of interest the resolution of which by orderly processes of compromise is what international order is all about ... Conflicts are exacerbated, or created, by differences in values when the difference is not accurately perceived - as when successive British governments failed to appreciate either the strength of Argentine nationalism or the extent to which the claim to the Falklands was a central expression of it. It may also be exacerbated or created when the difference is perceived, but the values of the other side are denounced as 'unreasonable' - as when, at the opening of Japan, the Western powers declared that the value Japan's rulers placed on their seclusion served only unreasonably to deprive the Japanese people of the benefits of international trade. Hitherto, as in that case, claims that another state's value priorities were unreasonable have usually been used simply as justification for the challenging state's self-interest. Lately, however, with the emergence of embryo notions of a world community, states have begun urging their own values on others for moral rather than self-interested reasons - as in the brief[2] American concern with human rights, or the attempts to urge the Japanese to abjure the wickedness of catching whales.

Another special case of the substantive nature of values leading to conflict is when the value-system of a particular state gives great weight to war activities themselves as one of the highest manifestations of the state's existence. As the appeasement policies of the 1930s showed, it would have been hard for any peace-loving state, whatever its accurate perception of the values of Hitler's Germany and its forebearance from denouncing them as unreasonable, to avoid conflict leading to war.

So conflicts of values obviously do make the maintenance of a peaceful international order more difficult. In fact, the very distinction between 'interests' and 'values' is spurious. An interest is not an interest until it concerns something which is valued. And even dyed-in-the-wool militarism as a value can be translated into an 'interest' in gaining opportunities for warlike self-expression – which is why Weber used to talk about 'ideal and material interests' and economists talk about 'psychic income'. What is really at issue here is the distinction not between values and interests, but between *universal* values/interests like territory or opportunities for trade (one can safely assume that for all states the more of them the better) and *idiosyncratic* values/interests which some states have and others do not depending on their 'culture'.

What has to be guarded against, however, is the assumption that this culture is an implastic unity, that the interest-defining values relevant to international behaviour are the expression of some deep-rooted all-of-a-piece culture. The difference in the value priorities relevant to international behaviour of Helmut Schmidt's Germany and Hitler's Germany should be enough to undermine that notion.

Nor are the core values of a society necessarily best deduced from its admired scriptures. Someone setting out for Teheran might, indeed, gain some insight if not exactly from the Koran, at least from what Khomeini says about, or quotes from, it. But …, he will probably gain even greater insights by reading, instead, in the general sociology of nationalism and nativist reactions. It is, indeed, true that … the principles of traditional religions like Islam or modern religions like Marxism are more likely in some societies than in others to have an effect on foreign policy, but even in such societies it generally is a matter of action being provided with justification, rather than of action being dictated by the central moral imperatives, by the internal logic, of the religious tradition. All the large (literate) religious traditions in question are extremely diverse. Japan, in the twelfth and thirteenth centuries alone, spawned one version of Buddhism very similar to evangelical Christianity and another very similar to militant Islam. The available inventory is generally large – even Marxism is already a house with many mansions – and which items are drawn from stock is very much a discretionary matter.

Discretionary, but not arbitrary. In the last century, whether in the form of the Mahdis, the Boxers, Shinto patriots, Ghandians, or modern Islamic fundamentalists, the point being made by the revivalists is generally a nationalist point.[3] The attribution of value to a traditional religion is a claim to parity of respect asserted against 'dominant other' nations, and often, simultaneously and more proximately, against a local ruling class which has embraced the values and life-styles of those dominant other nations. The tradition to be reasserted can be crafted out of the available inventory to provide the maximum dimensions of differentiation from the oppressors. Thus Gellner, describing the variety of traditional Islam in terms of an austere Great Tradition and a more indulgent superstitious Little Tradition notes that it is from the former that the urbanizing or urban-aspiring revivalists draw their new Islamic fundamentalism, because 'it does a triple job. It defines them against the foreigner. It defines them . . . against a Westernized and envied elite, and it . . . defines them against their own rural past of which they are openly ashamed'.[4] Just as, one might say, the castelessness of Ghandiism allowed its followers to assert the virtues of rural simplicity while disavowing those elements of traditional rurality of which – under Western influence – they no longer approved.

So let us grant some causal force to the overt *doctrinal* traditions of formal religious faiths – just as it makes some difference to the shape of the pantomime horse whether there are fat men or thin men inside. And perhaps one should grant even more force to the less overt, less avowed subtleties of culturally-determined patterns of interpersonal relations and the way they work through to the value priorities of states. For example, the considerable concern in Japan's foreign policy with the international reputation of the country, is surely very largely the product of a century's struggle to gain recognition as an equal member of the white-skinned club of Great Powers; but it is also, probably, a reflection of the fact that Japan has traditionally been, and to some extent remains, a hierarchical society in which people more often show a concern to establish who ranks above or below whom than they do in more egalitarian countries. But the motive force (to strain the metaphor a bit further, the pay-off which persuades both fat men and thin men to get into the pantomime horse) remains interests defined by *universal* values – the resentful urge to correct one's nation's perceived deprivations of prestige, power, income, territory, or economic opportunity which has always formed the issue between *status quo* and *non-status quo* powers.

Those who doubt this, particularly those whose doubts rest on the perception that much of the Third World, once Europeanized by imperial masters, has partly reverted to idiosyncratic traditional cultures and thereby become less accessible to the appeals of an order based on Western civilization, should look at Tucker's examination of the collective claims of the Third World to a redistributive New Economic Order.[5] The arguments of 'the new political sensibility' (which he is concerned to scotch) are all couched in terms wholly familiar from the claims of, or on behalf of, the poor and underprivileged *within* Western societies (even the 'reparations' argument is used in the case of American blacks). They are arguments appealing to principles of morality familiar within Western civilization. The only novelty – extending those principles 'beyond the confines of the state' – is a novelty which owes nothing to any non-Western culture: Boulding, Myrdal,

MacNamara, and the other authors of the authoritative statements of this novel principle whom Tucker quotes are not noted as exponents of any traditional non-Western culture.

FELLOW-FEELING

Finally we come to the third, the 'fellow-feeling' mechanism. The main questions to be asked are: first, how genuinely important is it; second, are there reasons to think that the cultural bases for fellow-feeling are increasing, or decreasing?

There are many who would answer the first question with a firm: 'of minimal importance'. Thus Morgenthau:

> Let us suppose that American and Russian education and culture could be brought to the same level of excellence or completely amalgamated, and that Russians would take to Mark Twain as Americans would take to Gogol. If that were the case, the problem of who should control Central Europe would still stand between the United States and the Soviet Union as it does today.[6]

I would beg to differ. Quite apart from the ambiguities of the phrase 'control Central Europe', and the fact that there have been times when there was an influential view in both Moscow and Washington that the two powers had a *shared* interest in not encouraging any Warsaw Pact state to think it could swing to NATO, or vice versa, there is surely plenty of evidence that an increase in fellow-feeling does enhance the propensity to perceive shared interests, and lessen the tendency to exacerbate conflicts of interest by attributing malevolence or moral turpitude to opponents. No French observer would deny that as a result of this fellow-feeling, there is something of a special relationship between the United States and the United Kingdom. No Japanese observer would deny that there is equally something special in the relation between the USA and all European countries that is not present in relations between the USA and Japan – and they might well ascribe to that difference the fact that Europe makes such a conflictual thing about its trade deficit with Japan, but not about its equally large deficit with the USA. Similarly, most Japanese would agree that the phrase which resounds in the speeches of friendship delegations – the Japanese and Chinese 'are of the same culture, the same stock' – has some meaning, even if it is difficult to specify how much it has meant in terms of concrete concessions rather than in demands for symbolic assertions of solidarity (as in the famous dispute over the anti-hegemony clause in the Treaty of Friendship).

All that is contended is that it *would* make a difference to the possibilities of international order if 'people in Maine should feel the same degree of responsibility toward the people of Japan or Chile or Indo-China as they feel towards California' – a sense of responsibility for which 'fellow-feeling' is an obvious precondition. This proposition is equally accepted by Boulding who thinks that state of affairs desirable and even possible, and by Tucker who would find it abhorrent if he were not convinced of its impossibility. It would, of course, be naïve to attribute the fact that there has been no civil war between Maine and California while the USA *has* been engaged in major wars with Japan and Indo-China to differences in degree of fellow-feeling. The system of order which regulates conflicts of interests between Maine and California is one enforced by the whole apparatus of a federal state with a well-honed constitution, a system of justice, and a monopoly (or near-monopoly) of violence. But the development of those federal institutions, as any historian of the USA would affirm, did depend on the existence, the cultivation of, and the appeal to, fellow-feeling as well as shared material interest. And it is to the same dialectical feedback between strengthening institutions and strengthening fellow-feeling that optimists must look for prospects of the establishment of world order.

But fellow-feeling between whom? Most importantly, clearly, between those who formulate foreign policies. One has to make a distinction, as Bull does [see note 11], between those directly involved in state-to-state contacts, who participate in a diplomatic society and are inducted into a world diplomatic culture, and the larger urban elite within whom they interact and inter-marry and from whom come the interest-group pressures on their policies. Diplomats can be overruled and rapidly replaced (more especially where bureaucratic traditions are shallow). Hence the possibilities of fellow-feeling between these wider urban elites of the world are what become important if one is thinking of building *sustained* commitment to the conventions of an international order.

Beyond them lie the men on the Clapham omnibus. The extent to which the stretch of *their* sympathies counts varies, of course, from country to country, depending on whether they are indeed men who ride on omnibuses and read daily newspapers, or men who think themselves lucky to ride on a bullock cart and wouldn't know what to do with a newspaper if they had one. It depends, also, of course, on the extent to which the political system is such as to allow the popular sentiments to have an effect on policy.

These answers to the 'fellow-feeling between whom?' question become important as soon as we begin to address ourselves to the second question, the possibility of an increasing volume and more widespread distribution of fellow-feeling in the world. Hitherto, in the guise of enunciating a single proposition, I have covertly been using two, viz.:

1. Increased fellow-feeling between state representatives in a society of

states, and between the national groups of their compatriots who influence or control them, increases the likelihood that they will have some moral commitment to the rules of order established in that international society and subordinate the pursuit of national interests in conflicts with other states to those rules.

2. Ego is more likely to experience fellow-feeling towards alter the more he perceives him to be similar to himself (if I may phrase the matter in the jargon of the psychologists who have provided evidence for this proposition - though they would add the qualification: up to the point at which the similarity becomes close enough to evoke the eerie discomfort of the *doppelganger* echo effect) (Snyder and Fromkin, 1980).[7]

All one needs now as a preliminary to asking the important question about change in the modern world is a third proposition:

3. People are more likely to perceive similarities between themselves and others (a) the more similar they in fact are, (b) the more they have a chance to observe each other, and (c) the less actual contact is preceded by the absorption of hostile stereotypes of each other.

INCREASING CULTURAL HOMOGENEITY?

There are two kinds of arguments in support of the view that similarity is increasing. The first is the popular assumption about cultural diffusion - about the Westernization, Americanization, cocacolanization, etc. of the world. The second is a family of arguments of a social evolutionary kind about the unfolding logic of industrialism. Let us take the more complex second family of arguments first.

They come in many versions, from the more obviously ethnocentric argument that 'moral progress (i.e. *their* becoming more like us) follows material progress', to more subtle arguments to the effect that the material interest which nations have in adopting the principles of scientific rationality in matters of technology or business accounting so firmly roots those principles in the society - in the first place in the schools - that they are diffused to politics, to law and administration (leading to the universal growth of bureaucracy), to family life (leading to family planning, etc.) to religion (leading to a decline in superstition), and so on. At the same time the growing division of labour with economic development, increased specialization in ever more sophisticated occupations, greater spatial and social mobility, all lead to greater individuation and an expansion of individual choice, the growth of the nuclear family, the weakening of community ties, egalitarianism, the switch from particularistic to universalistic norms, from principles of ascription to those of achievement, etc.

Convergence of cultures occurs, in other words, because (broadly speaking) there is only one way of organizing societies to make an industrial system work efficiently, and all societies do want to get an efficient industrial system.

These versions of the convergence theory were most influential in the late 1950s and early 1960s when it was possible to argue that the Japanese, poor souls, were not very efficient industrially because they somehow could not get their societies organized according to the best principles of individualism and scientific rationality in the way that Americans did. (Clark Kerr and his fellow authors[8] were among the more influential exponents of the view.) It is rather awkward for the thesis that, while still failing to organize themselves properly, the Japanese have perversely managed to achieve a considerable level of industrial efficiency.

But if hopes of increasing similarity arising from the inner logic of industrialism must be tempered, there are also the *diffusion* processes at work. These proceed at two levels. First there is the direct spread of fashions and tastes, of architectural styles and wallpaper patterns, of pop songs and Kentucky Fried Chicken, along established commercial channels; the spread of religions by missionaries, of ideologies of self-determination or racial equality through academic and political congresses and by tired journalists who find it easier to purloin ideas by translation from a foreign journal than to think of something new. Second, diffusion takes place through the directly imitative transplant of institutions, usually from countries considered more, to countries considered less, advanced – the implantations of bureaucratic systems of civil service organization, of school and health systems, are examples. These institutions shape the behaviour, the aspirations and sensibilities of those who are involved in them as surely as do those of industrialism itself, and in ways which probably, on balance, make for greater similarity with people in the countries where those institutions first evolved.

There is, indeed, some empirical evidence to show that increasing similarity of outlooks and values does result from these processes. A study of urban workers in six developing countries sought to measure the extent to which they held a set of attitudes and values (stressing individual choice and responsibility, belief in rationality and the possibility of controlling one's fate, etc.) which were labelled by that question-begging term 'modern'. Their responses showed clearly a greater incidence of these modern attitudes the longer the exposure to schools, to factories, and to urban living.[9]

These advances in similarity are still limited: British, Chinese, and Pakistani factory workers may all live in nuclear families, have educational ambitions for their children, limit their families, and plan household expenditures, but still behave very differently towards their wives or their foremen or their politicians. Nevertheless they *are* advances in similarity stretching to social strata beyond the middle class elites, if not yet very far into the rural hinterlands where the bulk of the population of some states lives.

For these real advances in similarity to affect perceptions of similarity, and hence fellow-feeling, the second of the conditions in proposition 3 must be fulfilled - viz., increasing contact. That the density of such contacts is in fact increasing is clear enough. Inkeles [and Smith] uses a variety of statistics to prove the point - for university students overseas, for volumes of foreign mail, telephone calls, tourist travel, world trade, overseas investment, and the number of non-governmental international organizations (increasing in the early 1970s at 5 per cent p.a.). And to physical movements must be added the worldwide exchange of television films. That factory workers are less affected than middle classes is obvious, but then they are, as argued above, less important to the argument about cultural homogeneity, fellow-feeling, and world order.

TRANSNATIONAL CONTACTS

One particular form of international contact relates to the earlier argument about industrialization and individuation as well as to the distinction, as Bull draws it, between a 'society of states' and 'world society'. One version of the view that we are moving towards a world society is what Pettman calls the structuralist view of the world as a global capitalist system in which divisions between states are seen as ('ultimately'?) of lesser consequence than divisions between classes.[10] There may, indeed, be rare manifestations of global working class solidarity - Swedish workers, perhaps the world's most internationally travelled workers, have been known to strike in support of the Brazilian employees of their Swedish multinational - but the chances of growing cultural homogeneity and an emerging sense of solidarity are probably somewhat greater in the international capitalist bourgeoisie.

But greater still (since international capitalists are often competing directly with each other) are the chances of such cross-frontier solidarity among professional groups. The arguments go as follows. One universal feature of the transformations of industrialization and modernization is a switch from family production in hereditary lines of business to wage/salary employment in *chosen* occupations … This opportunity, even necessity, for choice … leads to some increase in individuation, some increase in … the degree to which people are committed to the choices they have made. Men and women who *choose* their loyalties are more likely to define their identity in terms of their chosen occupation, more likely to be self-consciously committed to a religious or ethnic group.

And this, together with the increase in communications and travel leads to some transnationalization of inter-personal allegiances: people who are musicians to their fingertips may feel a greater sense of brotherhood with foreign musicians than with tone deaf fellow-countrymen. Frontier-crossing ties of community of this type can develop among physicists, boy scouts, Orientalist scholars, Jews, tennis players, engineers, and bird-watchers. These allegiances can lead, for example, to an intensified concern of UK musicians for USSR musical dissidents. Multiple pressures from musicians, writers, Jews, Baptists, etc., can prompt the US government to make human rights representations to the USSR which can lead to Helsinki agreements, and some continuing pressure to reinforce them.

The underlying process is arguably a movement towards a world society, a frontier-eroding process inimical to the institutionalization of a society of states. Yet the effective expression of this process is in inter-state agreements, and the society of states is also strengthened by the increase in the scope and diversity of the binding ties of international agreements, and by the strengthening pressures within the states to see that agreements are kept. The distinction between movement towards a world society and movement towards a society of states is a useful one, but *(pace* Bull[11]), the two trends can be complementary rather than contradictory.

THE CONSTITUENTS OF CULTURE

So far in this argument I have left the concept of 'cultural similarities' unexamined. It can, perhaps, remain that way to be understood at a common-sense level. If we are concerned with the stretch of sympathy, the degree of fellow-feeling which provides the impulse occasionally to try to see the world from the other person's point of view, which prompts the diffusion of positive rather than negative stereotypes of foreign counterparts, and the willingness to take risks in, say, disarmament agreements, gambling on the other side's good faith and thereby building relations of trust, then almost any kind of similarity can contribute to it: similarity in material and artistic and intellectual culture - shared tastes for blue jeans, Polish films, hamburgers, or Japanese pottery, the shared appreciation of engineering skills or sportsmanship on the soccer field - can be as important as deeper and more private matters like religious faiths or moral principles.

The 'world culture' which is emerging as the common elements of middle-class life-styles in Washington and Moscow, Havana and Caracas, Dakar and Tokyo, may indeed be a rather superficial matter of parallel tastes and snob values in cars or domestic architecture, classical music, or patent medicines; similar concerns about children's education and lung cancer; a similar familiarity with the Hilton Hotel coffee-shop culture of muzak and orange juice, discos and cheesecloth blouses. But that does not necessarily reduce its importance for the diffusion of fellow-feeling. And there seems no reason to doubt that the increasing density of communications (slower though that process may be in the recent years of economic stagnation than in the previous three decades) is leading to an increasing similarity of these urban middle-class cultures – an increasing fleshing out of a skeletal 'world culture', and its diffusion to larger numbers of people.

INHIBITORS

Except where explicit obstacles are interposed to hinder this 'natural' process. One can include Moscow and Havana in a list of 'world culture' capitals, as I did above, a little more easily than one can include Peking. All countries which call themselves Communist try to limit the penetration of this 'world culture' to some degree, but the Chinese more strenuously, more publicly, and more self-consciously than most for reasons which tell us something about the nature of the phenomenon. It is not just a matter of the rejection of symbols of bourgeois ideology: there is nothing more intrinsically bourgeois about blue jeans than about dachas. It has a lot to do, also, with the nativist reaction in have-not countries which was mentioned earlier as prompting, and shaping the form of, the revival of traditional religions. When Islamic fundamentalists in Iran burn down night clubs and insist that their women veil their faces, they are not only expressing religious convictions but also the resentments bred of the deprivations of have-not status.

In poor societies, world culture, especially the material aspect of it, is a luxury culture, predominantly enjoyed by those who hold power and their friends. They are the objects of envy. This envy becomes significant when the anti-government opposition tries, as oppositions naturally do, to use nationalism against its opponents and accuse them of allowing rich and powerful countries to exploit and slight the nation with impunity. Perhaps, borrowing the paradigms of the dependency theorists, the opposition will brand the ruling group as a comprador bourgeoisie clasped in a profitable symbiotic embrace with foreign capital – an embrace which they seek to justify as a means to economic development, not understanding what sins they commit by defining development as a process of (servile) imitation of the West. Such a nationalist appeal finds it only too easy to mobilize the envy just referred to. To say that the out-of-reach grapes are immoral and forbidden is even more satisfying than claiming that they are sour. So the ruling class can be denounced for its mistaken objectives, for its lack of proper national pride in accepting subordination to foreigners, *and* for betraying the national culture by whoring after Western fads and fancies - pop music, female emancipation, eating cow meat, foreign religions, or whatever shows the most heinous contrast with local traditions.

There is a very particular twist to the process just described which can, if I may be forgiven the jargon, be called the 'second-generation indigenization phenomenon'. This brings the split between the adherents and the denouncers of Western values and life-styles into the elite groups themselves - between older and younger generations. The phenomenon can be observed in ex-colonial societies, but also in societies like Japan in the last century or China after 1949, or even, perhaps, Quebec after World War II, which are suddenly opened to catching-up 'modernization'. The first 'modernizer' or 'post-independence' generation has often received its training in foreign (Western) universities in a Western cosmopolitan language. Partly because they first go abroad as impressionable teenagers, their absorption of Western values and life-styles may well be profound - far more than the superficial veneer which, after a couple of decades' experience as a sergeant in a British African regiment, made Idi Amin a half plausible president of a modern state.

But the far more numerous second generation get their intellectual training at home in the new universities which the first generation have set up. They get their Western culture at second hand, and only a fraction of them get abroad, the majority for postgraduate study in their twenties when they are no longer plastically impressionable. At first the universities may use a metropolitan language (as is still the case in Singapore, in some universities or some faculties in India and Sri Lanka, and in French West Africa). At that stage the written-word contact is still first hand, and only the verbal, personal intercourse, life-style transmission is second hand. But soon the demand for mass university education forces a switch to teaching in the native language: knowledge is indigenized by means of translations - usually of limited range and of poor quality. The new universities provide a much more diluted contact with metropolitan world culture. Their products are likely to resent the superior sophistication of the older generation - who are also likely to be seen as blocking their chances of promotion in the hierarchies of the modern sector organizations into which they are recruited (or into which, as graduate unemployment increases, they fail to get recruited). Their proneness to succumb to the appeals of nativist opposition movements is naturally enhanced. In Japan, as the second home-trained generation gained power, this process resulted, by the early decades of [the twentieth] century, in a situation in which the graduates of Western universities were severely disadvantaged in the competition for jobs in the bureaucracy and leading modern sector organizations. The diplomatic elite of the mid-century was arguably a good deal less cosmopolitan than its counterparts at the beginning of the century. However, over the long run, the underlying processes of absorption of world culture have continued through the medium of Japanese-language education. It takes longer than direct foreign study and metropolitan-language transmission, but is more far reaching, and lasting in its effects.

The reactions just discussed can have a *general* effect in inhibiting the spread of world culture. They have a particular and acute effect on the diplomatic representatives of non-Western countries – the people whose ability to generate fellow-feeling with their opposite numbers has the most direct effect on the chances of creating and sustaining some kind of commitment to the rules of a world order. Their situation makes them peculiarly liable to schizophrenia. While being, by and large, the members of their country most likely to have absorbed, and to have a personal taste for, world culture, they paradoxically have the strongest motives for disavowing it – for two reasons. First, being most often in contact with foreigners they are most vulnerable to the charge of betraying the national interest and national culture. If the British Foreign Office smarts under the charge that it was almost traitorously willing to see the 'Argie' point of view over the Falklands, its travails are as nothing compared with those of Chinese diplomats during the Cultural Revolution who were forced to prove their Mao-loving Chineseness and hatred for the corrupt culture of the West in all sorts of humiliating ways.

The second reason is more complicated. The whole culture of diplomatic intercourse, of bilateral talks, international conferences, nobbling in the lobbies, and partying in the reception rooms – the arts of chairmanship, of cocktail party charm and conference rhetoric, of knowing when to be incisive and when to bore the time away, of judging what will count as a joke and what as an insult – is all part of a world culture as Western in its origins as apple pie. Diplomats from non-Western countries are often not very good at it. This can be for two reasons: first, because they have often had to start learning this kind of social intercourse in adulthood and then with limited chances of practice solely in professional contexts, whereas their opposite numbers have often been learning those, or highly cognate social skills, from childhood – in their middle-class Western families as well as in schools. Second, doing all these things well requires confidence, especially in the crucial early stages, and it is much easier to develop that confidence if you start with the halo worn by the representative of a top nation than if you represent a nation low down in the prestige scale. The delegate from Ecuador, coming straight from his Swiss school and seigneurial holidays on his hacienda, soon known to the diplomatic hostesses as that charming Dr Oliviera, may suffer from the low-prestige-nation disability, but never, at all, from the personal confidence one. For the Japanese delegate the former gives fewer problems, but the latter, compounded by sheer language-fluency difficulties, is likely to disadvantage him for all his professional life. For the Indonesian or the Malian delegate, both disabilities can bite with equal force.

As a result two things can happen, both inhibitive of fellow-feeling. Sensing that he does not cut much of a figure by the values of that small specialist bit of world (Western) culture in which he is engaged, he may reject those values and the values of the whole world culture of which it is a part. Second, since his contacts with his opposite numbers do not advance far in intimacy, since he does not get beyond being 'that boring Malian chap' (to be approached by such conversational gambits as 'would it be raining in your country at this time of year'), he is in effect treated in terms of his national identity rather than as a person in his own right. And that means that his national identity *does* become a more salient part of his personal sense of identity: in that context he is a Malian first, and the individual Dr Mbanka second. As such, every slight to his nation *is* a personal slight to himself. In New York, perhaps he suddenly discovers for the first time what the xenophobia of the opposition's nativist nationalism back at home was all about. So he may withdraw, start insisting on wearing national costume, using interpreters, and keeping his socializing to the formal minimum - and have as little sense of belonging to a world community linked by ties of fellow-feeling as a fully clothed Martian suddenly precipitated into the middle of a human nudist colony.

WORLD CULTURE: WESTERN CULTURE

So when one says that, *other things being equal*, an increasing density of communication should ensure an increasing basis for fellow-feeling between the nations, or at least the middle classes, or at the very least the diplomats of the world, one has to acknowledge that some of the things that may not be equal can be very important indeed.

It will be noted, however, that all the inhibiting factors listed above spring from the fact that the emergent 'world culture' is perceived as Western culture. And by and large that perception is correct. The addition of a few 'exotic' elements - Chinese cooking, vodka, soul music, the fad for Japanese quality circles in American business schools, the incorporation of Zen Buddhism and Indian Art into the catalogue of things the man of taste should appreciate, make a very small contribution to that stock of what it is that the middle-class culture of Tokyo, Bonn, Dakar, etc. have in common. But the Western character of that shared culture only matters - in all the ways just described - because the Western nations identified as having a proprietary claim to that culture are clustered around the top of the international power/prestige hierarchy and seen as exercising unfair domination over the others.

When that ceases to be the case—when, say, the Japanese or the Chinese or the Koreans perfect the first cheap and effective ABM system and secure military as well as economic dominance, when it is the Tokyo or the Peking autumn collections that dominate the fashion magazines, and the computers churn out more translations from Japanese into English than vice versa, and Japanese or Chinese universities become the goal of the world's ambitious youth – then that situation will change. World culture will still be basically Western culture. Many post-Confucian elements may be absorbed: geisha parties might replace cocktail parties at the UN and there may be more talk of benevolence and less of justice in the rhetoric. But the modes of international law and conference procedure, the *idea* of autumn collections and annual art shows, the shape of the novel and the structure and functioning of universities will still be Western in origin. But if the Western nations have been clearly demoted from their position at the top of the power/prestige hierarchy that will not matter so much. The blockages to the steady diffusion of world culture which arise from the various manifestations of the nativist reactions described above will be dissolved – not least the very important blockages to be found at present in the nations of the Sinic culture area themselves.

So, in the long term, the prospects of the structure of a world order receiving reinforcement from the binding ties of a world culture might improve. The more immediate problem is to prevent the chain reactions set off by somebody's anti-Western nativism from embroiling the super-powers into a conflict which blows up the world's chance of having that long a term.

NOTES

1. K. Ogura, 'How the "inscrutable" negotiate with the "inscrutable": Chinese neotiating tactics vis-a-vis the Japanese', *China Quarterly*, Sept. 1979, pp. 529–55.
2. [Another hindsight note. This referred to the Carter episode, long before it was discovered how effective human rights arguments could be for beating the Chinese over the head.]
3. M. Matossian, 'Ideologies of delayed industrialization', *Economic Development and Cultural Change*, **VI**(3), April 1958.
4. E.A. Gellner, 'State and revolution in Islam', *Millennium*, **VIII**(3), winter 1979–80.
5. R.W. Tucker, *The Inequality of Nations*, New York, 1977.
6. H.J. Morgenthau, *Politics Among Nations*, New York, 4th edn. 1966, p. 505.
7. C.R. Snyder and H. Fromkin, *Uniqueness: the Human Pursuit of Difference*, New York and London, 1980.
8. C. Kerr, *et al.*, *Industrialism and Industrial Man*, London, 1974.
9. A. Inkeles and D.H. Smith, *Becoming Modern*, Cambridge, MA, 1974.
10. R. Pettman, *State and Class: A Sociology of International Relations*, London, 1979.
11. H. Bull, 'Human rights and world politics', in R. Pettman (ed.), *Moral Claims in World Affairs*, London, 1979.

PART IV

Polemics: For All the Constraints of Structure and Culture, Is There Still Room For Hope and Reason?

21. White papers*

Can there be another country with so many annual government white papers? I can claim some minor responsibility. In a lifetime of writing agitated 'letters to the editor' and advocacy articles, the only evidence I have of ever having had the least scintilla of influence on any government's behaviour was when a manifesto drafted with some Japanese friends on the then chaotic nature of Japanese government publications got to the Ishibashi cabinet in 1956 and led to the setting up of the present government publications system. We offered as a model the British Stationery Office on whose exemplary finances at the time I did some research. Now, of course, the British Stationery Office is cruelly privatized and unfriendly to all but money-spinning users, while its Japanese equivalent, with its 72 branch shops all over Japan, goes from strength to strength.

* From Preface to new edition of *City Life in Japan*, Curzon Press, 1999, p. xiii, *à propos* the *Japanese White Paper on the Nation's Livelihood* (Kokumin seikatsu hakusho).

22. The diploma disease: some modest proposals*

Clearly, to deschool is to throw the baby out with the bath water, for there genuinely is an educational baby worth preserving and nurturing in the institution called school. The cure for the problems which beset developing country school systems must be sought in less drastic measures - but measures perhaps only a little less drastic.

One element lies at the heart of nearly all the problems discussed in this book: the diploma disease. ... It should, surely, be there that one should look for the possibilities of reform. Somehow, to be sure, society has to find ways of deciding who does what job, and they have to be the ways which (a) are considered by the people of that society just and acceptable ways of awarding the privileges and amenities that go with different jobs, and (b) ensure that the productive efficiency of society is not too much impaired by having too many round pegs in square holes - what may be referred to as the equity requirement and the efficiency requirement. The efficiency requirement, of course, has two parts: choosing pegs from wood of the right grain in the first place, and shaping them to a proper roundness in the second; the selection and the training aspects respectively. The solution which most societies have adopted throughout most of human history - hereditary succession - is not likely to find acceptance anywhere today; it solves the efficiency problem only in societies with a relatively simple and non-progressive technology where the chief division of labour is between those who always give orders and those who are always on the taking end (family upbringing being the best sort of shaping tool for the attitudes and self-perceptions required for efficient job performance in those respects). And equally, by 1975, hereditary succession was no longer an acceptable answer to the equity problem either, except, perhaps, in a few backwaters of Latin America and North-West Asia which are still very largely unaffected by the flood of egalitarian ideas spreading out from the industrial societies in which they

* Extracted from *The Diploma Disease*, London: Allen & Unwin/Berkeley: University of California Press, 1976, pp. 141–67. The chapter follows a highly critical examination of what was perhaps the most widely read piece of educational radicalism of the 1970s, Ivan Illich's *Deschooling Society*, London: Calder and Boyars, 1971.

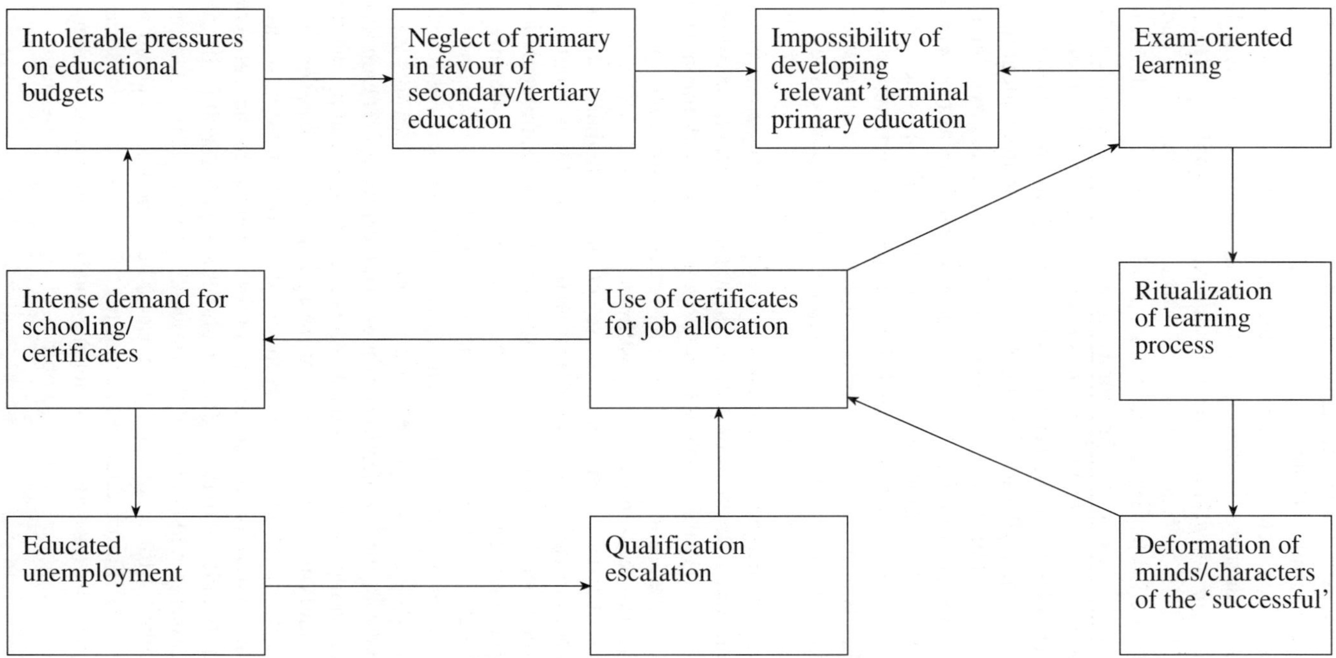

Figure 22.1 The diploma disease

first developed. And if the alternative which has developed in the industrial 'models of modernity' (both capitalist and socialist) – the alternative of relying largely on selection through the educational system – has such disastrous consequences when transplanted to developing countries, then it is time to search for something better. Even more is this so if we reflect on two points which I hope were established earlier: first [that] the certificate-selection alternative developed in the industrial countries largely ad hoc and unplanned, as a result of the cumulation of individual calculations of private rationality, not from any considerations of social rationality; and, second [that] in so far as the system does work roughly in a socially rational way, it does so chiefly by identifying the able rather than by creating ability, and that we are fooling ourselves if we think that it is necessary to keep a man at Bouleian geometry until the age of 21 just in order to test his capacity to learn (on the job, after he starts work) to write pithy position papers or plan a sales campaign. Alternatives exist. It is possible to think of something better. And as we shall see in the next chapter there are countries which are trying it, if, so far, only partially. The essential elements of that alternative are two:

1. Start careers earlier – around the ages of 15–17 – doing as much of the selection as possible within work organizations, and transforming all tertiary education and training into in-career learning, either part-time or full-time, in special educational institutes.
2. At all points where there has to be selection – particularly all-important decisions as to which work organization people are to enter initially at the end of their period of basic schooling – avoid using learning achievement tests: whether the alternative be aptitude tests, lotteries, special 'encapsulated' tests (see below), the essential thing is that they be tests which cannot be (or cannot much be) crammed for.

Let us spell out the implications of these suggestions…. The civil service, for instance, would no longer recruit graduates. There would, instead, be a single major entry port for all grades at the age of 16 (or whatever were fixed as the school leaving age) and everyone would start as a clerk; some, on the results of internal tests, or on the basis of work performance, would be promoted fairly quickly to the executive grades and given such further training as was necessary, and some of those would similarly be selected – and educated/trained – for administrative posts. The same pattern could apply to other professions. Future engineers could train first as craftsmen; some of the craftsmen could be trained as technicians, and the ablest of those sent off for full training as engineers. Doctors could begin as medical assistants; teachers as pupil-teachers …

[The Advantages ...:]

A cure for educated unemployment.... There would be no point in a student in India or Sri Lanka slogging relentlessly on taking O levels three times and A levels four times, putting himself through the wholly joyless and uneducational grind of a ritualistic four-year university course solely in order to qualify for an outside chance of a graduate job....

The morale of the technical school. The vocational secondary schools [would no longer be] blighted by their reputation of being the dumping ground for the 'failures' who could not qualify for academic secondary schools....

More mature students.... Those who get into the tertiary institutes for professional training would be more mature; ... they would have an idea of the use to which the knowledge they gain might be put, they would have their own clear purposes, their own criteria of the value of learning. At present ... the world is full of 'misfits' channelled into their occupations solely by virtue of the fortuitous circumstance that their position in an achievement-test mark hierarchy corresponded with a certain point in the hierarchy of jobs, as those jobs were ranked by scarcity, income, power and prestige.

Greater flexibility. A further, and not the least, advantage is that the present institutionalized concept of different 'levels' of courses would disappear ... Anyone who has observed the shifting sands of pomposity in which university teachers mire themselves when they discuss whether a certain course is to be considered a 'genuinely graduate-level course', or rather is only 'of undergraduate level', will know how wholly conventional these distinctions are....

Early Recruitment into Work - Possible Objections:

... many groups in society would have strong vested interests which would be threatened by such a change. But it must be admitted that there are also a number of objections which one might make on more objective grounds of social equity and efficacy. Some ... weighty.

Loss of a dynamic spin-off? [Perhaps] educated unemployment represents one of those beneficent imbalances celebrated by such economists as Albert Hirschman, imbalances which will give dynamism to the economy by somehow making their own backward and forward linkages.

The bureaucratization of society? The scheme assumes a corporate structure of society; it assumes that all middle-level and professional careers are made within large organizations.... [but] the pass is already sold. In most developing countries the modern sector which employs the products of secondary schools and universities is already highly bureaucratized ...

Objective and subjective criteria ... University degree qualifications do, at present, offer some kind of relatively corruption-proof objective criterion for allocating these all-important life-chances. [True,] many developing societies are so riddled with 'personalism' and patronage that one would have to abandon the hope of placing much emphasis on work performance in [selecting those to be sent for further professional training and education] and rely instead on external agencies – most obviously the educational institutions which would provide the training courses – to do the selection by aptitude tests of their own devising.

Training and education.... The system might work well enough for vocational training, but how about education? If tertiary education was merely a matter of being sent on courses to become better at doing particular jobs, who would learn Amharic, who would study philosophy? ... Universities which offer genuine education could continue to exist. If non-vocational courses cease to offer certificates which could be used for job-getting purposes, ... and if, as a consequence, these courses were attended only by those who wish to learn rather than by those who wish to obtain a job-entitling certificate, the quality of the education given and received could be vastly improved. If such courses were thrown open to anyone, the numbers seeking education for its own sake might be sufficiently limited for it to be possible for the state and employing organizations to allow them to take leave from their jobs at little or no financial loss. For many professions a period of such education could become conventional, even required....

Too costly? The possible cost of such a scheme might constitute a fifth objection. Extending the period of education, having older and more mature people in full-time training, increases the social opportunity cost in production forgone; and if those who are sent for training in their twenties and thirties are to continue to receive their salaries while being educated or trained, the direct cost will be considerable. On the other hand, there would be two very important sorts of savings which in many societies would amply offset these increases in cost. The first is the reduction in the total amount of schooling required when it no longer becomes sensible to press on to ever higher levels of general education in order to get more certificates and slight improvements in job chances. Second, much more learning will be done 'on the job' so that the vocational courses which systematize practical knowledge and teach the theory behind it could be shortened. Moreover, once the idea is abandoned that all higher education has to come in two- or three- or four-year packages called degree or diploma courses, and it becomes easier to take specific 'learning modules' as suggested earlier, one could stop teaching a good deal of what is now taught in professional courses only because convention requires it ...

The specially gifted. Some talents require continuous cultivation, mature early and spoil early – the highest mathematical and musical talent, for instance. For musicians and artists there would presumably be no problem, since in those fields the distinction between training and work performance is blurred anyway. But to set a gifted mathematician at a work bench doing repetitive work for the good of his soul - even to give him a job as a junior demonstrator in a university - would be to waste the nation's stock of human talent. It should not be too difficult to make special exceptions to allow the exceptionally gifted in these fields to continue in full-time study. The more problematic question is how great would be the loss if the much larger numbers of those destined to become 'ordinary' scientists and technologists spent a good deal of their late adolescence in fairly routine work, [especially] in those cumulative branches of study like mathematics in which each new step must be built on an understanding of the step that has gone before ... It should not be beyond the wit of man to deal with the problem by providing day-release continuation classes for all those jobs which could lead to professional scientific work.

SELECTION TESTS

The second part of our modest proposal is not an essential concomitant of the early-recruitment-into-work system, but it is one which could greatly enhance its effectiveness. Society still has to select. Some of the selection will be done within work organizations, but in societies where the modern-sector work organizations that everyone wants to get into - including teaching, the jobs of salaried co-operative secretaries and village clerks - can at best absorb only 20 per cent of each age group reaching the school leaving age, how is that 20 per cent to be selected?

And also, when? There are a number of developing countries which can already reasonably hope, as Sri Lanka does, to give every child a basic nine-year education lasting up to the job-recruitment age of 15 or 16, depending on whether schooling starts at 6 or 7. In most, however, it is hardly feasible to provide truly universal primary education for more than five or six years. Given that it would be unreasonable either to delay the start of schooling much beyond the age of 6, or (given the culture gap problem, too, between the modern and traditional sectors) to make the point of job recruitment earlier than 16, or at the most 15, this suggests a two-tier system - a universal and compulsory five or six years of primary schooling, followed by a selective secondary school for three or four years with (the only realistic assumption) most of the modern sector jobs being open only to secondary graduates. This would imply a double selection process: first for entry into secondary school, and second for entry into jobs.

These selection procedures ... should employ, not achievement tests, but instead tests which cannot be, or cannot much be, specifically coached and crammed for. The rationale for this suggestion should be obvious to those who have followed the argument so far. If the primary schools are to develop curricula which are genuinely helpful in preparing that majority of their students who are destined to spend the rest of their lives as self-employed farmers and craftsmen and fishermen and retailers, the schools have to be liberated from the 'backwash effect' of examinations which, as we saw when discussing Sri Lanka's experiments with pre-vocational courses, effectively prevent 'relevant' curricula either from being taken seriously, or else from being genuinely relevant (rather than additional intellectualized packages of knowledge made artificially examinable for selection purposes).

[The remainder of the chapter considers the various alternatives - aptitude tests of various kinds; academic tests confined to maths and native language, or 'encapsulated achievement tests'('example … a recent innovation of the Ceylon Institute of Chartered Accountants which gives applicants for articling a three-week course at the end of which they are tested on what they have learned. [This was] an achievement test; it tested the ability to learn; it tested it in a specifically relevant field, and it had no backwash effect on the school curriculum'). Another alternative was qualifying tests plus lotteries - an idea 'some people may find shocking. But lotteries have been used in Japan and Korea for distributing children among high schools, and in Holland for deciding who can and who cannot be admitted to universities.' It continues with a discussion of how teachers might adapt if the examinations they would still need for feedback were no longer a crucial determinant of their pupils' life chances, and concludes a pessimistic assessment of the forces that would line up against such change with a summary of the 'radical structural reform package' as it appeared in a special report on education and employment in ECAFE's 1973 Annual Survey. That summary follows. The handful of people who ever read it would have had little difficulty in discerning that the Dore seeking to borrow the authority of that august body's anonymous author was its anonymous author.]

Alter the public sector recruitment patterns to do all bottom-of-the-ladder recruitment at 16–18, and give every incentive to the private sector to do likewise. Higher education beyond that age to consist of three types:

(i) In-service training, e.g. of future administrators to study politics, economics, public administration or sociology. Such training could be recurrent throughout life and in a variety of forms, not conventional degrees.
(ii) Training for self-employment. Non-certifiable courses in carpentry, business management, accountancy, etc. (but certifiable when there is a need to protect the public, e.g. in the case of druggists).
(iii) In-career education: again non-certifiable courses, again not

> conventional university degree packages of knowledge, again not confined to the beginning of a career. They would be part time or there could be a scheme of granting leave from work for these general education courses as much as for in-service training.

Use the resources released by the consequent natural shrinkage of tertiary-level education to make primary education as universal as possible, and extend the open-access span of universal schooling as long as possible.

Decisively shift the content of primary education to make it relevant to the work life of the community in which the school is situated. All tests which serve to ration life chances, e.g. occupational recruitment tests, and selection in the educational system (in societies which cannot afford to keep all children in school until the age of 16 or 17 so that there has to be selective education at the secondary level), to be something other than achievement tests to avoid distorting the school curriculum.

In all fields, an encouragement of on-the-job learning, decisively shifting the balance of the society's learning from pre-career qualification to in-career preparation for a future career which one has already chosen, and for which one has already been chosen.

23. Adjustment in process: a Lancashire town*

[This paper is an interim report from a field study. It concerns the structure of industry in the former textile town of Blackburn; how, why and in what manner are textiles going downhill? What is going uphill, and why? The focus of the research is on one particular kind of adjustment problem - that arising from the dynamics of trade between the NICs (and subsequent generations of NICs), and older industrial countries (hereafter OICs). The assumptions, positive and normative on which the investigation is based are as follows:]

1. The OICs have one set of (manufacturing) industries (A) which are losing domestic markets to imports because the NICs' potential comparative advantage from lower wage rates is being increasingly realized as they learn by doing (*and* by studying). These are industries well advanced in the product cycle where learning by doing and studying is easier. They also have (B) another 'Schumpeterian' set (mostly manufacturing, some services) at an earlier stage of the product cycle in which they retain comparative advantage, *and* in which productivity growth is more rapid, and hence they have most to gain in terms of growth in *per capita* income. Finally, they also have (C) an intermediate range of industries not clearly in either category, including, of course, poodle clipping and discos and retailing and emergency wards which provide non-internationally-traded goods and services.
2. It is assumed that the sort of dynamic change which would take place in the OICs in the absence of any market distortions except trade-union protection of wage levels would be roughly as follows: increasing import penetration of the markets of the A industries leads to employment decline in those industries (not a fall in wages), a consumer surplus is generated from the purchase of cheaper imports, demand in the exporting NICs for imports of the OICs' (B) industries increases, while this, plus the OIC consumers' surplus stimulate expansion in (B) and (C) industries, which absorbs the displaced labour, while the increased exports of the (B)

* Extracted from article in J.N. Bhagwati (ed.), *Import Competition and Response*, Chicago: Chicago University Press for the National Bureau of Economic Research, 1982, pp. 295–317.

industries balances the external accounts to pay for the increased imports.

3. Such an outcome is assumed to be desirable. Specifically, for all the reasons about shared interests in world stability and prosperity set out in the Brandt Commission report,[1] we assume that the policy objectives of the OIC governments should *also* give very positive weighting to the welfare gains accruing to the NICs from this process.
4. But to ask that, in order to achieve this desirable outcome, market forces should be let rip is to ask for the moon. In Europe, at least, in Japan, and increasingly in the United States, the political clout of the interests groups who lose in the process of writing off the (A) industries is too great to let that happen.
5. The only way to move toward this desirable outcome, therefore, is to buy off the opposition.
6. One can also … find arguments from justice for doing so. Current world norms concerning what citizens have a right to demand of governments have come to include the right to the protection of jobs against import competition. The entrepreneur who goes bankrupt or the worker who loses his job because the government fails to provide this protection has, on this argument, a claim to more consideration than someone who reaches the same plight through his own inefficiency.
7. But how best to provide that compensation? What formula will best (a) provide an inducement not to resist the run-down of (A) industries, (b) produce the least frictional hurt from that run-down, with (c) the most just graduation of hurt to compensation, and (d) at the same time optimizing distribution of the incremental flow of capital and labour respectively as between the (B) and the (C) industries?

The best way to work toward an answer to these questions, we thought, was by talking to people currently affected by the process.[2] [There follow 18 pages of empirical material reporting on what happened in the late 1970s to textiles firms in and around Blackburn, the views and reactions of the people who formerly managed and worked in them, the new industry start-ups, etc. and of the impact of various policy measures – the textile industry reorganization scheme of 1959, the Temporary Employment Subsidy and the Short Time Working Subsidy of the 1970s etc. It concludes that the industry's demands for 'temporary' protection while it restores competitive profitability have failed to have much beneficial effect; there are far fewer instances than in Japan and Germany of a genuine retention of competitiveness by moving up-market, and protection measures for a fixed term have generally turned out to be anything but non-renewable.]

A form of temporary protection for an import-threatened industry which might have better results is a degressive tariff tapering to zero in a fixed term of years, the revenue proceeds of which are used only to pay for scrapping and exit compensation … and not for re-equipment of firms which elect to stay in the business. [As was the case with the 1959 Act.] With a degressive tariff, the slide first gets established at a level at which it still holds off imports. By the time it ceases to do so and the threat increases, the degressive slide has an established legitimacy and it is hard for protesters to choose any rational point at which to cry halt. If the compensation amounts … were to vary with tariff revenue income, this would encourage early exit and create an interest group directly concerned with maximizing imports….

Most of the adjustment measures discussed above are aimed at firms or workers. We have seen that the real losers whom nobody thinks of compensating, are the officials of the [dwindling] textile associations and the unions – who are also the full-time organizers of the successful protectionist lobbies. Why should these associations and unions not also be compensated for lost membership fees? … Supposing compensation is to be paid to the losers, are there any devices which might increase the likelihood that the compensation paid is used to stimulate the growth of employment capacity in the (B) and (C) industries and export capacity in the (B) industries?…

Two possible devices exist. First, if exit compensation is paid to a firm which gets out of a threatened industry, an additional premium could be paid if, instead of closing, it retains the firm's identity and premises and at least some of its work-force and switches to production of a new product. If the society concerned is one like Japan where there is a belief in the ability of government officials to pick winners, the premiums might be adjusted according to the desirablity of the industry entered.

Second, redundant workers might be given a re-employment voucher. They give this to anyone who offers them a job, and their new employer can use each voucher as collateral for a capital equipment loan of £*x*. If the employee is still with the same firm after, say, twelve months, the voucher can then be cashed in by the employer for *y* per cent of £*x*. The worker's compensation is in the form of enhanced re-employment chances….

NOTES

1. W. Brandt *et al.*, *Programme for Survival*, London, Pan Books, 1980.
2. The 'we' who did the talking included collaborators, Geoffrey Shepherd, Gillian McHugh and Jill Eaton.

24. Unemployment, jobs and sharing*

A PROPER RECOGNITION STILL TO BE GIVEN TO THE UNEMPLOYMENT PROBLEM

(Letter, *Financial Times*, 15 June 1993)

That unemployment will not yield all that much to 'active macroeconomic policies' we've known for some time. Now, Edward Balls tells us (in his article 'A tide that's not for turning', 9 June) that the active labour market policies Richard Layard was advocating in his Personal View article (8 June) don't work either, except as political tokenism designed to show the problem is being taken seriously.

So what's left?'Less generous unemployment benefits'?Yes, indeed, push the welfare minimum down to American levels and you will force more people into jobs – at the poverty-level wages that now characterize so much work in America. Is that what we really want?

Surely we need to recognize that the unemployment problem is a result of the new 'labour market scissors'. On the one hand are the decent instincts which have made a welfare floor of 40 per cent of average income pretty well universal in European societies. On the other are those changes in society and technology which have changed the job structure. More and more jobs are beyond the learning capacity of people who did not do well in school, and fewer and fewer jobs are of the sort almost anybody can learn to do. The exceptions are serving and caring jobs that are only slowly becoming acceptable for able-bodied males.

And both of these factors are [continung, even accelerating] factors. Don't we need to think again about the nature of 'work' and how far doing it ought

* Sections A, B and C below are related to what I call the 'scissors effect' thesis, developed initially while working on the nature of youth unemployment in 1984, and around which I organized a conference at Farnham Castle in 1985. Very few of those present [who included David Donnison, Alan Little, Bruce Williams, Jay Gershuny, Charles Carter, Ray Pahl, Tom Schuller, Michael Young, Emma Rothschild, Michael White, Ken Young and Manfred Bienefeld] were convinced that the 'limitations on trainability', 'scissors effect' thesis had either validity or importance, but I was urged to write a book which developed the thesis, incorporating relevant passages from their sceptical papers. Failure to do this still produces occasional pangs of guilt, but I have frequently returned to the theme. A is a brief statement, B an exposition of the problem, C is an assault on those who in his eyes profit by shutting their eyes to the problem. D 'Sharing' is a recent exposition of what should be done about it.

to be a precondition for citizen dignity? The notion of a basic citizen income which effectively cuts that link, and makes extra money-earning work as much a voluntary activity for the lucky ones as amateur athletics, has been around for a long time. Shouldn't the prospect that the unemployment problem will force us into some such solution by 2020 start concentrating our minds on how to get from here to there?

At present the only people thinking about this are the members of the Citizens Income Study Centre [which has since become the Citizens' Income Trust] and we are considered slightly dotty by our academic colleagues. Isn't it time to take, if not us, at least the problem seriously, and for those who have a different perspective on the year 2020 to come clean and tell us what it is?

B GOOD JOBS, LOUSY JOBS AND NO JOBS

(From *Hitachi Lecture*, University of Sussex, 21 November 1996 [UNCRIR paper], abridged)

Whether more unemployment or an increase in ill-paid Mcjobs, it is all perfectly understandable, says the economist. There is an over-supply at the unskilled level and under-supply at the level of the highly skilled. Those with scarce skills are able to command ever higher incomes, while those with over-abundant skills command ever lower ones. The correction is obvious. Make the unskilled more skilled. Invest in human capital.

The recent OECD study on technology, productivity and employment (specially written for the second G7 'employment summit' in March 1996) talks about the need to find 'innovative solutions for those who are low-skilled or who are excluded from the labour market for other reasons'[1] but appears to have no such innovative solutions to offer beyond 'a concerted effort ... to identify those young persons who leave school with inadequate vocational preparation ..., and to develop the teaching and learning methods and settings (and supportive services) to ensure that their learning needs are met.[2]

The efforts made by Britain's National Council on Vocational Qualifications to develop these innovative learning methods and settings have recently come in for some devastating criticism, and justly so, [see below]. [But even if that were not so,] the problem with the call for better education and training that our economists resort to so readily is that it does not take account of the unequal distribution in all human populations of untrainability – of that mix of brains and the culturally transmitted will to learn which makes some people capable of significant breakthroughs in atomic physics and other people unable to figure out percentages. The displaced agricultural workers of the nineteenth century did not have much problem mastering the skills required for the factory jobs they found. Those displaced from unskilled jobs today may not be able to learn to perform adequately in the more demanding jobs which remain in our technically much more complex society. The whole spectrum of what one might call the 'ability-demandingness' of jobs has shifted upwards.

No national statistics office counts the number of lousy jobs, except in terms of wages, but they all count the number of unemployed. So about unemployment and the characteristics of unemployment common to most European countries we know a fair amount. We know, for instance, that as compared with unemployment twenty years ago, there is a much higher proportion of long-term unemployed who have been out of work for more than a year. We know that the propensity to become unemployed, and especially a member of the long-term unemployed, is highly correlated with low scholastic achievement, and we know that the jobs being sought by the majority of the unemployed are in the wholly unskilled category. We know that the hard-to-employ can easily become the unemployable - discouraged workers whose discouragement amounts to a paralysing loss of self-confidence. We know that unemployment tends to be concentrated in families - if the husband is unemployed there is a greater probability that the wife or adolescent child will be unemployed also than in families where the husband has a job, and that the gap is growing.[3]

To be sure, the fact that there is a correlation between finding it difficult to get a job and low scholastic achievement, does not mean that cognitive ability is the only, or even the major determinant of who wins in the competition for jobs which require little theoretical knowledge and none of the skills which require extensive pre-employment preparation. The range of such jobs is wide; cleaning, catering, care and sales jobs, mail delivery, security, to name but a few (though, according to a British Office for National Statistics survey, the jobs sought by most men without work in Britain fall into as few as 12 out of the 371 classified occupations[4]). Even those jobs nearly all today require at least literacy - which, according to one estimate, 600 000 adults in Britain today lack while ten times that number read and write only with difficulty.[5] They also require what is often called 'common sense' - the ability to draw inferences and take initiatives when something goes wrong. But they also require other qualities which begin to count for more as the competition for such jobs increases.

Energy, for instance, as one may realize if one observes the bustling of workers in a privatized garbage collection firm. As compared with the previous municipal service workers they are fewer in number and of higher productivity. They work more minutes in each paid-for-hour, and only the tough former municipal garbage men can stand the pace. Other jobs, particularly in the growing sector of care for the elderly, require primarily a capacity for caring sympathy, sensitivity to others' feelings and at least an appearance of caring for their welfare. In other jobs, for instance in that other

– alas – fast-growing sector of security jobs, reliability and a sense of responsibility is the prime requirement. And in sales and the service industries which require contact with customers, increasingly as managements compete in developing customer service orientation programmes, the jobs of those who have adequate social skills, the capacity for confident self-presentation, verbal fluency, *chutzpah*, the ability to say 'Have a nice day' as if you really meant it. A more general requirement, also not very clearly related to cognitive achievement, is 'getting on with people' – co-operativeness, and particularly the willingness to co-operate with, to defer to, organizational superiors. A survey of employers' perceptions of the value of qualifications in recruitment, showed very clearly that it was their judgement of this kind of personal quality which counted for far more than formal qualifications in their recruitment decisions.[6]

[One might sum up the pessimistic perspective on employment as follows:] unemployment *per se* is not the real problem; the real problem is a growing mismatch between the occupational structure dictated by technological development and international trade on the one hand, and the distribution of trainability for those occupations on the other. That growing mismatch, if left to market forces, will have the effect of consigning an increasing proportion of the labour force to an alternation between lousy jobs and no jobs at all, while paying an increasingly handsome premium to those who have the scarce learning abilities which the more difficult jobs demand.

C ONE NATION: TWO PROBLEMS

(from *Prospect*, June 1996, pp. 14–16)

Most people who have decided they will vote for Tony Blair in the modest expectation that his lot will have marginally more decent instincts than the present lot, would agree that Britain has two big problems; a competitiveness problem and a social polarization/poverty/social exclusion problem. They would probably agree also with the report of the Dahrendorf Commission that solving the one is not going to solve the other. 'Trickle down', 'the rising tide that lifts all boats', may have some relevance in the fast-growing economies of agrarian Asia, but in our mature and technically advanced industrial society tends to mean little more than sending the day's left-over sandwiches to the soup kitchens for the homeless. As the full title of the Dahrendorf Commission suggested, 'wealth creation' and 'social cohesion' are two problems not one, and they require different solutions.

No harm, perhaps, if the proffered solutions go under the same slogan. Like, for instance, 'the stakeholder economy' of Tony Blair's Singapore speech, the multiple interpretations of which were apparent in the next day's newspapers.

Will Hutton, in the *Guardian*, latching on to the passage about a shift in the corporate ethos, 'a vision of the company as a community or partnership in which each employee has a stake', declared that we had at last 'a credible ideology that stands up effectively to *laissez-faire* capitalism'. Not only a more decent society, but a more efficient one. Frank Field in *The Times*, on the other hand, with his social cohesion concerns, seized the opportunity to offer exegesis on a different passage in the speech about 'a stakeholder economy which involves all our people, not a privileged few', and outlined his plans to give everybody a personal 'stake' in a universal and compulsory pensions scheme, with the state paying the premiums for those who cannot pay for themselves.

But the fact that solutions to the competitiveness problem and solutions to the social cohesion problem can be comfortably accommodated under the same slogan, does not necessarily mean that they are complementary, or even compatible. The 'stakeholders' firm' certainly has advantages over the 'shareholders' firm'. As came to be a dominant view in the 'flexibility' debates a decade ago, if you make firms a bit more like communities, by treating 'core' employees as full members of the firm, guaranteeing stability of employment, offering profit-sharing schemes, etc., you can thereby gain 'commitment', 'involvement' and flexibility. But that involved the polarizing distinction between the privileged core – which the wise employer keeps as restricted as possible – and a dispensable 'periphery' of part-time, temporary and contract workers whose 'flexibility' is still of the easy-hire-easy-fire kind.

Fraternity can only too easily begin, and end, in the home firm. Nowhere are firms more like communities than in Japan, where even the unions are fragmented single-firm organizations, thus encouraging 'enterprise egotism' to a point which precludes much concern on the part of 'insiders' for the 'outsiders'. People have not fogotten the Minamata pollution case in which the Showa Denko union co-operated with the management in a disgraceful attempt at cover-up. German unions, by contrast – as in the proposed Alliance for Jobs, trading off wage increases for employment – do show broader social concerns, responding, in effect, to those economists, like the late James Meade, who first made a point of the insider/outsider distinction to argue that the growing advantages of privileged insiders is one cause of intractable unemployment.

David Soskice, writing in these pages a couple of months ago, suggested that this capacity of the German unions to take on board the cause of the unemployed was symptom of a broader sense of social cohesion and capacity for co-operative action in Germany, manifested also in the strength of chambers of commerce and employers' associations, co-operation in the apprentice training system, etc. And further that this sort of social cohesion was a necessary precondition for any kind of Will Huttonish stakeholder firm

– which was therefore ruled out of practical British politics because Britain is incapable of developing such national institutions.

It is not obvious that he has identified his chicken and egg correctly. It might be that a change in company law which acknowledges the claims of other stakeholders, enjoining co-operation and compromise rather than individualistic unilateralism, could be the place for Britain to start building a sense of social cohesion. And, once built, that sense of social cohesion could measurably enhance the chance of building an electoral majority for the kind of redistributive taxes and public spending which the Frank Field version of 'stakeholder economy', i.e., individual citizen stakes in pension funds or the NHS, will inevitably entail – as David Willets correctly argued in *Prospect*.

Utopian, perhaps. Inheriting a sense of social cohesion from a closed nineteenth-century Germany is one thing. Creating it anew in an increasingly open, individualistic, twenty-first century British society is something else. But in any case, the two versions of 'stakeholder economy', the 'change the corporate ethos' version and the Frank Field version, *are* different. They might in the very long run be mutually reinforcing but in the short run are more likely to work against each other. Those who are lucky enough to arrive in the privileged 'core' employment sector, with their BUPA membership and their company pensions, will have less reason to look with 'there but for the grace of God' sympathy on the less fortunate inhabitants of the periphery, more likely to wonder whether Clare Short or Tony Blair is the better guide to how much a Labour Government's pursuit of Social Justice is likely to cost them.

The Great Training Illusion

Incompatible solutions to what are clearly recognized as different problems are one thing. Muddled solutions to what are in fact different problems but are not recognized as such are another. That – though neither New Labour nor the present government seem to recognize it – seems to be the case with the revamping of our skill training and certification system which has gone on over the last ten years. And once again it is the competitiveness problem and the social cohesion problem which are conflated.

We have all heard the diagnosis. There are two routes to international competitiveness: the low-pay, low-skill, price-competitive route, or the high-quality, high-skills, high-wage route. Failure to invest in training is giving us the wrong kind of competitiveness and doing nothing to stop the enormous waste of resources implied in high unemployment. Unemployment comes from a skills mismatch; a shortage of highly-qualified people and a superfluity of the unskilled. So give the unskilled skills, or Britain will forever flounder in its 'low-skill equilibrium trap'.

But in fact Britain doesn't have a skills problem; it has two rather different skills problems. One is the problem of the operational efficiency of 'qualified' people in the work force who don't do their jobs as well as they might; the people who design engines for inter-city trains that break down every ten thousand miles; the software writers who can't deliver what they promised the Stock Exchange; the maintenance mechanic who doesn't recognize an anomalous noise in a machine and is responsible for hours of expensive down-time; the doctors who misdiagnose; the Job Centre clerk who gets his records mixed up.

The other is the problem of rescuing the socially marginalized for the world of work – those slow learners who come out of the school system with little capacity for manipulating numbers or words, without the self-confidence which that capacity confers, and often without the self-discipline – the basic ability to turn up at a job at half-past-eight every morning – which self-confidence, and a belief that the world of work offers a future, can confer.

Two problems; the efficiency problem and the social rescue problem, in short. And they require different solutions. The efficiency problem may require some institutional improvements in the training system itself, the work of the professional bodies and universities that give the initial pre-employment training to bankers and radiographers, accountants and master-brewers. But what it needs even more is, within firms and *after* people have got jobs, a tightening of standards, a 'cultural revolution' to eliminate sloppiness, more systematic training on the job – in respect of all of which, incidentally, the 'community firms' of Japan and Germany seem to do better than British firms, if only because there is more willing sharing of knowledge, more co-operative pooling of ideas, and greater legitimacy, and hence greater effectiveness in the discipline which eliminates inferior work.

But in fact, the vast bulk of the steadily mounting expenditure on 'vocational education and training' over the last ten years has been on the other, the social rescue, problem. Under a succession of labels – YOPS, YTS, YT – courses specifically for 16–17-year-olds who have had their fill of school and cannot get jobs – have absorbed the lion's share of public training funds. (The ineffable Sir Ron Dearing, in his recent report on the rationalization of education and training provision for the 16–18-year-olds, now suggests yet a new name – National Traineeships. One is reminded of the Sri Lankan joke. Why did Ceylon change its name? Because it's so difficult to change anything else.) A small part of that money has been captured – e.g. by the construction industry, or for managerial training in the supermarket industry – to support the apprenticeship-type training which the industry ought to be doing anyway, but otherwise might not. As such it addresses the efficiency problem. But the bulk of the expenditure has been directed at trying to rescue for the world of work – against the day when the economy will actually provide jobs they can do at wages sufficiently far above benefit levels to attract them – rescuing for the world of work those whom the labour market cannot absorb and whom school has discouraged (probably realistically) from aspiring to more education and better-paid careers. The French cynically call this *formation parking* – 'put 'em on hold training'. It is a matter of keeping work aspirations alive in people who can't get jobs, persuading those who have opted out to opt back in, boosting the confidence of those who haven't made it into 'proper jobs' by giving them certificates of accomplishment. And yet the fiction that this is 'quality training' is sedulously preserved, endorsed again by Sir Ron in his recent report when he deplores the fact that YT has only a 46 per cent completion rate, as if he were blissfully unaware of the realistic popular perception that staying two years to the bitter end is a mark of failure and that the 44 per cent who 'came out of the parking zone' and left YT for jobs (which according to an official survey he himself quotes they still held six months later) were doing better for themselves than those who 'completed' their training.

Where the money goes, there go the professionals. The old MSC's YTS curriculum and certifying experts had the resources to capture a large part of the British training industry, and they were by no means lacking in public relations skills. They succeeded, first of all, in concealing the duality of the training problem and presenting their social rescue efforts as the main thrust in a government effort to tackle the efficiency problem. When the YTS was extended from one year to two in the mid-1980s, the MSC took a full-page advertisement in the national papers. Two years of 'quality training', was the message, reinforced by a photograph of an attractive lass with a computer manual and the caption: 'Look out Japan. Lindy's coming!'

There are two quite separate aspects to the failure to distinguish the efficiency problem and the social rescue problem. One is the way the public and those who represent it at Westminster are conned into spending large sums of money on social rescue in the pretence that these schemes are making important contributions to Britain's competitiveness. I am easily persuaded that this is a constructive and necesary con; if truth were in fact told, the money would not be forthcoming, and the plight of the inadequate school-leavers would be worse than it was before. On the other hand, if the social rescue purpose were fully acknowledged, better ways of fulfilling it might be devised – much more intense remedial education in reading and arithmetic in the early years of primary school, for instance, to ensure that people do not get to school-leaving age with their ability and will to learn permanently damaged.

But there is a much more serious consequence of the 'single skills problem' fallacy; the fact that training doctrines and certification methodologies devised specifically for social rescue work, are now being generalized up the occupational scale to, for example, craftsman training – the areas where improvements are indeed needed on efficiency, not social rescue, grounds.

And in being so applied these new doctrines, propagated with missionary zeal by the National Council for Vocational Qualifications, endorsed by the Beaumont Report issued in the middle of January this year and again in the Dearing Report in March, actually serve to fudge standards rather than improve them, to substitute vague and ill-tested criteria of competence for exact and objectively tested knowledge.

It happened like this. The YTS, it was decided, was to be about 'quality training'. Quality training obviously deserves certification, but a scheme like the YTS which could refuse no entrants of whatever level of illiteracy, but had a highly diverse intake (which in areas of high unemployment could include some young people not much below average in the learning-ability distribution), obviously had difficulty in setting standards for the YTS 'Certificate of Accomplishment' which would simultaneously, (a) have some fiduciary value in the labour market - would actually be taken by employers as an indication of what the certificate's possessors could do, and (b) not set such standards as would require labelling a lot of inadequate people as failures.

The final compromise was to sacrifice the first objective for the second. No objective tests, no external assessors, - assessment, in effect, by those responsible for training - and all legitimized by the importation from the United States of the ideology of 'competence training' developed around the Community Colleges which also had 'slow-learner' problems. Work competence, the creed begins, plausibly enough, can only be defined in a work context; by analysing what is actually done, breaking down the functions a worker performs into their sub-functions and their sub-sub-functions. And, it goes on, likewise work competence can only be *assessed* in the work context in which that competence has to be deployed. Moreover, full occupational competence involves all sorts of interpersonal as well as material-manipulative skills which cannot possibly be tested by objective tests or simulations, certainly not by external examiners who do not have intimate knowledge of the work tasks. In any case; some people don't do well in examinations. There are many different styles of learning....

As Alan Smithers remarked in a Channel 4 programme which did an Emperor's Clothes job on the whole NCVQ testing system two years ago and momentarily sent Whitehall into a state of shock; many styles of learning indeed. There is the plumber who has been taught and tested for knowledge of the formula for calculating the minimum slope of a drain. And that formula will stand him in good stead in any situation he is likely to meet. And there is the plumber whose Record of Achievement records him as having competently set the slope of a drain, leaving us to guess whether he derived this once demonstrated competence from calculation, feel, or trial and error. And we know which one we'd rather have mend our pipes.

What allowed the doctrines and methods worked out for YTS social rescue work to spread upwards to plumber training was the creation, in 1989, of the National Council for Vocational Qualifications with a general competence to co-ordinate - and in effect to control spending on - the crucial certification functions of the British training industry. Let me be clear what I mean by the 'training industry' - not those teachers involved in passing on specific expertise on courses for bankers or fitters or solicitors or plumbers, but the army of experts on training principles and methods, the consultants, occupational psychologists, academic researchers, editors of training magazines, personnel managers, etc., and, significantly, those who, having made a career in that industry, had become the spokesmen on training for the CBI and the TUC. By the time that Council was created the training industry had become largely dependent on the major source of government spending which was the MSC, and on the YTS which made up such a major part of the MSC's activity. There's nothing like subsidy for diffusing doctrinal orthodoxy: dependency breeds conformity. It is hard, otherwise, to account for the spread of this 'competence training' orthodoxy, or why it and its 'trainer assessment; no external tests' principles, should have captured the NCVQ.

But capture it, they did. The idea of a central Council was sensible enough. It arose from an understandable and very un-British desire to clear up the topsy-grown maze of qualifications, knock the heads of City & Guilds, BTEC and RSA, etc. together, save wasteful duplication and produce a system of qualifications intelligible both to individuals seeking skills and employers buying them - qualifications of easily ascertainable fiduciary value. But we should have been warned by the Report which recommended its creation; precious little about fiduciary value and a lot about 'the assessment of competence directly relevant to the needs of employment and the individual'. As it turns out, better the pre-existing jungle and all its ad hocery than a powerful unified body driven by such a perverse orthodoxy as that which has replaced it.

The low-level NVQs, as the new qualifications are called, for all the impossible jargon in which their standards are couched, can actually do their social-rescue, confidence-building job reasonably well - not for the really seriously hard-to-employ, but at least for those who get jobs. Thus, a personnel manager who spoke well of the new system: 'take somebody who perhaps hasn't done very well at school and who'd be paralysed if she had to take an examination. After all, some people can't handle exams and there *are* different styles of learning. So she embarks on an NVQ and she persists and persists in working through this enormous wodge of stuff, and she comes through. And there's a presentation. It does your heart good to see the glow of pride. We had a woman of 59 who'd never done anything much; it gave her a new lease on life.' And the fiduciary value of such a qualification if he were recruiting a new employee? 'A kind of character reference.'

Splendid, and fortunately the NCVQ has hitherto operated primarily at that level. It is only now that it is actually getting round to the more serious 'Level 3' and 'Level 4' qualifications which are supposed to carry a fiduciary value actually relevant to knowledge and skills and not just character. It is seeking to hijack the older type of City & Guilds craftsman qualifications (with externally tested written and practical exams), an imperialistic ambition which the Beaumont Report and the Dearing report endorse *en passant* in astonishingly cavalier fashion, as if they were unaware of the fact that these traditional qualifications remain popular, and the preferred form of qualification for employers who are seriously concerned about their young employees gaining substantial skills.

It simply needs to be stopped in its tracks. I can see lots of good pragmatic, reasons to do with practical politics for tolerating ambiguity about the difference between competitiveness objectives and social cohesion/social rescue objectives – whether it be about stakeholders or about training. Fictions can be functional, but one has to ask 'functional for whom?' For society as a whole in some kind of 'greatest good of greatest number' terms? For the trainees who get psychic satisfaction from their certificates but precious little career advancement? For their possible employers? Or for the training industry whose livelihoods are staked on the present system and its expansion?

D SHARING: WHAT, WITH WHOM, HOW MUCH AND WHY?

(Address to the annual meeting of the Society for Advancement of Socio-Economics, Madison, Wisconsin, July 1999)

For middle-class British children, at least, getting a concept of 'sharing' is what first introduces them to the pains of moral behaviour; the way they first learn that impulses of self-gratification have to be restrained not only in obedience to the authority of the elders they depend on, but also in deference to the needs and wishes of their peers. Share your chocolate with Tommy. Give Mary a ride on your tricycle: you must learn to share.

It's true, of course, that particularly in American speech, 'sharing' can also be anything but altruistic, an expression of one's self-gratifying right to bore the pants off other people. As in 'Tommy will now share with us the story of his gerbil who died' or 'I want to share with you this evening my thoughts on sharing'. The link is some notion of community, of agglomerations of individuals which are more than crowds or single-purpose associations: the community of the play group, of the show-and-tell classroom, of people dedicated to the advancement of socio-economics.

It is in such communities or quasi-communities that children also learn the concept of property. In fact 'property' has to be prior to the concept of 'sharing'. 'It's *my* chocolate I'm giving you.' When we went to the Italian seaside, the first Italian words my three-year-old daughter learned were *E'l mio*. It's mine. But the tricycle may also be the playgroup's tricycle, a public good, part of the commons. Children may learn to distinguish between the altruism of sharing private goods, and the respect for the rights of others involved in sharing public goods. Noblesse oblige may come into it too. The tricycle-rich child of well-off parents may find that giving rides to the tricycle-poor can turn away envy and resentment, earn friendliness and even gratitude. But will he feel the same later about his BMW, not a gift from his wealthy parents, but earned by the sweat of his brow – or by the sweat of his clenched fists as he gives a boardroom presentation, or his clever quick thinking in front of the trading-room computer screens?

That is where we move from playgroup to globalizing societies. The key question suggested to me by our conference theme, Globalization and the Good Society, is what forms of wealth and income redistribution are going to be viable in the societies of the twenty-first century: what forms are needed if those societies are going to be judged by their members as good societies? Globalization erodes not only nation-states' economic and political, but also their cultural, frontiers. It changes individuals' sense of the community or communities they belong to, may even encourage them to think of themselves as free-standing individuals, engaged not at all with communities but only with markets and individual friends. It changes the resonance of words like 'the national community', hollows out rhetorical flourishes like 'ask not what your country can do for you, but what you can do for your country'.

And at the same time the arguments for redistribution grow stronger: the inequalities of income and of life-chances are increasing as the technology our economies use places an ever-increasing premium on skills which it takes a good endowment of learning ability to acquire, while giving poor rewards to those who can only learn to do what just about anybody can learn to do. Do not be deceived by those who tell you that the American goldilocks economy, its low unemployment and the recent modest increase in bottom-level wages, disproves any such secular tendency. Only one country at a time can sustain such an astonishing level of consumer demand by sucking in loose liquidity from the whole of the rest of the world. And, as a former governor of the Fed said in the *Wall Street Journal* a couple of days ago, productivity and GDP measures, as good society indicators, are confused anyway because, he said, 'we are not correctly measuring the decline in quality of customer service' which comes not only from labour shortage and downsizing to increase profits, but also 'the increasing use of workers with sub-par language, math and social skills.'[7]

It was possible for an as acute and economic observer as Keynes to predict in 1929, in his 'Economics of our Grandchildren', that by the end of the century we would all be working only 5 hours a week. I repeat, 'all', not 'on average'. He did not foresee societies in which the gifted spend 80 hours a week at what they call work, much of which is enjoyable problem-solving, self-expression, ego-assertion or whatever, and the least gifted 30 per cent would have time on their hands, in and out - some of them mostly out - of lousy jobs.

This issue, and the whole 'rethinking the welfare state' movement in European politics, has a particular poignancy for Englishmen of my generation. I remember, just 50 years ago, listening to a public lecture by R.H. Tawney, the author of 1920s tracts on the gross inequalities of British society. His lecture was a celebration of that society's transformation. Thanks to wartime taxation and in particular inheritance taxes, only a few dinosaurs survived among the great landed magnates of traditional England, and they would soon be extinct. Britain could now afford decent education, a decent health service and decent pensions for everyone. It was in the same year that T.H. Marshall was delivering the lectures subsequently published as *Citizenship and Social Class* (Cambridge University Press, 1950). When I went to Japan a year later, I had friends in the Tokyo Fabian Society whose main topic of concern was: how soon could Japan emulate Britain's Beveridge social security system?

It was possible for Tawney, and for his audience doubtless, to see all this in quasi-playgroup terms, an an institutionalized form of sharing within the national community. But it is a long way from getting off a tricycle so that Tommy can have a go, to the bureaucratic modalities of welfare state sharing. It was not a personally known Tommy asking for sacrifice but the coercive state, the hated taxman to be avoided if you can, evaded if you can't. And on the other side, as Michael Ignatieff observed: 'Only someone who has not actually been on the receiving end of the welfare state would dare call it an instance of civil altruism at work.[8]

It was clear from the start that the Beveridge system had problems. The idea of the social pooling of the risks of illness and old age, of unemployment in what was expected to be a full-employment society, benefits earned as of right by universal contributions from all those whose circumstances permitted contribution, was fine as an ideal. But the full employment assumption was betrayed. The universal insurance benefits were pegged at inadequate levels and needed increasing topping up from means-tested social assistance. Means-testing produced benefit fraud. Benefit fraud - and the alarmist accounts of benefit fraud in the popular tabloid press - fed the tax allergy of voters, leading particularly to the erosion of the state pension and a further increase in social assistance and means-testing. And so the spiral accelerated downwards – downwards in satisfaction delivered, though upward in social expenditure, a trend which even 18 years of Thatcherite conservative government could not reverse.

So rethinking the welfare state is, to be sure, essential. But in Europe, the actual current rethink is one that largely precludes any notion of sharing or community, with strong support for tax privileges to facilitate private insurance and private pension provision. I believe that this has a lot to do with the control of the ideological airspace exercised by the financial services industry – in London and in Brussels, at least. I am less sure about Rome, Bonn or Paris. There is less doubt about that dominance in Washington and New York. It all started, said an American friend, when American newspapers started paying their senior journalists with stock options.

Most discussions of pensions start off, as if stating an unassailable fact, from the notion that it is impossible to continue the traditional pay-as-you-go system of paying this year's pension largely out of this year's contributions, with only a small invested float if any at all. Pay-as-you-go is dead. 'Today we have three and a half people working for every pensioner. In thirty years time it will be only two and a half. It is unreasonable to expect that two and a half to bear the tax and social security contributions to pay a whole person's pension. So people must be self-reliant and save for their old age themselves.' What few people bother to ask is where are the returns on those savings going to come from? The savers have a choice. Either they send their savings to Brazil or China and build up claims to the production of future generations of Chinese and Brazilians – which could be quite risky given the volatility of exchange rates. And, as a *Financial Times* leader-writer suggested, 'the successful Asians' … readiness to pay for pensions in the west rests on a rosy western perception of mutual interest that could yet be confounded by realpolitik.' Anyway the savings might be needed for economic growth at home. But if they do keep them at home, it is still the work of the same two and a half producers that they will be depending on for their rentier income as pensioners.

In other words, a pension system will be viable if it depends on the property system – on the legal liabililities of those two and a half workers to pay bondholders their coupons, to pay shareholders their dividends and landowners their rents. But not if it depends on the political system, on the willingness and ability of electorally competing politicians to persuade those two and a half workers to pay taxes and social security contributions.

But what a funded pension system does to the capital and labour shares of national income in 2030, when two-sevenths of the population have become rentiers, and how what it would have to do to make the system viable, squares with the relative factor scarcities of capital and labour, and the organizational requirements for decent and workable relations between managers and managed, is something that seems never to get discussed. Who wants to bother with such issues when the banks and mutual funds can make such rich pickings out of the tax-privileged equity savings accounts? It is estimated that the competing providers of the British equivalent of the American 401(K) plans, the Individual Savings Accounts, spend 60 million sterling a year on advertising alone.

Globalization clearly has something to do with the decline in the sense of social solidarity which gave rise to the Beveridge social security system and the National Health Service in 1940s Britain. The banks and investment houses whose chairmen lunch with British cabinet ministers are global; so are the media empires which reflect their assumptions about the limits of the possible; so is the international quasi-community of professional economists which blesses those assumptions *ex cathedra*. The hegemonic culture of Davos man gets steadily more hegemonic, at least among the mobile elites. But Huntington is right in arguing that one should not exaggerate the impact on the bulk of the world's population. Soccer may be globalized. The British football cup competition may be eclipsed by the World Cup, but that only gives the punters more occasions deeply to feel their Englishness, rather than their local identity as fans of Sheffield Wednesday. Globalized Britain still, after all, has enough of a sense of community to support a system of universal child benefit. The National Health System is still hugely popular.

Clearly there are other factors involved in the erosion of social solidarity in Britain since the 1940s, not just globalization. The depleting legacy of wartime solidarity is one; people's wars do tend to unite peoples. Then there are the slow processes of internal cultural differentiation, probably reinforced by declining rates of social mobility. The gap between the culture of the popular tabloids and TV programmes and that of the broadsheet newspapers read by 10 per cent of the population, has never been greater.

The other big difference between Britain of the 1940s and now - thinking back to that Tawney lecture - is that the redistributive taxation was then seen primarily to hit inherited wealth: unearned income, especially that of the landed aristocracy. Today it is primarily earned incomes, and the savings out of earned income - wealth that its possessors think their own efforts have deserved - which is on the line.

So preserving in individual nation-states something of the character of communities-which-share, is clearly difficult for reasons which go beyond globalization. Nevertheless, I think it is just within the bounds of possibility that within 30 or 40 years, we shall see the sort of citizens income arrangement - the expansion of universal child benefit to universal adult benefit - that Philippe van Parijs has been so eloquently advocating for years.[9] For the basic income to be sufficient for what would then count as a non-excluding level of expenditure, some 40 per cent of GDP would probably have to be siphoned out of the economy. The expansion of automatic citizens' rights might be matched, though not necessarily made conditional on, an expansion of duties of civic service. Not only would the poverty problem of unemployment be removed, but the stigma problem too, if those who chose not to do paid work included not only those hardly capable of earning much, but also those who could very well earn good money but prefer to spend their time writing poetry or digging their garden.

What factors do I have in mind when I say, 'just within the bounds of possibility'? First, the increasing resort to in-work benefits as a means of tackling unemployment – letting unskilled labour be paid its ever-lower market-clearing rate and for those with dependants top up with welfare benefits. In Britain this used to be called Family Income Supplement. The Blair government has revamped it, following the USA, as Working Families Tax Credit, a device to shift responsibility for administration from the Department of Health and Social Security to the Treasury in order to control its growth and to change its impact on the PSBR. But it is highly unlikely that the Treasury will be able to exercise the control it would like to, and 40 per cent of GDP may soon come to look like a not unlikely prospective cost.

Second, in-work benefits require means tests. So do all the other targeted benefits increasingly replacing or supplementing social security insurance payments. Means tests breed benefit fraud, an increasingly hot political issue which a universal citizens' income system could eliminate at a stroke.

And the third factor, of course, is that, as more beggars pester, and more thieves snatch and more muggers mug, the declining quality of urban life, for all those who don't want to, or cannot afford to, live in walled ghettos protected by security guards, other people's poverty becomes a matter of increasing importance.

There is a fourth factor putting a citizens' income scheme just within bounds of possibility, if a more problematic one, namely the possibility that change in the occupational structure might alter the complex of our ideas about work, effort, earning and just desserts. As compared, say, with hewing at a coal face or totting up rows of figures in a back room, a high proportion of the jobs left to be done, by people rather than by machines, offer a better balance of satisfaction to pain – the satisfaction of solving problems, exercising skill, wielding power, making people smile and go away happy. Could that permit a change in our view of the relation of job performance, effort and reward?

Think back to Tawney again. The nineteenth century, by and large, assumed that it was part of the order of nature that the rich man should be in his castle and the poor man begging at his gate. By the mid-1940s, the demand for equality of opportunity, the onslaughts of people like Tawney, had made such rich men suitable targets for punitive taxation. Could the same sort of shift in evaluations as took place with respect to unearned incomes happen with respect to earned incomes too? What would be the arguments of the new Tawneys? Primarily, I suppose, that those who have got the brains which allow them to learn the skills that earn them interesting and satisfying jobs, should count themselves lucky rather than deserving. They should, of course, get extra money as an incentive to extra effort, but shouldn't need too much. They should also take some satisfaction from sharing their contributions to the economy with the rest of us.

Looking around the world, it seems to me that Japan has not a bad chance of leading the world into such a citizens' income regime. It is not just that its racial and cultural separateness sharpen its citizens' sense of the frontiers of shared Japaneseness. There is another reason. It is plausible - plausible to anybody who has watched the different behaviour of different kids on tricycles at least - to think of a general 'propensity to share' as a personality trait. The willingness to see the national community as a sharing community may be developed and enhanced in a society where there is also a lot of sharing in the 'little platoons' to use Burke's phrase, in the micro-units of societies. Japan has not only stronger neighbourhood and parish associations than most societies, but also firms which are only dubiously capitalist - much more like communities of employees than organizations in which manager agents hire their labour at the combination of price, quantity and quality that will maximize the profits of their shareholder principals.

Let me illustrate. Wage negotiations in a Japanese firm look very much like wage negotiations in a properly capitalist firm. Managers on one side of the table, union representatives on the other. But when the manager of a British or American firm talks a wage demand of 5 per cent down to 3 per cent, he knows that there will be more leeway for managerial bonuses, and that his meritorious work in holding down costs should get its reward. A Japanese manager, by contrast, can expect that his success will mean that his own salary too will go up by only 3 per cent not 5. One principle of the firm as community is that the permanent lifetime members, each according to his proper place in the hierarachy, should share at least proportionately if not equally, in both the good times and the bad times.

But times are indeed changing. Capitalism is global. The California Public Employees Retirement Scheme, CREF, and the Harvard Business School are all bent on teaching Japanese managers about shareholder value. Stock options are coming in, and annual salary contracts for managers instead of civil-service-like fixed pay scales. How far it will go I cannot predict. Much will hinge on the relative growth performance of the US and the Japanese economies over the next decade, and God alone knows what will determine that - what mix of technological excellence, the cleverness of macroeconomic policy, the herd behaviour which shifts exchange rates, the whims and winds of consumer confidence, the iconic leadership of Greenspans and his Japanese opposite numbers - or butterfly wing-flaps.

I have not fully covered the agenda of my title. I have explored the 'what and the how much' and to some extent the 'why'. But the 'with whom' remains as probably the most difficult question of all. Why sharing only within nation-states, with fellow-Brits and fellow-Frenchmen? What about migration and the right to choose the community in which one will share? Can state-to-state foreign aid be a morally reasonable substitute for human rather than national solidarity? These questions I can only, lamely, leave to others.

NOTES

1. Geoff Mason, *The New Graduate Supply Shock: Recruitment and Utilisation of Graduates in British Industry*, National Institute of Economic and Social Research (London), 1995, p. 123, para 549.
2. *Ibid.*, p. 125, para. 562.
3. See Jonathan Wadsworth and Paul Gregg, 'The rise of the no-job household', *Centrepiece*, 2, June 1996.
4. *Financial Times*, 29 May 1996.
5. B. Holmes, 'Literacy and numeracy: what cause for concern?', *Employment Gazette*, 1989, pp. 133–9, as cited in K. Ducatel, 'The future of low-skill jobs' in H. Metcalf (ed.), *Future Skill Demand and Supply*, London, Policy Studies Institute, 1995.
6. Sally Dench, 'What types of people are employers seeking to employ? Some evidence from the Employers' Manpower and Skills Practices Survey', Paper for the ES/PSI conference, 'Unemployment in Focus', Rotherham, November 1993.
7. Lawrence B. Lindsey, *Wall Street Journal,* 7 July 1999.
8. Quoted by Peter Saunders, 'Citizenship in a liberal society' in Bryan S. Turner (ed.), *Citizenship and Social Theory*, London, Sage, 1993.
9. See his *Freedom For All: What (if anything) Can Justify Capitalism?* Oxford, OUP, 1995 and any issue of the Basic Income European Network of which he has been a principal organizer.

25. The firm as community: the road to industrial democracy*

This chapter has a simple thesis. On several counts the Community model firm is superior to the Company Law model firm: innovativeness, efficiency, competitiveness, the quality of life and kinds of satisfaction it delivers to those who work in it. Japan manages to have firms which are predominantly of this type, partly because they were clever enough to understand about these things, and lucky enough to have industrialized late when it was easier to do something about them; partly because the employee interest is quite strong vis-à-vis the shareholder interest in the Japanese form of capitalism for a variety of historical reasons; and partly because Japan is a society where authority is not *in principle* problematical, where hierarchy is more acceptable than in Britain, and subordinates are more willing to assume competence in their superiors and to accept instructions from them when the assumption appears to be confirmed.

How can Britain, with none of these advantages, get more Community model firms? Once again, as in the case of incomes policies, we need deliberate social-engineering legislation to achieve by artifice what the Japanese enjoy largely by historical and cultural inheritance....

[The favourite British prescription: give employees a piece of the owners' action - a tiny portion of the company's shares - has severe limitations, so what can] alternatively be done to give employees a stake in their firm by giving them a share in the shareholders' controlling power, and giving it to them *qua* employees? What, in other words, should be done about industrial democracy?

Debate about industrial democracy in Britain must surely be due for a revival, nearly a decade after the abortion of the last attempt to introduce some measure of legal compulsion (the Bullock Report, 1977, and the subsequent White Paper). In practically every country in Europe some form of limitation of the shareholder interest in favour of the employee interest has been on the statute books for many years. West Germany built the postwar miracle on a structure of co-determination, a part of the landscape of German society for the best part of four decades.

* Extracted from *Taking Japan Seriously: A Confucian Perspective on Leading Economic Issues*, Stanford: Stanford University Press, 1987, pp. 145–65.

And what do we have in Britain? A government dedicated to undying opposition to the European Communities' draft Fifth Directive which would make shareholder–employee power-sharing mandatory. And elsewhere a deafening silence. The managerial optimists of the One-Nation Tory/Alliance/right-wing Labour centre are silent because still discouraged by the Bullock debate. The Labour Party is silent because the trade unions are not interested. And the trade unions are not interested because they have other fights on their minds.

One trade union, the Electrical, Electronic, Telecommunications and Plumbing Union (EETPU), has taken a decisive step towards endorsement of the Community model firm. The pattern has, significantly, been worked out in deals with Japanese subsidiaries in this country: one single all-embracing plant-based union; pendulum arbitration without strikes or lock-outs; wide-ranging works-council consultation; factory-wide grading schemes; elaborate management–union contracts incorporating all basic factory rules. The recognition agreement at the Hitachi Hirwaun factory says, in its second clause:

> In this joint approach, the company and EETPU recognize that there is a common objective to continue to ensure the efficiency and prosperity of the Company for the benefit of its members, its customers, its shareholders and its community.

Note the order, with shareholders in third place. 'Members' here means [not 'shareholders' as in the British Company Act, but] employees. EETPU represents 'all company members below middle management level'.

The EETPU, possibly to be followed by the Amalgamated Union of Engineering Workers (AUEW), is of course very much a minority element in the union movement. Its acceptance – advocacy even – of what is regarded by many TUC members as an attitude of abject collusion with the capitalist enemy is not likely to become dominant TUC strategy for some years yet. It represents, however, through its acceptance of an organization-oriented (see Chapter 2) employment system, an approach to the Community model by the Japanese method, quietly elbowing the shareholders aside, accepting 'management' not as shareholders' agents, but as trustees of the interests of 'the company and all its members', allowing the potential for adversarial division to arise only from possible differences between 'short-term-interested subordinates' versus 'long-term-vision seniors and experts', and in any case making sure that this opposition is muted by an ideology of basic identity of interest.

That Japanese method can work fairly well in the wholly owned subsidiary of a Japanese multinational because the 'shareholders' who come number three on the interest group list are, in fact, the managerial colleagues in Tokyo of the 'managerial members' running the subsidiary in Britain. Will it work as well, will the shareholders be as willing to be elbowed aside, when 'the shareholders' means, say, a Tiny Rowlands, a Charles Ronson, a Robert Maxwell or some other of our City buccaneers?

For the average British firm it is unlikely that the EETPU-type Japanese approach to the Community model will get very far. But there is little interest, indeed some hostility, in the trade-union movement to the alternative route by which a more Community-type of firm might be reached: the traditional 'industrial democracy' route of power sharing between employees and shareholders within the board structure of the firm. The TUC's antipathy to such arrangements was overt until the early 1970s. The creation of Community-type enterprises is not good news in the least for unions who see their *raison d'être* as lying precisely in the adversarial relations of the Company Law-type enterprise. The unions were persuaded to go along with the establishment of the Bullock Committee only because they believed that industrial democracy could be an extension of collective bargaining. And so it would have become if the Bullock arrangements, giving unions pre-eminent control over the selection of employee representatives on company boards, had been carried into effect, thereby preserving Company-Law stances and producing little pay-off in efficiency or co-operation. Opposition was understandably great; there was a long delay; a White Paper which again shirked the essential issues, and the matter was dropped to general relief …

[But there are] good reasons for thinking that industrial democracy is 'on the cards', bound to come.[1] … The Bullock Committee itself hinted at something of this [the] underlying logic [of this forecast] when it spoke of a higher material standard of living having made people less tolerant of poor safety and health conditions, redundancy and unemployment (Bullock, Report of the Committee of Inquiry on Industrial Democracy, UK Department of Trade, June 1977, p. 22). It identified as other trends:

1. More education, and particularly education which stimulated independent and questioning approaches to authority.
2. The slow-down of growth and diversion of aspirations to other fields. (A kind of 'sublimation' variant of the Maslow thesis of a hierarchy of needs from lower-level physical ones to higher-level needs for autonomy and self-actualization, a hierarchy up which societies and individuals move with increasing affluence and security.)
3. Increasing complexity of business organizations, remoteness and concentration of decision-making power, calling forth countervailing forces and calls for business corporations to recognize general social responsibilities.
4. Accelerating pace of invention and concomitantly increasing role of

innovation in competition leads to increasing need for adaptability in the work force.

5. This adaptability can only be speedily obtained with the consent of workers, given the increasing power of trade unions (Bullock, pp. 20–23).

A constant theme in the chorus of management criticism which greeted the Bullock Report was the argument that trade-union representatives on the board would contribute only delay and inefficiency. (They were, it will be recalled, to be equal in numbers to shareholders' representatives with a minority of neutrals to hold the balance: the $2x + y$ formula.) I do not recall reading any half-way analytical account of why this should be so – these, after all, were still the days when a certain hangover of wet Toryism prevented even the Institute of Directors from being too insulting about trade unionists as a category – but the implicit reasons were, presumably, that:

1. Trade unionists would not have acquired the necessary experience to understand the complex issues on which boards have to take decisions. Probably true, but do the politicians, retired admirals and ambassadors on the boards of our companies understand, say, the electronics industry in which the companies whose boards they adorn operate?
2. The admirals, diplomats, and so on, are intelligent, quick learners, aware of what they understand and what they do not understand, capable of contributing useful reasoning power and freshness of mind to problems (as well as experience-based 'feel' for the way organizations work). Trade unionists will be less intelligent, less able to contribute. There was absolutely no reason to suppose this to be the case in the generation of Ernie Bevin, when highly intelligent people were leaving school for a milk-round at the age of 12, and dunderheads were leaving Wellington for a successful army career. With the increase in equality of educational opportunity, the argument becomes increasingly plausible.
3. Employee representatives elected through trade-union channels would be lifelong trade unionists, the people most successful at the militant prosecution of the *sectional* interests of the groups within the firm whom they represent, trained to give the reflex action 'that's your problem!' to any attempt by managers to invoke in argument the interests of 'the company as a whole'. (And quite rightly in the Company Law model firm, where the rules of adversarial bargaining should forbid sympathetic consideration of 'the other side's' problems.) It is too late in life to expect them to change and suddenly, as board members, begin to take a 'for the good of the company as a whole' point of view. They would tend to sit silent through all discussions about the desirability of breaking into this or

that market, developing this or that product, and spring into life only when an issue directly affecting workers' wages or well-being is discussed.

There is a good deal to be said for arguments 2 and 3 (though 3 is an exaggerated caricature of the truth: pure Company Law firms are rare in the private sector, and a good many works' convenors are in fact closer to the Community model in the way they perceive their role). There really is a problem of ensuring, on the one hand, that decisions are taken by those most *competent* to take them (in terms of their grasp of details, ability to do the reasoning which predicts the consequences of alternative courses of action, and so on) and, on the other hand, that they are *accountable* to the employees of the firm for their responsibility to try to work for the 'good of the company as a whole' (i.e. not to sacrifice the common interest of all parties for the disproportionate interests of one group, e.g. the managers, or the shareholders). Competence is necessary if the firm (and the economy) are to survive and prosper; accountability is necessary if the effort-evoking, co-operation-evoking, properties of the Community model are to be achieved. Getting the right balance between competence and accountability is extremely difficult for at least three reasons. First is the problem already discussed *à propos* the Bullock proposals: how can the men and women likely to be most effective as accountability watchdogs on behalf of the manual-worker majority (those least able to understand difficult boardroom decisions) have, not only the trust of those they represent, but *also* the competence to understand what is going on?

Second is the sheer time and effort problem. Time spent being accountable, explaining decisions and the considerations on which they were based, demonstrating good faith, persuading, is time which cannot be spent on gathering the information and doing the analysis necessary to make decisions better.

And third, there is the balance in the accountability devices between suspicion and trust. All forms of accountability – from the parliamentary question to the audit of the tennis club books – are forms of institutionalized suspicion. If the suspicion is too overt, if the checks are not just the conscientious following of the audit rules in the expectation that all will be in order, but a relentless 'they'll get away with anything if you don't keep your eye on them' pursuit of incriminating evidence, then the motivations which make decision-makers competent will be destroyed. Their effort-input will diminish and so, more definitively, will their willingness to take initiatives and to back risky entrepreneurial ventures. In order not to destroy competence, accountability has got to be based 90 per cent on trust, only 10 per cent on evidence that the trust is well placed.

Choosing the right 10 per cent, and making sure that the channels by which the evidence is gathered and diffused are right, is what all the debates about the correct forms of industrial democracy are about. The German model supervisory-board/executive-board hierarchy is one way of achieving the 10 per cent/90 per cent division and keeping the accountability watchdogs out of the top managers' hair for most of the time.

I would suggest an alternative to a hierarchy of boards which has the advantage of specifying more clearly *which* 10 per cent of the array of top-level decisions the accountability devices should focus on. It seems fairly safe to assume that the crucial decisions are the 'who gets what' decisions and that the quickest way of changing gear from a Company Law mode to a Community mode is to set up a system whereby *workers' representatives have as much right to a say in determining managers' pay and conditions of work as representatives of management now have in determining workers' pay and conditions.*

This could be done by a system of parallel boards with divided functions. Let the main board be dominated by senior executives as it is now (with perhaps some changes in the other members to be considered later). But let there also be established what one might call a Fairness Council. (Recall the arguments in Chapters 3 and 4 about the crucial role of the concept of 'fairness' in British industrial conflict.) This should be made up of representatives of shareholders and various groups of workers, *including managers as one interest group among others.* (Consumers might also be represented in some large firms.) The Fairness Council (hereafter FC) would scrutinize, and within certain limits have veto powers over, all decisions of the board which have implications for the *distribution* of the rewards given to, and the burdens placed on or contributions expected from, the groups represented. Members of the Board *(not* the manager interest group representatives on the FC itself) would be in attendance at meetings of the FC in order to 'sell' the Board's proposals to the FC, but would not vote. The chairman of the FC might well be independent – one of the outside directors, perhaps, chosen by the other FC members by unanimous vote.

This suggestion rests on an attempt to do what, in its sketchy couple of pages on the subject, the Bullock Report notably fails to do: namely to think through what boards actually *do.* One way of categorizing the decisions they take is in terms of their:

1. *Efficiency implications:* the bearing of the decision on the firm's capacity to grow, increase its operating profit, its market share, value-added per employee, or whatever is accepted (by the FC) as being a reasonable measure or set of measures of the success of the enterprise, i.e. a reasonable definition of the *common* objectives of everyone involved;
2. *Equity implications:* their meaning in terms of the likelihood of

increased income or fringe benefits, the possibility of redundancy, harder or less pleasant work, etc., for members of the enterprise.

A wide range of management decisions (both those which do and those which do not normally reach board level) involve both kinds of implications: wage settlements (primarily an equity matter) affect the firm's ability to get efficient people in the labour market; the choice between dividends and retaining earnings involves the firm's power to raise new capital if it needs it as well as the question of what is fair to the shareholders; a new productivity-enhancing machine puts some people out of their familiar jobs and perhaps out of a job altogether; the finance manager's Rover is not only nice for the manager (equity) but possibly a determinant of his bargaining effectiveness with the banks if it is read as an indication of his status in the firm.

In the Company Law model managers are supposed to be single-mindedly concerned with maximizing the profit of the shareholders and to hell with everyone else. Most of our fly-blown rhetoric (hard-nosed conflict sociologists' rhetoric as well as politicians' and businessmen's) preserves this assumption in the talk about the 'two sides' of industry. Mainline management-school business ideology, however, has moved on from there to a rather dubious version of the Community model. Managers are now spoken of as the guardians of the interests of 'the company as a whole'. They are supposed to take decisions which judiciously weigh the differing interests of everyone involved and find the fairest point of compromise without ever, ever giving special consideration to their own *self*-interest in higher salaries, better fringe benefits, more managerial jobs, better returns on their stock options. The suggestion made here for a Fairness Council parallel to the board rests on the view that:

1. The 'Platonic guardians' view of managers is neither wholly true nor wholly false.
2. The best way to flush out the 'managers' self-interest' aspects of (manager-dominated) Board decisions is to have managers' representatives defend them in a Fairness Council where they are *expected* to act in an avowedly self-interested way.
3. Workers' representatives, after many years of work much closer to the shop floor than most managers get (in Britain), may well have the experience and expertise to make valuable contributions to efficiency decisions. Boards ought to have some places for ex-manual and ex-clerical workers, both for this reason and as a symbolic affirmation (like suggestions schemes) that everybody's knowledge and experience counts.
4. But the people best able to contribute to efficiency decisions are not necessarily the people who have achieved prominence in the company by

the firmness with which, as shop stewards, they have stood up for the sectional interests of the workers they represent. The anti-Bullock argument mentioned earlier has some truth. It *would* be a sudden and not easy transition if they were required to step outside their representative role and simply contribute expertise to efficiency decisions. They should be appointed to the Fairness Council where they could continue to do what they are good at.

5. But there are good grounds for believing that they would do it rather differently and that the atmosphere of industrial relations would greatly improve because:

   (a) Suspicion often poisons bargaining encounters at present precisely because of the ambiguity of the managers' role both as guardians and as self-interest-maximizers. A forum in which everyone avowedly speaks self-interest will clear the air.
   (b) The other thing which often poisons bargaining encounters is the status differential and the resentment it arouses, worker resentment of the fact that workers are always the supplicant proposers, managers the disposers. The symmetrical arrangement making managers' pay increases as much a matter for the FC as workers' should cure that.
   (c) Equally it should diminish diffuse resentment directed at what are thought to be excessive management pay and privileges if the extent of such privileges were known and differentials the subject of explicit decision. The system proposed might in fact alter the distribution of rewards in our society over time; it would almost certainly 'harmonize' status-linked differences like length of holidays, pensions and sick-pay rights, hours of work, free lunches, and so on. But one might expect that it should generate a sufficient atmosphere of respect for reality for differentials not to be reduced to the point at which there is a large-scale brain-drain of able managers to other countries.

6. The dynamics of small groups are such that the FC should build up a certain *esprit de corps*. The sentiments which its members might come to feel (of attachment to the FC, and by extension to the corporation of which it is part) might not be easy to achieve simply by the mutual pursuit of rationally calculated self-interest.

What would such a system do to collective bargaining? The short answer is: extend it. Additional matters will be brought within the scope of trade unionists' influence, such as dividend payments and managers salaries. Much of the mainline pay bargaining will take place *within* FCs (and may evolve into an annual company kitty bargaining procedure). The articulation of this with industry-wide bargaining procedures and the national trade-union structure (what Donovan's Royal Commission called the 'formal system' [Donovan Report, Report of the Royal Commission on Trades Unions and Employers' Associations 1965–8, London, HMSO, 1968]) will present some problems, but they can be resolved as they have been resolved where conventional company bargaining structures have been set up: at Ford's or at Pilkington's or at British Leyland.

There will remain two sorts of industrial disputes to be dealt with 'through procedure', possibly involving use of the strike weapon. The first will arise over matters dealt with by the FC, when the FC itself fails to reach an acceptable compromise and an overruled minority digs its heels in, or when members of one of the representatives' constituencies repudiate his [or her!] acceptance of an FC decision. The procedures for such disputes will have to involve some outside mediation or arbitration and it should, presumably, be a sub-committee of the FC (drawn from the overruling majority in the case of a matter unresolved in the FC) which acts for 'the company' in the dispute. The second will be disputes arising from the day-to-day decisions of managers within their delegated powers. The FC itself would play an important part in the procedures for the second kind of dispute.

It all sounds a bit bizarre, perhaps, a bit too neat and tidy for an industrial world brought up to respect the illogicalities of 'custom and practice'. 'Fairness Council' perhaps sounds a bit soppy. Well, 'equity commission' might sound a little more pompous and proper, but there is no great harm in trying to persuade people to talk frankly of underlying realities and to do so in the language of everyday discourse.

Some, I know, will disagree: 'A bit of pompousness, a bit of fudging, a bit of illogical respect for custom and practice are really the only ways you ever get anything done in this world. All this attempt at neat, rational, separation of the issues will never work in Britain. It is precisely because what you call the efficiency issues and the equity issues *are* mixed up and *stay* mixed up that we manage to get the compromises that keep things ticking over. Your Fairness Council will only sharpen up differences that could be papered over with an appeal to the interests of the whole. You've got to have people accepting a lot of blurring at the edges; you can't have *every* management decision questioned from a "so what's he going to get out of it" point of view; it's going to erode what little authority management's got left, and when that's gone we're going to be really in the soup. You can't run industry without some sort of authority.'

My answer to that is twofold. First I would challenge the conception of authority which such criticism implies, on the grounds set out in Chapter 5.

Authority does not *have* to rest on status ascription, or on some 'aura' which impresses the groundlings. It can be rooted in subordinates' perceptions of managers' competence, in their recognition that the competence is being directed to common, shared purposes not to private purposes, in their judgement of managers' honesty, fairness and concern for other people. Second, I think beliefs about the limits of rationality are overdone. I see no reason why the ability to reach compromises through rational argument - by separating appraisal-of-fact questions from interest questions - should somehow be a monopoly of people like the Swedes.

NOTES

1. [With all my optimism, I would have never dared to make this assertion if I had been able to imagine the possibility of a Blairite Britain more likely to become the 51st state than a full member of Europe. The change from the Britain of 1986–7 to a Britain in which the 'maximization of shareholder value' is almost universally accepted as the purpose of business firms and the stock market plays a pivotal role in the economy - and the inroads of that ideology in Japan and Germany - is the subject of my latest book. For the grounds of the 'bound to come' assertion, see Chapter 6 (Trade Unions).]

26. Rethinking free trade*

The international trading system needs a Copernican revolution. Or rather, Free Trade Orthodoxy needs a Lutheran Reformation. Consider Britain's recent history. From the first impact of Honda's arrival to the death of the British motorbike industry was about a decade. By the time the colour TVs and cars began to come from Japan we had learned our lesson. We trumped up charges of dumping to justify punitive tariffs, and thereby pushed the Japanese into VERs - 'voluntary' export restrictions. They responded - resentfully and reluctantly - by manufacturing inside our market. The result: we now have a flourishing CTV and a flourishing car industry.

True, sad things have happened to British firms in those industries. But they would have happened anyway - faster and more brutally - under free trade. And at least a very large chunk of the value-adding activity which goes into making our cars and TVs takes place in the UK and generates labour incomes in the UK. As for the profits, British insurance companies and pension funds long ago shifted their investments out of BL and into Toyota and Nissan.

Sensible and effective pragmatism. But how will the economist High Priests of the Free Trade Orthodoxy describe it? As the unprincipled and self-defeating expediency of short-sighted politicians. They will tell you precisely how much cheaper the cars would have been if we had just gone on importing them. They will not only tell you how much extra this protectionism makes us pay for our cars; but also how big are the extra profits of Nissan and British Rover. What they will not tell you is how much of the 'consumer surplus' yielded by cheaper cars would have been mopped up in unemployment pay, or how many fewer pounds we would have had for spending on cars if the car industry had gone the way of the motorbike industry.

The High Priests frequently affect to despise such a nationalistic calculus. What has happened to global output, they will ask. The answer: probably enhanced. Thanks to the chicanery of anti-dumping tariffs, less of the Japanese surplus has been channelled into buying US Treasury bonds and real estate, more into direct overseas investment, thereby doing more to add to world efficiency by diffusing their work practices around the world.

* Contributed article to the *Financial Times*, 8 July 1992; cf. also the article of the same title in R. Morgan, J. Lorentzen, A. Leander and S. Guzzini (eds), *New Diplomacy in the Post-Cold War World: Essays for Susan Strange*, Basingstoke: Macmillan and New York: St Martin's, 1993, pp. 83–118.

Suppose we did reform GATT to allow for such sensible pragmatism. What might it mean in practice?

1. Drop all the provisions which allow protectionist measures to be justified by charges of dumping or hidden subsidies (but not those that permit it for infant-industry, gaining-learning-time reasons). Anti-trust prosecution of predatory pricing can still continue - without discrimination between imported and domestically produced goods.
2. Substitute IIIQRs - Investment Inviting Import Quantity Restrictions. A Triple IQR does not, like an anti-dumping action, say 'You are cheats and we are going to block your imports.' It says: 'You are clearly more efficient than us. But we don't want to lose the industry. We shall import only *x* of your widgets per year for the next ten years. But by all means come and manufacture here. We shall give you all the facilities available to domestic start-ups, though we shall insist on phased-in local content rules.'

   The trigger conditions for permissible Triple IQRs should be defined tightly in the GATT - in terms of an industry's share in GNP, its linkages as measured in input–output tables, the growth rate of import penetration, etc. - taking care, probably by some measure of labour-intensitivity, that IIIQRs cannot be used against developing countries' attempts to escape poverty by trading on their sole - cheap labour - advantage. (Try telling a Mauritian peasant; we won't take your sugar, but by all means come and grow beet in Norfolk.)

What are the implications of what would amount to a Lutheran shift, making Free Trade no longer absolute virtue, and discrimination no longer absolute vice?

1. An end to the most poisonous feature of our current hypocritical orthodoxy; the fact that the only way to practise (frequently sensible) protection is by calling a trading partner a cheat. It takes experts to expose the dishonest chicanery of anti-dumping suits.[1] But every newspaper reader can see how unhealthy Japan-bashing is for American party politics, let alone international relations.
2. Japanese firms would come to Europe, not resentful at being bludgeoned by charges of unfairness, but flattered at the acknowledgement of their solid competitive strengths. They would be more ready to comply honestly with local content rules.

Discrimination against states with an in-built structural surplus (as Keynes argued in the 1940s when it was the USA which was the obvious target for discrimination) is a recognition that we live in a world community - just as the universal practice of progressive taxation which discriminates against the wealthy is a recognition that the nation is a community.

The problems? Triple IQRs protect industries not the existing domestic firms in an industry. But unfortunately it is existing firms which finance pressure group lobbies and political parties, and often actually *believe* that the Japanese win by cheating and not by exercise of the solid Victorian virtues of thrift, diligence, long-term planning and managerial efficiency. Reform needs politicians with the Lutheran toughness to resist the lobbies.

The Japanese won't like discrimination either. But they are great golfers. Tell them: sorry; we've been using the wrong metaphor about 'level playing fields'. The game's not football, but golf. Handicapping is the only way you get a good fair game.

Orthodoxies are powerful. Free Trade Orthodoxy rests on three things; an admirable spirit of internationalism; the self-interest of the dominant rule-making nations over the last century (first Britain, then the USA, now Japan); and the arguments of trade theory about the *mutual* benefits - to weaker as well as stronger trading partners - of Free Trade.

Accelerating investment through Triple IQRs shows an even stronger spirit of internationalism. As for trade theory, the bankruptcy of the comparative advantage paradigm with its assumptions of competitive markets and 'undistorted' prices is apparent even to some of its High Priests. A world in which one country's export drive can destroy another country's industry in the space of half a decade is no longer Ricardo's world.

NOTE

1. J.R. Boltuck and R.E. Litan (eds), *Down in the Dumps*, Washington, Brookings, 1992.

27. Convergence in whose interest?*

Why were we - the contributors - interested in globalization and convergence? It seems to me that one can crudely classify the approaches adopted under three heads:

The Analytic;
The Implicit Normative;
The Explicit Mandarin Normative.

I would like to elaborate briefly on the differences as I see them, declare my allegiance in this particular context to the explicit mandarin normative mode, and present one particular example of the sort of messy dilemma such an approach gets one into.

The pure and consistent examples of the analytic mode [examples cited] are concerned, above all, with teasing out causal connections, with showing the multiplicity of forces that cause economic institutions to be different in different countries and might in the future cause them to converge or diverge, and with seeking generalizations about the way those forces interact and which are likely to be stronger.

[Of two typical examples of the implicit normative category,] the one expresses its norms more frequently in the form of prescriptive 'shoulds' and the other in predictive 'wills', but it does not take much reading between the lines to infer that the values that direct their analysis are similar. The two goods on which both agree are 'fairness' and 'efficiency'. But because 'fairness' turns out to be defined as that which maximizes the openness of competition by giving everyone an equal chance to take part in it, and competition is valued because it leads to greater efficiency, eventually it is efficiency that is king - the ur-value from which all other values are derived.

But when the underlying values of normative reasoning are left unargued and implicit, they can be more easily partisan. Efficiency, which presumably means improving the ratio of outputs to inputs, is all very well, but outputs for whom from inputs by whom? [Consider the questions asked and the questions

* Extracted from R. Dore and S. Berger (eds), *National Diversity and Global Capitalism*, Ithaca: Cornell University Press, 1996, pp. 366–74.

not asked in the paper about 'corporate governance' which asserts that the American system emphasizes the reduction of agency costs, and the Japanese system reduces transaction costs.] The question asked is: which offers 'genuine economic efficiency', which the least 'unfair restraint of trade that ultimately reduces global economic welfare'. The questions not asked are 'which leads to a more equal or a more equitable distribution of income in society,' 'which to a more democratic distribution of political power', 'which to an atmosphere more conducive to the peaceful and costless resolution of clashes of interest'.

I say 'partisan' because the viewpoint taken is that of the owner of capital. The fact is that agency costs - the costs to shareholders of managerial behaviour not wholly devoted to their interests - may well, in the United States, take the form of the famous fleet of jets run by Mr Johnson of RJR Nabisco,[1] whereas in Japan they are more likely to take the form of keeping underemployed workers on the books in a recession instead of laying them off. But such considerations [are treated as] irrelevant to the argument. They are, indeed, irrelevant from the point of view of the owner of capital who bears those costs and has no interest except in minimizing them.

I called this approach 'partisan' because there is a long-standing debate, and in some quarters ongoing debate (particularly quarters where very little capital is owned), as to whether the owners of capital actually deserve such exclusive consideration.[2]

It is in making its partisanship explicit that the third category, what I called the explicit mandarin normative category [example cited], differs. Because my own brief discussion of trade policy which follows falls into the same category, it is perhaps worthwhile to spell out the assumptions of this approach.

1. It is not meaningless to speak of a 'public interest' and of 'fair' criteria for adjudicating between clashing private interests, even though any definition of that interest must be a reflection of the definer's own values.
2. The values of people who talk about the public interest and about fairness do frequently go beyond the Pecksniffian rationalization of private interest. This can happen even for those who have not had the training in detachment given to mandarins in the best civil services, whose role is explicitly defined as guardians of the public interest, and *a fortiori* for those who have.
3. Where there is a consensus on what public interest or criteria of fairness mean (and therefore by definition on the values that define them) within a society or among the politically active members of society, this consensus can have an effect on policy that is not always and necessarily

overwhelmed by the self-interest maximization of group lobbies (the more so, obviously, in more socially cohesive societies).

4. Seeking to create such a consensus by persuading others to accept one's own values (frequently described as the political process par excellence in ideal or idealistic conceptions of democracy) can actually occur in practice. Politics in the industrial democracies are not all about interest assertion and horse trading. There are competing altruisms as well as competing egoisms.
5. There is reason to think that the altruism quotient may be steadily diminishing in most industrial societies, a thesis encapsulated in Fred Hirsch's phrase about the 'depleting moral legacy of capitalism.'[3] Capitalism may be undermining itself because it depends for its functioning on the force of certain moral constraints that derive from precapitalist society and that capitalism itself works steadily to erode. Part of that notion, its relation to politics and the conception of a 'general interest', is neatly summarized by Hirschmann: 'With macro-management, Keynesian or otherwise, assuming an important role in the functioning of the [capitalist] system, the macromanagers must be motivated by the "general interest" rather than by their self-interest, and the system, being based on self-interest, has no way of generating the proper motivation. To the extent such motivation does exist, it is a residue of previous value systems that are likely to "erode".'[4]
6. The tendency to nail one's colours to the mast is exacerbated by a contemporary *trahison des clercs,* the propensity among academic analysts to elevate the importance of self-interest among the factors that make the world go round. This seems to spring either from the pursuit of some hard-nosed macho self-image or from the envious desire to do game theory just like the economists.
7. Even if one is fighting a losing battle and the world is going to the dogs, it is worth trying to resist these tendencies, even if all one gains is temporary respite from the inevitable.
8. Any definition of the public interest or of fairness is properly open to attack on the nonintellectual, moral-judgemental grounds that they are repulsive/uncongenial/fascist/infantile/*fin de siècle*/neoliberal/unregenerate-Marxist, or whatever. But we make those judgements as citizens. The only intellectual job to be done is that of uncovering the underlying value judgements and assessing their logical consistency.
9. But that job of sorting out the logical consistency or otherwise of different value positions and the policy prescriptions that follow from them is indeed a useful intellectual or academic activity – as useful as the (different) intellectual activity of causal analysis.

10. Any intellectual's selection of the value positions to be analysed is bound to be (and, alas, his or her conclusions about their consistency may well be) affected by what her or his own values are, so that Trade Description Act considerations require one to make one's values explicit (quite apart from any proselytizing zeal to make converts). The frequent use of the first-person singular that this entails may give such writing a certain let-it-all-hang-out, me-decade air that not everyone will find tasteful, but that cannot be helped.

In principle there is no reason why the causal analysis of political economists and mandarin normative analysis of value consistency should ever be in conflict. The latter also requires causal analysis, insisting only that it should be kept separate from the normative consistency analysis.

However, in practice, when mandarin normative analysts do such causal analysis, their sensitivity to (and wish to believe in the causal efficacy of) public interest and fairness arguments may cause them to give slightly different causal interpretations from those of full-time political economists of the same situation. This reflection occurred to me when I read Gourevitch's account of the Structural Impediments Initiative Talks in Japan and found myself balking slightly at his suggestion that the success of US negotiators in urging institutional reforms on Japan was determined by whether or not they were supported by articulate domestic interest groups. I would suggest, however, that what one might call 'strength-of-the-argument' considerations also played a part in determining outcomes. Examples include: (1) A widely shared sense that it was in the public interest to mollify the Americans lest worse (Super-301, etc.) befall; hence some especially rapid concessions in areas that seemed dearest to American hearts, such as quick licences for Toys-R-Us. (2) A sense that the institutionalized deviations from legal procedures involved in the Large Retail Stores Law ... were an affront to administrative rectitude and could not be defended. (3) On land taxation a sense that the redistribution of wealth through phenomenal land price rises was inequitable (I mean inequitable, not just bad for the losers) – a sense made all the stronger by the dominance of a 'productivist' ethic that looks suspiciously on unearned speculative gains of any kind. (4) An 'absurdity level' effect. Defending a domestic rice price that is five times the international level is harder than defending one that is only three times higher through mechanisms that have nothing to do with the rice-eaters' assessment of the consumer surplus they are being denied.

The point is that the coincidence between foreign and domestic pressures involves something wider than domestic pressures driven by group self-interest. To put it in Weberian terms, democratic pluralism involves a plurality of ideal as well as of material interests.

BUT WHOSE PUBLIC?

One problem with notions such as the 'public' interest is to define one's public. Should it be fellow-citizens or fellow-human beings everywhere? Real mandarins have no difficulty: the answer is that public who pays their salary, whose civil 'servant' they are. But for free-floating would-be ventriloquist mandarins in academia and the media, the dilemma is real. One could see it lurking in the background to many comments on NAFTA during the American debate in the fall of 1993. Is an extra dollar's welfare to a citizen of Chiapas to be treated as of equal or less value than an extra dollar for a citizen of Peoria? It was not a question that made much difference to the American debate, but in a similar debate in, say, Norway, where the aggressive assertion of national self-interest is less admired as an expression of proud masculine patriotism, it would have been frequently heard.

THE DILEMMA WHERE IT HURTS

What public? is a question that must be confronted in any reasonable argument about protectionism and free trade. I have long been an advocate of protectionism against Japan. Not at all because I think the Japanese unfair. It is one of the follies of the GATT system that the only way it allows an industry threatened by Japanese imports to fight even for the temporary protection it needs to survive at all is by hurling charges of unfairness – trumped-up charges of dumping, collusive targeting, and so on – to justify anti-dumping duties or the demand for VERs, 'voluntary' export restrictions.

I am in favour of protection against Japanese exports. I am also in favour of the Japanese defending themselves against us by refusing to deregulate in fields such as finance and insurance where they might feel threatened by our superior ruthlessness or expertise in inventing arcane derivatives and by our tendency to turn the insurance industry into something less like a means of socializing risks and more like a means of speculative gambling. I take this position not on any grounds of unfairness, because the playing field is tilted, or whatever, but because of the need for mutual recognition of different definitions of the public interest, deriving from different value conceptions of what life is about.

To begin with our case in Europe and North America (theirs, with respect to finance, would be somewhat different) it seems to me that the Japanese expand their market shares so rapidly in our markets as well as in third markets partly because they are more clever and efficient (in organizational as well as material technology) but also partly because they work harder, give more of their time and loving care to their work life, and have fewer and less dominant outside interests beyond their work lives than we do. (The competitive advantage this confers is not a question of 'wage costs per hour' but, rather, of the total 'put-work-demands-first' flexibility with which the hours are offered. The debate on 'lean production' among German unions recognizes how much this is an ingredient of Japanese success, something glossed over in the MIT book[5] that gave that concept such wide diffusion.) The Japanese often *seem* to be happier that way than we are, leading a more 'balanced' life, seeing more of our friends and families, spending more time in front of the television or whatever. But that's their affair. We would, on the whole, not like to sacrifice our weekends whenever our job required it the way they seem to do.

[So, I do not think that doctrinaire adherence to the principle of maximization of global welfare through free trade should stand in the way of defending ourselves against having to become workaholics (see Chapter 26 for a way we might manage to have our cake and eat it in the matter of trade barriers against Japan). Nor should it stand in the way of the Japanese who want to have the sort of (possibly quite costly) insurance system that has a high element of social risk pooling which competing American firms would diminish. National groups are entitled to value goals other than income maximization, and mandarins are entitled to endorse them (across borders, as it were) provided that they say explicitly what their value premises are.

The real problem for mandarins with a lingering attachment to ideals of equality comes when 'free trade or protectionism' presents a stark dilemma. Should one be as open as possible to developing country imports in order to contribute to reducing inequality *among* nations, when one knows that such imports are likely to exacerbate the growth of inequality *within* nations which technological change is already accelerating? Better ways of redistributing income within the rich countries would resolve the dilemma, but are they likely?]

NOTES

1. See Bryan Burrough and John Helyar, *Barbarians at the Gate: The Fall of RJR Nabisco,* New York, Harper and Row, 1991.
2. See, for example, L.E. Preston, H.J. Sapienza and R.D. Miller, 'Stakeholders, Shareholders, Managers', in A. Etzioni and P.R. Lawrence (eds), *Socio-economics: Toward a New Synthesis,* Armonk, NY, M.E. Sharpe, 1991.
3. F. Hirsch, *Social Limits to Growth,* London, Routledge, 1977.
4. A.O. Hirschmann, *Rival Views of Market Society,* Cambridge, Harvard University Press, 1992, p. 111.
5. J. Womack, D.T. Jones and D. Roos, *The Machine That Changed the World: The Story of Lean Production,* New York, Harper, 1991. For the German debate, see G. Schienstock and B. Steffensen, 'Lean Production: The German Debate', mimeo, Akademie fur Technikfolgenabschatzung, Stuttgart, n.d.

28. Why bother about our grandchildren?*

There was a time when sociologists believed in progress. They were not fearful that any suggestion on their part that today might be better than the yesterdays of earlier decades and centuries would be taken as an endorsement of the contemporary structure of society. But a lot of things have happened since the days when Spencer and Comte and Mill, and sometimes even Marx, could write under the confident assumption that they lived in the best days there had ever been, and that there were better days to come.

It is not just that sociology has been established as a university subject and sociologists have discovered the attractions of taking on the role of vanguard of the intellectual proletariat, too preoccupied with critical analysis of the evils of the present to be much concerned with trends in the past and how they might be extrapolated into the future. It is not just that. Other factors have affected the credibility of the doctrine of progress. The two world wars of this century, the scale of the carnage in the first and the programme of cold-blooded genocide which developed in Germany in the second, gave a hollow ring to the self-assured pronouncements of Victorian philosophers about the moral evolution of mankind, supposedly a concomitant of the increasing differentiation and rationalization of social structures, the development of new bases for social solidarity, and the steady expansion of internalized moral control over behaviour with the increasing perfection of education systems. By the mid-twentieth century 'the progress of mankind' was the kind of phrase which intellectuals left to publicists and politicians.

PROGRESS AND THE ADVANCE OF SCIENCE

To be sure, the assumption of a continuing accumulation of scientific knowledge, a continuing flow of invention, and cumulating possibilities of material abundance, were more widely taken for granted than ever before, more a part of mother's-milk common sense. It was only in the 1950s, for

* Extracted from 'Why Bother About Our Grandchildren?', Smyth Memorial Lecture, New University of Ulster, 24 November 1983.

example, that wage-bargaining came to be based on the expectation of an annual increase in wages as the workers' share in what was expected to be a steadily maintained trajectory of economic growth.

This assumption of continuing material progress was taken for granted, indeed was a major starting point, for the writers of our famous distopias. It was what made possible the efficient deprivation of liberty and personal fulfilment in the interests of political aggrandizement which a Huxley or an Orwell foresaw.

Nowadays, we may have our doubts even about that. Even the likelihood of continuing material progress seems something by no means to be taken for granted after a decade of inflation and stagflation, culminating in three years of deep recession. Inevitably our long-term expectations are coloured by our short-term experiences. It needs only five dollars off the price of a barrel of oil, and the oil companies drop their coal liquefaction projects, and governments cut back all their energy conservation programmes.

And yet no one really doubts the core assumption which underlies the expectation of increasing material affluence - the assumption that, short of the man-made cataclysm which science has now made possible, scientific knowledge will continue to accumulate and so will the power to control the material universe as that knowledge is applied. No one can disinvent the role of the inventor, unless by destroying most of civilization. The university researcher, the research department of public and private enterprises, those new creations of the twentieth century, will not go away. And carrying forward the advance of scientific knowledge is their in-built mission.

The possible social and political consequences of this one reasonably reliable long-run trend are worth a good deal of thought. Some sociologists have, in fact, given it a lot of thought, but generally, futurology has a bad name. It is seen as a kind of journalism designed to bemuse the groundlings and perhaps even to take their minds off the exploitation of the present with the seductive allure of gee-whiz dreams about the future. This is a pity. It is a pity because imagining the future is as fascinating a game in its own right as the archaeologist's attempt to imagine the shape of the past - and there is no reason why the one should count as one of the purest forms of scholarship and the other as a suspect activity. It is a pity also because there are going to be people living in that future - our children and our children's children - and because the decisions we are taking today will have consequences for the shape of their future.

Of the literature on the future which exists, one part involves forecasting the consequences of current decisions to build nuclear power stations or to interfere with the environment, and is concerned primarily with persuading us to act one way or the other. Another part is concerned with the extrapolation of trends and largely invites us simply to contemplate what will be, either with joy or with horror. The two activities are not always brought into conjunction. Often our perception of the dangers of nuclear wastes or the risks of oil or food supplies being exhausted is based on the assumption that the world of the future which we are putting at risk will be very much the same as ours. But it may not be, and a clear perception of the way the future might change may alter the assessment of risks. Equally, and more important, as I shall argue, our inability to imagine the social and political possibilities of the future may lead us to ignore the ways in which some of our actions now are in fact pre-empting possible choices for our children and grandchildren. A barrel of reactor waste caked in glass and put in a crack in a mountain to radiate potential death for several thousand years we can visualize and demonstrate vociferously about. A decision on nuclear arms or the law of the sea which may have much more devastating consequences in preventing our children from having the chance to conquer world hunger or escape nuclear annihilation – a chance which a different decision on our part would have afforded them – is much less likely to attract attention. This is understandable, perhaps, because the possibilities in question are much less precisely calculable than the half-life of plutonium oxide or the probability of natural selection reproducing a new species of sperm whale when once the first one is extinct. But for all that greater uncertainty, they are not by any means to be considered as matters of lesser importance....

MAKING OURSELVES THINK OF THE FUTURE

... [I]f we do agree in principle [with what I have said about a duty to consider the welfare of future generations], if it is a case of the spirit being willing and only the flesh being weak, then why not seek ways of fortifying the flesh? Various societies have found various ways of doing that sort of thing: sticking admonitory slogans like 'The buck stops here' above one's desk, for instance, or establishing the custom of periodic rituals at which better selves can be preached to. Within administrations, a nation's better self is often represented in a monitoring role, in the form of a watchdog council, a Supreme Court, or an Ombudsman.

So why not have a monitoring agency specifically concerned with our duties to future generations? The Foreign Office, to start with, might establish a '2050 Department', charged specifically with the task of evaluating all current policies for their probable long-run consequences on our descendants in 70 years time. If we did this, we might conceivably reduce the possibility that our thoughtlessness, our adventurism, or our intransigent unwillingness to take the risk of trusting in others' good faith, will deprive our descendants of options they might otherwise have, including the option of survival.

List of Ronald Dore's publications

This Bibliography covers Ronald Dore's main publications. Excluded from the list are newspaper columns, except where published as books (1994, 1997), articles based on panel discussions or interviews (there are quite a few of these in Japanese), reviews, except for review articles, and most working papers and conference papers which were subsequently published as articles. Translations are not listed separately, but book translations are noted along with the original publication.

1949

Review of A.R. Nykl (Kanji: a New Method Comprising 2700 Sinico-Japanese Characters) in *Bulletin of SOAS*, **13**(1), pp. 253–4.

1950

'Poole Grammar School Overseas', (Letter from Tokyo) in Magazine of Poole Grammar School, July, pp. 51–3.

1952

'The Ethics of the New Japan' in *Pacific Affairs*, **25**(2), pp. 147–59.

1953

'Japanese Rural Fertility: Some Social and Economic Factors', in *Population Studies*, **7**(1), pp. 62–88.

'The Tokyo Institute for the Science of Thought', in *Far Eastern Quarterly*, **13**(1), pp. 23–36.

1956

'Jinkō mondai no shakaiteki kiban' (The Social Foundations of the Population Problem) in S. Tahata (ed.), *Nōgyō ni okeru senzai shitsugyō* (Latent Unemployment in Agriculture), Tokyo: Nihon hyōronsha.

'Japanese Election Candidates in 1955', in *Pacific Affairs,* **29**(2), pp. 174–81.

'Left and Right in Japan' in *International Affairs*, **32**(1), January, pp. 11–26.
'The Day the Fire Brigade Went Fishing', in *Japan Quarterly*, **3**, pp. 347–55.

1957

(Review article) 'Japan - Attitudes, Power and Ideas', in *Pacific Affairs,* **30**(3), pp. 260–65.

1958

City Life in Japan, London: Routledge & Kegan Paul; and Berkeley: University of California Press (also in Japanese).
'The Japanese Land Reform in Retrospect', in *Far Eastern Survey*, **27**(2), pp. 183–8.
'Is Japan Asian?', in *Mankind* (Hyderabad), **3**(2), pp. 108–13.
'Tōzai no bunka to nanboku no keizai' (East–West Culture and North–South Economics), in *Shōwa dōjin*, **4**, pp. 25–30.
'"Musuko no dai" no nai nōgyō' (Farming Without the Son's Generation) in *Chido*, April, pp. 90–94.
'Kanada ni okeru Nihon kenkyū' (Japanese Research in Canada) in *Kokuritsu kokkai toshokan kokusai kōkan tsūshin*, **26**, September, pp. 1–2.

1959

Land Reform in Japan, Oxford: Oxford University Press; and Berkeley: University of California Press (also in Japanese).
(Review article) 'Japan: Country of Accelerated Transition', in *Population Studies*, **13**(1), pp. 103–11.
'The Meiji Landlord: Good or Bad?', in *Journal of Asian Studies*, **18**(3), pp. 343–55.
'Teachers to the Barricades: Japanese Politics in 1958', in *Canadian Forum*, **38**, pp. 256–7.
'Kanbun kyōiku to aikokushin' (Classical Chinese Education and Patriotism), in *Shisō*, **418**, April, pp. 108–13.

1960

'Agricultural Improvement in Japan, 1870–1900', in *Economic Development and Cultural Change*, **9**(1), part 2. (Reprinted in E. Jones and S. Woolf (eds), *Agrarian Change and Economic Development: The Historical Problems*, London: Methuen, 1969.)
'Shinchūgun no nōchi kaikaku kōsō: rekishi no ichi danmen' (The Concept of

Land Reform of the Occupation Forces: a Cross Section of History), in *Nōgyō sōgō kenkyū*, **14**(1), pp. 175–94.
'Daieiteikoku ōgon jidai no gaikōkan' (Diplomats of the Golden Age of the British Empire), in *Tosho*, **135**, pp. 30–31.

1961

'Function and Cause', in *American Sociological Review*, **26**(6), pp. 843–53 (reprinted in A. Ryan (ed.), *The Philosophy of Social Explanation*, Oxford University Press, 1973; R. Denisoff *et al.*, *Theories and Paradigms in Contemporary Sociology*, Hasca IL: Peacock, 1973; and M. Martin and L. McIntyre (eds), *Readings in the Philosophy of Social Science*, Cambridge MA: MIT Press, 1994).
'Japanese Politics and the Approach of Prosperity', in *The World Today*, July, pp. 289–99.
'The Japanese Socialist Party and "Structural Reform"', in *Asian Survey*, **1**(8), pp. 3–15.
'Meijiki ni okeru Nihon no jinushi' (Landlords of the Meiji Period), in *Shisō no kagaku*, **29**, pp. 66–71; **30**, pp. 62–71.
'Surōgan ni hanran suru kuni' (Nation Deluged With Slogans), in *Chūō kōron*.

1962

'Ie to kazoku: Nihonjin sutairu to hakujin sutairu' (Household and Family: Japanese Style and Caucasian Style), and 'Shūkyō: nichiyō gakkō no bon odori' (Religion: Bon Dancing at Sunday School), in M. Gamo (ed.), *Umi o watatta Nihon no mura* (Japanese Village Overseas), Tokyo: Chūō kōronsha.
'Sociology in Japan', in *British Journal of Sociology*, **13**(2), pp. 116–23.
'Talent and the Social Order in Tokugawa Japan', in *Past and Present*, **21**, April, pp. 60–72.
'The Thought of Men, the Thought of Society', in *Asian Cultural Studies*, **3**, (ICU, special issue), October, pp. 73–86.
'Class and the Economy in Japan', in *New Society*, **4**(25).
'The Administration of Japanese Land Reform', in *Journal of Local Administration Overseas*, **1**(4), pp. 231–8.

1963

'Beyond the Land Reform: Japan's Agricultural Prospects', in *Pacific Affairs*, **36**(3), pp. 267–76.
'Some Comparisons of Latin American and Asian Studies, With Special

Reference to Research on Japan', in *Items*, **17**(2), pp. 13–20.
(Review article) 'Social Thought in Japan', in *New Left Review*, **25**, pp. 77–83.

1964

Education in Tokugawa Japan, London: Routledge & Kegan Paul; and Berkeley: University of California Press (also in Japanese).
'Education in Japan', in R. Ward and D. Rustow (eds), *Political Modernization in Japan and Turkey*, Princeton: Princeton University Press.
'Latin America and Japan Compared', in J. Johnson (ed.), *Continuity and Change in Latin America*, Stanford: Stanford University Press.
'Japan as a Model of Economic Development', in *European Journal of Sociology*, **5**(1), pp. 138–54.
'Education in Japan's Growth', in *Pacific Affairs*, **37**(1), pp. 66–79.
'Le Réveil Religieux et la Politique', in *Archives de Sociologie des Religions*, **17**, pp. 45–51.
'Analysis of the Japanese Election Results', in *The World Today*, January, pp. 4–8.
(Review article) 'The Search for Modernity in Asia and Africa', in *Pacific Affairs*, **37**(2), pp. 161–5.

1965

'The Legacy of Tokugawa Education', in M. Jansen (ed.), *Changing Japanese Attitudes toward Modernization*, Princeton: Princeton University Press.
'Japanese Personality', in *Asia: A Handbook*, G. Wint (ed.), London: Anthony Blunt Ltd, pp. 491–96.
with K. Aoyagi, 'The Buraku Minority in Urban Japan', in A. Rose and C. Rose (eds), *Minority Problems: A Textbook of Readings in Inter-Group Relations*, New York: Harper & Row.
'Land Reform and Japan's Economic Development', in *Developing Economies*, **3**(4), pp. 487–96.
'Schools and States in Africa and Asia', in *Pacific Affairs*, **38**(3–4), pp. 345–52.
'Happy Families', in *Japan Quarterly*, **12**(4), pp. 495–97.
'How Asian is Japan?', in *New Society*, 27 May (no. 139), pp. 14–15.
'Japan and China', in *New Society*, 3 June (no. 140), pp. 16–17.
'The Special Problem of Agriculture', in *The Listener*, 9 September (reprinted in A. Shonfield (ed.), *Second Thoughts on Aid*, London: BBC Publications, 1965).
'New Ideas and Old Habits', in International House of Japan *Bulletin*, August.

1966

Chief author of United Nations, *Progress in Land Reform: Fourth Report*, New York.

'The Socialist Party and the Farmers', in A. Cole, G. Totten and C. Uyehara, *Socialist Parties in Postwar Japan*, New Haven: Yale University Press.

'Watashi no Nihon keizairon' (My View of the Japanese Economy) in Nikkei Shimbun (ed.), *Watashi no Nihon keizairon*, Tokyo.

'Japan's Place in the World', in *The World Tod*ay, July, pp. 293–306.

'On the Possibility and Desirability of a Theory of Modernization', in Asiatic Research Centre, Korea University (ed.), *International Conference on the Problems of Modernization in Asia: Report*, Seoul, pp. 157–66.

'The Case of the Wholesale Modernizer', in *The Listener*, 24 February.

1967

(Ed.), *Aspects of Social Change in Modern Japan*, Princeton: Princeton University Press ('Introduction' and 'Mobility, Equality and Individualism' in same).

'Sociological Aspects of Land Valuation and Land Reform', in A. Woodruff, J. Brown and S. Lin (eds), *International Seminar on Land Taxation, Land Tenure and Land Reform in Developing Countries*, Hartford: Lincoln Institute.

'Comments on Land Reform', in H. Southworth and B. Johnston (eds), *Agricultural Development and Economic Growth*, Ithaca: Cornell University Press.

'Japan Votes in a Black Mist', in *New Society*, 26 January, pp. 133–4.

1968

'Modernization: the Middle Class', in *International Encyclopaedia of the Social Sciences*, New York: Macmillan.

'Climate and Agriculture: the Intervening Variables', in UNESCO (ed.), *Agroclimatological Methods - Proceedings of the Reading Symposium.*

'General Introduction to Land Reform', *Report of the Conference on Land Reform*, Agromisa, Wageningen.

1969

'The Tenancy System in Prewar Japan', in A. Beteille (ed.), *Social Inequality*, Harmondsworth: Penguin.

'Agricultural Improvement in Japan 1870–1900', in E. Jones and S. Woolf (eds), *Agrarian Change and Economic Development*, London: Methuen.

'The Modernizer as a Special Case: Japanese Factory Legislation, 1882-1912', in *Comparative Studies in Society and History*, **11**(4), pp. 433-50.

'Social Planning for the Family', in *Journal of Development Studies*, **6**(4), pp. 57-66.

'On Learning to Live With the Second Best', in *Economic and Political Weekly*, 8 November, pp. 1781-5.

'On the Possibility and Desirability of a Theory of Modernization', Institute of Development Studies, *Communication*, **38**.

'How Modern is Japan?', in *Interplay*, Dec. 1969-Jan. 1970, pp. 12-16.

(Review article) 'Making Sense of History', in *European Journal of Sociology*, **10**(2), pp. 295-305.

1970

'City Life in Japan: Life in a Tokyo Ward', in H.M. Lindquist (ed.), *Education: Readings in the Process of Cultural Transmission*, Boston: Houghton Mifflin.

'Interests, Purposes and Payoffs', in E. Norbeck and S. Parman (eds), *The Study of Japan in the Behavioural Sciences*, Rice University Studies, 56/4.

'Nihon kindaikaron no saikentō' (Reconsidering Theories of Japanese Modernization) in T. Kondo and K. Takeda (eds), *Hikaku kindaikaron* (Comparative Modernization Theories), Tokyo: Miraisha.

'Textbook Censorship in Japan: the Ienaga Case', in *Pacific Affairs*, **43**(4), pp. 548-56.

'Sangyō to kyōiku: daigaku nyūshi wa kuji de kimeyō' (Industry and Education: Let's Decide University Entrance by Lottery), in *Ajichō geppō*, **1**(10), pp. 19-34.

'Keizai kaihatsu to Nihon no yakuwari' (Economic Development and Japan's Role), in *IDE minshu kyōiku kyōkaishi*, **102**, pp. 23-7.

'Hajime ni moji ari' (In the Beginning Was the Written Word), in *Tosho*, **253**, September, pp. 46-9.

'The Future of Japan's Meritocracy', in International House of Japan *Bulletin*, **26**, October, pp. 30-50.

'Put it in Writing', in Asahi Press (ed.), *This is Japan*, Tokyo.

1971

'Modern Co-operatives in Traditional Communities', in P. Worsley (ed.), *Two Blades of Grass: Rural Co-operatives in Agricultural Modernization*, Manchester: Manchester University Press.

'Land Reform and Japan's Economic Development: a Reactionary Thesis', in T. Shanin (ed.), *Peasants and Peasant Societies*, Harmondsworth: Penguin.

'Interests, Purposes and Payoffs', in E. Norbeck and S. Parman (eds), *The Study of Japan in the Behavioural Sciences*, Rice University Studies 56/4.

With T. Ouchi, 'Rural Origins of Japanese Fascism', in J.M. Morley (ed.), *Dilemmas of Growth in Prewar Japan*, Princeton: Princeton University Press.

'Japanese Industrialization and the Developing Countries: Model, Warning or Source of Healthy Doubts?', Institute of Southeast Asian Studies (Singapore) Occasional Paper No. 8, August, pp. 1–18.

'The Late Development Effect', paper for Modernization in Southeast Asia Conference, Institute of Southeast Asian Studies (Singapore), January.

'Teaching and Testing: Education in the Developing World', IDS Discussion Paper No. 6.

1972

Translation, *Japanese Rural Society*, Tadashi Fukutake (orig. *Nihon nōson shakai ron*, Tokyo University Press, 1964), Ithaca: Cornell University Press. ('Preface' in same, reprinted in T. Megarry (ed.), *The Making of Modern Japan: A Reader*, Dartford: Greenwich University Press, 1995.)

With E. Faure, J. Galtung, E. Reischauer and J. Ben-David, *Reviews of Education: Japan*, Paris: OECD.

'The Importance of Educational Traditions: Japan and Elsewhere', in *Pacific Affairs*, **45**(4), pp. 491–507.

'How Modern is Japan?' and 'Education' in BBC, *The Asian Phoenix*, London: BBC Publications.

With T. Machida, 'Shakai hoshō kinō no ninaite: kokka to kigyō' (Shouldering Social Security Functions: State and Enterprise), in *Kikan shakai hoshō kenkyū*, **8**(3), pp. 46–57.

'Commitment – to What, By Whom, and Why?', in *The Social and Cultural Background of Labour-Management Relations in Asian Countries* (Conference proceedings), Tokyo: Japan Institute of Labour.

'Rhodesia: the Settlement and After', IDS Discussion Paper, 13 pp.

'False Prophets: the Cuernavaca Critique of School', IDS Discussion Paper No. 12.

1973

British Factory-Japanese Factory: the Origins of National Diversity in Industrial Relations, London: Allen & Unwin; and Berkeley: University of California Press (also in Japanese and Spanish).

Chief author of *Education and Employment in Asia*, ECAFE, Annual Survey 1973, Vol. 1.

'The Late Development Effect', in H.D. Evers (ed.), *Modernization in S.E. Asia*, Singapore: Oxford University Press.

'L'Effetto di Sviluppo Ritardato e il Giappone', *in Rivista Internazionale di Scienze Economiche e Commerciali*, **20**(8–9), pp. 738–57.

'Kōhatsu kōka to Nihon' (The Late Development Effect and Japan) in *Fukuoka UNESCO*, **8**.

'Pre-Vocational Studies: a Comment on Recent Developments in Ceylonese Education', IDS Discussion Paper No. 13, pp. 1–22 (reprinted in *Marga*, **2**(2), 1973).

1974

'The Labour Market and Patterns of Employment in the Wage Sector of LDCs: Implications for the Volume of Employment Generated', in *World Development*, **2**(4–5), pp. 1–7.

'The Educational Rat-Race of the Third World', in *New Society*, 30 May, pp. 502–4.

'Late Development – Or Something Else? Industrial Relations in Britain, Japan, Mexico, Sri Lanka, Senegal', IDS Discussion Paper No. 61, 44 pp.

'Deschool? Try Using Schools for Education First: The Educational Impasse in the Developing World', IDS Discussion Paper No. 6, 17 pp.

1975

'The Future of Japan's Meritocracy' in G. Fodella (ed.), *Social Structures and Economic Dynamics in Japan up to 1980*, Milan: Università Bocconi (also in *Rivista Internationale di Scienze Economiche e Commerciali*, **22**(7–8), pp. 762–82).

'The Prestige Factor in International Affairs', in *International Affairs*, **51**(2), pp. 190–207.

'The Future of Formal Education in Developing Countries', in *International Development Review*, **17**(2), pp. 7–11.

'Authority, Function and Status in British and Japanese Factories', in *International Studies of Management and Organizations*, **5**(1).

'Selection Function of Schools Seen as Ignored by Educators', in *Report* (World Bank), May–June, R-4.

'Underdevelopment in Theoretical and Comparative Perspective', in *Problems of Development in Atlantic Canada*, Royal Society of Canada.

'Nihon no shakai to igirisu no shakai ni tsuite' (About Japanese Society and British Society), in *Komyunitei*, **40**, pp. 96–152.

'Some Reflections on the Late Development Hypothesis' and 'The Late Development Effect: A Reply', in IDS *Bulletin*, **6**(3), pp. 32–7; 50–73.

'Special Issues in Developing Countries', Keynote Address to 3rd International Conference on Higher Education at the University of Lancaster, 1-5 September, 10 pp.

1976

The Diploma Disease: Education, Qualification and Development, London: Allen & Unwin; and Berkeley: University of California Press (also Japanese and Spanish translations).

'Human Capital Theory, the Diversity of Societies and the Problem of Quality in Education', in *Higher Education*, **5**, pp. 79-102.

With J. Humphreys and P. West, 'The Basic Arithmetic of Youth Unemployment', Geneva: ILO.

'The Almighty Certificate', in *Times Educational Supplement*, 17 September.

(Review article), 'East is East and West is West', in *Government and Opposition*, **11**(2).

'Toshi no Nihonjin o kaita koro no koto' (About the Times When I Wrote City Life in Japan) and 'Hajime ni moji ari' (In the Beginning Was the Written Word), in G. Itasaka *et al.* (eds), *Modern Japanese: a Reader*, Tokyo: Kōdansha.

1977

'South Korean Development in Wider Perspective', in *Pacific Affairs*, **50**(2), pp. 189-207.

'Gakurekibyō jidai' (Age of the Diploma Disease), in *Nobi nobi*, 4/8 pp. 48-51; 4/9 pp. 60-63; 4/10 pp. 60-63; 4/11 pp. 52-5; 4/12 pp. 58-61; 5/1 (1978) 64-7; 5/2 pp. 52-5; 5/3 pp. 64-7.

'Minutes of Evidence' to The Select Committee on Science and Technology (Japan Sub-Committee), pp. 71-88.

'Underdevelopment in Theoretical Perspective', IDS Discussion Paper No. 109.

1978

Shinohata: Portrait of a Japanese Village, London: Allen Lane and Pantheon.

With S. Katō, chief eds for Fukuoka UNESCO, *Sengo no Nihon: tenkanki o mukaete: kokusai shinpojiumu* (Postwar Japan: Towards a Period of Transition), Fukuoka.

'Desperation Ratios and Pressure Groups in the Selection Process', in L. Dove and J. Cameron (eds), *Selection for Post-Primary Education in Developing Countries*, London: Institute of Education.

'Learning From China: Reflections on Transferability', in *World Develop-*

ment, **6**(5), pp. 715–18.
'Scholars and Preachers', in IDS *Bulletin*, **9**(4), pp. 12–15.
'The Role of Universities in National Development', Association of Commonwealth Universities Occasional Papers, July (also in *University News*, Association of Indian Universities).
With C. Deraniyagala and A. Little, *Qualifications and Employment in Sri Lanka*, Brighton: Institute of Development Studies.

1979

'Industrial Relations in Japan and Elsewhere', in A. Craig (ed.), *Japan: A Comparative View*, Princeton: Princeton University Press.
'Credentials in a More Expressive Future', in *Oxford Review of Education*, **5**(3), pp. 227–335.
'The Economic Miracle of Shinohata', in *Human Nature*, February, pp. 74–80.
'More About Late Development', in *Journal of Japanese Studies*, **5**(1), pp. 137–51.
'The Internationalization of Japan', in *Pacific Affairs*, **52**(4), Winter, pp. 595–611.
'Datsu kōgyōka shakai wa gakureki shakaika' (Is Post-industrial Society a Diploma Society?), in *Daigaku ronshū*, Collection No. 7, pp. 191–204.
'Foreword' to S. Katō, *A History of Japanese Literature: the First Thousand Years* (trans. D. Chibbett), London: Macmillan/Paul Norbury.

1980

'South Korean Development in a Wider Perspective', in Y. Chang (ed.), *Korea: A Decade of Development*, Seoul: Seoul National University Press.
'The Internationalization of Japan' in *Pacific Affairs*, **52**(4), pp. 595–611.
'Daikigyō to minshu shugi' (Large Firms and Democracy), in *Nihon rōdō kyōkai zasshi*, **259**, pp. 2–11.
'Daisan sekai to Nihon no kokueki' (The Third World and Japan's National Interest), in *Kokusai kaihatsu jyānaru*, **284**, pp. 32–52.
'Kyoiku ni okeru dentō no juyōsei' (The Importance of Educational Traditions), in Nagoya University, *Kyōiku 60 nendai kenkyū*, **3**, pp. 64–7.
The Diploma Disease Revisited', in *IDS Bulletin*, **11**(2), pp. 55–61.

1981

Ed. with Z. Mars and V.S.R. Brandt, *Community Development: Comparative Case Studies in India, the Republic of Korea, Mexico and Tanzania*, London: Croom Helm; and Paris: UNESCO.

Certification, Education and Work, course book for Open University, Open University Press (with contributions from Angela Little).

'Nihonteki keiei shisutemu no isō' (A Topology of Japanese-style Management) in *Keizai hyōron*, **30**(7), pp. 2–22.

'What Happened to QWL: a Kink in the Evolutionary Trend or the Wheel Coming Full Circle?', Sophia University Symposium, May.

'The Future Role of the Advanced Industrial Countries in the Development of the Third World', paper for Technova Conference, Paris.

'Energy Conservation and the Social Structure' paper for International Symposium on Energy Conservation, Tokyo, December.

1982

'Japan and the Third World: Coincidence or Divergence of Interests?', in R. Cassen, R. Jolly, J. Sewell and R. Wood (eds), *Rich Country Interests and Third World Development*, London: Croom Helm.

'Adjustment in Progress: a Lancashire Town' in J. Bhagwati (ed.), *Import Competition and Response*, Chicago: NBER.

'Recent Trends in Japanese Industrial Policy', in *Policy Studies*, **3** part 2, October, pp. 104–120.

Energy Conservation in Japanese Industry, London: Policy Studies Institute (Energy paper No. 3 [British Institute's Joint Energy Policy Programme])

With A. Little, *Resource Booklet* for the Film 'The Diploma Disease', Brighton: IDS Publications.

1983

'Goodwill and the Spirit of Market Capitalism', in *British Journal of Sociology*, **34**(4), pp. 459–82 (reprinted in M. Granovetter and R. Swedberg (eds), *The Sociology of Economic Life*, Boulder, CO: Westview Press, 1992; J. Ravenhill (ed.), *Japan*, Aldershot: Edward Elgar, 1995; W. Lazonick and W. Mass (eds), *Organizational Capability and Competitive Advantage*, Aldershot: Edward Elgar, 1995; P. Buckley and J. Michie (eds), *Firms, Organizations and Contracts: A Reader in Industrial Organization*, Oxford: Oxford University Press, 1996; S. Beechler and K. Stucker (eds), *Japanese Business*, London: Routledge, 1997; also in Italian in M. Margatti (ed.), *Azione Economica Come Azione Sociale*, Milano: FrancoAngeli, 1991).

'A Case Study Technology Forecasting in Japan: the Next Generation Base Technologies Development Programme', London: Technical Change Centre Report.

'Education' and 'Terakoya' in *Kodansha Encyclopedia of Japan*, Tokyo: Kodansha, Vol. 2, pp. 171–5; Vol. 8, pp. 11–12.

'Quality circles and their transferability to Britain', *in Rivista Internazionale di Scienze Economiche e Commerciali*, **30**(8), pp. 696–702.

'An Incomes Policy Built to Last', *Tawney Pamphlets*, **6**, pp. 1–23.

'The Social Sources of the Will to Innovate', in *Papers in Science, Technology and Public Policy*, **4**, Imperial College/SPRU/TCC.

'Watashi no Nihon shakai kenkyū: hitotsu no chiteki jiden' (My Research on Japanese Society: an Intellectual Autobiography), in *Hōsei*, **10**(3), pp. 26–38.

'Chikyūka shakai to Nihon no yakuwari' (Globalizing Society and Japan's Role), in *Shakai rōdō kenkyu* (Hōsei University), **29**(3–4), pp. 163–80.

'Daigaku wa nan no tameni sonzai suru no ka' (What Do Universities Exist For?), in *Waseda fōramu daigaku mondai ronshū*, **40**, pp. 4–13.

'Reflections on the "Learn from Japan" Boom', in International House of Japan *Bulletin*, **3**(2).

'Introduction' to S. Kamata, *Japan in the Passing Lane: an Insider's Account of Life in a Japanese Auto Factory*, London: Allen & Unwin.

'Why Bother About Our Grandchildren?', Smyth Memorial Lecture, New University of Ulster, 19 pp.

'Labour Markets, People and Power: a Plea for Small Innovation in Consensus-talking and National Accounting', Institute of Economic Growth (India) Occasional Papers, New Series No. 8, pp. 1–57.

'Workshop on British Competitiveness: An Agenda for Sociologists', paper for the ESRC Workshop on the Contribution of Social Science to the Study of Competitiveness of the Economy.

1984

'Preface' to reprinting of *Land Reform in Japan*, London: Athlone.

'Preface' to reprinting of *Education in Tokugawa, Japan*, London: Athlone.

'Technological Self reliance: Sturdy Ideal or Self-serving Rhetoric?', in M. Fransman and K. King (eds), *Technological Capability in the Third World*, Basingstoke: Macmillan.

'Unity and Diversity in World Culture', in H. Bull and A. Watson (eds), *Expansion of International Society*, Oxford: Clarendon Press.

'The Learn From Japan Boom', in *Speaking of Japan*, **5**(47).

'Nihon wa seiyō no atooi o suru noka: atarashii komyunitei o mosaku suru (Will Japan Follow the West: In Search of a New Community), in Fukuoka International Seminar Committee (ed.), *Ningen to gijutsu: sono chōwa o motomete*, Seibonsha.

1985

With K. Taira, *Structural Adjustment in Japan*, Geneva: ILO.

'Authority and Benevolence: the Confucian Recipe for Industrial Success', in *Government and Opposition*, **20**(2), pp. 196–217.
'Financial Structures and the Long-term View', in *Policy Studies*, **6**(1), pp. 10–29.
'Technical change and Cultural Adaptation', in *Compare*, **14**(1).
'Ruminations on Speculation', in *Tawney Journal*, Summer, pp. 13–17.
'Chūsan kaikyū no toshi, puroretaria no toshi' (The Year of the Middle Class, the Year of the Proletariat), in T. Umezao and T Moriya (eds), *Toshika no bunmeigaku*, Tokyo: Chūō kōronsha.
'Chingin kōshō ni okeru kōsei no gainen' (The Concept of Fairness in Wage Bargaining) in *Nihon rōdō kenkyū zasshi*, January, pp .4–13.
With C. Pratten, M. Sako and A. Silberston, 'Outward Direct Investment and the "Hollow Economy" Syndrome', JEIRC, Imperial College, 70 pp.
With Z. Mars, 'Technical Change and Inter-industry Wage Differentials', in *Work and Society*, **7**, January, p. 6.

1986

Flexible Rigidities: Industrial Policy and Structural Adjustment in the Japanese Economy 1970–1980. London: Athlone; and Stanford: Stanford University Press.
Bōeki masatsu no shakaigaku (The Sociology of Trade Friction), Tokyo: Iwanami shoten.
'Where Will the Japanese Nobel Prizes Come From?', in *Science and Public Policy*, **3**(6), pp. 347–61.
'Blackburn and Kishiwada: Proletarian Towns and Middle Class Towns', in T. Umesao, H. Smith II, T. Moriya and R. Ogawa (eds), *Japanese Civilization in the Modern World II: Cities and Urbanization*, Osaka: National Museum of Ethnology.
'Industrial Policy and How the Japanese Do It', in *Catalyst*, **2**(1), pp. 45–56.
'Commentary' (on Japan's Science Policy), in *Japan Economic Survey*, **10**(5), pp. 6–11.
With M. Sako, 'How the Youth Training Scheme Helps Employers', in *Employment Gazette*, June, pp. 195–204.
With M. Dodgson, 'Efficiency and Skills in the Use of CNC Machining Centres', Technical Change Centre.

1987

Taking Japan Seriously: A Confucian Perspective on Leading Economic Issues. London: Athlone; and Stanford: Stanford University Press (also in Italian).

Ed. with R. Sinha and M. Sako, *Japan and World Depression, Then and Now: Essays in Memory of E.F. Penrose*, Basingstoke: Macmillan ('How Fragile a Super State?' in same).

'Late Capitalism, Corporatism and Other-isms', in W. Outhwaite and M. Mulkay (eds.), *Social Theory and Social Criticism: Essays for Tom Bottomore*, Oxford: Basil Blackwell.

'Citizenship and Employment in an Age of High Technology', in *British Journal of Industrial Relations*, **25**(2), pp. 201–25 (reprinted in B. Turner and P. Hamilton, *Citizenship: Critical Concepts*, London: Routledge, 1994; and M. Bulmer and A.M. Rees (eds), *Citizenship Today*, London: UCL Press, 1996).

'Checks and balances', in *New Democrat*, **5**(4), pp. 20–21.

'Shinsōsai tanjō de nani ga kawaruka' (What Will Change With the Advent of the New (LDP) President?), in *Newsweek (Japan)*, 5 November, pp. 44–5.

1988

'Rigidities in the Labour Market', in *Government and Opposition*, **23**(4), pp. 394–412 (also in Italian in *Stato e Mercato*, Spring).

With M. Sakō, 'Teaching or Testing: the Role of the State in Japan', in *Oxford Review of Economic Policy*, **4**(3), pp. 72–81.

'Unions in a Technically Mature Society', paper for IIRA International Conference, Tokyo, (published in Japanese as 'Gijutsu seijuku shakai ni okeru rōdō kumiai', in Rōdō mondai risāchi sentā (ed.), *Seijuku gijutsu shakai ni okeru rōdō mondai ni kanṣuru kōkusai kaigi hōkokusho*, Tokyo, pp. 131–47.

1989

With M. Sako, *How the Japanese Learn to Work* , London and New York: Routledge (also in Italian, 1993).

With K. Tapiola and E. Bounine-Cabal, *Japan at Work: Markets, Management and Flexibility*, Paris: OECD.

Translation and 'Foreword', in *The Japanese Social Structure: its Evolution in the Modern Century*, Tadashi Fukutake (orig. Nihon shakai no kōzō, Tokyo, University Press), Tokyo: Tokyo University Press.

'Tipi di Impresa e Strategie della Partecipazione' in P. Ceri (ed.), *Impresa e lavoro in trasformazione*, Bologna: il Mulino.

'Where are We Now: Musings of an Evolutionist', in *Work, Employment and Society*, **3**(4), pp. 425–46 (cf. 'Afterword' of 1990 edition of *British Factory-Japanese Factory*. Also in Italian in *Sociología del Trabajo*, **15**, Spring 1992).

'Latecomers' Problems', in *The European Journal of Development Research*, **1**(1), pp. 100–107.

'Technology in a World of National Frontiers', in *World Development*, **17**(11), pp. 1665–75.

'Meritocracy, Employment and Citizenship in Japan and Elsewhere', in *Rivista Internazionale di Scienze Economiche e Commerciali*, **36**(2), pp. 101–6.

'How Democratic is Modern Japan?', paper for International Conference on 'Asia in the 21st Century: Challenges and Prospects', Seoul.

'Relationship Between Business Organization and Culture', in Seiko Epson (ed.), *Japan and Europe: Changing Contexts and Perspectives*, Brussels: Seiko Epson.

With M. Dodgson and D.H. Whittaker, 'Innovation and Industrial Relations in the UK Pump Industry', Imperial College, JEIRC Occasional Papers, 90 pp.

With D. Cairncross, 'Employee Training in Japan', Report for the Office of Technology Assessment, 49 pp.

1990

Will the 21st Century be the Age of Individualism? (in English and Japanese), Tokyo: Simul.

Ed. with C. Crouch, *Corporatism and Accountability: Organized Interests in British Public Life*, Oxford: Clarendon Press ('Japan: A Nation Made for Corporatism?' and with C. Crouch, 'Whatever Happened to Corporatism?' in same).

'Afterword' to reprinting of *British Factory–Japanese Factory*, Berkeley: University of California Press.

'Two Kinds of Rigidity: Corporate Communities and Collectivism' in R. Brunetta and C. Dell'Aringa (eds), *Labour Relations and Economic Performance*, Basingstoke: Macmillan/International Economic Association.

'An Outsider's View', in K. Yamamura (ed.), *Japan's Economic Structure: Should it Change?*, Seattle: Society for Japanese Studies.

'The World as Seen From Tokyo', in G. Casadio (ed.), *Cooperation Between Europe – Italy – China – Korea and Southeast Asian Countries*, Milano: FrancoAngeli.

'Reflections on Culture and Social Change', in G. Gereffi and D. Wyman (eds), *Manufacturing Miracles: Paths of Industrialization in Latin America and East Asia*, Princeton: Princeton University Press.

'Support and be Supported: Japan's Strategies of Interdependence', in *Government and Opposition*, **25**(4), pp. 438–45.

'Introduction' to new edition of G.C. Allen, *Modern Japan and Its Problems*, London: Athlone.

'Foreword' to I. Amano, *Education and Examination in Modern Japan*, Tokyo: Tokyo University Press.

'Foreword' to M. Saso, *Women in the Japanese Workplace*, London: Hilary Shipman.

'Foreword' to D.H. Whittaker, *Managing Innovation: A Study of British and Japanese Factories*, Cambridge: Cambridge University Press.

1991

Improving Britain's Industrial Performance, London: Employment Institute.

'Un Modello Utile per L'Occidente?' (Japan as an Industrial Relations Model?) in *Il Progetto*, **11**(66), pp. 15–17.

'When Will Japan Slow Down', in *Cornell Enterprise*, Winter/Spring, pp. 34–8.

With T. Inagami and M. Sako, 'Japan's Annual Economic Assessment', Campaign for Work Research Report, **3**(7).

1992

'Sovereign Individuals' in John A. Hall and Ian Jarvie (eds), *Transition to Modernity: Essays on Power, Wealth and Belief*, Cambridge: Cambridge University Press (also in Hall and Jarvie (eds), *The Social Philosophy of Ernest Gellner*, Poznan Studies in the Philosophy of the Sciences and the Humanities, 48).

'Japan's Version of Managerial Capitalism', in T. Kochan and M. Useem (eds), *Transforming Organizations*, New York: Oxford University Press.

'Politiche, Istituzionie e Sviluppo Economico' (The Management of Hierarchy) in C. Tolomelli (ed.), *Le Politiche Industriali Regionali; Espeirenze, Sogetti, Modelli,* Bologna: CLUEB.

'International Markets and National Traditions', University of Hong Kong, Dept of Sociology Occasional Paper.

(Review article) 'Social Relations and Social Contexts', in *Contemporary Sociology*, **21**, pp. 766–8.

'Nihonjin no kachikan to kōdō yōshiki' (The Values and Behavioural Patterns of the Japanese), in *Kokusai bunka shinpojiamu (proceedings)*, pp. 28–40.

1993

'"*Kō shiyō" to ieru Nihon*' (The Japan That Can Say 'Let's Do This'), Tokyo: Asahi shinbunsha.

With Y. Fukada, *Nihongata shihonshugi nakushite nan no Nihonka* (What is Japan if it Loses Japanese-style Capitalism?), Tokyo: Kōbunsha.

'What Makes the Japanese Different' in C. Crouch and D. Marquand (eds), *Ethics and Markets: Co-operation and Competition Within Capitalist Economies*, Oxford: Blackwell/Political Quarterly.

'Rethinking Free Trade', in R. Morgan, J. Lorentzen, A. Leander and S. Guzzini (eds), *New Diplomacy in the Post-Cold War World: Essays for Susan Strange*, Basingstoke: Macmillan; and New York: St Martin's. (Also in Italian in *Il Mulino*, **343**, Sept.-Oct. 1992, pp. 934–48, and summarized as 'Preaching Pragmatism to Free Trade Church', *Financial Times*, 8 July, 1992.)

'Nihonteki keiei shisutemu no shogensen' (The Roots of Japanese-style Management), in H. Itami, T. Kagono and M. Itō (eds), *Nihon no kigyō shisutemu daisankan: jinteki shigen*, Tokyo: Yuhikaku.

'Elitism and Democracy', in *The Tocqueville Review*, **14**(2).

'The World Economy in the 21st Century and Japan: Beyond the Economic Crisis', in *JCER Report*, **5**(6–7), Special Report, pp. 2–4.

'Kokusai kōken no shinario to tōjisha ishiki' (Scenarios for International Contributions and a Sense of Involvement), in *Ushio* June, pp. 110–19.

'Nihongata kaishashugi no fuhensei to tokushusei' (The Universality and Distinctiveness of Japanese-style Company-ism), in *Keidanren kurabu kaihō* August–September, pp. 2–30.

'Japan: Institutional and Regulatory Framework', paper for Human Capital Investments and Economic Performance Conference, Santa Barbara, 17–19 November.

1994

Nihon to no taiwa: fufuku no shosō (Dialogue With Japan: Faces of Discontent), Tokyo: Iwanami shoten.

Fushigi na kuni Nihon (Japan, a Peculiar Country), Tokyo: Chikuma shobō.

Ed. with M. Aoki, *The Japanese Firm: Sources of Competitive Strength*, Oxford: Oxford University Press (and 'Equality-Efficiency Trade-offs: Japanese Perceptions and Choices' in same; also in Japanese).

Ed. with R. Boyer and Z. Mars, *The Return to Incomes Policy*, London: Frances Pinter ('Incomes Policy, Why Now?' Introduction in same. Also in French).

Trans. ed. and 'Introduction' with D.H. Whittaker, *Business Enterprise in Japan*, K. Imai and R. Komiya (eds) (orig. *Nihon no Kigyō*, Tokyo University Press), Cambridge MA, MIT Press.

'Afterword' for reprinting of *Shinohata*, Berkeley: University of California Press.

'Japanese Capitalism, Anglo-Saxon Capitalism: How Will the Darwinian Contest Turn Out?', in N. Campbell and F. Burton (eds), *Japanese*

Multinationals: Strategies and Management in the Global Kaisha, London: Routledge.

'Sollecitazione e Penseri sui Concetti di "Coinvolgimento" e "Fudicia"' (Thoughts on 'Involvement' and 'Trust'), in G. Bonazzi and M. La Rosa (eds), *Modello Giapponese e Produzione Snella: La Prospettiva Europea*, Rome: FrancoAngeli.

'World Markets and Institutional Uniformity', in G. Parry (ed.), *Politics in an Interdependent World: Essays Presented to Ghita Ionesu*, Aldershot: Edward Elgar.

'Learning and Life Chances in Japan', in L. Mazzetti (ed.), *L'educazione al Lavoro Nella Societa di Consumo*, Rome: Armandi.

'Competition in Japanese Capitalism', in A. Beria di Argentina (ed.), *The Value of Competition*, Milano: Observatorio Giordano dell'Amore.

'Incurable Unemployment: A Progressive Disease of Modern Societies?' in *Political Quarterly*, **65**(3), pp. 285–301. (Also in Italian in *Il Mulino*, **352**, March–April, 1994 and 'Riposta', in *Economia e Politica Industriale* (Milano), **85**, 1995, pp. 5–11.)

'Why Visiting Sociologists Fail', in *World Development*, **22**(9), pp. 1425–36.

'Otome and Frank Daniels', in I. Nish (ed.), *Britain and Japan: Biographical Portraits*, London: Japan Library.

'Jinrui to kagaku tono chowa aru kyōzon' (Harmonious Co-existence Between Man and Science) in Genshiryoku anzen shisutemu kenkyūjo (ed.), *21 seiki Nihon no sentaku: enerugi, ekorojī, ekonomī no chōwa o motomete*, Tokyo: Daiyamondosha.

1995

'Man of Merit' in G. Dench, T. Flower and K. Gavron (eds), *Young at Eighty: the Prolific Public Life of Michael Young*, Manchester: Carcanet Press.

'Maruyama san tono 45 nen' (45 Years With Maruyama san), in *Maruyama Masao shū*, **3**, September, pp. 6–8.

'21 seiki no sekai ni okeru Nihon soshite kansai' (Japan and Kansai in the 21st Century World), in *Kikan orora*, **1**(1), pp. 130–49.

'Comment on Dr Jong's European Capitalism: Between Freedom and Social Justice', in *Review of Industrial Organisation*, **10**(4), pp. 421–727.

'Comment on the Kosai Paper', in The Japan Foundation Centre for Global Partnership (ed.), *The End of the Century: the Future in the Past*, Tokyo: Kōdansha, pp. 96–106.

'Japanese Bureaucracy' in ISESAO (Università Bocconi), *Policy Decision-making: the Relevance of the Japanese Experience for Italy.*

'The Limits of Discontinuity', paper for European Association for Comparative Economics Meeting at Trento.

'The "Employee Sovereignty" Pattern in Japan', DeVries Symposium on Asian Forms of Capitalism, Erasmus University, Holland, October.

'Western Concepts and Eastern Realities: Will the Twain Ever Meet?', World Bank Conference, Hakone, November.

'Japan and Europe: a Barely Existent Relationship', University of Bologna, Department of Political Science, Conference on Japan as a Superpower: Politics and Economy, September.

1996

Ed. with Suzanne Berger, *National Diversity and Global Capitalism*, Ithaca: Cornell University Press (and 'Convergence in Whose Interests?' in same).

'Confucianism, Economic Growth and Social Development' in J. Kreiner (ed.), *The Impact of Traditional Thought on Present-Day Japan*, Munich: Iudicium-Verl.

'La particularité du Japon', in C. Crouch and W. Streeck (eds.), *Les Capitalismes en Europe*, Paris: La Decouverte. (Also as 'The Distinctiveness of Japan', in C. Crouch and W. Streeck (eds), *Political Economy of Modern Capitalism: Mapping Convergence and Diversity*, London, Sage, 1997.)

'One Nation: Two Problems', in *Prospect*, June, pp. 14–16.

'A feasible Jerusalem?', in *Political Quarterly*, **67**(1), pp. 58–63.

'Unions between class and enterprise', in *Industrielle Beziehungen*, **3**(2), pp. 154–72.

'Cambiamento Tecnologico e Solidarietà Sociale', in *Stato e Mercato*, **46**, April, pp. 157–68.

'Globalizzazione dei Mercati e Diversità dei Capitalismi', in *Il Mulino*, **45**(368).

'Keizai dōyūkai no anpokan o utagau (Doubts on Dōyūkai's US–Japan Security Treaty View), in *Chūō kōron*, June, pp. 70–75.

Japan's 20th Century Trends: Looking East or West?', in *Asia-Pacific Review*, **3**(1), Tokyo: Institute for International Policy Studies.

'Nihon no kyōiku shisutemu to jinteki shigen no kaihatsu' (Japan's Education System and Human Resource development), in *Gekkan zensen*, December, pp. 39–44.

'What line should the optimist take in an age of pessimism?', in *Prime* (Tokyo, Meiji Gakuin), **4**, April.

'The End of Jobs for Life? Corporate Employment Systems in Japan and Elsewhere', Centre for Economic Performance (LSE) Occasional Paper No. 11, March, 32 pp.

'Good Jobs, Lousy Jobs and No Jobs', 15th Hitachi Lecture, University of Sussex, November.

'Market Failure, Government Failure: an Undisciplined View', Conference on Government and Market: Friend or Foe?, Hitotsubashi University, Tokyo, February.

'Still Capitalism With Such Feeble Capitalists?', Conference on the Future of Capitalism, Sussex University, April 1996.

'Faiths and Fashions: Neoliberalism in Britain and Japan', Conference on The Restructuring of the Economic and Political System in Japan and Europe, Bocconi University, Milan, June.

1997

Japan, Internationalism and the UN, London: Routledge.

Nihon o tou: Nihon ni tou: zoku fufuku no shosō (Asking About Japan, Asking to Japan: Faces of Discontent Sequel), Tokyo: Iwanami shoten.

'Ōyake' o 'watakushi' subekarazu: Yappari fushigi na kuni Nihon ('Public' Should Not be Made 'Private': Japan Really is a Peculiar Country), Tokyo: Chikuma shobō.

'Preface' to new edition of *The Diploma Disease*, London: Institute of Education.

'The Asian Form of Capitalism', in P. Admiraal (ed.), *The Corporate Triangle: the Structure and Performance of Corporate Systems in a Global Economy*, Oxford: Blackwell.

'The Argument of The Diploma Disease: a Summary' and 'Reflections on The Diploma Disease Twenty Years Later', in *Assessment in Education*, **4**(1), pp. 23–32 and 189–206.

'Good Jobs, Bad Jobs and No Jobs', in *Industrial Relations Journal,* **28**(4), pp. 262–8.

With T. Hanami, 'Nihon keizai no gurōbaru-ka to rōshi-kankei no shōrai' (The Globalization of the Japanese Economy and the Future of Industrial Relations), in *Nihon rōdō kenkyū zasshi*, **39**(5), pp. 44–52.

'Hashimoto 'gyōkaku' to shinjiyushugi e no gimon' (Doubts About the Hashimoto 'Administrative Reform' and Neo-liberalism), in *Chūō kōron*, November, pp. 28–38.

'Comparative Economics: The Agenda', in *Economic Systems*, **21**(1), pp. 68–71.

'Swings of Self-confidence, Swings of Training Policy', in *Economia e Lavoro*, **31**(3–4), pp. 309–16.

'Babel' in *Prospect*, March, pp. 69–71.

'Concorrenza Regolamentata, Tutela dei Deboli e Ricerca di Flessibilità: Dove va il Modello Giapponese?' (Competition, Flexibility and the Disadvantaged: Whither the Japanese Model?), in *Economia Marche*, **16**(2).

'Market Failure, Government Failure: an Undisciplined View', in Hitotsubashi University Institute of Economic Research (ed.), *Market and Government: In Search of Better Co-ordination*, Tokyo: Maruzen.

'21 seiki no sekai, ajia ni okeru Nihon' (Japan in 21st Century Asia and the World), in *Meiji daigaku kōkai kokusai seminā*, March.

'Igirisu, Amerika to Nihon no kōtō kyōiku (Higher Education in the UK, USA and Japan) in *Recruit College Management*, 82, January-February, pp. 68-73.

'The Deregulation Debate in Britain and Japan', in *Proceedings of the Japan Society* No. 129, London.

'The Limits of Discontinuity', Università di Trento Centre on the Evolution in Eastern European Countries Working Paper 97/1.

1998

'Innovation and Corporate Structures: USA and Japan', in J. Michie and J. Grieve Smith (eds), *Globalism, Growth and Governance*, Oxford: Oxford University Press.

'Asian Crisis and the Future of the Japanese Model', in *Cambridge Journal of Economics*, **22**(6), pp. 773-87.

'Nenkin seido o manē gēmu ni makikomu na' (Keep the Pension System out of the Money Game), *Chūō kōron*, March, pp. 112-19.

'Nihongata shihonshugi jizoku no kanōsei: 21 seiki e ikinokoreruka' (Can Japanese-style Capitalism Survive Into the 21st Century?'), in Fukuoka UNESCO iinkai ed. *21 seiki e no kadai to tenbō*, Fukuoka, pp. 14-24.

'Will Japan Convert to Capitalism?', in London School of Economics CEP, *Centrepiece*, Autumn, pp. 6-9.

'Trust and the Workings of Market Capitalism', University of Edinburgh International Social Sciences Institute paper, 14 pp.

1999

'Kaikakuron dairyūkō no Nihon: kaikakuronsha no honne' (Fashionable Reform Talk in Japan: the Reformers' True Intentions), in S. Inuzuka and N. Hoshi (eds), *Nihon no seido kaikaku*, Tokyo: Yushindo.

'Japan's Reform Debate: Patriotic Concern or Class Interest? Or Both?', in *Journal of Japanese Studies*, **25**, i, pp. 65-89. (Also as Università degli Studi di Ferrara, Collana Quaderni del Dipartimento di Economia, Istituzioni Territorio, No. 16.)

'21 seiki no rōdō kenkyu: "Rōdō mondai" yori "kigyō mondai"' (Labour Studies in the 21st Century: the 'Enterprise Problem' Rather Than the 'Labour Problem'), in *Nihon rōdō kenkyu zasshi*, **41**(4), pp. 70-72.

'Miryokuteki na shimin kyūfusei no kōsō' (The Attractions of a Citizen's Income Scheme) in *Shūkan rōdō nyūsu*, 5 April.

'Hendō no hageshii hanseiki o furikaeru' (Reflecting on a Half Century of Turbulent Change) in Fukuoka Unesco Association (ed.), Daikyūkai Nihon kankyu kokusai semina, Fukuoka, pp. 1–7.

'Koporēto gabanansu to rōdō kumiai: Ōbei de no rongi to Nihon e no kyōkun' (Corporate Governance and Trade Unions: the European and American debate and its Lessons for Japan), in *Rengō Sōken Repōto*, **127**, pp. 6–14.

'Cronies and Capitalism in Japan's Future', in Daiwa Anglo-Japanese Foundation (ed), *Bridging the Millennium, Bridging the Countries: Anglo-Japanese Concerns*, London.

With H. Ushio, 'Nihonteki keiei ronsō' (The Debate About Japanese-style Management) (with Ushio Haruo), *Chūō kōron*, January, pp. 84–97 (translated as 'Constancy and Change in Japanese Management', in *Japan Echo*, **26**(2)).

2000

Stock Market Capitalism, Welfare Capitalism: Japan and Germany Versus the Anglo-Saxons, Oxford: Oxford University Press.

With W. Lazonick and M. O'Sullivan, 'Varieties of Capitalism in the Twentieth Century', in *Oxford Review of Economic Policy*, **15**(4), pp. 102–20.

'Effort and Reward', in *Prospect*, July, pp. 34–7.

'Kabunushi ga daijika, jūgyōin ga daijika' (Are Shareholders Important, or are Employees Important?), debate with I. Nakatani, *Chūō kōron*, February, pp. 68–75.

Index